D1568191

Desk Reference on the

FEDERAL BUDGET

CONGRESSIONAL QUARTERLY'S

Desk Reference on the FEDERAL BUDGET

BRUCE WETTERAU

Congressional Quarterly Inc.
Washington, D.C.

Printed in the United States of America

Cover design: Ann Masters Design, Inc., Washington, D.C.
Interior design: Ann Masters Design, Inc., Washington, D.C.
Barton Matheson Willse & Worthington, Baltimore, Maryland

Library of Congress Cataloging-in-Publication Data

Wetterau, Bruce.
Congressional Quarterly's desk reference on the federal budget : over 500 uncomplicated answers to questions about taxes and spending / Bruce Wetterau.
p. cm.
Includes bibliographical references and index.
ISBN: 1-56802-378-2
1. Budget—United States—Handbooks, manuals, etc. 2. Taxation—United States—Handbooks, manuals, etc. 3. Government spending policy—United States—Handbooks, manuals, etc. 4. Fiscal policy—United States—Handbooks, manuals, etc. I. Title.
HJ2051.W43 1998
336.73—dc21 97-49135

CONTENTS

Tables and Figures **vi**

Preface **vii**

I Uncle Sam's Budget, the Economy, and Us 1

Budget Basics **1**

The Economy, Our Playing Field **14**

Tilting the Playing Field **34**

II Uncle Sam's Wallet—Where the Money Comes From 52

In General **52**

The IRS **71**

Raising the Revenue **73**

Borrowing and the Ever-Mounting Debt **81**

III What the Money Is Spent On 92

In General **92**

Social Spending **114**

Defense Spending **144**

Spending Potpourri **148**

IV The Budgeting Process 164

In General **164**

Executive Branch **179**

Congress **192**

Legislative Process **206**

Spending Control and Budget Cutting **219**

V Budget Timeline—Highlights From the Past 65 Years 237

In General **237**

Roosevelt Administration (1933–1945) **245**

Truman Administration (1945–1953) **250**

Eisenhower Administration (1953–1961) **255**

Kennedy Administration (1961–1963) **257**

Johnson Administration (1963–1969) **258**

Nixon Administration (1969–1974) **263**

Ford Administration (1974–1977) **270**

Carter Administration (1977–1981) **272**

Reagan Administration (1981–1989) **278**

Bush Administration (1989–1993) **286**

Clinton Administration (1993–) **289**

VI The Government in the Banking Business 296

In General **296**

Beyond Our Borders **308**

Bibliography 316

Index 321

TABLES AND FIGURES

Tables

1-1 Changes in Productivity and Wages, 1960–1996 **17**
1-2 Our Economic Growth **19**
1-3 Our Expanding Civilian Workforce **23**
1-4 Per Capita Disposable Income **26**
1-5 Year-to-Year Rises in Prices **29**
1-6 The Consumer Price Index, 1954–1996 **30**
1-7 The Misery Index, Ups and Downs **42**
2-1 Revenue and Spending Growth **58**
2-2 Trust Fund Balances **67**
2-3 Savings and Investment **77**
2-4 Making a Mountain of Debt **88**
2-5 Our Growing Dependency on Foreign Capital **90**
3-1 New Directions for Federal Spending **96**
3-2 The Deficit's Upward March **110**
3-3 The Rising Cost of Social Security **132**
3-4 Where the Money Is—Social Security Trust Fund Investments **136**
6-1 Money Supply Growth **299**
6-2 Key Interest Rates, 1940–1996 **301**
6-3 Treasury Bill and Bond Interest Rates, 1940–1996 **306**
6-4 Balance of Payments—Going Out of Balance **312**
6-5 The High Cost of Trade With Japan **313**

Figures

1-1 Past and Future Budget Deficits or Surpluses **7**
1-2 Growth in Real GDP **21**
2-1 The Federal Government Dollar—Where It Comes From **54**
2-2 Composition of Revenues **61**
2-3 Tax Rate for Married Couple with Combined Family Income of $100,000 **74**
2-4 Estimated Ownership of Debt Held by the Public **84**
3-1 Annual Federal Budget Growth, 1960–1997 **94**
3-2 The Federal Government Dollar—Where It Goes **99**
3-3 Growth in Entitlement Spending **116**
3-4 Composition of Social Security Recipients **130**
3-5 Portion of Beneficiaries that Rely Heavily on Social Security **131**
4-1 Growth of Academic Earmarks **213**
4-2 Executive Branch Civilian Employment, 1965–1996 **233**
5-1 Net Interest, 1960–2000 **285**
5-2 Poverty Rates, 1989–1995 **289**

PREFACE

Tax cuts, tax hikes, spending cuts, and spending increases—the 1997 Balanced Budget Agreement seemed to do something for everyone in the budget debate and yet miraculously lived up to its name by promising to balance the budget in five years. For the average American, the long and sometimes bitter debate leading up to the agreement was undeniably confusing and divisive. A blizzard of questions and counter-arguments swirled through the media coverage. Should we raise taxes or lower them, spend more on education or less on health care, cut federal programs or preserve government services and jobs? Difficult as they are, budget issues like these are crucial to the well-being of our nation, and sooner or later decisions on things like taxes and federal spending affect us all.

Given all these competing priorities, hammering out an acceptable plan for balancing the budget was truly a monumental achievement, and it is all the more tempting—for some even a relief—to think that the nation's budget worries have been completely solved. Budget controversies will not be disappearing from the headlines anytime soon, however. True, eliminating the deficit was a big step toward putting federal finances in order. But serious problems, including the $5 trillion mountain of federal debt and the impending insolvency of Social Security and Medicare, will be with us some years to come.

CQ's Desk Reference on the Federal Budget provides an invaluable guide to the complexities of the budget and budget economics—past, present, and future. It is the second in a series of Congressional Quarterly reference books written to give general readers ready access to otherwise unwieldy subjects.

Few people would argue that the budget is a huge and complex subject, and many think it impossibly so. But it need not be. This book, like *CQ's Desk Reference on American Government* before it, presents a wealth of information in an easy-to-understand, question-and-answer format. If necessary, the five hundred–plus questions and their clear, fact-filled answers can guide readers through the budget maze step by step. Or the answers, along with accompanying tables and figures, can serve equally well as a ready reference to an amazing array of budget facts, figures, procedures, events, and issues that have dominated news headlines and will continue to do so.

That is the beauty of *CQ's Desk Reference on the Federal Budget*—it is both a much needed self-teaching guide to the federal budget and a convenient reference for factual, procedural, and historical material about this crucial, often controversial aspect of government. Until now, readers usually had to rely on newspaper and magazine articles about hot-button issues for budget information. But these articles understandably focus on the one issue, and generally on just the latest twists and turns. Scholarly articles and books supply a more complete picture and broader perspective, but they are not written for the general reader and usually are not widely available anyway. Many of the books listed in the bibliography, for example, would not be available in the average local library. For that matter, readers would probably be hard-pressed to find even a copy of the current federal budget at many.

How then do you learn about such things as budgeting procedures and past budget issues, or find out about budget facts and figures without spending hours hunting up sources? *CQ's Desk Reference* is designed to fill this void in library collections and to provide a reliable, non-technical source of information for anyone who wants or needs to know about federal budget matters—from librarians themselves to the general reader, students, concerned citizens, writers, editors, and other professionals, including newspaper, radio, and television journalists. The basic question-and-answer approach can help any reader navigate through budget complexities, because it reduces puzzling budget issues to more manageable chunks, which can be tackled one at a time. These focused entries are then grouped together according to topic to make getting the broader picture easier. But entries usually have cross-references as well, leading readers to still other related questions elsewhere in the book. Stand-alone cross-references between entries serve the same purpose. Meanwhile, readers can also rely on the book's extensive index to quickly locate specific facts, definitions, events, and so on, allowing them to use the book as a ready reference, even though they do not necessarily have a question in mind.

Transforming a concept such as this into a bound book necessarily involves many people. I want to thank my editor at Congressional Quarterly, Dave Tarr, who saw the potential in the original idea and whose advice and recommendations helped keep it on track. Once again, the Alderman and Clemons Libraries at the University of Virginia proved an invaluable resource, and the government information resources staff—Barbara Selby, Jon Rice, and staff director Walter Newsome—found answers to even the most baffling research questions. Prof. Dan Franklin of Georgia State University and budget expert John Cranford were kind enough to review the manuscript, and their suggestions for improving the book in various areas were greatly appreciated. CQ project editor Christopher Karlsten also deserves thanks for ironing out a multitude of last-minute problems in both the manuscript and composed pages.

—Bruce Wetterau

1

UNCLE SAM'S BUDGET, THE ECONOMY, AND US

BUDGET BASICS

Q 1. What is the budget?

A Each year the federal government spends well over a trillion dollars on a mind-boggling array of expenses, ranging from paper clips, park maintenance, and employee paychecks to supercomputers and the multi-billion dollar space program. Everything about the federal budget seems outsized—even the printed version of the president's annual proposed budget runs over 2,000 pages.

The annual budget tries to control the huge outpouring of federal dollars by specifying ahead of time how much will be spent during the coming year, what programs will be funded, and by how much. In addition, the budget estimates how much income the government will take in from taxes, user fees, customs duties, and other revenues. You should remember, though, that the budget is just an estimate of what the government expects to spend and what revenues it hopes to collect. Unexpected emergencies and even small miscalculations in budget estimates can add many billions to federal expenses for a year. Or those miscalculations can also result in unexpected revenues or outright savings amounting to billions of dollars.

And though the budget is always written for a specific year, it is actually a hostage of Congress's past spending commitments. By law, entitlement programs like Social Security, Medicare, and Medicaid must be fully funded no matter how many eligible recipients there are in a given year, for example, and entitlements now account for 52 percent of all federal spending. Coupled with the mountain of federal debt and interest payments amounting to another 15 percent of federal spending, these prior commitments will dictate what the government can and cannot do for years to come.

(See 13 Why does the government spend more than it takes in? 20 Should the budget be balanced? 147 Who got what in a recent budget? 271 How is Uncle Sam's budget dif-

ferent from mine? 272 How is the budget prepared? 286 How much of the budget is now subject to annual approval by Congress? 397 What was the 1997 balanced budget agreement?)

Q 2. Who actually approves the budget?

A Though the president proposes a budget each year, Congress alone holds the power to authorize federal spending and to actually appropriate the money by passing laws to that effect. This broad authority is called "the power of the purse," and it makes Congress responsible for all the final decisions on federal taxing, spending, borrowing, and budget balancing. The president, of course, can veto the spending bills Congress passes, a power that allows the executive branch to influence the shape of legislation Congress approves.

(See 124 Where does Congress get the authority to borrow money? 272 How is the budget prepared? 286 How much of the budget is now subject to annual approval by Congress? 304 What role does a presidential veto play in the budget process? 320 What is "the power of the purse"? 322 Why is it that Congress has so much trouble keeping spending within a budget?)

Q 3. Who actually spends the money?

A Congress controls all federal money but does not actually spend what it budgets (except for its own administrative expenses). For the most part that responsibility falls on departments and agencies within, or in some way responsible to, the executive branch—such as the Department of Defense, the Social Security Administration, and the Environmental Protection Agency.

The funding bills Congress passes give departments and agencies what is called *budget authority,* allowing them to spend money or make financial obligations the government will have to pay. Even so, they do not actually write the checks for their employees' wages, for goods and services they use, or for direct payments to individuals, such as Social Security and veterans' benefits. That is the job of the Treasury Department's Financial Management Service, which each year cuts about 500 million Treasury checks and makes about 250 million electronic transfer payments.

(See 147 Who got what in a recent budget? 154 How does Congress spend the money it gets? 274 Are authorization and appropriations bills the same? 289 What is budget authority? 292 What are functions? 498 Why is Treasury's Financial Management Service (FMS) important?)

Q 4. How much does the government spend in a year?

A Spending for fiscal 1997 was about $1.6 trillion, or slightly less than $3 million a minute. That was up slightly from fiscal 1996, despite the blistering political battle between Republicans and Democrats over cutting spending and balancing the budget. The deficit, the shortfall between what the government spends and what it collects in revenue during a year, was down dramatically from the $200 billion-plus deficits of the early 1990s. But the government expects deficits will continue for several years. And costs for Medicare, Social Security, and other entitlement programs continued to rise.

(See 20 Should the budget be balanced? 146 How have federal spending patterns changed since 1960? 147 Who got what in a recent budget? 167 What has the deficit been, year by year since 1901? 171 Why has social spending risen by so much?)

Q 5. Is there enough gold in Fort Knox to pay for all of that?

A No, not nearly. Fort Knox, the government's main depository for gold reserves, contains about $51.5 billion worth of gold bullion (at current market value), and the total U.S. gold reserves are valued at about $92 billion. That is not even enough to keep the government running for a single month at its current spending rate.

But the real source of the country's wealth and an important part of the solution to the federal government's budget problems is not gold; rather, it is the economy. The United States economy produces goods and services worth trillions of dollars, year in and year out. These days federal taxes on business profits, wages, and such generate revenues of over a trillion dollars a year, and with each passing year the economy grows ever larger, producing still more tax dollars.

(See 13 Why does the government spend more than it takes in? 22 Just how big is the U.S. economy? 73 What are the government's major sources of revenue?)

Q 6. Why do I have to pay taxes?

A The federal government could not operate without the money it gets from various taxes, especially personal income taxes. There would be no money to pay salaries of public officials and employees, much less provide for services and federal benefits we now take for granted. Highways, the National Weather Service, the military services, and numerous other agencies would never have come into existence without tax dollars, and benefits such as Social Security, unemployment compensation, and Medicare would be out of the question.

Another reason we pay income taxes is to redistribute money from wealthier people to those with less income and to the poor who have little or none. Though not all people agree with the principle of income redistribution—taxing those who are better off to help those who are not—it has been an important aspect of tax policy for many years. The Democratic party especially has favored the idea of income redistribution through taxes.

Although the income taxes we pay represent the single largest share of federal revenues, they are not the government's only source of money (others include excise taxes, fees, interest income, and so on). And the idea of replacing the income tax with some other form of tax, such as a national sales tax, has recently gained some attention.

(See also: 73 What are the government's major sources of revenue? 74 What percent of federal revenues do my income taxes amount to? 85 What is tax fairness? 102 How do the proposed flat tax, sales tax, and value-added tax plans work? 111 How much per capita do we pay in taxes?)

Q **7. Have we always had to pay income taxes?**

A No. For the first century or so of its existence, the federal government used tariffs (taxes on imported goods) to raise most of its revenue. Congress imposed the first income tax in 1862 to help pay expenses for the Civil War, but that tax was allowed to expire in 1872. Later, after a depression cut federal revenues, Congress returned to the idea of an income tax, passing a 2 percent tax on personal incomes over $3,000 in 1894. The Supreme Court ruled the tax unconstitutional, however, in *Pollock v. Farmers' Loan & Trust Co.*, and no revenue was ever collected.

Congress eventually had to pass the Sixteenth Amendment to the Constitution to overcome the Court's objections. Shortly after the amendment was ratified in 1913, Congress established a modest 1 percent tax on incomes. The inevitable tax increases came a few years later during World War I, greatly expanding federal revenues and transforming income taxes into the government's main revenue source.

(See 14 Why doesn't the government just keep raising taxes to meet its expenses? 73 What are the government's major sources of revenue? 75 When did our income taxes become the government's main revenue source? 78 What articles of the Constitution grant Congress the power to tax and spend? 80 Why was the Sixteenth Amendment necessary? 81 When was the corporate income tax instituted? 103 What is a Laffer curve?)

8. How much did people pay during the first year of federal income taxes?

Compared to today, not very much. In the beginning, the tax on an individual's annual income was just 1 percent, but those with high earnings also paid a surtax of 1 percent to 6 percent. The tax code exempted the first $3,000 of a single person's income and $4,000 for married couples, while also allowing deductions for business expenses, interest income, and tax payments.

(See 111 How much per capita do we pay in taxes?)

9. Who was the first president to submit a budget to Congress?

President Warren Harding submitted the first formal budget proposal to Congress in December 1921 (for fiscal 1923). Until the 1921 Budget and Accounting Act, the president had not been required to prepare a budget, and for the most part presidents had little to do with setting spending levels.

In fact, for its first 132 years the government operated without a budget at all. Customs duties on imports (tariffs) provided ample income, and the size and scope of government, which spent less than $800 million a year, allowed Congress to handle federal finances in a haphazard way. Generally, departments and agencies within the executive branch submitted their annual budget requests directly to Congress, without the president's direct involvement.

The explosive growth of spending during World War I—topping $18 billion in 1919 alone—finally forced Congress to reconsider its handling of public finances. That resulted in the 1921 Budget and Accounting Act, requiring the president to submit an annual budget request to Congress. It also created the Bureau of the Budget and Congress's auditing agency, the General Accounting Office.

(See 272 How is the budget prepared? 283 What did the 1921 Budget and Accounting Act do? 284 What have been the major turning points in the history of federal budgeting? 305 What does the Office of Management and Budget do? 311 What was the Bureau of the Budget? 342 What does the General Accounting Office (GAO) do?)

10. What is a fiscal year and why does it start October 1?

A fiscal year is the year used for accounting purposes. Most businesses use a year that runs from July 1 to the following June 30 and figure their annual expenses, income, and losses on the basis of that time period. The federal government did so as well until 1976, when it switched to a fiscal year beginning on October 1 and ending the following September 30. Congress authorized the change to give itself more time to draft and vote on the appropriations bills that outlay funds for the fiscal year.

Fiscal years can be somewhat confusing for the average person. For example, fiscal 1998 actually begins in 1997 (October 1) and ends in 1998 (September 30). An easy way to avoid confusion is to remember that the fiscal year always ends in the year stated (fiscal 1998 ends in 1998).

Q 11. Is there a difference between the budget deficit and the debt?

A The *budget deficit* is the red ink the federal government accumulates in a single year. Specifically it is the amount of money spent over and above what it collects in taxes and other revenue for the year. These days that is no small matter, and even with the balanced budget deal in place deficits are expected to run in the billions of dollars until the year 2000.

The *debt* is the result of continued deficits. For the past twenty-eight years the government has outspent revenue and each year has had to borrow money to make up for the shortfall. The total of borrowed money yet to be repaid is the debt, and it has reached dizzying proportions—trillions of dollars. That may be the reason why Republicans and Democrats alike talk about reducing the deficit, rather than the debt. The mountain of debt will be with us long after the deficit has been eliminated.

(See 16 What is the longest period of consecutive budget deficits? 17 How big is the national debt? 126 Is there any limit on how much Congress can borrow? 133 What has the federal debt been over the years? 167 What has the deficit been, year by year since 1901? 374 When did efforts to control spending begin in Congress?)

Q 12. When did the government post the largest deficit in its history?

A Because Democrats focused so much attention on the large deficits of the 1980s, many people might think that the largest occurred during the Reagan administration. But the government's largest deficit to date, $290.4 billion, actually occurred in fiscal 1992, the year President George Bush unsuccessfully sought reelection (see Figure 1-1). The Bush administration also posted deficits over $200 billion in 1990 ($221 billion) and 1991 ($269 billion). In fact, the 1990s saw the high water mark of the deficit problem, with President Bill Clinton recording deficits of $255 billion (1993) and $203 billion (1994). But the push in Congress to eliminate the deficit, an improving economy, an end to the savings and loan crisis, and Clinton's efforts at downsizing government combined to pull the annual deficit below $200 billion.

Figure 1-1 Past and Future Budget Deficits or Surpluses

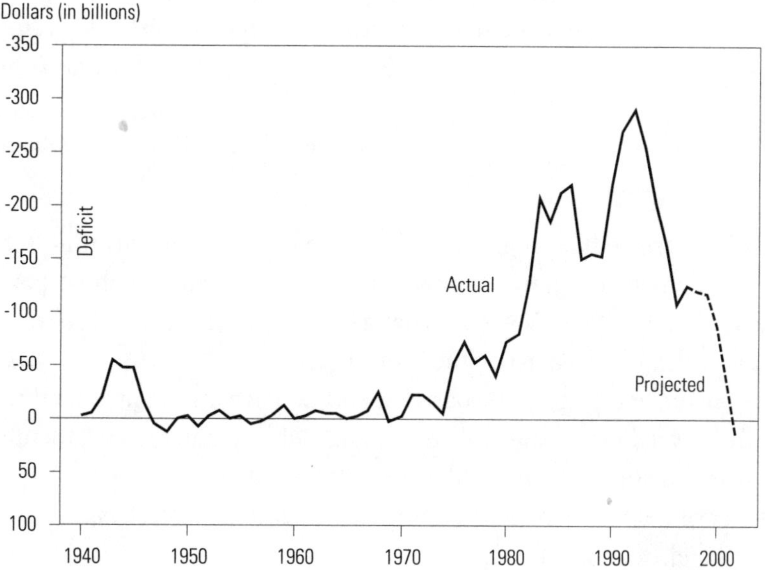

The eight years of the Reagan administration saw budget deficits climb over $200 billion three times—$207.8 billion in 1983, $212 billion in 1985, and $221.2 billion in 1986.

Experts also look at the deficit in relation to the Gross Domestic Product (GDP). For a table of deficits given in both dollar figures and as a percentage of GDP, see 167 What has the deficit been, year by year since 1901?

(See 16 What is the longest period of consecutive budget deficits? 17 How big is the national debt? 133 What has the federal debt been over the years? 135 How long might it take to pay off the national debt?)

Q 13. Why does the government spend more than it takes in?

A First, remember that the budget is a political statement, crafted by politicians, who sometimes consider costs secondary to policy, their own interests, or their constituents' demands. Decisions by the president and Congress on spending levels for defense or social programs, for example, have added billions to the budget. These decisions can create large deficits all by themselves and substantially increase the debt. If the new spending is set up as an entitlement program, the problem of controlling spending is even greater. Costs can mushroom decades after the initial decision has

"Congress will begin to restrain its spending the day its constituents say, 'Stop spending or we're going to take away your favorite toy: your seat in Congress.' Until then, they will spend because it profits them."

—Bill Frenzel, former congressman
[as quoted in Brian Kelly's *Adventures in Porkland*]

been made to create the program (as happened with Medicaid). But because spending for entitlement programs is mandatory, the government must pay whatever is necessary until Congress votes to change laws governing the programs. That can make it very difficult to balance the budget.

Waste, inefficiency, and pork-barrel spending have also contributed to overspending by the government. And the competing political interests of members of Congress, their constituents, and their respective parties—as well as special interest groups—have helped increase spending for programs, projects, and perks that benefit only a small number of voters.

But the budgeting process itself also contributes to the government's overspending problems. Budget writing actually begins well in advance of the fiscal year, when things like tax revenue and outlays for Social Security can only be estimated. Even a slight miscalculation in a forecast of tax revenues can add billions to the deficit. And misjudging the future cost of a program, as happened with Medicare and Medicaid, for example, also can drive up spending.

The government sometimes intentionally increases spending over the budget just to soften the effects of a recession ("deficit spending"). Then, too, expenses for unexpected emergencies, such as disaster relief and troop deployments overseas, may throw the budget out of kilter for the year.

(See 25 What are business cycles? 64 What is "stabilization policy"? 66 Do big deficits limit fiscal policy options? 146 How have federal spending patterns changed since 1960? 272 How is the budget prepared? 284 What have been the major turning points in the history of federal budgeting? 359 What is pork-barrel spending? 374 When did efforts to control spending begin in Congress?)

Q 14. Why doesn't the government just keep raising taxes to meet its expenses?

A Many Democrats and some Republicans have urged this solution—they believe the only way to eliminate the budget deficit is to raise taxes. Conservative Republicans on the other hand generally believe that raising taxes only slows economic growth and discourages people from working harder to make extra money (why work overtime if the government is only going to take more in taxes?). They, and some economists, think raising taxes actually costs the government revenue because a slower economy produces less tax revenue. For those reasons Republicans would rather attack the deficit problem at the source—by cutting spending—as well as by lowering taxes to stimulate the economy.

There is a third element in this equation, though, and probably the most important—the voters. While many of us like the federal benefits we receive and think the government should do all kinds of helpful things, we do not like seeing our paychecks disappear in taxes. We like tax increases even less. In the end all the arguments about what government should or should not be paying for, and how much taxpayers should be paying, come down to the question of what we voters are willing to accept. When it comes to taxing, spending, and politicians' careers, that is the bottom line, and the limit to raising taxes.

(See 20 Should the budget be balanced? 23 What impact does the government have on the economy? 71 What is supply-side economics? 103 What is a Laffer curve? 111 How much per capita do we pay in taxes? 117 What do critics say is wrong with the current tax system? 393 What cuts in the federal government has President Bill Clinton made?)

Q 15. How many times have there been budget surpluses since the depression era?

A The federal government posted budget surpluses—that is, it spent *less than* its revenues for the year—just seven times since 1931. Spending for depression-era programs and World War II ruled out surpluses in the 1930s and much of the 1940s. Then came a brief flurry of surpluses between 1947 and 1949 while President Harry Truman was in office. There was another budget surplus during the Truman administration in 1951. While President Dwight Eisenhower was in office, the government posted surpluses in 1956, 1957, and 1960. The last surplus to date was $3.2 billion in 1969, the first year of Richard Nixon's presidency.

The years between 1900 and 1931 saw a string of eleven consecutive budget surpluses running from 1920 to 1930, the first full year of the depression. That eleven-year string of surpluses is the century's longest.

(See 17 How big is the national debt? 133 What has the federal debt been over the years? 146 How have federal spending patterns changed since 1960? 167 What has the deficit been, year by year since 1901? 374 When did efforts to control spending begin in Congress?)

16. What is the longest period of consecutive budget deficits?

The longest string of budget deficits is the current one, which began in 1970 and as of fiscal 1997 numbers twenty-eight years. If the balanced budget package agreed to by President Bill Clinton and Congress works as intended, the pattern of deficits will finally end no later than 2002. If the economy performs better than expected the government may post a surplus sooner than that.

The second-longest period of back-to-back deficits is sixteen years, from 1931 to 1946. The period includes the Great Depression and World War II years, both times of emergency when government spending was unusually high. Another eight-year string of deficits occurred from 1961 to 1968 during the Kennedy-Johnson years.

(See 167 What has the deficit been, year by year since 1901? 461 Why were deficits so high during the Carter years? 475 Why were deficits so high during the Reagan years? 477 What was President Bush's economic record? 481 Did the deficit grow smaller during Clinton's first term?)

17. How big is the national debt?

Government estimates of the total debt at the end of fiscal 1997 stood at a whopping $5.4 trillion dollars. Getting a figure that large into perspective can be difficult, but try imagining the debt in dollar bills laid end to end. You would have enough to stretch more than five times the distance from the earth to the sun!

Astronomical terms are all too appropriate when it comes to the debt, and until the budget is actually balanced, the debt will go nowhere but up. The estimated total for the debt at the close of fiscal 1998 is $5.74 trillion, or about 3.6 times the total amount of revenue the government estimated it will collect that year.

(See 130 When did the federal debt top $1 trillion? $3 trillion? 131 When did the federal debt actually begin to mushroom? 132 How much does the interest on the federal debt cost now? 133 What has the federal debt been over the years? 135 How long might it take to pay off the national debt?)

18. Where did the national debt come from?

The debt is the direct result of the government spending more than it collects in revenue. Overspending is not new to the twentieth century. The government was in debt through much of the 1800s, but there was strong sentiment then for keeping spending in line with revenues (except during wartime). Generally speaking, the government managed enough budget surpluses in some years to pay back much of what was owed and that kept the federal debt from getting too large.

During the Great Depression of the 1930s, though, the Roosevelt administration broke with past practice and began a deliberate policy of deficit spending to pump up the economy and help people who were struggling to survive without jobs. The depression and the emergency of World War II that followed did end eventually, but the habit of deficit spending developed during the emergencies did not. Freed of the need to balance the budget, the president and Congress could skirt around hard decisions about whether the country could actually afford various new programs. Politically it was far easier to authorize spending and not worry about deficits (or worry about them later) than to impose higher taxes needed to keep the budget in balance.

The long string of budget deficits, large and small, that began in the 1930s depression era started the upward trend in the federal debt. Wars (Korea and Vietnam), cold war defense spending, unexpected drops in revenue and vast increases in social spending—especially for the new and enlarged entitlement programs of the 1960s—all contributed to the deficit problem over the years.

Even so, the debt did not begin mushrooming toward its current levels until the mid-1970s, when a lagging economy and rapidly rising costs for entitlement programs combined to produce the first big peacetime deficits.

The deficits only got bigger during the 1980s while Republican President Ronald Reagan and the Democratically controlled Congress battled over what to do about them. President Reagan's defense budgets certainly contributed to the deficit problem, and short term his tax cut probably did as well, but a larger share of federal spending increases—and hence the deficits—during his two terms came from the continued runup in entitlement spending. What began as $40–$50 billion-plus annual deficits during the Ford and Carter years blossomed into $100–$200 billion-plus in red ink during the Reagan-Bush administrations.

(See 11 Is there a difference between the budget deficit and the debt? 13 Why does the government spend more than it takes in? 14 Why doesn't the government just keep raising taxes to meet its expenses? 131 When did the federal debt actually begin to mushroom? 133 What has the federal debt been over the years? 135 How long might it take to pay off the national debt? 167 What has the deficit been, year by year since 1901?)

Q 19. Can't we just ignore the debt?

A For many years Congress largely ignored the debt, allowing it to get bigger and bigger. But the $5.4-trillion debt is now large enough that it hobbles the economy and the government in various ways.

* The $241 billion interest payment on the national debt for 1996 was the third largest budget expense and was more than the budget deficit for the year. That

drain on federal funds cuts into the amount the government can spend on social programs for health, education, and welfare, as well as defense needs and other spending priorities. In addition, the budget strain limits what the government can do to stimulate the economy during a recession.

* Government borrowing to finance the huge debt increases competition for credit and drives up interest rates. At the very least it costs the government and everyone else who borrows more in interest payments.
* High interest rates slow economic growth. Because borrowing money costs more, individuals have less to spend on big-ticket items like new cars and houses. Businesses also have less to invest in new plants and equipment, and that can translate into slower growth. In fact, the country's 2.5 percent average growth rate over the past two decades is markedly slower than the rate over previous decades.
* The huge debt has forced the government to borrow from foreign as well as domestic sources. Such borrowing raises the remote possibility that, as the government becomes more dependent on foreign investors, a stabilization crisis could occur. The economic effects of foreigners suddenly liquidating their U.S. investments could be severe.

(See 13 Why does the government spend more than it takes in? 17 How big is the national debt? 28 How fast has the economy been growing over the years? 66 Do big deficits limit fiscal policy options? 123 Will the government be going broke anytime soon? 126 Is there any limit on how much Congress can borrow? 129 Is a credit crunch good or bad? 133 What has the federal debt been over the years? 516 What is a stabilization crisis?)

Q 20. Should the budget be balanced?

A Despite real differences over how much the federal government should spend and on what programs, most people agree that, ideally, the government should not consistently spend more than it collects in taxes and other revenue. In practice, though, the government's habit of overspending has thrown the budget out of whack almost every year since before World War II.

In the short run, overspending—deficit spending in budgetspeak—sometimes can help the economy. For example, the federal government may help keep a recession from getting worse by stepping up purchases of goods and services. Among other things, the extra federal dollars provide work for people who might otherwise have been laid off because of the recession. Also, increased unemployment compensation and welfare benefits for workers who are thrown out of work help ease the personal hardship and add extra federal spending to boost the economy. The government could make up for this temporary excess spending later, by cutting back when the economy is good. During those years it would take in more money than it spent, creating a budget surplus that could be used to pay off the debt.

But most years, in good times and bad, the president and Congress have been unable to agree on a balanced federal budget, much less one that produced a surplus. Conservative Republicans especially have railed against deficit spending and the mounting debt for decades. But only in recent years has the debt become large enough to force serious consideration of politically unpopular remedies—tax increases, cuts in federal programs, or some combination of both—to restore the balance.

(See 13 Why does the government spend more than it takes in? 14 Why doesn't the government just keep raising taxes to meet its expenses? 16 What is the longest period of consecutive budget deficits? 17 How big is the national debt? 19 Can't we just ignore the debt? 60 Do entitlement programs help dampen recessions? 73 What are the government's major sources of revenue? 131 When did the federal debt actually begin to mushroom? 322 Why is it that Congress has so much trouble keeping spending within a budget? 397 What was the 1997 balanced budget agreement? 488 What did the 1997 balanced budget agreement do to cut taxes?)

Q 21. Where can I find information on the current year's budget?

A The Government Printing Office publishes the president's proposed budget in book form immediately after the president delivers it to Congress in January. The following volumes are issued as a set each year and are also available on the World Wide Web at *http://www.access.gpo.gov/su_docs/budget/index.html.*

A Citizen's Guide to the Federal Budget, Fiscal Year 19—. Provides a brief overview of the budget and some budget statistics in an easy-to-understand style for the general reader.

Budget of the United States Government, Fiscal Year 19—. Presents the president's proposed budget and spending goals, along with text discussion of federal programs.

Analytical Perspectives, Budget of the United States Fiscal 19—. Provides text discussion and statistics on trends in federal spending (by agency and account), revenue, borrowing, and so on. Also discusses budget concepts.

Historical Tables, Budget of the United States Government, Fiscal Year 19—. Detailed statistics on federal spending, receipts, and so on, from 1940 to the present, and current estimates through 2002.

Appendix, Budget of the United States Government, Fiscal Year 19—. Presents the budget in greatest available detail, including budget schedules for each account and text on work to be performed by various programs.

Budget System and Concepts, Fiscal 19—. Explains the system and concepts connected with formulation of the current budget proposals.

(See 310 Is the president's budget the only source of information on the current budget?)

THE ECONOMY, OUR PLAYING FIELD

Q 22. Just how big is the U.S. economy?

A If you added up the value of all the goods and services produced in the United States during just one year's time, it would amount to a staggering $7.8 trillion. That represents about $29,400 for every man, woman, and child in the country. Our economy is far and away the world's biggest. The total money value of goods and services it produced in a recent year was roughly two and a half times that of Japan and over four and a half times that of Germany.

(See 24 How does the economy affect me? 46 What happens in an economic expansion? 55 What is a recession? A depression? 64 What is "stabilization policy"?)

Q 23. What impact does the government have on the economy?

A The government is the big kid on the block when it comes to the economy—its $1.631 trillion in spending amounted to about 20 percent of the country's entire Gross Domestic Product for 1997. That much spending power means, in theory, the federal government could help push the economy up, down, or sideways if it wanted. The government also controls the money supply, taxes, and regulations that affect business and the economy as a whole. But there are limits to these powers, and the economy does not always react as expected. Listed below are some of the ways the government affects the economy.

* Controls the money supply and influences some interest rates, making investments more or less expensive.
* Uses increased spending and/or tax cuts ("fiscal stimulus") to increase business activity and consumer spending to boost the economy. It also sometimes takes steps to cool off an "overheated" economy, by raising taxes or cutting spending.
* Redistributes wealth by increasing taxes on the rich to pay for social programs for the poor.
* Uses regulations to outlaw certain practices, control competition, or protect those at a disadvantage. Regulations sometimes have a negative effect, pushing up prices unnecessarily by stifling competition or imposing wasteful practices.

* Competes with businesses and private individuals for available goods and services. Government borrowing to finance the mountain of federal debt, for example, has put a strain on the private credit market.
* Provides jobs for an entire sector of the economy (public employees) and sets basic standards of employment and compensation for the business world (minimum wages, eight-hour day, and so forth).

(See 6 Why do I have to pay taxes? 37 Do federal regulations affect the economy? 44 What can the economy do to the budget? 64 What is "stabilization policy"? 65 What is fiscal policy? 129 Is a credit crunch good or bad? 435 What were the economic policy successes and failures of the 1960s? 459 What were the new economic realities of the 1970s? 471 What caused the 1981–1982 recession? 490 How does the Federal Reserve affect the economy?)

Q 24. How does the economy affect me?

A Many things become easier when the economy is growing and business is good. You are more likely to land a job or win a promotion because new jobs are being created at a faster rate and companies are expanding. If you run your own business, a better economy could mean more customers and higher profits. And when interest rates are lower, getting loans for a new car or a house becomes easier.

One way or another you will probably feel the effects of economic problems as well. Many people in manufacturing and construction industries are laid off when business drops off because of an economic slump, for example, and you may postpone buying big-ticket items because you are suddenly uncertain about your own job. Or, during times of high inflation the prices of items you buy may be rising faster than your paycheck.

(See 46 What happens in an economic expansion? 48 How does inflation affect my paycheck? 56 How do we know when a recession has begun? 59 What is the Misery Index? 64 What is "stabilization policy"?)

Q 25. What are business cycles?

A Swings in economic activity from boom times to recession and back are called business cycles. Economists track business cycles by following the rise and fall of economic indicators, which signal the direction of economic activity. For example, a recessionary phase in the business cycle often begins when the output of goods and services fall, unemployment rises, and new housing starts drop. Then, when the direction of these and other indicators finally reverses, the expansionary phase usually gets underway.

The word *cycle* can be misleading because the swings do not occur at regular intervals and because the booms and recessions vary so much in duration. The country enjoyed an eight-year boom following recessions in 1980 and 1982, and an unbroken, if modest expansion since the 1991 recession. Many economists believe the length and severity of recessions since World War II have been limited by the federal government's fiscal and monetary policies.

(See 33 Does full employment help or hurt the economy? 39 What is the Index of Leading Economic Indicators? 46 What happens in an economic expansion? 55 What is a recession? A depression? 56 How do we know when a recession has begun?)

Q 26. Who or what determines supply and demand?

A We do, at least in part. Every time we decide to buy something, we add to the demand for the product or service. And when we go to work each day, we add to the labor supply. In fact, the economy is something like a gigantic marketplace in which millions of decisions about buying and selling things actually determine what supply and demand will be.

Supply and demand are the two most basic concepts in economics, and the law of demand is probably the most important to the science. It says that when the price of a good or service rises, the quantity demanded will decline; when the price drops, the quantity demanded will rise. There is no formal law of supply, but economists describe the action of supply this way: The amount of goods or services offered for sale increases as the price paid goes up; the amount declines as the price goes down.

Q 27. Why is productivity important?

A Productivity measures how much workers are producing. Technically speaking, it is the dollar value of output they produce per hour worked, and economists consider the size of yearly productivity gains (or losses) a sign of how healthy the economy is. When productivity improves, workers produce more in fewer hours and at less cost to employers. That means businesses can increase wages without raising prices, and long term, improved productivity has been important for income gains. Falling productivity, on the other hand, means higher labor costs for businesses, greater resistance to wage increases, and higher prices for consumers (inflation).

Falling productivity became a serious economic problem in the 1970s and helped fuel high inflation then. Between 1947 and 1965, productivity had grown at a healthy average of 3 percent a year. But it slipped from 1965 onward, scarcely increasing between 1973 and 1980, and averaged up just 0.8 percent a year (see Table 1-1). It actually fell three years in a row from 1978 to 1980. Economists blamed falling productivity on a number of things, including the massive influx of inexperienced (and

Table 1-1 Changes in Productivity and Wages, 1960–1996

	Changes in productivity		*Changes in hourly wages*	
	Business sector (%)	*Nonfarm business sector (%)*	*Business sector (%)*	*Adjusted for inflation (%)*
1960	1.6	1.2	4.3	2.6
1961	3.3	3.1	4.0	2.9
1962	4.6	4.6	4.5	3.5
1963	3.9	3.4	3.7	2.3
1964	4.6	4.3	5.2	3.8
1965	3.5	3.0	3.7	2.1
1966	3.9	3.5	6.7	3.7
1967	2.3	1.7	5.7	2.5
1968	3.5	3.4	8.1	3.8
1969	0.4	0.1	7.0	1.5
1970	1.8	1.4	7.8	1.9
1971	4.3	4.1	6.4	1.9
1972	3.3	3.4	6.3	3.0
1973	3.1	3.1	8.6	2.2
1974	–1.3	–1.6	9.7	–1.2
1975	3.3	2.7	10.3	1.1
1976	3.7	3.6	8.8	2.9
1977	1.9	1.6	7.9	1.3
1978	0.7	1.3	9.0	1.3
1979	–0.3	–0.8	9.7	–1.5
1980	–0.2	–0.4	10.8	–2.4
1981	2.0	1.1	9.5	–0.7
1982	–0.6	–0.8	7.5	1.2
1983	3.3	4.2	4.2	0.9
1984	2.3	1.7	4.4	0.0
1985	1.8	1.0	4.9	1.3
1986	2.5	2.6	5.2	3.3

(Continued on next page)

Table 1-1 *(Continued)*

	Changes in productivity		*Changes in hourly wages*	
	Business sector (%)	*Nonfarm business sector (%)*	*Business sector (%)*	*Adjusted for inflation (%)*
1987	–0.2	–0.3	3.8	0.2
1988	0.5	0.6	4.5	0.3
1989	0.8	0.5	2.8	–2.0
1990	0.8	0.5	5.7	0.3
1991	0.6	0.7	4.8	0.6
1992	3.4	3.2	5.2	2.1
1993	0.2	0.2	2.5	–0.5
1994	0.5	0.5	1.9	–0.6
1995	0.1	0.3	3.1	0.3
1996	1.5	1.3	3.3	0.3

Note: Productivity is dollar value of output per hour worked.
Source: Economic Report of the President 1997; Bureau of Labor Statistics.

therefore less productive) baby-boomers and women into the labor force, higher energy prices, and increased federal regulation of business.

(See 33 Does full employment help or hurt the economy? 37 Do federal regulations affect the economy? 52 What does inflation do to the economy? 459 What were the new economic realities of the 1970s?)

Q **28. How fast has the economy been growing over the years?**

A On average, our economic growth since 1946 has been about 3 percent a year in 1992 constant dollars (dollars adjusted for inflation). Between 1952 and 1969 GDP growth was stronger, about 3.4 percent average, with a sustained high growth rate of 4–6 percent from 1962 to 1966. Growth began to drop off in the late 1960s though, and since 1970 GDP growth has been lower, averaging just 2.5 percent or so (see Table 1-2 and Figure 1-2).

(See 404 How strong has economic growth been since World War II? 405 Under which president was economic growth the highest?)

Table 1-2 Our Economic Growth

	GDP in current dollars (billions)	*Percentage change*	*GDP in 1992 constant dollars (billions)*	*Percentage change*
1959	507.2	—	2,212.3	—
1960	526.6	3.8	2,261.7	2.2
1961	544.8	3.5	2,309.8	2.1
1962	585.2	7.4	2,449.1	6.0
1963	617.4	5.5	2,554.0	4.3
1964	663.0	7.4	2,702.9	5.8
1965	719.1	8.5	2,874.8	6.4
1966	787.8	9.5	3,060.2	6.4
1967	833.6	5.8	3,140.2	2.6
1968	910.6	9.2	3,288.6	4.7
1969	982.2	7.9	3,388.0	3.0
1970	1,035.6	5.4	3,388.2	0.0
1971	1,125.4	8.7	3,500.1	3.3
1972	1,237.3	9.9	3,690.3	5.4
1973	1,382.6	11.7	3,902.3	5.7
1974	1,496.9	8.3	3,888.2	–0.4
1975	1,630.6	8.9	3,865.1	–0.6
1976	1,819.0	11.5	4,081.1	5.6
1977	2,026.9	11.4	4,279.3	4.9
1978	2,291.4	13.0	4,493.7	5.0
1979	2,557.5	11.6	4,624.0	2.9
1980	2,784.2	8.9	4,611.9	–0.3
1981	3,115.9	11.9	4,724.9	2.5
1982	3,242.1	4.1	4,623.6	–2.1
1983	3,514.5	8.4	4,810.0	4.0
1984	3,902.4	11.0	5,138.2	6.8
1985	4,180.7	7.1	5,329.5	3.7
1986	4,422.2	5.8	5,489.9	3.0

(Continued on next page)

Table 1-2 *(Continued)*

	GDP in current dollars (billions)	*Percentage change*	*GDP in 1992 constant dollars (billions)*	*Percentage change*
1987	4,692.3	6.1	5,648.4	2.9
1988	5,049.6	7.6	5,862.9	3.8
1989	5,438.7	7.7	6,060.4	3.4
1990	5,743.8	5.6	6,138.7	1.3
1991	5,916.7	3.0	6,079.0	–1.0
1992	6,244.4	5.5	6,244.4	2.7
1993	6,553.0	4.9	6,386.4	2.3
1994	6,935.7	5.8	6,608.7	3.5
1995	7,253.8	4.6	6,742.9	2.0
1996	7,484.7	3.1	6,928.4	2.8

Source: Economic Report of the President 1997; Bureau of Economic Analysis.

Q 29. What exactly is Gross Domestic Product?

A Gross Domestic Product (GDP) is the total money value of all goods and services produced in a country during a year (or other time period). Economists and government officials use GDP as the basic yardstick for measuring the performance of the economy.

Only the value of finished products is counted in GDP. For example, the cost of flour to make a loaf of bread and the cheese in a cheeseburger are excluded from GDP because they are reflected in the price of the finished product. Also left out are exchanges of existing assets and so-called transfer payments, such as Social Security or welfare payments. Economists do include an estimate of the value of unreported activities like bartering and working "off the books."

(See 46 What happens in an economic expansion?)

Q 30. Is Gross National Product different from Gross Domestic Product?

A Gross National Product (GNP) provides a somewhat different gauge of a country's economic performance for a given time period. GNP includes Gross Domestic Product (the money value of all finished goods and services produced in a country) plus

Figure 1-2 Growth in Real GDP

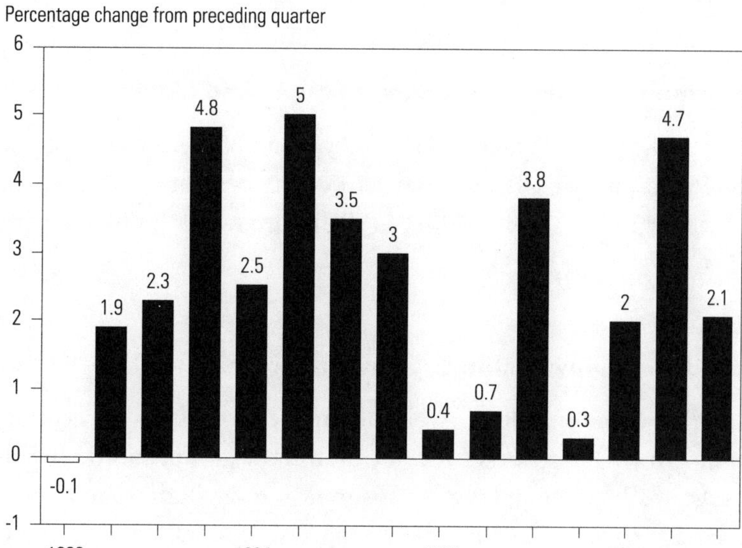

Source: Department of Commerce.
Note: Changes are at annual rates.

net foreign and domestic investment (the income the country's residents receive from production abroad minus foreign investment in the country). For that reason GNP emphasizes the total of goods and services produced by U.S. capital and labor worldwide, while Gross Domestic Product (GDP) focuses on just those goods and services produced within the country.

The amount received from abroad is small for the United States, just 0.2 percent of GDP in 1991. The federal government recently shifted from GNP to GDP for its basic economic yardstick, to comply with international accounting practices.

Q 31. How much of our economy is driven by government spending?

A Federal, state, and local government spending amounted to the equivalent of nearly one-third of GDP in 1996. State and local spending made up 10 percent and federal spending added another 21 percent for a total of 31 percent.

Thirty-one percent of GDP is a sizable amount of spending. But government spending by other developed countries is higher on a percentage basis. Government spending in Canada is the equivalent of about 42 percent of GDP; in Great Britain, about 45 percent; and in France, almost 55 percent.

(See 4 How much does the government spend in a year? 112 Do we pay more in taxes than people in other countries?)

Q 32. How many people are working in the United States?

A Over 100 million people are working, more than 65 percent of the entire population. Almost 76 percent of all men and almost 60 percent of women have jobs today. Employment growth since World War II has averaged about 1.8 percent a year (see Table 1-3).

Q 33. Does full employment help or hurt the economy?

A Generally, the more people are working, the better it is for the economy. Production, economic growth, and worker income all usually go up, and the need for social support programs like unemployment insurance, food stamps, and welfare drops when jobs are easy to get. But like everything else, too much of a good thing can be unhealthy. Beyond a certain point the demand for more workers feeds inflation.

Full employment is something less than 100 percent of the workforce actually working in a job. Seasonal factors, job changes, and changes in technology make for a fairly constant amount of unemployment even when the economy is booming. During the 1960s, for example, 96 percent employment (with 4 percent unemployment) was considered full employment. More recently, 93.5 percent to 94 percent employment (6 percent to 6.5 percent unemployment) has been considered a more realistic number for full employment.

Achieving full employment has been a major goal of federal fiscal policy ever since the New Deal, and the Employment Act of 1946 established specific objectives. Fiscal measures to stimulate business (and so expand employment) proved inflationary though, and between 1950 and 1975 inflation rose sharply whenever unemployment dropped much below 4 percent.

(See 44 What can the economy do to the budget? 49 What causes inflation? 64 What is "stabilization policy"? 422 Why did Congress pass the Employment Act of 1946? 458 What was the Humphrey-Hawkins full employment bill?)

Q 34. Is there a difference between consumer goods and capital goods?

A Food, clothing, home appliances, and anything else you use to satisfy your needs or desires are called *consumer goods.* Machinery, equipment, raw materials, and other things used to produce another product or service are called *capital goods.* The differ-

Table 1-3 Our Expanding Civilian Workforce

	Labor force (millions)	Percentage of population	Total employed (millions)	Employment growth (%)	Unemployment rate (%)
1946	56.7	57.3	54.5	4.6	3.9
1947	59.4	58.3	57.0	4.6	3.9
1948	60.6	58.8	58.3	2.3	3.8
1949	61.3	58.9	57.6	–1.2	5.9
1950	62.2	59.2	58.9	2.2	5.3
1951	62.0	59.2	60.0	1.8	3.3
1952	62.1	59.0	60.3	0.5	3.0
1953	63.0	58.9	61.2	1.5	2.9
1954	63.6	58.8	60.1	–1.7	5.5
1955	65.0	59.3	62.2	3.4	4.4
1956	66.6	60.0	63.8	2.6	4.1
1957	66.9	59.6	64.1	0.4	4.3
1958	67.6	59.5	63.0	–1.6	6.8
1959	68.4	59.3	64.6	2.5	5.5
1960	69.6	59.4	65.8	1.8	5.5
1961	70.5	59.3	65.7	0.0	6.7
1962	70.6	58.8	66.7	1.5	5.5
1963	71.8	58.7	67.8	1.6	5.7
1964	73.1	58.7	69.3	2.3	5.2
1965	74.5	58.9	71.1	2.6	4.5
1966	75.8	59.2	72.9	2.5	3.8
1967	77.3	59.6	74.4	2.0	3.8
1968	78.7	59.6	75.9	2.1	3.6
1969	80.7	60.1	77.9	2.6	3.5
1970	82.8	60.4	78.7	1.0	4.9
1971	84.4	60.2	79.4	0.9	5.9
1972	87.0	60.4	82.2	3.5	5.6
1973	89.4	60.8	85.1	3.5	4.9
1974	91.9	61.3	86.8	2.0	5.6

(Continued on next page)

Table 1-3 *(Continued)*

	Labor force (millions)	*Percentage of population*	*Total employed (millions)*	*Employment growth (%)*	*Unemployment rate (%)*
1975	93.8	61.2	85.8	–1.1	8.5
1976	96.2	61.6	88.8	3.4	7.7
1977	99.0	62.3	92.0	3.7	7.1
1978	102.3	63.2	96.0	4.4	6.1
1979	105.0	63.7	98.8	2.9	5.8
1980	106.9	63.8	99.3	0.5	7.1
1981	108.7	63.9	100.4	1.1	7.6
1982	110.2	64.0	99.5	–0.9	9.7
1983	111.6	64.0	100.8	1.3	9.6
1984	113.5	64.4	105.0	4.1	7.5
1985	115.5	64.8	107.1	2.0	7.2
1986	117.8	65.3	109.6	2.3	7.0
1987	119.9	65.6	112.4	2.6	6.2
1988	121.7	65.9	115.0	2.2	5.5
1989	123.9	66.5	117.3	2.1	5.3
1990	124.8	66.5	118.8	0.5	5.6
1991	125.3	66.2	117.7	–0.9	6.8
1992	127.0	66.4	118.5	0.6	7.5
1993	128.0	66.3	120.3	1.5	6.9
1994	131.0	66.6	123.0	2.2	6.1
1995	132.3	66.6	124.9	1.5	5.6
1996	133.9	66.8	126.7	1.4	5.4

Source: Economic Report of the President 1997; The Economic Record of Presidential Performance: From Truman to Bush, Richard J. Carroll.

ence is based on what the item is used for—a stove you use at home for cooking meals is a consumer good, for example. But use the same stove in your new restaurant and it would be classified as a capital good. Why? Because now you are making meals (a product) for paying customers.

Both consumer and capital goods can be either *nondurable goods* or *durable goods.* Nondurable goods, such as food, clothing, and gasoline, usually last under three years. Durable goods, such as appliances, cars, and furniture, last longer than that. The distinction becomes especially important in times of recession. We tend to postpone purchases of durable goods like cars and furniture when the economy is bad, but continue buying nondurable goods to satisfy our immediate needs.

Q 35. What is disposable income?

A Disposable income is not money you throw away. It is the term economists use for the income you have left over after your taxes and all other payments to federal, state, or local governments are deducted (see Table 1-4). (Those other payments include license fees, fines, and even state college tuition payments—all money that winds up in government coffers.) Our disposable income is a good yardstick of just how well off we are, and it helps economists estimate our spending for consumer goods and services, as well as how much we will put into savings. The United States Department of Commerce publishes statistics on disposable income in the *Survey of Current Business.*

(See 14 Why doesn't the government just keep raising taxes to meet its expenses? 103 What is a Laffer curve?)

Q 36. Why are housing starts an important economic indicator?

A A decline in housing starts is usually one of the first indicators of a coming economic downturn and so is considered an important leading indicator. Some experts think counting housing starts exaggerates construction activity, because finishing a house may take months or years and because in bad times work on the house may even stop altogether.

Housing starts are calculated monthly by the United States Bureau of the Census. The bureau counts only private housing units on which actual construction has begun.

(See 38 What are "leading" and "lagging" indicators? 39 What is the Index of Leading Economic Indicators?)

Q 37. Do federal regulations affect the economy?

A Deregulation has been an important issue for the Republican party, which has taken aim at inefficiencies and extra costs created by federal regulations. In the past the gov-

Table 1-4 Per Capita Disposable Income

	Current dollars	*1992 constant dollars*
1959	1,970	8,638
1960	2,008	8,660
1961	2,062	8,794
1962	2,151	9,077
1963	2,225	9,274
1964	2,384	9,805
1965	2,541	10,292
1966	2,715	10,715
1967	2,877	11,061
1968	3,096	11,448
1969	3,297	11,708
1970	3,545	12,022
1971	3,805	12,345
1972	4,074	12,770
1973	4,553	13,539
1974	4,928	13,310
1975	5,367	13,404
1976	5,837	13,793
1977	6,362	14,095
1978	7,097	14,662
1979	7,861	14,899
1980	8,665	14,813
1981	9,566	15,009
1982	10,108	14,999
1983	10,764	15,277
1984	11,887	16,252
1985	12,587	16,597
1986	13,244	16,981
1987	13,849	17,106
1988	14,857	17,621
1989	15,742	17,801

Table 1-4 *(Continued)*

	Current dollars	*1992 constant dollars*
1990	16,670	17,941
1991	17,191	17,756
1992	18,062	18,062
1993	18,555	18,078
1994	19,264	18,330
1995	20,224	18,799
1996*	21,177	19,242

*to third quarter.
Source: Economic Report of the President 1997.

ernment sought to control industries that were believed essential to the public (like airlines) or that were "natural monopolies" like telephones and the electric power system. In return for protecting the companies from competition, the government set prices and required companies to provide services even if they were unprofitable.

Just how much did those regulations cost? A recent study of deregulation in the airline, telecommunications, trucking, railroad, and natural gas industries shows rate reductions after deregulation saved consumers an estimated $40 to $60 billion a year. These savings are undeniably substantial, but the study did not include the botched deregulation of the savings and loan industry, which only made a bad situation worse (high interest rates had already seriously weakened S & Ls). Similarly, if the government were suddenly to abandon all environmental, health, and safety regulations, there might be considerable savings for the consumer. But at what long-term cost to workers and to society generally? Some regulations, obviously, are worth keeping.

(See 500 When did Congress deregulate the banking industry?)

Q **38. What are "leading" and "lagging" indicators?**

A Changes in certain economic statistics, such as a rise or fall in new unemployment insurance claims, can signal a coming upswing or downswing in the economy. These statistics are called "leading" indicators because they may change anywhere from one to twelve months before the overall economy does. By contrast, "lagging" indicators, like interest rates and unit labor costs, are statistics that rise or fall sometime after the change in the economy.

While these indicators are important in making economic forecasts, they have limitations and are only two of the tools economists use. The Conference Board compiles figures on leading and lagging indicators.

Q 39. What is the Index of Leading Economic Indicators?

This index helps economists predict what the economy will be doing six months to a year later. It is a composite of ten different economic indicators that tend to move up or down well before the overall economy enters a new phase in the business cycle. The indicators are: average weekly new unemployment insurance claims, index of consumer expectations, a stock price index, manufacturers' new consumer goods orders (in 1992 dollars), manufacturers' new orders (nondefense capital goods), average workweek of manufacturing production workers, interest rate spread (ten-year treasury bonds less federal funds), vendor performance (slowdown in delivery by vendors), money supply (M-2, in 1992 dollars), and the index of new housing starts.

(See 36 Why are housing starts an important economic indicator? 493 What is the money supply?)

Q 40. Does the Consumer Price Index (CPI) overstate inflation?

A A panel of economists appointed to study the CPI reported in 1997 that the index overstates inflation by about 1.1 percent a year (see Tables 1-5 and 1-6). That in turn has affected a wide range of economic statistics, they said, producing a ripple effect on both government finances and the private sector economy.

The CPI itself is calculated by the Bureau of Labor Statistics and is based on a monthly survey of 71,000 items at 22,000 stores. But the congressionally appointed panel, the Advisory Commission to Study the Consumer Price Index, concluded the CPI overstated inflation because the method of figuring the CPI was flawed in three ways:

* First, it underestimates improvement in quality as a factor in price increases (if something lasts longer or works better, a higher price is not really due to inflation).
* Second, the CPI surveys a fixed basket of goods and services (based on a standard set in 1982–1984). But consumers often substitute another item when the price of one gets too high (more chicken when beef prices rise, for example).
* Third, the CPI does not take into account consumers switching to discount stores.

(See 48 How does inflation affect my paycheck? 49 What causes inflation? 114 How has tax indexation changed tax policy? 171 Why has social spending risen by so much?)

Table 1-5 Year-to-Year Rises in Prices

	Percentage change in prices (all urban consumers)		*Percentage change in prices (all urban consumers)*
1940	0.7	1968	4.2
1941	5.0	1969	5.5
1942	10.9		
1943	6.1	1970	5.7
1944	1.7	1971	4.4
		1972	3.2
1945	2.3	1973	6.2
1946	8.3	1974	11.0
1947	14.4		
1948	8.1	1975	9.1
1949	–1.2	1976	5.8
		1977	6.5
1950	1.3	1978	7.6
1951	7.9	1979	11.3
1952	1.9		
1953	0.8	1980	13.5
1954	0.7	1981	10.3
		1982	6.2
1955	–0.4	1983	3.2
1956	1.5	1984	4.3
1957	3.3		
1958	2.8	1985	3.6
1959	0.7	1986	1.9
		1987	3.6
1960	1.7	1988	4.1
1961	1.0	1989	4.8
1962	1.0		
1963	1.3	1990	5.4
1964	1.3	1991	4.2
		1992	3.0
1965	1.6	1993	3.0
1966	2.9	1994	2.6
1967	3.1		
		1995	2.8
		1996	3.0

Source: Economic Report of the President 1997.

Table 1-6 The Consumer Price Index, 1954–1996 (all items)

Year	CPI	Year	CPI
1954	26.9	1975	53.8
1955	26.8	1976	56.9
1956	27.2	1977	60.6
1957	28.1	1978	65.2
1958	28.9	1979	72.6
1959	29.1		
		1980	82.4
1960	29.6	1981	90.9
1961	29.9	1982	96.5
1962	30.2	1983	99.6
1963	30.6	1984	103.9
1964	31.0		
		1985	107.6
1965	31.5	1986	109.6
1966	32.4	1987	113.6
1967	33.4	1988	118.3
1968	34.8	1989	124.0
1969	36.7		
		1990	130.7
1970	38.8	1991	136.2
1971	40.5	1992	140.3
1972	41.8	1993	144.5
1973	44.4	1994	148.2
1974	49.3		
		1995	152.4
		1996	156.9

Note: Table data are based on prices for urban consumers (CPI-U).
Source: Economic Report of the President 1997.

Q 41. What impact does the inflated CPI have?

A If the CPI were being used only for its original intended purpose—as a rough guide to prices of things consumers buy—the overstated inflation would probably have little effect on the economy. But the government and economists tend to use the CPI as a cost-of-living index, which they rely on to tell them how much inflation there has been over any given year. Because of this key role in measuring inflation, the CPI affects many important statistical measures of the economy—real (inflation-adjusted) GDP, real annual growth rates, and so on.

Effects of overstating inflation go far beyond a few abstract economic statistics, though. Tax brackets and government spending for various entitlement programs are automatically adjusted for inflation as measured by the CPI. Because of that, experts estimated that overstating inflation by just 1.1 percent will add a stunning $1 trillion to the national debt over the next twelve years.

How? The government uses the CPI to figure cost-of-living adjustments (COLAs), which protect the fixed benefits of some 45 million retirees and disabled workers from the effects of inflation. The higher inflation is, the more benefits increase, so that each time inflation is overstated Social Security recipients get what is actually a hike in benefits that was not voted on by Congress. Among the other federal programs with COLAs based on the CPI are Supplemental Security Income (6.5 million beneficiaries), federal civilian and military retirement plans (4 million beneficiaries), veterans' disability and pension benefits (3.3 million beneficiaries), and the railroad retirement plan (800,000 beneficiaries).

The inflated CPI is also costing the government much needed revenue Tax bracket break points are adjusted each year based on the CPI, to protect taxpayers from "bracket creep" associated with inflation. Adjustments to the personal exemption, standard deduction, Earned Income Tax Credit, limit on itemized deductions, excess pension distribution tax, and limits on pension contributions are all dependent on the CPI. Taxpayers are actually paying less than they would otherwise because of the inflated CPI.

Meanwhile, the CPI has an effect on the private sector, too. Many labor union contracts, some state and local employee wages and pensions, some commercial rental rates, and even some alimony and child support payments are pegged to the CPI.

(See 48 How does inflation affect my paycheck? 49 What causes inflation? 114 How has tax indexation changed tax policy? 171 Why has social spending risen by so much?)

Q 42. How is the Producer Price Index figured?

A The U.S. Bureau of Labor Statistics compiles the Producer Price Index each month from prices of about three thousand selected commodities. Current prices are compared to those in a previous year and the change is reported as a percentage. Among the monthly Producer Price Indexes are those for raw materials, intermediate products, and finished goods, but the Producer Price Index people usually refer to is the finished goods index. The bureau publishes the various indexes in the *Monthly Labor Review* and *Survey of Current Business.*

Originally compiled as the Wholesale Price Index, the Producer Price Index has been in existence since 1902 and was renamed in 1978. No other U.S. price index has been in continuous publication as long.

(See 38 What are "leading" and "lagging" indicators? 39 What is the Index of Leading Economic Indicators?)

Q 43. Do Americans vote their pocketbooks?

A A good economy can do wonders for an election campaign. Presidential approval ratings and presidential election campaigns are especially dependent on how satisfied voters are with the overall economy. An economic slump and the voter resentment it produces can give the challenger a definite edge on election day, while a good economy can strengthen an incumbent's chances despite lackluster performance or outright mistakes in other areas. Even mid-term congressional elections, in which a third of senators and all members of the House of Representatives are up for election, can be affected by a sagging economy or persistent economic problems like inflation.

Among the recent presidential elections, some clearly hinged on voters' concern about the economy. Richard Nixon was convinced he lost his 1960 presidential bid to John F. Kennedy because of an economic slump that fall. (Nixon was probably right; unemployment rose by 452,000 in October, just before the election). Persistent stagflation (stagnant economy plus inflation) and soaring interest rates contributed to incumbent president Jimmy Carter's loss to challenger Ronald Reagan in the 1980 election. And the economy's anemic recovery from the 1990–1991 recession was also a factor in President George Bush's loss to challenger Bill Clinton in 1992.

(See 58 What is stagflation? 61 How can politics in a presidential election year impact the economy?)

Q 44. What can the economy do to the budget?

A Federal revenues and expenses are closely tied to how well the economy is performing. Tax revenues, for example, are much higher during an economic boom because more people are working (and paying taxes), taxable business profits are rising, and individual tax payments go up when wages and salaries do. All that reverses during a recession, which delivers a one-two punch. First, the recession pulls down federal revenues because profits go down and fewer people work. Second, it pushes up federal expenditures. Outlays for unemployment compensation, food stamps, welfare, and other social safety programs all rise as more people lose their jobs during an economic slump.

Since changes in the economy mean billions of dollars in unexpected revenues or expenses, budget planners devote considerable energy to estimating how the economy will perform during the year covered by the budget. Better-than-expected growth in the economy can produce a revenue surplus that helps reduce the deficit. But an unexpectedly long recession can wreak havoc, pushing the deficit far above what was expected.

(See 13 Why does the government spend more than it takes in? 23 What impact does the government have on the economy? 64 What is "stabilization policy"? 65 What is fiscal policy? 69 What is monetary policy? 281 Are the government's budget projections accurate?)

Q 45. What did President Bill Clinton mean when he said the era of big government is over?

A The view that government can, and should, take responsibility for solving a widening array of social and economic problems has led to a vast expansion of the federal government since the 1930s. Where government once limited itself to such basic concerns as maintaining the currency, providing for the national defense, and collecting taxes, today's activist government funds programs that touch most every aspect of American life. Since the 1970s especially, conservatives have questioned the effectiveness and mushrooming cost of big government and have campaigned for reducing both its size and scope. Liberals have been buoyed by the fact that many federal programs provided help to millions and remain popular with voters. They argued strenuously against cutting social programs throughout the 1970s and 1980s. But the huge budget deficits of the 1980s and 1990s forced the question, Can we afford the cost of big government?

President Clinton, a Democrat, answered that question in his 1996 State of the Union address by saying:

"We know big government does not have all the answers. We know there's not a program for every problem. We have worked to give the American people a smaller, less bureaucratic government in Washington. And we have to give the American people one that lives within its means.

"The era of big government is over. But we cannot go back to the time when our citizens were left to fend for themselves. Instead we must go forward . . . to meet the challenges we face together. Self-reliance and teamwork are not opposing virtues; we must have both."

How much can government do?

"Government cannot solve all our problems, it can't set our goals, it cannot define our vision. Government cannot eliminate poverty, or provide a bountiful economy or reduce inflation or save our cities or cure illiteracy or provide energy, and government cannot mandate goodness."

—President Jimmy Carter, in his inaugural address, January 20, 1977

(See 372 What are the pros and cons of stricter budget control? 392 What is downsizing? 393 What cuts in the federal government has President Bill Clinton made? 396 If we are downsizing the government and cutting the deficit, why is federal spending still growing? 400 What effect did the 1930s depression have on the fundamental philosophy behind federal spending? 484 What did the Republican Contract with America try to do?)

TILTING THE PLAYING FIELD

Q 46. What happens in an economic expansion?

A When the economy is expanding, the total amount of goods and services produced by businesses and industries goes up. More workers are needed to increase production, so overall employment also rises and unemployment decreases. Typically certain sectors of the economy—but not necessarily all of them—benefit from an economic expansion. Sales of new homes and automobiles usually increase, for example, and prices generally go higher at a faster clip as an economic boom develops. Surges in consumer or federal spending are among the economic factors that can stimulate an expansion.

(See 55 What is a recession? A depression? 58 What is stagflation? 64 What is "stabilization policy"?)

Q 47. When was the last expansion? The longest?

A The economy has been expanding, although painfully slowly at times, since about April 1991, the end of the most recent recession. That makes the current expansion just over six years old, as of mid-1997, and a fairly long one. But two others in this century have been longer, including one lasting almost eight full years from about December 1982 to July 1990 during the Reagan-Bush administrations. The longest, though, occurred during the Kennedy-Johnson years. It continued for almost nine years from about February 1961 to December 1969.

(See 24 How does the economy affect me? 25 What are business cycles? 43 Do Americans vote their pocketbooks? 44 What can the economy do to the budget? 55 What is a recession? A depression? 64 What is "stabilization policy"? 69 What is monetary policy? 435 What were the economic policy successes and failures of the 1960s?)

Q 48. How does inflation affect my paycheck?

A Your paycheck may not change at all, or it may actually get larger when inflation is high. But generally speaking your paycheck will not buy as much as before, because inflation has been pushing prices up faster than your pay is increasing. That loss of buying power is one of the serious effects of inflation, and it usually takes some years for wages and salaries to catch up after a round of inflation (some wage earners and people on fixed incomes are permanently left behind). Another problem is that any savings you have will be worth less too, unless the interest you are getting is higher than the inflation rate.

(See 52 What does inflation do to the economy? 54 Who cured high inflation? 58 What is stagflation? 69 What is monetary policy? 443 What change in inflation did economists say occurred in the 1970s? 454 How did the oil shortages and other "supply shocks" affect inflation? 456 What was President Gerald Ford's economic record?)

Q 49. What causes inflation?

A Generally speaking economists are divided into two basic schools of thought on just what sets off inflation—a general rise in prices. Monetarists think inflation follows whenever the supply of money in the economy rises too fast. As leading monetarist economist Milton Friedman put it, "Inflation is always and everywhere a monetary problem."

Other economists think inflation stems from economic forces other than money, such as when demand for goods and services exceeds the economy's capacity to produce them (the excess demand of an overheated economy). In this scenario, typical of Keynesian economic theory, people have too much purchasing power and so bid up the price of available goods and services. Government efforts to promote full employment were generally believed to push up inflation for just that reason—with so many people working there was too much money available for buying things. Other non-monetary explanations for inflation include such economic forces as the "wage-price spiral" (higher wages increase demand, causing higher prices and new demands for higher wages), oil price increases, and the effect of monopolies on the economy.

(See 54 Who cured high inflation? 58 What is stagflation? 63 What exactly is Keynesian economics? 69 What is monetary policy? 443 What change in inflation did economists say occurred in the 1970s? 454 How did the oil shortages and other "supply shocks" affect inflation? 456 What was President Gerald Ford's economic record? 460 What was President Carter's economic record? 490 How does the Federal Reserve affect the economy?)

Q 50. When have there been bouts of inflation since World War II?

A Except for the 1970s, the economy has experienced only relatively brief periods of high inflation, and on average inflation has been about 4.3 percent a year since World War II.

The first bout with high inflation came immediately after the war, between 1946 and 1948, when it jumped to a high of 14.4 percent (in 1947). Inflation rose to 7.9 percent in 1951, largely because of the Korean War, and then nearly disappeared for the next sixteen years. During that time inflation never got above 3.3 percent a year.

Inflation reappeared in the mid-1960s, because the Johnson administration was spending heavily for the Vietnam War and many new social programs. After peaking briefly at 5.7 percent in 1970, inflation eased for two years and then spurted up to 11 percent (in 1974). It remained a serious economic problem throughout the 1970s and did not drop below 5 percent a year again until 1983.

Inflation hit a twenty-three-year high of 13.5 percent in 1980 during the Carter administration. It reached the lowest level in two decades, 1.9 percent, in 1986.

(See 49 What causes inflation? 52 What does inflation do to the economy? 54 Who cured high inflation? 69 What is monetary policy?)

Q 51. Under which presidents has average inflation been highest and lowest?

A Presidents do not always enjoy as much control over the economy as many people would think. But to some degree their policies can contribute to inflation and other economic problems during their administrations (or to those of succeeding administrations). President John F. Kennedy enjoyed the lowest average inflation rate since World War II—1.2 percent per year—during his three years in office, even though fighting inflation was not a high priority. President Dwight Eisenhower, who was concerned about inflation, averaged slightly higher during his eight years as president—1.4 percent. President Jimmy Carter, whose economic policies have been criticized for contributing to inflation, fared the worst—10.1 percent a year inflation on average.

President Richard Nixon, who battled with Congress over "inflationary" federal spending connected with his predecessor's Great Society programs, was next to last with an inflation rate of 6.4 percent a year.

(See 49 What causes inflation? 65 What is fiscal policy? 70 Are there political advantages to monetary policy?)

Q 52. What does inflation do to the economy?

A Economists are as divided on inflation's effects as they are on its causes. Some believe steady inflation rates of 10 percent a year have no real economic cost other than the inconvenience of constantly changing prices. And inflation has been a fairly constant feature of the post–World War II economy. The effects of the 1930s depression notwithstanding, the level of consumer prices in 1940 was about the same as it had been in 1778. But between 1940 and 1980 inflation drove consumer prices up over 400 percent.

Other economists think inflation has real economic consequences. Some see subtle costs, like an "inflation tax"—inflation steadily erodes the purchasing power of cash balances and so puts a drag on the economy. In fact, periods of high inflation in recent years have been linked with low economic growth.

Federal taxes on personal and corporate income posed a not-so-subtle inflation-oriented drain on taxpayers and businesses during the 1970s. As wages and corporate profits rose with inflation, individuals and businesses were pushed into higher income brackets and so paid more in taxes—as well as more for inflated prices of goods and services. Tax indexing, the automatic adjustment of tax brackets, eliminated much but not all the effects of inflation on taxes.

Another important consequence of inflation is upward pressure on government spending. Benefit programs like Social Security have automatic cost-of-living adjustments (COLAs) that increase automatically as inflation rises. While these adjustments help retirees and others receiving payments keep pace with inflation, increased benefits also have added to inflationary pressures and, according to some, helped put the program in financial jeopardy.

(See 58 What is stagflation? 65 What is fiscal policy? 69 What is monetary policy? 114 How has tax indexation changed tax policy? 298 What have been the successes and failures of past fiscal policy? 443 What change in inflation did economists say occurred in the 1970s? 454 How did the oil shortages and other "supply shocks" affect inflation? 468 What did the Reagan tax cut and budget reduction package do? 490 How does the Federal Reserve affect the economy?)

"... Inflation hurts the weak and so do the orthodox measures for controlling it. Inflation takes from the old, the unorganized and the poor and gives to those who are strongly in control of their own incomes. Monetary policy works by putting people out of jobs and by depressing the prices of those who have the least control. Also, it denies loans to the smaller man, who depends on borrowed money for his business, but it gives the corporations which have capital from their own earnings a free run."

—John Kenneth Galbraith, in *Almost Everyone's Guide to Economics*

Q 53. What are constant dollars?

A When inflation pushes up prices of things you buy, the value of your dollar actually shrinks—it buys less at the new higher prices than before. Constant dollars represent a way to compare what your dollar is worth now with what it would buy before inflation cut your buying power. Though seeing the actual difference may be somewhat depressing for you, it does help economists compare things like today's federal spending with past levels.

To find constant dollars, economists simply calculate what the overall inflation has been since (or before) a given benchmark year, say 1987. Then they use that figure to adjust the "current dollar" amount. For example, total federal spending for 1994 was $1.46 trillion in current dollars, but only $0.98 trillion in 1987 constant dollars. Inflation since 1987 puffed up the 1994 current dollar figure.

Things work in reverse for years before the 1987 benchmark. Actual federal spending in 1945, which marked the height of World War II expenditures, was $92.7 billion. But in 1987 constant dollars, 1945 spending was equal to $396 billion. As you can see, the cumulative effect of inflation since World War II has been substantial.

Q 54. Who cured high inflation?

A Federal Reserve chairman Paul Volcker, appointed by President Jimmy Carter in 1979, is generally credited with finally having ended the persistent high inflation that plagued the economy during the 1970s and early 1980s. Chairman Volcker did so by shifting the Federal Reserve's focus from trying to fine-tune interest rates to increasing bank reserves.

Forcing banks to keep more of their deposits in reserve (as opposed to loaning the money out) was the Fed's way of restricting the growth of the money supply. Slower money supply growth would make borrowing money more expensive (interest rates would rise) because there would be less money available. That in turn would slow economic growth and—eventually—inflation. In the past, money supply growth had been allowed to vary widely while the Fed focused on controlling interest rates.

Volcker announced the new policy on October 6, 1979, but it took several years to finally wring inflation out of the economy. Nineteen seventy-nine closed out with inflation boosting prices by 13.5 percent, even though the prime interest rate had hit 15.25 percent. Interest rates would go even higher the next year, hitting 20 percent in 1980 and 1981. Volcker continued his tight money policy though, relaxing only briefly during the mild 1980 recession before tightening the money supply again.

Volcker's anti-inflation measures proved so harsh they finally sent the economy into a deep recession in 1981–1982, early in President Ronald Reagan's first term. But it turned out that the recession dealt the final blow to high inflation. Since then Volcker's basic monetarist strategy, continued by his successor Alan Greenspan, has kept inflation in check.

(See 49 What causes inflation? 58 What is stagflation? 69 What is monetary policy? 490 How does the Federal Reserve affect the economy? 493 What is the money supply?)

Q 55. What is a recession? A depression?

A Recession is an economic slowdown. As business activity drops off because of it, factories cut back production, layoffs increase, jobs become harder to find, workers' incomes shrink, and consumers spend less. But recessions do not necessarily hit all parts of the economy to the same degree. The consumer products industry tends to be less sensitive to recessions, for example, and the housing industry more so.

An especially long, severe economic slowdown is called a depression, but there is no clear-cut way to determine when a recession has become a depression. An old saying gives the problem a personal spin, though: If your neighbor loses his or her job, it is a recession. If you lose yours, it's a depression.

Recent Recessions:
April 1960–February 1961 10 months
December 1969–November 1970 11 months
November 1973–March 1975 16 months
January 1980–July 1980 6 months
July 1981–November 1982 16 months
July 1990–March 1991 8 months

(See 25 What are business cycles? 38 What are "leading" and "lagging" indicators? 465 What first appeared in President Carter's annual economic report? 466 What was President Reagan's economic record? 471 What caused the 1981–1982 recession?)

56. How do we know when a recession has begun?

There is no hard and fast rule for determining exactly when a recession has begun, but a change in leading economic indicators (such as a drop in new housing starts and a rise in unemployment claims) for two or three consecutive quarters can signal a recession is on the way.

Part of the problem with identifying the start of a recession is that recessions themselves do not always fit a standard model. Newspapers have helped spread a popular definition of a recession, which holds that the economy is in a recession when GDP has declined for two or more quarters. The National Bureau of Economic Research, which makes the official determination of a recession for the federal government, relies on a more complicated definition: it calls a recession "a recurring period of declining total national output, income, employment, and trade, usually lasting from 6 months to a year and marked by widespread contractions in many sectors of the economy."

(See 25 What are business cycles? 38 What are "leading" and "lagging" indicators? 39 What is the Index of Leading Economic Indicators?)

57. Does disinflation always come with a recession?

Some disinflation—an easing of inflation—usually accompanies a recession. That is because, as the amount of money in circulation declines during a recession, the dollar is worth more and so buys more in goods and services. *Usually* is a key word, though. During the 1970s the United States, and the world at large, experienced episodes of continued inflation even though economic growth was stagnant. Economists labeled the problem "stagflation."

Deflation is distinct from disinflation and has been rare in the U.S. economy since World War II. Deflation is an actual drop in prices, as compared to a slowdown of price increases.

(See 25 What are business cycles? 44 What can the economy do to the budget? 52 What does inflation do to the economy? 69 What is monetary policy?)

58. What is stagflation?

Stagflation is an unusual mix of inflation, economic stagnation, and rising unemployment. It is unusual because prices keep going up (the inflation) even though economic growth has stalled and unemployment is rising—conditions economists once thought would always bring on a drop in prices. Stagflation first became a serious problem in the United States and other developed countries during the 1970s. Possible causes of stagflation in the United States include effects of government spending for both the Vietnam War and Great Society social programs, and the sharp increases in oil prices imposed by the Organization of Petroleum Exporting Countries (OPEC) during the 1970s. Some economists also think the government's success in preventing long recessions has encouraged businesses to ride out the downturns without lowering prices. Increases in unemployment posed both economic and political problems, and inflation-fighting fiscal measures used in the past failed to cure stagflation. The government instead turned to monetarist policies to attack the problem. (At the end of the 1970s the Federal Reserve pushed up key interest rates in an effort to halt inflation, a policy that proved successful.)

(See 52 What does inflation do to the economy? 69 What is monetary policy? 443 What change in inflation did economists say occurred in the 1970s? 454 How did the oil shortages and other "supply shocks" affect inflation? 456 What was President Gerald Ford's economic record? 490 How does the Federal Reserve affect the economy?

Q 59. What is the Misery Index?

A The Misery Index is a rough indicator of just how uncomfortable a bad economy has made life for the average person. It is computed by adding the inflation rate to the unemployment rate (see Table 1-7). Jimmy Carter exploited the Misery Index idea in his successful 1976 campaign for the presidency. Carter embarrassed President Gerald Ford by pointing out the Misery Index had reached unacceptably high levels while Ford was in office. But four years later during the 1980 presidential election campaign, challenger Ronald Reagan used the Misery Index to turn the tables on President Carter. Under Carter the Misery Index hit a postwar high.

(See 24 How does the economy affect me? 33 Does full employment help or hurt the economy? 43 Do Americans vote their pocketbooks? 48 How does inflation affect my paycheck? 52 What does inflation do to the economy? 61 How can politics in a presidential election year impact the economy? 64 What is "stabilization policy"?)

Q 60. Do entitlement programs help dampen recessions?

A Yes. When people lose their jobs during a recession, payments from federally backed programs such as unemployment compensation, food stamps, and welfare provide a safety net that eases their personal hardships. That is the primary goal of these programs, but on a larger scale the federal dollars also help soften the overall effects of a

Table 1-7 The Misery Index, Ups and Downs

	Misery Index	*Inflation*	*Unemployment*
Roosevelt administration, war years			
1939	15.8	–1.4	17.2
1940	15.3	0.7	14.6
1941	14.9	5.0	9.9
1942	15.6	10.9	4.7
1943	8.0	6.1	1.9
1944	2.9	1.7	1.2
Truman administration			
1945	4.2	2.3	1.9
1946	12.2	8.3	3.9
1947	18.3	14.4	3.9
1948	11.9	8.1	3.8
1949	4.7	–1.2	5.9
1950	6.6	1.3	5.3
1951	11.2	7.9	3.3
1952	4.9	1.9	3.0
Eisenhower administration			
1953	3.7	0.8	2.9
1954	6.2	0.7	5.5
1955	4.0	–0.4	4.4
1956	5.6	1.5	4.1
1957	7.6	3.3	4.3
1958	9.6	2.8	6.8
1959	6.2	0.7	5.5
1960	7.2	1.7	5.5
Kennedy administration			
1961	7.7	1.0	6.7
1962	6.5	1.0	5.5
1963	7.0	1.3	5.7

Table 1-7 *(Continued)*

	Misery Index	*Inflation*	*Unemployment*
Johnson administration			
1964	6.5	1.3	5.2
1965	6.1	1.6	4.5
1966	6.7	2.9	3.8
1967	6.9	3.1	3.8
1968	7.8	4.2	3.6
Nixon administration			
1969	9.0	5.5	3.5
1970	10.6	5.7	4.9
1971	10.3	4.4	5.9
1972	8.8	3.2	5.6
1973	11.1	6.2	4.9
Ford administration			
1974	16.6	11.0	5.6
1975	17.6	9.1	8.5
1976	13.5	5.8	7.7
Carter administration			
1977	13.6	6.5	7.1
1978	13.7	7.6	6.1
1979	17.1	11.3	5.8
1980	20.6	13.5	7.1
Reagan administration			
1981	17.9	10.3	7.6
1982	15.9	6.2	9.7
1983	12.8	3.2	9.6
1984	11.8	4.3	7.5
1985	10.8	3.6	7.2
1986	8.9	1.9	7.0
1987	9.8	3.6	6.2
1988	9.6	4.1	5.5

(Continued on next page)

Table 1-7 *(Continued)*

	Misery Index	*Inflation*	*Unemployment*
Bush administration			
1989	10.1	4.8	5.3
1990	10.9	5.4	5.5
1991	10.9	4.2	6.7
1992	10.4	3.0	7.4
Clinton administration			
1993	9.8	3.0	6.8
1994	8.7	2.6	6.1
1995	8.4	2.8	5.6
1996	8.1	2.7	5.4

Source: Economic Report of the President 1997 (for data).

recession. The programs are "automatic stabilizers" for the economy, because when a recession starts more people need unemployment insurance and other safety net benefits. That automatically pumps extra federal money into the economy and helps keep demand for goods and services from falling off too sharply, which would only make the recession worse.

(See 6 Why do I have to pay taxes? 13 Why does the government spend more than it takes in? 20 Should the budget be balanced? 65 What is fiscal policy? 147 Who got what in a recent budget? 160 What are entitlement programs? 171 Why has social spending risen by so much?)

Q 61. How can politics in a presidential election year impact the economy?

A Because Americans tend to "vote their pocketbooks," presidents and their parties have compelling reasons to promote an election-year upswing in the economy. Various options for a short-term stimulus have been used. For example, pre-election tax cuts (or delayed tax hikes), direct benefit increases, and increases in federal spending for various programs all can create an election-year economic upswing.

Another election-year gambit once used called for arranging a Social Security benefit increase early in the election year. That way the president and a willing Congress could put extra dollars in the pockets of millions of Americans and create a short-term fiscal stimulus to the economy. Taxpayers would not begin paying the extra payroll taxes required to make up for the increases until the following year, when the election had already been decided.

(Automatic cost-of-living increases for Social Security benefits, which began in 1975, undercut this particular politically motivated increase.)

These dodges give the economy a short-term boost but for the most part all have hidden long-term costs, like pushing up inflation and contributing to budget deficits.

(See 43 Do Americans vote their pocketbooks? 52 What does inflation do to the economy? 65 What is fiscal policy? 67 What role does Congress play in setting fiscal policy?)

Q 62. Does "laissez-faire" mean more or less government intervention in the economy?

A Less. Laissez-faire is an economic doctrine that arose in eighteenth-century France, where excessive government regulation of business reached all the way down to the local level. A French official named Jean Baptiste Colbert supposedly once asked a manufacturer how the government might help business, only to receive the disgruntled response, "laissez nous faire," or "leave us alone"! Laissez-faire, the idea of freeing business and the economy from the yoke of government interference, became the leading economic doctrine of the eighteenth and nineteenth centuries.

Here in the United States, the federal government gave more or less free rein to farmers, merchants, and manufacturers during much of the 1800s. The president had few economic responsibilities. But the industrialization of America toward the end of the 1800s brought such problems as bouts of severe unemployment, financial panics, powerful monopolies that took unfair advantage of workers and consumers alike, and grinding poverty in the cities. By the early 1900s the laissez-faire doctrine was giving way to demands for government regulation of industry and a new, more activist outlook in government. The public reaction to the Great Depression in the 1930s, which left 25 percent of the American workforce jobless, and the popularity of President Franklin Roosevelt's New Deal policies firmly established the view that government should be responsible for the country's overall economic and social well-being.

(See 64 What is "stabilization policy"? 69 What is monetary policy? 71 What is supply-side economics? 398 What was the "classical" view of the economy? 399 How have fundamental attitudes about federal budget policy changed since the country was formed? 400 What effect did the 1930s depression have on the fundamental philosophy behind federal spending? 401 What was the impact of the new federal spending policy? 412 What caused the Great Depression?)

Q 63. What exactly is Keynesian economics?

A Developed by the British economist John Maynard Keynes, Keynesian economics focuses on total demand in the economy (called aggregate demand). Put simply, when total demand for goods and services drops sharply in either the consumer, industrial, or government sector, a recession will occur. That is because as demand falls off, the growing backlog of unsold inventory forces businesses to cut back production and lay off employees.

Keynes's views became popular during the Great Depression because they offered an explanation for what had happened to the economy. Keynes also proposed federal spending as a solution to massive unemployment during the depression era. Keynes argued that increasing government spending would raise total demand in the economy and so force employers to hire more workers to boost production. For every dollar the government spent (or returned to the economy through tax cuts), there would be a "multiplier effect" as the federal dollars rippled through the economy. Keynes predicted it would create a far greater stimulus, and many more jobs, than could be expected from the original dollar alone.

The economic recovery that followed the sudden increase in federal spending during World War II is generally taken as proof of Keynes's ideas. And after World War II Keynesian theories provided justification for substantial federal intervention aimed at controlling the economy (stabilization policy). By raising and lowering taxes and spending, the government hoped to minimize unemployment and produce the highest possible level of prosperity, even if that meant deficit spending. While the government had success in controlling recessions, it came at a price—inflation and chronic high deficits.

(See 68 Can we fine-tune the economy? 298 What have been the successes and failures of past fiscal policy? 400 What effect did the 1930s depression have on the fundamental philosophy behind federal spending? 412 What caused the Great Depression? 418 Did President Roosevelt's policies deepen the 1937–1938 recession? 435 What were the economic policy successes and failures of the 1960s?)

Q 64. What is "stabilization policy"?

A The federal government's efforts to smooth out swings in the business cycle are called stabilization policy. Our economy naturally adjusts itself by means of economic expansions and recessions. But the American people have come to expect government intervention—particularly by the president—to produce the best possible economic conditions whether times are good or bad. During recessions, for example, the government's stabilization policy tries to keep unemployment from becoming too severe, and during boom times to hold inflation in check.

The government uses both fiscal policy and monetary policy (see questions below) to promote more stable economic conditions, but over the years its success has been mixed. Inflation proved a major stumbling block in the 1970s, for example, because Congress was unwilling to impose politically unpopular, inflation-fighting measures like spending cuts and tax hikes. Action by the Federal Reserve, which raised interest rates sharply, finally brought inflation under control during the 1980s.

(See 25 What are business cycles? 43 Do Americans vote their pocketbooks? 48 How does inflation affect my paycheck? 66 Do big deficits limit fiscal policy options? 69 What is monetary policy? 489 What is the Federal Reserve?)

Q 65. What is fiscal policy?

A Fiscal policy is the sum of taxing and spending decisions the government makes to pump up, slow down, or otherwise stabilize the economy. An inflation-fighting fiscal policy, for example, might try to slow the economy by imposing deep federal spending cuts or unpopular tax increases. A policy aimed at economic stimulation, on the other hand, would use higher federal spending levels and politically popular tax cuts to help pull the economy out of a recession. In either case, timing is important, however, because the economy changes quickly. The amount of money in the fiscal policy package may also affect the results.

Actually implementing fiscal policy is an unwieldy process. The president usually proposes spending increases, tax cuts, and other measures that make fiscal policy, but Congress must approve them. That means the president and his advisors have to decide not only what measures will help the economy, and in what amount, but also which ones Congress is likely to accept. The president and his party face longer-term political consequences as well, if the fiscal policy fails to prevent a recession or is otherwise unpopular with the electorate.

(See 23 What impact does the government have on the economy? 43 Do Americans vote their pocketbooks? 69 What is monetary policy? 295 Do we look to Congress or the president for leadership on economic issues? 298 What have been the successes and failures of past fiscal policy? 435 What were the economic policy successes and failures of the 1960s?)

"Fiscal policy is somewhat more equitable than monetary policy. But it also works by restricting production and employment, and it does this before prices are affected. So it, too, puts the burden of controlling inflation on those who lose their jobs. It works better on prices of small businessmen and farmers, those who are least able to maintain their prices and incomes."

—John Kenneth Galbraith, *Almost Everyone's Guide to Economics*

Q 66. Do big deficits limit fiscal policy options?

A Big deficits and the overhanging burden of a big national debt do restrict what the government can do to fight a recession with tax cuts and deficit spending, fiscal policy tools frequently used in the past. During a recession the budget is normally strained because tax revenues drop at the very time expenses are increasing for unemployment insurance, welfare, and other social "safety net" benefits. This is the reason why deficits tend to get much larger during recessions.

When the government even runs large deficits in good economic times, and then there is a recession, the drain on the budget can be severe. With so much red ink already flowing because of the recession, the government suddenly finds it cannot spend more money to stimulate the economy (deficit spending) to end the recession quickly. The extra spending would only swell the deficit to politically unacceptable highs and add to the mountain of federal debt. Passing a tax cut to stimulate the economy would have the same effect of reducing federal revenues at the worst possible time. (This tax-cut-during-a-recession scenario is just what happened with President Ronald Reagan's big tax cut in 1981. Republicans and Democrats alike in Congress became so worried about a big drop in revenues that they undid about 25 percent of the tax cut a few months later.)

(See 17 How big is the national debt? 19 Can't we just ignore the debt? 20 Should the budget be balanced? 65 What is fiscal policy? 126 Is there any limit on how much Congress can borrow? 133 What has the federal debt been over the years? 516 What is a stabilization crisis?)

Q 67. What role does Congress play in setting fiscal policy?

A Fiscal policy—taxing and spending decisions—must be approved in legislative form by Congress, which means the 535 members of the House and Senate will debate and ultimately vote on the measures. While that ensures taxing and spending decisions are subject to the democratic process, it has often hampered the president's ability to stabilize the economy through fiscal policy. By the time a fiscal package is approved by Congress, it often is a blend of middle-of-the road decisions reflecting the political realities and social attitudes of the day. What is really needed, though, is a fiscal package aimed at the economic realities of the moment.

The time it takes to pass the legislation—months to over a year—also can render the spending or taxing initiative irrelevant because economic conditions usually change more quickly. A classic example of this legislative "lag" is the tax cut first proposed by President John F. Kennedy in mid-1962. The tax was intended to counter an economic slump, but by the time the bill became law in 1964 (under President Lyndon Johnson), the economy was growing again.

Individual members of Congress tend to be sensitive to how broad fiscal policy decisions affect their constituents. Legislation that cuts jobs in a particular district, for example, will usually be opposed by the House member serving that district. This narrow focus can make passing tough fiscal policy measures unlikely, even though they are badly needed for the economy as a whole.

(See 13 Why does the government spend more than it takes in? 64 What is "stabilization policy"? 65 What is fiscal policy? 295 Do we look to Congress or the president for leadership on economic issues? 436 What was unusual about President Johnson's tax cut?)

Q 68. Can we fine-tune the economy?

A At one time during the 1960s, economists thought it would be possible for the government to "fine-tune" the economy—to adjust the money supply, federal spending, and taxes every few months to achieve continued full employment. Most economists now think fine-tuning through fiscal policy just is not possible in the real world of politics and imperfect knowledge of the economy.

That is because the timing of changes is so critical. An economic stimulus or an inflation-fighting spending cutback delivered too soon or too late could have serious unintended effects—or no effect at all.

Economic indicators being what they are, the government often does not find out a change is needed until the time for action has passed. Then, too, there is usually a long delay in putting fiscal policy into action. The president and Congress must both agree on the changes in spending or taxes, and then enact a bill to actually make the policy change. Even then it may take months or years before the fiscal policy takes full effect.

(See 65 What is fiscal policy?)

69. What is monetary policy?

The Federal Reserve sets monetary policy by raising or lowering the growth rate of the money supply, the amount of money circulating in the economy. The money supply, many economists think, directly affects economic activity. Increasing its rate of growth forces down interest rates because more money is available. That in turn stimulates investment and the economy generally. Decreasing the growth rate has the opposite effect—interest rates go up, discouraging investment and slowing the economy. But a slowing economy also helps bring down inflation.

So the Fed's monetary policy can wield considerable power over the economy. Decisions to lower interest rates helped spark the economic booms of the 1960s and 1980s, for example, and pushing up interest rates helped bring on recessions in the early 1970s and early 1980s. Beginning in the late 1970s, the Fed took a tough and sometimes unpopular stand against inflation that pushed up interest rates dramatically and slowed economic growth. But the persistent high inflation of the 1970s and early 1980s is now a thing of the past.

(See 48 How does inflation affect my paycheck? 49 What causes inflation? 54 Who cured high inflation? 58 What is stagflation? 459 What were the new economic realities of the 1970s? 489 What is the Federal Reserve? 490 How does the Federal Reserve affect the economy? 493 What is the money supply? 502 Why is money sometimes "tight" and sometimes "loose"?)

70. Are there political advantages to monetary policy?

One reason monetary policy is such a useful tool, especially for fighting inflation, is that the Federal Reserve can react relatively quickly to changing economic conditions. Fiscal policy might also be used against inflation, but the president must get approval from Congress before imposing inflation-fighting measures like cutting spending or raising taxes. That takes time. The measures may not be approved until long after economic conditions have changed, or Congress may even render them ineffective by watering down tough provisions.

Tough fiscal measures are also unpopular with voters, which only makes getting them through Congress even harder. Members of the Federal Reserve board of governors, on the other hand, are not elected to office, and the Federal Reserve itself can act independently of the president and Congress. So members do not have to worry (as much) about the political effects of a tough inflation-fighting monetary policy—rising unemployment and slowing economic growth—which may take several years to be fully effective. That greater insulation from politics gives monetary policy a huge political advantage over fiscal measures.

(65 What is fiscal policy? 489 What is the Federal Reserve? 491 Does the president control the Federal Reserve?)

Q **71. What is supply-side economics?**

A A controversial economic theory that gained acceptance among many conservative Republicans during the late 1970s, supply-side economics promised to quickly increase personal and corporate productivity without raising inflation or adding to the deficit. The solution, supply-siders maintained, was to cut taxes. High taxes discourage people from working harder and take money away from businesses that could be used to invest in new plants and equipment. By cutting taxes, especially the high "marginal" rates on the wealthy and businesses, supply-siders believed the government would put money into the hands of those who could invest it in ways to increase output of goods and services.

Supply-side theory appeared at an opportune time. The seventies had been beset by sagging productivity, chronic inflation, and a rising deficit brought on by increased social spending. In addition, the share of GDP taken as taxes by the government had been rising steadily during the Carter administration until it reached a post–World War II high of 19.7 percent in 1981.

Though the supply-side theory had many critics, presidential contender Ronald Reagan seized on the idea of cutting federal spending, reducing taxes, and balancing the budget, ideas that proved popular with voters. President Reagan ultimately won a large tax cut. In the end, however, his supply-side program was largely overwhelmed by the partisan battles over tax cuts vs. tax increases and defense spending vs. social spending priorities, not to mention a severe recession that began shortly after Reagan took office. Ultimately government spending, which had been rising since the 1970s because of the rapid growth of entitlement programs, grew much faster than the rise in federal revenues during the Reagan years.

(See 466 What was President Reagan's economic record? 468 What did the Reagan tax cut and budget reduction package do? 470 What was the 1982 tax hike?)

II

UNCLE SAM'S WALLET—WHERE THE MONEY COMES FROM

IN GENERAL

Q 72. What does the term revenue mean?

A Revenue is the government's income—money it takes in from taxes, fees, and other sources. It is the lifeblood of the federal government, and the Constitution gives Congress clear authority to levy taxes to raise money. The taxes and other revenue the Treasury collects pay the salaries of government workers, support the armed forces, fund various social programs, and make possible the federal government's many other activities.

(See 6 Why do I have to pay taxes? 14 Why doesn't the government just keep raising taxes to meet its expenses? 75 When did our income taxes become the government's main revenue source? 76 When did Congress pass its first revenue-raising bill? 78 What articles of the Constitution grant Congress the power to tax and spend? 82 When did federal revenues top $100 billion a year? A trillion? 83 How have federal revenue and outlays grown over the years?)

Q 73. What are the government's major sources of revenue?

A Taxes and borrowing provide the federal government with the bulk of the money it needs to operate. In fiscal 1996, for example, just over 45 percent of all revenue came from individual income taxes. Corporate taxes produced nearly 12 percent more and social insurance taxes 35 percent. Federal taxes on gasoline, telephone service, and the like (excise taxes) brought in about 4 percent, and other miscellaneous taxes and receipts (such as customs duties, estate and gift taxes) just over 4 percent. The government borrowed about 7 percent more to make up the difference between total revenue and what it actually spent (see Figure 2-1). Actual figures for 1996, and estimates for 1997 to 2000, are as follows:

Source	*1996*	*1997 (est.)*	*1998 (est.)*	*1999 (est.)*	*2000 (est.)*
			(In billions of dollars)		
Personal income tax	656.4	672.7	691.2	721.6	755.6
Corporate tax	171.8	176.1	189.7	199.6	212
Social Security tax	509.4	535.8	557.8	585.2	614.4
Excise tax	54	57.2	61.2	64.5	64.9
Estate & gift tax	17.2	17.6	18.9	20	21.4
Customs duties	18.7	17.3	18.3	18.5	19.6
Fed. Reserve deposits	20.5	23.2	23	23	23.7
Other misc. recpts.	5	5.4	6.8	11	16.1
Totals	1,453	1,505.3	1,567	1,643.4	1,727.7

Source: Budget of the United States, Historical Tables.

(See 408 How have tax revenues as a share of GDP changed since World War II?)

Q 74. What percent of federal revenues do my income taxes amount to?

A Though your income taxes probably seem like a lot to you, they are just a tiny fraction of what Uncle Sam collects in a year. Suppose you are a married taxpayer filing jointly and reported taxable income of $70,000 for 1996. Your $14,394 in personal income taxes would amount to just .0000000099 percent of the $1.45 trillion Uncle Sam collected in 1996. That may seem a drop in the bucket, but then that is the point of taxes—and the bucket: to catch as many drops as possible!

(See 6 Why do I have to pay taxes? 7 Have we always had to pay income taxes? 85 What is tax fairness? 112 Do we pay more taxes than people in other countries? 117 What do critics say is wrong with the current tax system? 118 How much do we pay, just to file our taxes? 410 Under which presidents did we have the largest personal income tax cuts? Tax increases?)

Q 75. When did our income taxes become the government's main revenue source?

A Congress first passed steep increases in income tax rates to help pay for expenses in World War I, and revenues jumped from just $360 million in fiscal 1917 to $2.3 billion

Figure 2-1 The Federal Government Dollar—Where It Comes From

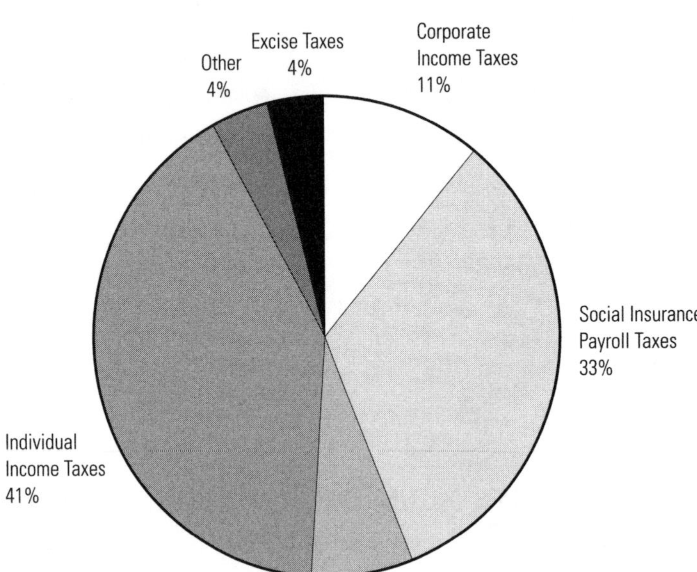

the following year. The proportion of federal revenues coming from income taxes rose throughout the 1920s, until in 1930 they amounted to over half of all revenues collected by the Treasury. Temporary excise taxes, enacted during the depression to make up for lost revenue, supplanted income taxes as the leading revenue source during the fiscal years 1933 to 1941. But since then income taxes have remained the government's single largest revenue source.

(See 7 Have we always had to pay income taxes? 8 How much did people pay during the first year of federal income taxes? 408 How have tax revenues as a share of GDP changed since World War II? 409 Under which presidents have average tax revenues been lowest? Highest?

Q **76. When did Congress pass its first revenue-raising bill?**

A The first money raising bill was approved by Congress July 4, 1789, just four months after the first Congress convened under the Constitution. The measure levied tariffs (customs duties) on goods imported into the United States. Tariffs remained the federal government's chief revenue source until the Civil War, supplying over 90 percent of what it collected each year.

(See 7 Have we always had to pay income taxes? 73 What are the government's major sources of revenue? 78 What articles of the Constitution grant Congress the power to tax and spend? 99 What are customs duties and who pays them?

Q 77. How much money did the federal government take in during its first years of existence?

A The newly created federal government took in a grand total of $4.42 million during its first three years of operation (1789–1791). For 1792 the federal government collected $3.7 million, and revenue climbed during much of the remainder of the 1700s, even though the total U.S. population numbered only about 4 million people. By 1800 annual revenue had reached $10.8 million.

(See 75 When did our income taxes become the government's main revenue source? 140 What did the government spend in its first year of operation? 145 When did the federal government post its first deficit?)

Q 78. What articles of the Constitution grant Congress the power to tax and spend?

A Three clauses of Article I of the Constitution spell out congressional powers to raise money, to borrow, and to spend. Article I, Section 8, begins, "The Congress shall have power to lay and collect taxes, duties, imposts and excises, to pay the debts and provide for the common defense and general welfare of the United States. . . ." A second clause in Section 8 grants Congress the power "to borrow money on the credit of the United States." The third clause appears in Article I, Section 9, and states, "No money shall be drawn from the Treasury, but in consequence of appropriations made by law. . . ."

(See 2 Who actually approves the budget? 3 Who actually spends the money? 7 Have we always had to pay income taxes? 80 Why was the Sixteenth Amendment necessary? 83 How have federal revenue and outlays grown over the years? 126 Is there any limit on how much Congress can borrow?)

Q 79. Can Congress pass any tax it wants?

A The Constitution grants Congress the power to enact almost any tax, and the courts have generally supported this broad taxing authority. The Constitution expressly forbids only export taxes (in Article I, Section 9) and requires that any taxes be "uniform throughout the land." One further limitation in Article I, Section 9, requires that direct taxes be collected in proportion to the population. That stipulation blocked establishment of the current income tax until the Sixteenth Amendment was ratified in 1913. The Supreme Court decision in *McCulloch v. Maryland* (1819), which established the government's right to implied powers not expressly stated in the Constitution, also exempted state and local governments from federal taxes.

(See 7 Have we always had to pay income taxes? 14 Why doesn't the government just keep raising taxes to meet its expenses? 73 What are the government's major sources of revenue? 83 How have federal revenue and outlays grown over the years?)

Q 80. Why was the Sixteenth Amendment necessary?

A The 1895 Supreme Court decision *Pollock v. Farmers' Loan & Trust Co.* overturned an income tax Congress had enacted two years earlier. The tax imposed a 2 percent tax on personal incomes over $3,000, but before any money was collected the Court ruled it was a direct tax. The Constitution (Article I, Section 9) specifically prohibits direct taxes unless they are apportioned among the states according to population. Since it would be impossible to apportion an income tax that way, the Supreme Court held it was unconstitutional.

Congress wanted the income tax because it needed a new source of revenue, however, and a campaign to enact the Sixteenth Amendment began soon after. The one-sentence amendment expanding Congress's taxing powers went right to the point: "The Congress shall have power to lay and collect taxes on incomes, from whatever source derived, without apportionment among the several states, and without regard to any census or enumeration." The amendment was not ratified until February 23, 1913, but once Congress got the green light it quickly passed the Revenue Act of 1913 to establish the income tax.

(See 7 Have we always had to pay an income taxes? 8 How much did people pay during the first year of federal income taxes? 73 What are the government's major sources of revenue? 75 When did our income taxes become the government's main revenue source?)

Q 81. When was the corporate income tax instituted?

A Congress levied the first corporate income tax in 1909 by disguising it as a "special excise tax." Corporations were taxed 1 percent on net income over $5,000, and unlike the personal income tax, the Supreme Court refused to overturn the excise tax. The Revenue Act of 1913, passed after the Sixteenth Amendment expanded Congress's taxing powers, reenacted the tax as a corporate income tax. The rate remained the same, however.

(See 73 What are the government's major sources of revenue? 75 When did our income taxes become the government's main revenue source? 120 Why have corporate tax revenues declined over past decades? 164 What is "corporate welfare"? 287 How do interest groups influence the budget process?)

Q 82. When did federal revenues top $100 billion a year? A trillion?

A Revenues finally exceeded $100 billion for the first time in 1963, but took just thirty years more to pass the $1 trillion mark. Despite the breathtakingly fast growth in total dollars, federal revenues during this time stayed remarkably stable as a percentage of Gross Domestic Product—18.3 percent of GDP in 1960 and 18.8 percent in 1990. What changed between 1960 and 1990 was the economy itself. Thanks in part to the arrival of baby-boomers, the economy expanded, and personal and corporate incomes rose along with it. That, of course, meant more taxable income and automatic gains in the government's total tax revenue.

(See 22 Just how big is the U.S. economy? 28 How fast has the economy been growing over the years? 46 What happens in an economic expansion? 75 When did our income taxes become the government's main revenue source? 141 When did federal spending reach $1 billion a year? $1 trillion?)

Q 83. How have federal revenue and outlays grown over the years?

A During the fifty years following World War II, federal revenues have grown thirty-fold, topping $1.4 trillion by 1996 (see Table 2-1). While taxpayers may feel as though taxes are higher than ever before, in fact taxes as a percent of GDP have remained fairly steady. (Looking at total revenues relative to GDP compensates for economic growth.)

Though federal revenues have increased substantially most years since World War II, federal spending has risen faster. Since the mid-1970s spending has remained above 20 percent of GDP, and big deficits have been the norm.

Strong economic growth and increased taxes in the mid-1990s created a surge in revenue growth from 1993 to 1996—$100 billion a year for three straight years (for a look at federal revenue composition, see Figure 2-2). That coupled with new efforts at controlling federal spending helped bring about a major reduction in the deficit.

Table 2-1 Revenue and Spending Growth (dollar figures in millions)

	Revenue	*Percentage of GDP*	*Outlays*	*Percentage of GDP*	*Surplus/ Deficit*
1930	$4,058	4.1	$3,320	3.3	$738
1931	3,116	3.7	3,577	4.2	–462
1932	1,924	2.8	4,659	6.8	–2,735
1933	1,997	3.4	4,598	7.9	–2,602
1934	2,955	4.8	6,541	10.6	–3,586
1935	3,609	5.1	6,412	9.1	–2,803
1936	3,923	4.9	8,228	10.4	–4,304
1937	5,387	6.1	7,580	8.5	–2,193
1938	6,751	7.5	6,840	7.6	–89
1939	6,295	7.0	9,141	10.1	–2,846
1940	6,548	6.7	9,468	9.7	–2,920
1941	8,712	7.5	13,653	11.8	–4,941
1942	14,634	10.1	35,137	24.2	–20,503
1943	24,001	13.3	78,555	43.7	–54,554
1944	43,747	21.2	91,304	44.2	–47,557
1945	45,159	20.8	92,712	42.6	–47,553
1946	39,296	18.0	55,232	25.4	–15,936
1947	38,514	16.9	34,496	15.1	4,018
1948	41,560	16.4	29,764	11.7	11,796
1949	39,415	14.6	38,835	14.4	580
1950	39,443	14.5	42,562	15.6	–3,119
1951	51,616	16.1	45,514	14.2	6,102
1952	66,167	18.9	67,686	19.4	–1,519
1953	69,608	18.7	76,101	20.4	–6,493
1954	69,701	18.5	70,855	18.8	–1,154
1955	65,451	16.5	68,444	17.3	–2,993
1956	74,587	17.5	70,640	16.6	3,947
1957	79,990	17.8	76,578	17.0	3,412
1958	79,636	17.4	82,405	18.0	–2,769
1959	79,249	16.2	92,098	18.8	–12,849

Table 2-1 *(Continued)*

	Revenue	Percentage of GDP	Outlays	Percentage of GDP	Surplus/ Deficit
1960	92,492	17.8	92,191	17.8	301
1961	94,388	17.8	97,723	18.4	–3,335
1962	99,676	17.6	106,821	18.8	–7,146
1963	106,560	17.8	111,316	18.6	–4,756
1964	112,613	17.6	118,528	18.5	–5,915
1965	116,817	17.0	118,228	17.2	–1,411
1966	130,835	17.4	134,532	17.9	–3,698
1967	148,822	18.3	157,464	19.4	–8,643
1968	152,973	17.6	178,134	20.5	–25,161
1969	186,882	19.7	183,640	19.4	3,242
1970	192,807	19.1	195,649	19.4	–2,842
1971	187,139	17.4	210,172	19.5	–23,033
1972	207,309	17.6	230,681	19.6	–23,373
1973	230,799	17.7	245,707	18.8	–14,908
1974	263,224	18.3	269,359	18.7	–6,135
1975	279,090	18.0	332,332	21.4	–53,242
1976	298,060	17.2	371,792	21.5	–73,732
1977	355,559	18.0	409,218	20.8	–53,659
1978	399,561	18.1	458,746	20.7	–59,186
1979	463,302	18.6	504,032	20.2	–40,729
1980	517,112	19.0	590,947	21.7	–73,835
1981	599,272	19.7	678,249	22.2	–78,976
1982	617,766	19.2	745,755	23.2	–127,989
1983	600,562	17.6	808,380	23.6	–207,818
1984	666,499	17.5	851,888	22.3	–185,388
1985	734,165	17.9	946,499	23.1	–212,334
1986	769,260	17.6	990,505	22.6	–221,245
1987	854,396	18.6	1,004,164	21.8	–149,769
1988	909,303	18.4	1,064,489	21.5	–155,187
1989	991,190	18.5	1,143,671	21.4	–152,481

(Continued on next page)

Table 2-1 *(Continued)*

	Revenue	Percentage of GDP	Outlays	Percentage of GDP	Surplus/ Deficit
1990	1,031,969	18.2	1,253,163	22.0	–221,194
1991	1,055,041	18.0	1,324,400	22.6	–269,359
1992	1,091,279	17.8	1,381,681	22.5	–290,402
1993	1,154,401	17.8	1,409,414	21.8	–255,013
1994	1,258,627	18.4	1,461,731	21.4	–203,104
1995	1,351,830	18.8	1,515,729	21.1	–163,899
1996	1,453,062	19.4	1,560,330	20.8	–107,268
1997(e)	1,505,425	19.2	1,560,330	20.8	–107,268
1998(e)	1,566,842	19.1	1,687,475	20.5	–120,633
1999(e)	1,643,320	19.1	1,760,700	20.4	–117,380
2000(e)	1,727,304	19.1	1,814,427	20.1	–87,123

Note: (e) indicates estimates.
Source: Budget of the United States, Historical Tables; Economic Report of the President 1997.

Q 84. What is the difference between progressive and regressive taxes?

A A progressive tax system increases the tax rate on an individual's income as the total amount earned gets larger. That way people who earn less pay less in taxes, while high income earners pay more. This system is considered fairer because it puts more of the overall tax burden on people who are better able to afford it. The United States income tax system is progressive—it has brackets that start out at about 15 percent of taxable income and go up in steps to 39.6 percent as total income increases.

Regressive taxes are those with a fixed rate for all levels. Sales taxes, for example, are regressive because rich and poor alike pay the same amount of tax on items they buy, even though the extra expense is harder for the poor to bear. Payroll taxes are also regressive because they impose a flat rate on earnings. But the Social Security system they support is progressive because low income earners get higher benefits in relation to the money they paid in.

(See 6 Why do I have to pay taxes? 87 What are marginal tax rates? 103 What is a Laffer curve?)

"Taxes are what we pay for civilized society."

—Oliver Wendell Holmes, 1904.

Figure 2-2 Composition of Revenues

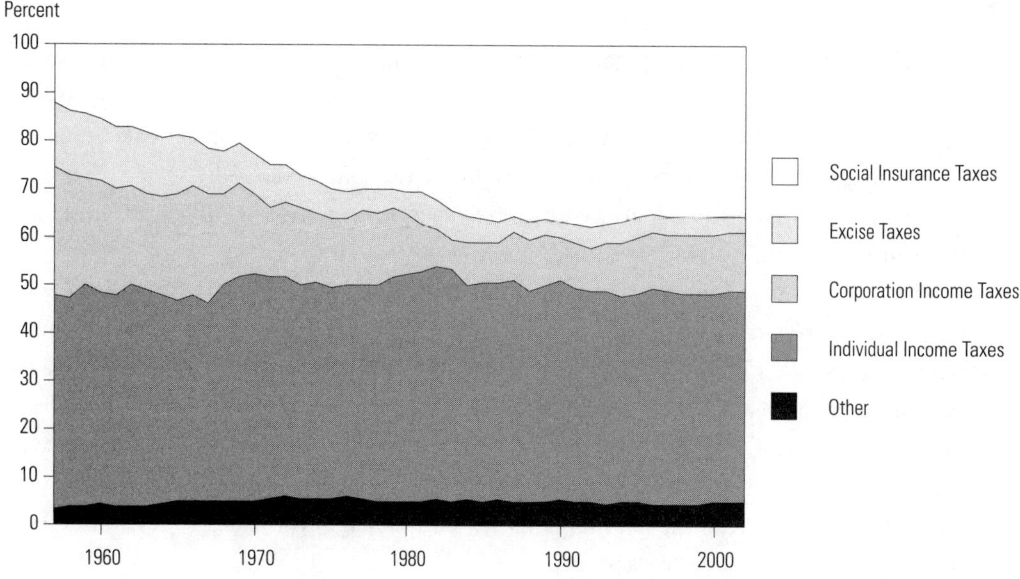

85. What is tax fairness?

To some degree, the definition of tax fairness depends on your point of view: For those who believe in the progressive tax system, tax fairness means the rich should bear the greater burden of taxes because they are better able to afford it. But others question how much of the tax burden the wealthy should have to pay. For them, tax fairness means the burden should be spread around more evenly.

Tax fairness in both these senses became a central issue in writing the Tax Reform Act of 1986, which cut top tax rates and various deductions and made income taxes less progressive. At the same time, though, the act also made it possible for about 6 million of the working poor to pay no taxes at all.

The issue of tax fairness has survived into the 1990s, used by both Republicans and Democrats in pushing for further reforms of the tax code.

(See 6 Why do I have to pay taxes? 87 What are marginal tax rates? 119 When was the last major overhaul of the tax code and what changed?)

▶ What is income redistribution? *See 6 Why do I have to pay taxes? 84 What is the difference between progressive and regressive taxes?* ◀

86. What is the capital gains tax?

For tax purposes, the government distinguishes between the money people earn in wages and the profits (capital gains) they make from investments, such as stocks and bonds, works of art and other collectibles, and real estate. Cutting the capital gains tax has been a major goal of conservative Republicans, who believe a lower rate will spur investment and promote economic growth. Critics have charged that a lower rate would not stimulate the economy (and tax revenues) enough to offset amounts the government would lose in taxes.

The 1997 balanced budget agreement cut the capital gains tax in a way that favors longer-term investments. Assets held for more than eighteen months, for example, will be taxed at 20 percent (instead of the current 28 percent). Profits on assets bought after the year 2000 and held for five years or more will be subject to a top rate of 18 percent. Homeowners who sell their primary residence for $250,000 or less will pay no capital gains tax. Taxable real estate profits will be subject to a 25 percent tax. According to estimates, the capital gains tax cut package will result in a revenue loss of $21.2 billion over ten years.

(See 488 What did the 1997 balanced budget agreement do to cut taxes?)

87. What are marginal tax rates?

A hot topic among proponents of supply-side economics during the 1980s, the marginal tax rate is the rate you pay on the top end of your income. For example, with tax brackets used in the 1970s, your first $10,000 of income would be subject to a 12 percent tax, the next $10,000 at the next tax level, and on up in steps until you reached the 50 percent level, the top tax rate. Any additional money you made was taxed at the 50 percent rate, the marginal rate.

Supply-siders pointed out that the high marginal rate discouraged people from putting in the extra effort to produce more or from taking risks to invest more, once they hit the marginal rate. It was actually easier to earn less than more. That, they argued, translated into slower growth for the economy as a whole and, ultimately, lower tax revenues because people were not earning as much as they could be.

Reductions in marginal tax rates in over fifty countries during the 1980s provided dramatic proof that the theory was in fact correct. Great Britain and Japan both saw substantial gains in economic growth after cutting marginal tax rates during the 1980s. President Ronald Reagan's 1981 tax cut dropped the top rate in the United States from 70 percent to 50 percent and sparked a surge in growth during the

"What is a loophole? That is something that benefits the other guy. If it benefits you, it is tax reform."

—Sen. Russell B. Long (D-La.), longtime Senate Finance Committee chairman

decade. Meanwhile, the top 5 percent of all taxpayers actually paid more in taxes after the marginal rate dropped. Under the old system, in 1979, they paid 37.6 percent of all income tax revenues; in 1988 they paid 45.9 percent.

(See 14 Why doesn't the government just keep raising taxes to meet its expenses? 103 What is a Laffer curve?)

88. How do "tax expenditures" affect revenues?

A At tax time we all like to see the tax loopholes—credits, exemptions, and deductions—that reduce our taxable income and save us money. But for the federal government these exceptions, called tax expenditures, cut two ways. On the one hand, tax expenditures are a useful policy tool—deductions for mortgage interest can help promote home ownership, for example, and tax breaks for businesses can spur on economic growth or even promote social policy. But they also cost the government billions of dollars that would have been collected if the deduction, credit, or exemption had not been allowed.

For that reason Congress has generally tried to limit, rather than expand, tax expenditures during the 1980s and 1990s. But some of the most costly tax expenditures have been around almost as long as the income tax itself, and the amount of lost revenues only rises with each passing year. The 1996 budget lists over one hundred tax expenditures, which cost the government anywhere from a few million dollars to over $64 billion.

(See 102 How do the proposed flat tax, sales tax, and value-added tax plans works?)

Q 89. What are the major tax expenditures and how much revenue is lost through them?

A Despite efforts in Congress to save money by closing tax loopholes, many still exist. Those listed below were among the biggest in fiscal 1996. Some curiosities can also be found among the deductions—the exclusion for reimbursed employee parking expenses ($1.25 billion in revenue losses), for example, was about the same as that for deferred interest on U.S. savings bonds ($1.3 billion lost).

Tax deduction/credit allowed	*Lost Tax Revenue (in millions)*
Employer contributions to employee medical insurance and medical care	$64,450
Employer pension contributions and earnings	55,410
Mortgage interest on owner-occupied homes	47,525
Accelerated depreciation	32,230
Step-up basis of capital gains at death	29,530
State and local taxes	28,265
Social Security income exemptions for retired workers	17,005
Charitable contributions	16,045
State and local property taxes	15,900
Interest on state and local debt	15,720
Capital gains on home sales deferred	14,410
Interest on life insurance savings	10,525

Source: Budget of the United States Government, 1998, Analytical Perspectives.

▶ How much revenue does the Earned Income Tax Credit cost? *See 182 What is the Earned Income Tax Credit?* ◀

Q 90. How many tax-exempt organizations are there?

A The IRS listed over 1.2 million tax-exempt organizations as of the mid-1990s. By far the largest categories were religious and charitable groups (about 600,000), social welfare groups (over 140,000), and fraternal societies (over 92,000). There were some 74,000 business leagues, 68,000 labor and agricultural groups, and over 30,000 war veterans' organizations, as well as some 5,300 state-chartered credit unions and almost 9,300 cemetery companies.

Q 91. Do individuals and companies get tax breaks on foreign earnings?

A When United States citizens work abroad they often do not have to pay taxes on up to $70,000 of their income and can deduct a part of their housing costs. Exporters can reduce their taxes by allocating earnings abroad, or get an outright exemption for part of their earnings if they work through foreign sales corporations. Foreign corporations controlled by United States firms or principals also benefit from tax deferrals. Their earnings are not taxed until shareholders in the United States receive them as stock dividends.

Q 92. What are excise taxes, and how much revenue do they generate?

A Taxes on the manufacture, sale, or consumption of goods are called excise taxes, and this form of taxation has been with us since the first years of the republic. Within a few years after ratification of the Constitution, the federal government levied excise taxes on such things as liquor, snuff, sugar, carriages, and auction sales. Because they pass on extra costs directly to the manufacturers or to purchasers of the goods, they have met with public disfavor from time to time. In fact, the federal excise tax on liquor, enacted in 1791, sparked the first abortive revolt against federal government authority—the Whiskey Rebellion of 1794.

Though excise taxes on tobacco and liquor remain perennial favorites, the government has imposed (and later repealed) excise taxes on various manufactured goods over the years, especially when money was needed to fight a war. Today federal excise taxes include those on gasoline, telephone service, and ozone depleting chemicals, as well as liquor and tobacco. The overall proportion of revenue remains small, about 4 percent of annual revenue, and in 1997 amounted to about $60 billion. Nevertheless, excise taxes are regressive taxes because everyone must pay a higher price for the goods. That puts what many regard as an unfair burden on the poor.

(See 73 What are the government's major sources of revenue? 84 What is the difference between progressive and regressive taxes? 115 Has the mix of federal tax revenues changed over the years?)

Q 93. What are the social insurance taxes?

A Also called payroll taxes, these taxes are deducted from wages and salaries to pay for the Social Security program, disability insurance, Medicare, and unemployment insurance. Both the employee and employer make contributions to these programs, and the employee portion is withheld from each paycheck (along with the amount for income taxes).

Payroll taxes amounted to about $509 billion in 1996, making them the federal government's second largest revenue source. Revenues have been rising about $20 billion a year during the 1990s and are expected to do so for the rest of the decade. The government estimates revenue from payroll taxes will top $614 billion by the year 2000.

(See 6 Why do I have to pay taxes? 95 What are the major federal trust funds and how much do they take in? 121 How has the tax rate for the employer's share of the payroll tax increased over the years? 171 Why has social spending risen by so much? 411 What happened with corporate and social insurance tax revenues?)

Q 94. What are general funds?

A General funds are revenues collected by the government that are not earmarked by law for some special purpose, such as Social Security. For budget purposes the government classifies as general funds nearly all receipts from income tax revenue, all excise taxes and some from other sources, and all borrowed money. It uses these funds to pay for such things as the operating expenses of federal agencies, the interest on the debt, and for national defense expenditures. The budget has two other important categories of funds—trust funds and special funds, which are discussed in Question 97, below.

The term "federal funds" includes general funds as well as special, intergovernmental, and public enterprise funds. Only money earmarked for trust funds is not counted as federal funds.

(See 72 What does the term revenue *mean? 73 What are the government's major sources of revenue? 97 What is the difference between special funds and trust funds?)*

Q 95. What are the major federal trust funds and how much do they take in?

A The government collects about $700 billion annually—nearly half of its gross receipts—for deposit into the 160-plus federal trust funds. About 97 percent of the money goes to the eight largest trusts, Social Security, Medicare (hospital insurance), Medicare (supplementary medical insurance), federal civilian employees retirement, military retirement, the highway trust, airports and airways trust, and the unemployment insurance trust (see Table 2-2). The two funds with far and away the largest balances are Social Security and the federal employee retirement trusts.

The proportion of federal revenues going into trust funds has grown significantly in past decades. In 1960, for example, trust funds got under 20 percent of what the government collected each year. As of 1996, about 57 percent of federal revenues went into trusts. The government held almost $1.4 trillion in trust fund accounts as of 1996, and that total was expected to reach almost $2 trillion by the year 2000.

(See 60 Do entitlement programs help dampen recessions? 93 What are the social insurance taxes? 165 What is "backdoor spending"? 171 Why has social spending risen by so much? 207 Has the government been using funds from Social Security for other purposes?)

Q 96. Can the money in trusts be diverted to other purposes?

A Congress can alter trusts, divert the funds, and even abolish them if enough votes can be found in both houses to pass the legislation. Funds in trusts almost always have

Table 2-2 Trust Fund Balances (in billions)

Fund	*1996*	*1997 (est.)*	*1998 (est.)*	*1999 (est.)*	*2000 (est.)*
Social Security (Old Age Survivors and Disability Trust)	$549.6	$625.4	$705.9	$794.1	$890.1
Federal employee retirement	401.7	430.9	461.1	491.0	520.7
Medicare—hospital insurance fund	125.3	115.3	117.4	119.7	124.6
Medicare—supplemental medical insurance	27.0	30.3	31.5	32.2	32.9
Military retirement	131.2	139.1	146.0	152.7	159.6
Unemployment	54.0	61.1	67.5	74.1	80.7
Highway trust	21.6	24.4	27.7	31.4	34.9
Airport and airway	7.9	7.8	7.7	5.2	3.9

Source: Budget of the United States Government, 1998, Analytical Perspectives.

been used for the specified purposes, but from time to time Congress has made alterations. It diverted money from the highway trust fund to finance mass transit, authorized payment of Federal Aviation Administration expenses out of the airways trust fund, and even terminated the revenue-sharing trust fund in 1980. Where diversions have occurred, the purposes usually have been related to the original mission of the trust. Diverting funds from the Social Security trust fund, as some have feared, is virtually out of the question, however, because the political opposition from senior citizens would be enormous.

The federal government does borrow surplus funds from the trusts and pays the trusts over $80 billion a year in interest. Though critics of this practice disagree, it represents a legitimate, revenue-producing investment of the funds, not a diversion. For example, the Social Security trust fund earned about $34 billion in interest payments during 1996 alone.

(See 197 Why is Social Security called the "third rail" of American politics? 207 Has the government been using funds from Social Security for other purposes?)

Q 97. What is the difference between special funds and trust funds?

A Though special funds are not officially designated as trusts, the money in them has been earmarked for special purposes. The budget gives a separate accounting of user fees collected for the National Wildlife Refuge Fund, Land and Water Conservation Fund, and other special funds. But unlike trust funds, this money is deposited in the general fund, and the government pays no interest for borrowing money from a special fund.

(See 94 What are general funds? 95 What are the major federal trust funds and how much do they take in?)

Q 98. How much revenue do estate and gift taxes produce?

A Benjamin Franklin once observed, "In this world nothing can be said to be certain except death and taxes." As if to confirm that, the federal government collects estate taxes, a final property tax on everything you own at the time of your death. The tax currently applies only to those people with estates worth more than $600,000 and has been a permanent fixture in the tax code since 1916. (The exemption will rise in steps to $1 million by 2006.) The gift tax, imposed on large gifts since 1932, became necessary to prevent people from giving away their property to avoid the estate tax. Together, estate and gift taxes produce only about 1 percent of the tax revenue and in 1996 amounted to about $16 billion.

(See 73 What are the government's major sources of revenue?)

Q 99. What are customs duties and who pays them?

A Customs duties, also known as tariffs, are taxes on goods imported into the United States. Ultimately, the person buying the item pays because the tax is usually passed on in the form of a higher price tag.

Historically, customs duties were used to protect American manufacturers from foreign competition—the added cost of customs duties kept the price of foreign imports high. Receipts from the duties also generated revenue, which was the federal government's main source for spending money from the late 1700s to the early 1900s. (Income taxes are now the largest revenue source.)

Total revenues from customs duties have risen slowly in past years (to about $18 billion), but personal and corporate tax revenues have risen so much faster that customs receipts now amount to only about 1 percent of all revenues collected by the government each year. Also, moves toward lowering trade barriers worldwide in recent decades have reduced or eliminated customs duties on many imported items.

(See 73 What are the government's major sources of revenue? 75 When did our income taxes become the government's main revenue source?)

Q 100. Has Congress imposed special taxes on corporate profits?

A Yes, special taxes on excess corporate profits have been levied on corporations during World War I, World War II, and the Korean War. The tax was designed to offset the government's expenses of fighting the wars and to tax extra profits corporations made from producing war materials. More recently, Congress passed a windfall profits tax on oil companies in 1980. Domestic oil production was being deregulated at the time, and the tax was designed to tap excess profits made from the resulting oil price rises.

(See 7 Have we always had to pay income taxes? 73 What are the government's major sources of revenue? 81 When was the corporate income tax instituted? 120 Why have corporate tax revenues declined over past decades? 411 What happened with corporate and social insurance tax revenues?)

Q 101. What is a negative income tax?

A This tax scheme is basically a mirror image of our current, progressive income tax, which taxes people with high incomes more heavily to help reduce the amount people with low incomes must pay. The negative income tax would still tax high income earners heavily, but people below a certain income level would no longer have to pay any tax at all. In fact, they would actually receive money from the government based on the negative tax rate and how far below the income threshold their earnings were.

For example, suppose $10,000 was the threshold income for the negative tax and a worker made only $6,000 during the year, $4,000 below the minimum income. If the negative tax rate were 20 percent, the worker would pay no taxes at all and get a check for $800 through the IRS. The government would in effect pay the worker 20 percent of the $4,000 he or she did not earn.

Experiments with the negative tax idea during the late 1960s revealed various potential problems, not the least of which was preventing cheating and widespread fraud. Other problems included a reduction in incentives to work, an unexpected increase in family instability, and the failure to offer cash benefits equal to existing welfare plans.

(See 170 Why spend tax dollars on social programs? 182 What is the Earned Income Tax Credit?)

Q 102. How do the proposed flat tax, sales tax, and value-added tax plans work?

A There are many variations, but the three basic tax reform plans are as follows. (Payroll taxes would still have to be paid under all these plans.)

* Flat tax. This plan would tax everyone at the same rate no matter how much they earned, doing away with the tax bracket system. It would also end all tax deductions, and eliminate taxation of investment income (including savings accounts and stock dividends). As a Republican presidential primary candidate in 1996, Steve Forbes championed a flat tax of 17 percent, complete tax exemption for low-income individuals, an end to taxes on investments, and promised to make filing returns so simple taxpayers could use a postcard. Critics charged flat-tax plans favor the rich and could wind up losing billions in tax revenues. That millions of homeowners would lose their mortgage deduction was also a concern.
* National sales tax. Retail stores would collect this tax the same way they collect state and local sales taxes. The problem here is that only a fairly high tax would generate enough revenues—rates of 13 percent and 17 percent have been suggested (on top of state and local sales taxes). A more serious argument, though, is that tax enforcement is nearly impossible. Both the seller and the buyer would have reason to avoid paying the tax, especially at the higher rates needed. Furthermore, sales taxes are less fair because they hit the poor harder than the wealthy.
* Value-added tax (VAT). This tax is paid by businesses and is imposed at each stage of production. A manufacturer is taxed based on its net profit, the difference between its expenses and gross revenue from sales of goods. There are no problems of enforcement with this system. But it is potentially disruptive to the economy in the short-term, and the increased costs to business will undoubtedly be passed on to consumers through price hikes. Also, the VAT is considered a regressive tax that will hit the poor harder than the wealthy.

(See 84 What is the difference between progressive and regressive taxes?)

Q 103. What is a Laffer curve?

A A controversial concept in supply-side economics, the Laffer curve charts the amount of tax revenue the federal government can expect to collect when the tax rate is at various levels. At one end of the curve the tax rate is zero, netting the government no revenue. At the other a 100 percent tax rate also yields no revenue, because without income people have no incentive to work. Economist Arthur Laffer, who developed this concept, theorized that at some point between the extremes taxes finally get high enough to discourage people from working. That in turn reduces people's income and, ultimately, federal tax revenues.

Although many mainstream economists doubted the Laffer curve concept, President Ronald Reagan and other Republican supply-siders used it to argue for tax cuts during the 1980s. Taxes had already become so high, they said, that people were being discouraged from working to earn more, and they pointed to the stagnant economic growth of the 1970s as proof.

(See 14 Why doesn't the government just keep raising taxes to meet its expenses? 58 What is stagflation? 87 What are marginal tax rates?)

▶ Do higher taxes slow down the economy? *See 14 Why doesn't the government just keep raising taxes to meet its expenses?* ◀

THE IRS

Q 104. How many tax forms does the IRS process each year?

A About 200 million tax forms a year pour into the IRS, including income tax, estimated tax, corporate tax, payroll tax, and estate tax forms. End-of-year income tax forms filed by individuals accounted for about 114.9 million of the forms processed in a recent year (18.9 million were 1040EZ). Corporate tax forms numbered about 4.6 million.

Q 105. What does the IRS collect in taxes and pay out in refunds?

A The IRS has collected over a trillion dollars in taxes each year since 1989 (almost $1.3 trillion in a recent year). It collected about $620 billion in individual income taxes, about $154 billion in corporate taxes, and almost $444 billion in payroll taxes. The IRS gives back over $90 billion in refunds a year. Most of that, almost $77 billion in a recent year, goes for refunds on personal income taxes.

Q 106. Whose tax forms are getting a closer look from the IRS?

A Of all the tax returns filed in a recent year, the IRS actually examined just a fraction, about 1.4 million or 0.93 percent overall. The average for individual tax returns was slightly higher, about 1.08 percent examined, and IRS examiners paid relatively more attention to returns in the upper income brackets. Corporate tax returns also received greater scrutiny—about 2.3 percent overall were checked—and the biggest corporations got the closest look of all. About 55 percent of returns filed by corporations with earnings over $250 million were examined.

Q 107. How much does it cost the government to collect $100 in taxes?

A The IRS spent over $7 billion collecting more than $1 trillion in personal and corporate income taxes in 1996. That works out to 58 cents for every $100 dollars it took in.

(See 118 How much do we pay, just to file our taxes?).

Q 108. Do people cheat on their taxes?

A Yes. According to IRS estimates, about 83 percent of all taxpayers comply with tax laws, and in 1996 they paid over $1.3 trillion in taxes. The IRS used "direct enforcement" to collect $38 billion more from another 3 percent of taxpayers, who for one reason or another failed to comply with tax laws. Between voluntary compliance and direct enforcement, the IRS estimates about 86 percent of taxpayers paid their fair share in 1996. That means the other 14 percent apparently are tax cheats who got away with it—at least for the time being.

Q 109. Does it really cost $28.6 billion just to collect the taxes?

A The IRS actually spends only a few billion ($7.3 billion in 1996) to collect over $1.3 trillion in taxes annually. It pays out the rest of the money in its budget to taxpayers. The bulk of the money, $19.2 billion in 1996, covers cash payments for earned income credits owed to low-income workers.

(See 105 What does the IRS collect in taxes and pay out in refunds? 107 How much does it cost the government to collect $100 in taxes? 182 What is the Earned Income Tax Credit?

Q 110. How many people work for the IRS?

A Computers have taken over much of the work in checking tax returns, but as of early 1997 the IRS still employed 102,000 people. This includes auditors, administrators, clerks, and others involved in processing tax forms and enforcing tax compliance.

(See 159 How many people work for the federal government? 393 What cuts in the federal government has President Bill Clinton made?)

"The art of taxation consists in so plucking the goose as to obtain the largest possible amount of feathers with the smallest possible amount of hissing."

—Jean Baptiste Colbert (1619–1683)

RAISING THE REVENUE

Q 111. How much per capita do we pay in taxes?

A The per capita tax is a "what if" figure that shows what every man, woman, and child in the United States would pay if they all chipped in an equal share of the government's actual total revenue for a year. In the mid-1990s, for example, the government took in $1.3 trillion, which means the per capita tax would have been $5,108. But the average tax bill for just those people who actually worked is almost double that: just over $10,000.

Q 112. Do we pay more in taxes than people in other countries?

A No, percentagewise we pay less than in some of the world's major nations (see Figure 2-3). In 1990, for example, total taxes in both France and Germany amounted to 43.7 percent of their GDP. Total taxes in the United States for 1990 amounted to 29.9 percent of GDP, which also ranked below Canada (37.1 percent), the United Kingdom (36.7 percent), and Japan (31.3 percent).

Q 113. How does inflation affect my taxes?

A Before tax indexation went into effect in 1985, inflation automatically pushed taxpayers into higher brackets, forcing them to pay a higher percentage of their earnings in taxes. "Bracket creep," as it was called, happened because in times of inflation wages tend to increase along with prices. The worker does not really gain any advantage—higher living costs absorb the extra income—but in the past tax brackets stayed at fixed levels until Congress decided to change them.

So long as the inflation rate was low, taxpayers did not notice the extra tax bite. From time to time Congress took credit for passing so-called "tax cuts," which actually just raised brackets to adjust for inflation. But between 1976 and 1981, surging inflation pushed so many people into higher tax brackets that federal tax receipts jumped from 17.2 percent of GDP to 19.7 percent. The 1981 tax cut, pushed

Figure 2-3 Tax Rate for Married Couple with Combined Family Income of $100,000

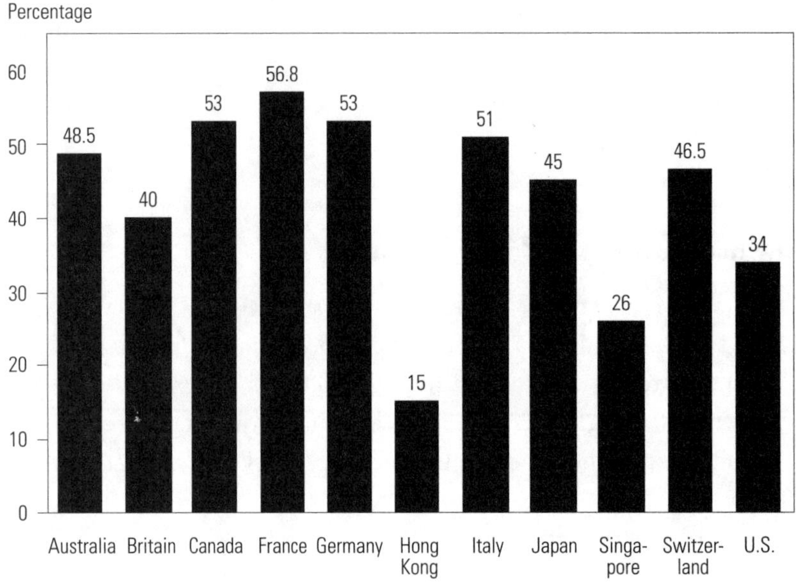

by the Reagan administration, readjusted tax brackets to account for inflation. But among other things it also provided for tax indexation—automatic annual adjustment of tax brackets to compensate for inflation—beginning in 1985.

Q 114. How has tax indexation changed tax policy?

A "Bracket creep" had provided the federal government with an ongoing revenue windfall before tax indexation went into effect in 1985: for every 1 percent increase in inflation, tax collections actually increased 1.5 percent. But because the windfall accumulated automatically (and most taxpayers did not know they were being charged more), Congress did not have to risk voting for what would normally be an unpopular tax hike. More money to fund new programs simply appeared with every uptick in inflation.

Little wonder, then, that some opponents claimed tax indexation would have "disastrous" effects on the budget, including huge deficits that would force Congress to take such politically unpopular steps as raising taxes or making deep spending cuts. Supporters countered by saying indexation would make Congress more "honest" about taxing and spending. Any major spending increases would ultimately force floor votes to raise new revenues.

To some degree everyone turned out to be right. Tax indexation has done away with hidden tax increases and gratuitous "tax cuts" that merely adjusted brackets for inflation—in fact, it was not until 1997 that Congress enacted the first significant tax cut since 1981. Instead, Congress has been forced to seek spending cuts and ways to increase tax revenues in the face of big deficits, caused in part by inflation and the disappearance of that extra revenue. Congress ultimately had to vote tax increases in 1982, 1990, and 1993, along with so-called revenue enhancements in 1984, 1986, and 1987.

Q 115. Has the mix of federal tax revenues changed over the years?

A Yes. Since World War II personal income taxes have consistently amounted to about 45 percent of the government's total annual revenue (within a percent or two), but receipts from other taxes have changed markedly. Corporate income taxes are now about half what they were in 1960, having shrunk from about 23 percent of all revenue to about 11.8 percent in 1996. Social insurance taxes did just the opposite. They more than doubled between 1960 and the mid-1990s, skyrocketing from 15.9 percent to 36.2 percent. Excise taxes, which the government routinely raises during wartime, also shriveled from a high of 19 percent during the Korean War to a low of 3.4 percent in 1990. Excise taxes have since risen slightly but are expected to remain in the 3 percent to 4 percent range throughout the 1990s.

(See 120 Why have corporate tax revenues declined over past decades?)

Q 116. When have personal income tax revenues been at their lowest?

A Measured in terms of percentage of GDP, revenues from personal income taxes hit their post–World War II low of 14.8 percent in 1950. The share had been only slightly higher in 1949 (15 percent), and since 1950 it has never again dipped below 16 percent of GDP.

Personal income tax revenues hit the postwar all-time high of 20.2 percent twice: in 1968 during the Johnson administration and in 1981, the year the Reagan administration took office. The average for personal income tax revenues during the postwar period is slightly more than 18 percent.

(See 410 Under which presidents did we have the largest personal income tax cuts? Tax increases?)

Q 117. What do critics say is wrong with the current tax system?

A Perhaps the most common criticism is that the system is too complicated. Considering that complying with the tax code costs taxpayers an estimated 3 billion hours in time each year, there just may be something to that complaint. Conservatives frequently blame the taxes on savings, dividends, and other capital gains for discouraging saving and investment and for favoring current consumption (for saving and investment data, see Table 2-3). Liberals meanwhile are concerned that the tax system is not progressive enough and want an increase in the tax burden for wealthy Americans. The system of tax expenditures (tax exemptions) has also come under attack as a source of tax breaks for the wealthy.

Q 118. How much do we pay, just to file our taxes?

A Because filing a tax return is so complicated, many families and businesses rely on paid professional help from accountants and tax preparers. One estimate put the total amount paid for complying with the federal tax code (including the cost of time spent learning about requirements and keeping records) at $225 billion a year.

Q 119. When was the last major overhaul of the tax code and what changed?

A The 1986 Tax Reform Act has sometimes been called the most important tax legislation since the Sixteenth Amendment to the Constitution established the personal income tax, and experts generally agree it made the tax code more fair. Tax reform had been President Ronald Reagan's top domestic priority during his second term, and the 1986 Reform Act as it emerged from Congress made sweeping changes to the tax code. Designed to produce neither more nor less revenue (revenue neutral), the act replaced the fifteen–tax bracket system with two brackets (15 percent and 28 percent of income), lowered the top tax rate (the marginal tax), eliminated many tax deductions and loopholes, and made it possible for 6 million of the working poor to pay no taxes at all. Among the deductions the act eliminated or curbed were those for sales tax, consumer loans, medical expenses, business lunch expenses, and charitable and political contributions. The investment tax credit was eliminated, and the advantages of tax shelters, long considered an unfair tax dodge for the very rich, were sharply reduced.

(See 85 What is tax fairness? 468 What did the Reagan tax cut and budget reduction package do? 482 What was President Clinton's 1993 tax increase designed to do? 488 What did the 1997 balanced budget agreement do to cut taxes?)

Table 2-3 Savings and Investment (dollar figures in billions)

	Gross savings	*Personal savings*	*Personal savings (% of disposable income)*	*Business savings*	*Government savings**
1959	$109.0	$24.3	7.0	$58.4	$26.2
1960	113.9	23.3	6.4	58.8	31.8
1961	116.8	28.3	7.5	60.2	28.3
1962	127.4	29.5	7.4	67.6	30.3
1963	135.4	28.6	6.8	71.7	35.1
1964	145.8	35.5	7.7	77.4	32.9
1965	161.0	37.8	7.6	86.6	36.6
1966	171.7	39.1	7.3	93.5	39.2
1967	174.4	48.9	8.5	95.9	29.7
1968	185.8	46.8	7.5	99.3	39.7
1969	202.9	46.9	7.0	102.1	53.9
1970	198.2	61.0	8.4	103.8	32.6
1971	215.3	68.6	8.7	122.1	23.9
1972	244.9	63.6	7.4	139.1	41.5
1973	297.5	89.6	9.3	152.7	55.1
1974	302.3	97.6	9.3	155.2	51.5
1975	298.3	104.4	9.0	197.8	–3.9
1976	340.9	96.4	7.6	221.1	23.5
1977	395.5	92.5	6.6	256.9	46.1
1978	477.4	112.6	7.1	292.4	72.4
1979	540.9	130.1	7.4	319.0	90.7
1980	547.4	161.8	8.2	327.6	56.8
1981	651.1	199.1	9.1	382.8	68.1
1982	604.7	205.5	8.8	404.6	–5.3
1983	589.6	167.0	6.6	452.1	–29.4
1984	751.5	235.7	8.4	501.9	14.0

(Continued on next page)

Table 2-3 *(Continued)*

	Gross savings	Personal savings	Personal savings (% of disposable income)	Business savings	Government savings*
1985	746.7	206.2	6.9	525.3	15.2
1986	721.0	196.5	6.2	513.6	10.8
1987	780.9	168.4	5.0	558.8	53.6
1988	877.2	189.1	5.2	619.3	68.8
1989	907.9	187.8	4.8	628.1	92.0
1990	904.4	208.7	5.0	653.0	42.7
1991	935.5	246.4	5.7	685.6	3.3
1992	905.4	272.6	5.9	699.2	–66.5
1993	935.5	214.4	4.5	748.0	–26.9
1994	1,056.3	189.4	3.8	817.3	49.6
1995	1,151.8	249.3	4.7	822.5	80.0
1996	1,267.8	239.6	4.3	886.0	142.3

	Gross private domestic investment	Gross government investment	Gross savings (% of GNP)
1959	$78.8	$29.3	21.4
1960	78.8	28.2	21.5
1961	77.9	31.3	21.3
1962	87.9	33.2	21.6
1963	93.4	33.5	21.8
1964	101.7	34.5	21.8
1965	118.0	35.4	22.2
1966	130.4	40.1	21.7
1967	128.0	43.5	20.8
1968	139.9	44.3	20.3
1969	155.0	43.9	20.5

Table 2-3 *(Continued)*

	Gross private domestic investment	*Gross government investment*	*Gross savings (% of GNP)*
1970	150.2	44.0	19.0
1971	176.0	43.1	19.0
1972	205.6	45.4	19.7
1973	242.9	48.3	21.3
1974	245.6	56.0	20.0
1975	225.4	62.7	18.1
1976	286.6	64.4	18.6
1977	356.6	65.4	19.3
1978	430.8	74.6	20.6
1979	480.9	85.3	20.9
1980	465.9	96.4	19.4
1981	556.2	102.1	20.7
1982	501.1	106.9	18.5
1983	547.1	116.5	16.6
1984	715.6	131.7	19.1
1985	715.1	149.9	17.8
1986	722.5	163.5	16.3
1987	747.2	173.5	16.6
1988	773.9	172.9	17.3
1989	829.2	182.7	16.6
1990	799.7	199.4	15.7
1991	736.2	200.5	15.8
1992	790.4	209.1	14.5
1993	871.1	210.6	14.3
1994	1,014.4	212.3	15.2
1995	1,065.3	221.9	15.9
1996	1,116.5	224.3	16.6

*Government savings includes federal, state, and local government savings.
Source: Economic Report of the President 1997.

120. Why have corporate tax revenues declined over past decades?

Corporate tax revenues, which amounted to 20 to 30 percent of federal revenues during the 1940s and 1950s, have declined fairly steadily since the late 1960s. In 1983 they hit a post–World War II low of 6.2 percent of federal revenues before moving upward again. Weak profits are the main reason for the long decline, but increased debt financing, greater use of tax dodges, and the drop in marginal tax rates during the 1980s all probably contributed as well. Corporate taxes yielded 11.8 percent of federal revenues in 1996.

Corporate income tax revenues of course do not include the substantial sums collected by the government for the employer's share of payroll taxes, which have been rising rapidly in recent years (See next question).

(See 115 Has the mix of federal tax revenues changed over the years? 411 What happened with corporate and social insurance tax revenues?)

121. How has the tax rate for the employer's share of the payroll tax increased over the years?

Though many people who are employed do not realize it, their employer matches dollar-for-dollar what they pay in payroll taxes for Social Security, disability, and hospital insurance. So business pays half of all revenue the government collects for payroll taxes (the self-employed pay both halves of the payroll taxes themselves).

Both the tax rate and the amount of income that can be taxed have increased sharply in recent years, as federal spending for Social Security and Medicare has mushroomed. When the Social Security program began in 1937, the employer/employee tax was 1 percent up to a maximum of $3,000 of income. The tax rate was up to 3 percent by 1960, although the taxable maximum had risen to only $4,800.

President Lyndon Johnson's sweeping changes in Social Security dramatically altered the program during the 1960s, and liberals in Congress further expanded benefits during the 1970s. By the mid-1970s, however, it was becoming clear that payroll tax increases were well short of what was needed to fund the expanded program (by 1975 the employer/employee rate was 5.85 percent on $14,100). With insolvency looming in the years ahead, the government focused primarily on increasing the maximum taxable income. For example, by 1980 the maximum taxable income was $25,900 while the tax rate was 6.13 percent; in 1997, $65,400 and 7.65 percent.

Q 122. How have revenues from "user charges" changed over the years?

A Federal revenues from user fees more than doubled from $55.6 million in 1981 to about $120 million in 1991. Congress has backed additional fee hikes since then as part of the effort to reduce the budget deficit. Park entrance fees, federal highway tolls, charges for postal services, and charges for other government goods and services generate about three-quarters of user fees. The remainder comes from other charges, such as regulatory fees (like those for copyrights and patents) and liability-based charges (such as the crude oil tax to pay for cleaning up oil spills).

Until the 1980s, fees covered only actual costs of the goods or services being offered. But that policy changed with the 1985 Consolidated Omnibus Budget Reconciliation Act and subsequent legislation, which directed agencies to begin recovering their operating costs as well through the fees. Charges by the Nuclear Regulatory Commission, for example, jumped from $46 million to $439 million between 1986 and 1991. More recently, the government also began phasing in new revenue-generating fees for various activities at national parks and historic sites.

BORROWING AND THE EVER-MOUNTING DEBT

Q 123. Will the government be going broke anytime soon?

A While there is reason for concern about the rising national debt, it is unlikely the government will ever have to declare bankruptcy. In fact, one reason why the government has been able to borrow so much money is that it is still a good risk. Despite its habit of overspending, and despite the awesome size of the federal debt, the government takes in a huge sum each year—about $1.5 trillion in 1997 alone—and that inspires confidence that loans can be repaid.

By another measure economists use, the debt in relation to gross domestic product (GDP), the government is still in considerably better shape than it was at the end of World War II. The fact that our government has substantial fiscal resources to draw on—continued borrowing and taxes it can raise to increase revenue—means bankruptcy is not really a question at this point. What has happened is that the debt has finally gotten large enough to become a fiscal and political liability that must be addressed. What once might have been fixed with some spending restraint or modest increases in taxes now requires much more painful and politically unpopular remedies.

(See 13 Why does the government spend more than it takes in? 14 Why doesn't the government just keep raising taxes to meet its expenses? 19 Can't we just ignore the debt?

"A national debt, if it is not excessive, will be to us a national blessing."

—Alexander Hamilton, 1781

73 What are the government's major sources of revenue? 131 When did the federal debt actually begin to mushroom? 132 How much does the interest on the federal debt cost now? 133 What has the federal debt been over the years?)

Q **124. Where does Congress get the authority to borrow money?**

A The second clause of Article I, Section 8, of the Constitution grants Congress the power "to borrow money on the credit of the United States." This brief clause effectively sets no restrictions on that power—Congress can borrow for any purpose and is free to borrow as much as it wants, to choose any lender, and to make the loan on any terms.

(See 78 What articles of the Constitution grant Congress the power to tax and spend? 320 What is "the power of the purse"?)

Q **125. Why does the government have to borrow money?**

A When the government spends more in a year than it collects in taxes and other revenue, the difference—called the deficit—must be made up by borrowing money. In theory, at least, the government pays back the loans in years when revenues are higher than expenses. But since 1931 the government has managed to eke out small surpluses in just a few years. Meanwhile, the ever-increasing need for borrowing in recent years has pushed the debt up to astronomical levels.

(See 13 Why does the government spend more than it takes in? 16 What is the longest period of consecutive budget deficits? 17 How big is the national debt? 18 Where did the national debt come from? 20 Should the budget be balanced? 133 What has the federal debt been over the years? 136 Have we mortgaged the country to foreign investors? 516 What is a stabilization crisis?)

"Our national debt, after all, is an internal debt owed not only by the nation but to the nation. If our children have to pay interest on it, they will pay that interest to themselves. A reasonable internal debt will not impoverish our children or put the nation into bankruptcy."

—President Franklin Roosevelt, 1939

Q 126. Is there any limit on how much Congress can borrow?

A The Constitution imposes no restrictions on the borrowing power of Congress, and attempts by Congress itself to set a ceiling on the national debt have failed for decades. Whenever borrowing pushed the debt close to the statutory debt ceiling, Congress simply passed new legislation to raise it (Congress has done so over eighty times since 1940).

The only practical limits on congressional borrowing power are political and financial considerations. In recent years the mushrooming debt has become a major political issue, effectively forcing Congress to find ways to cut spending and reduce the amount it borrows each year. Also, the debt has become so large that financing it puts the government in competition with private business for available funds in the credit market. Meanwhile, interest payments on the debt have also become so costly they now rank as a major budget expense each year.

(See 14 Why doesn't the government just keep raising taxes to meet its expenses? 17 How big is the national debt? 18 Where did the national debt come from? 123 Will the government be going broke anytime soon? 129 Is a credit crunch good or bad? 130 When did the federal debt top $1 trillion? $3 trillion? 377 What are debt ceilings?)

Q 127. When did Congress make an open-ended commitment to pay interest on the debt?

A Congress realized fairly soon that the only way to maintain its credibility as a borrower was to guarantee the government would always pay interest on the national debt as it came due. So in 1847 it passed a permanent appropriation authorizing payment of whatever interest was owed on the national debt, then and in the future. That effectively shielded interest expenses, now running hundreds of billions of dollars, from political controversy. The measure also made it possible to continue borrowing even though the national debt was reaching astronomical levels.

(See 123 Will the government be going broke anytime soon? 132 How much does the interest on the federal debt cost now? 133 What has the federal debt been over the years? 377 What are debt ceilings?)

Q 128. Where does the government get the money it borrows?

A The bulk of borrowed money is raised by the Treasury through the sale of notes, bonds, and Treasury bills in financial markets and to the government trust funds. For example, in 1995 the debt was $4.6 trillion and of that about $3.4 trillion was held by the public. The Social Security trust fund and other government trusts held over $1.2 trillion of the debt, most of it in the form of notes called special issues. Foreign

Figure 2-4 Estimated Ownership of Debt Held by the Public (September 30, 1995)

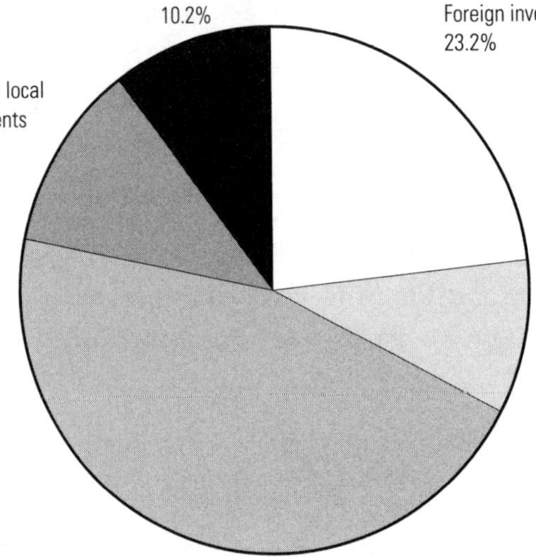

Federal Reserve banks 10.2%

Foreign investors 23.2%

State and local governments 11.6%

Private individuals 9.5%

Corporations, financial institutions, and other 45.5%

Source: U.S. Department of the Treasury.

investors are holding an increasingly larger share of the United States national debt. About 27.5 percent of the public debt in 1996 was held by foreigners, up from 18 percent in 1990 (see Figure 2-4).

(See 125 Why does the government have to borrow money? 126 Is there any limit on how much Congress can borrow? 137 What is the difference between public debt and agency debt? 138 What are marketable and non-marketable issues? 139 Who holds special issues?)

Q 129. Is a credit crunch good or bad?

A When the government has to borrow heavily to finance large deficits, it tends to crowd businesses and individuals out of the credit market. The resulting "credit crunch" drives up interest rates (because competition makes money available for borrowing more valuable). While this means lenders make more money, in the long run it hurts the economy and the federal budget.

In the first place, the higher interest rates make loans more expensive, forcing consumers to put off buying big-ticket items like cars and houses that must be financed.

Businesses are also forced to cut back on things like buying new equipment and buildings to modernize or expand their operations. Over the long run these decisions not to buy or expand drag down economic growth.

The credit crunch also hurts the federal government because high interest rates mean more tax revenues are swallowed up by the mounting debt. That limits federal policy options and also forces the government to turn to foreign investors for loans.

(See 66 Do big deficits limit fiscal policy options? 125 Why does the government have to borrow money? 133 What has the federal debt been over the years? 136 Have we mortgaged the country to foreign investors? 516 What is a stabilization crisis?)

Q 130. When did the federal debt top $1 trillion? $3 trillion?

A World War II ushered in the first big jump in the national debt, which went from about $51 billion in 1940 to $271 billion in 1946. Another 42 years passed before the debt finally topped the $1 trillion mark, though, and at the end of fiscal 1982 it stood at about $1.1 trillion. Annual deficits in the $100 billion to $200 billion a year range piled up the debt at a breathtaking pace throughout the remainder of the 1980s, so that it took only four years to go from $1 trillion to $2 trillion. After that the debt zipped by trillion dollar marks: $3 trillion in fiscal 1990, $4 trillion in 1992, and $5 trillion in 1996.

(See 17 How big is the national debt? 18 Where did the national debt come from? 123 Will the government be going broke anytime soon? 126 Is there any limit on how much Congress can borrow? 133 What has the federal debt been over the years? 167 What has the deficit been, year by year since 1901? 377 What are debt ceilings?)

Q 131. When did the federal debt actually begin to mushroom?

A The short answer is, earlier than most people think. We have heard often enough about how the federal debt mushroomed in the 1980s, but that growth spurt actually got started in the 1970s. The national debt stood at what now seems a paltry $381 billion in 1970. By 1980 it had swollen almost two and a half times to $909 billion, though, and at that rate was poised to break the $1 trillion mark within two years (which it did).

In the past the federal government had routinely run up the debt during wars, only to gradually pay the money back during peacetime. But that did not happen after World War II or the Korean War. The debt hovered around the World War II peak of $271 billion throughout the 1950s and finished the decade up slightly at $291 billion. The Vietnam War and subsequent defense spending certainly contributed to the rising debt (up $90 billion during the 1960s), but Great Society social programs enacted in the 1960s proved far more costly than anyone expected. During the 1970s and 1980s mandatory spending each year for entitlement programs such as Social Security, Medicare, and Medicaid rose astronomically (from $61 billion in 1970 to $262 billion in 1980, $568 billion in 1990, and $785 billion in 1996). Entitlement spending became an underlying cause of the debt's dizzying rise.

(See 13 Why does the government spend more than it takes in? 17 How big is the national debt? 18 Where did the national debt come from? 93 What are the social insurance taxes? 160 What are entitlement programs? 171 Why has social spending risen by so much?)

Q 132. How much does the interest on the federal debt cost now?

A The federal government paid out a net $241 billion for interest during fiscal 1996—about $1,000 for every man, woman, and child in the country. Experts believe interest costs will continue rising, topping $250 billion by fiscal 1998. Payments for interest on the debt began rising during the 1970s and shot up during the 1980s as the federal debt piled up. From $69 billion in 1981, net interest nearly doubled to about $139 billion by 1987. By 1998 spending on interest is expected to be almost what the government spends on national defense and will account for more than the entire annual deficit.

(See 123 Will the government be going broke anytime soon? 135 How long might it take to pay off the national debt? 136 Have we mortgaged the country to foreign investors?)

Q 133. What has the federal debt been over the years?

A Since 1970 the national debt has gone nowhere but up, and in the past thirty-six years it has increased almost eighteen times more than all the debt accumulated in the federal government's first 184 years. Although efforts by Congress and the Clinton administration have trimmed annual deficits, the debt will continue to grow at least into the next century. Meanwhile, interest on the mountain of debt has reached the $250 billion-a-year range, a sum large enough to curb federal spending for other needs.

Another way to look at the debt is to compare it with Gross Domestic Product (GDP), in effect measuring the debt against what the economy can produce in a year's time. In that one regard at least, the debt is not as serious a problem as it has been. Currently the debt is 69.2 percent of GDP and is expected to remain in the 69 percent range into the next century. In 1940 the debt was 51.8 percent of GDP, and at its highest since then it has topped 124 percent of GDP (1946). From 1943 to 1955, a period embracing emergency spending for World War II and the Korean War, the debt as a percentage of GDP was consistently above current levels. In fact, between 1945 and 1947 it was actually larger than GDP (see Table 2-4).

(See 13 Why does the government spend more than it takes in? 15 How many times have there been budget surpluses since the depression era? 16 What is the longest period of consecutive budget deficits? 20 Should the budget be balanced?)

Q 134. Has the national debt ever gone down in recent years?

A Since 1940 the flood tide of federal red ink has ebbed only six times—1947, 1948, 1951, 1956, 1957, and 1969. It is not expected to decrease again in this century.

Q 135. How long might it take to pay off the national debt?

A The debt stood at about $5.45 trillion by the close of fiscal 1997. If the government did not borrow another nickel, and while covering the interest also started paying off what it owes at a dollar a second, it would take almost 173,000 years to wipe out the debt. As a practical matter, the government is not likely to go ten years without borrowing money, much less 173,000, and in fact the government has carried at least a small amount of debt throughout most of its history. For the foreseeable future the best we probably can hope for is that the government will cut the annual deficits and slow the accumulation of debt.

(See 13 Why does the government spend more than it takes in? 17 How big is the national debt? 18 Where did the national debt come from? 123 Will the government be going broke anytime soon?)

Q 136. Have we mortgaged the country to foreign investors?

A Until fairly recently, individuals and institutions here in the United States held almost all of the federal debt. But beginning in 1970, foreign banks and investors began buying up federal government securities issued to finance the debt, even though no effort had been made to market the securities overseas.

As late as 1969, foreign investment accounted for just $10.3 billion of the debt—only about 3.7 percent of the total then. By 1972, though, foreign investment had shot up to $49.2 billion, or 15.2 percent of the debt. Foreigners held anywhere from 14 percent to 18 percent of the debt throughout the 1970s, 1980s, and early 1990s. But in 1995 and 1996 they again dramatically increased their share of the debt, pushing it up to an all-time high of $1.03 trillion, or about 27.5 percent (see Table 2-5). Half of all

Table 2-4 Making a Mountain of Debt

	Gross debt (in millions)	*Percentage of GDP*	*Net interest paid (in millions)*
1940	$ 50,696	51.8	$ 899
1941	57,531	49.9	943
1942	79,200	54.5	1,052
1943	142,648	79.3	1,529
1944	204,079	98.7	2,219
1945	260,123	119.7	3,112
1946	270,991	124.4	4,111
1947	257,149	112.5	4,204
1948	252,031	99.4	4,341
1949	252,610	93.7	4,523
1950	256,853	94.2	4,812
1951	255,288	79.5	4,665
1952	259,097	74.2	4,701
1953	265,963	71.4	5,156
1954	270,812	71.8	4,811
1955	274,366	69.4	4,850
1956	272,693	63.9	5,079
1957	272,252	60.5	5,354
1958	279,666	61.0	5,604
1959	287,465	58.7	5,762
1960	290,525	56.1	6,947
1961	292,648	55.2	6,716
1962	302,928	53.4	6,889
1963	310,324	51.8	7,740
1964	316,059	49.4	8,199
1965	322,318	46.9	8,591
1966	328,498	43.6	9,386
1967	340,445	41.9	10,268
1968	368,685	42.5	11,090
1969	365,769	38.6	12,699

Table 2-4 *(Continued)*

	Gross debt (in millions)	*Percentage of GDP*	*Net interest paid (in millions)*
1970	380,921	37.7	14,380
1971	408,176	37.9	14,841
1972	435,936	37.0	15,478
1973	466,291	35.7	17,349
1974	483,893	33.6	21,449
1975	541,925	34.9	23,244
1976	628,970	36.3	26,727
1977	706,398	35.8	29,901
1978	776,602	35.1	35,458
1979	829,470	33.2	42,636
1980	909,050	33.4	52,538
1981	994,845	32.6	68,774
1982	1,137,345	35.4	85,044
1983	1,371,710	40.1	89,828
1984	1,564,657	41.0	111,123
1985	1,817,521	44.3	129,504
1986	2,120,629	48.5	136,047
1987	2,346,125	50.9	138,652
1988	2,601,307	52.5	151,838
1989	2,868,039	53.6	169,266
1990	3,206,564	56.4	184,221
1991	3,598,498	61.4	194,541
1992	4,002,136	65.1	199,421
1993	4,351,416	67.2	198,811
1994	4,643,705	68.0	202,957
1995	4,921,018	68.5	232,169
1996	5,181,930	69.2	241,090
1997	5,453,677 (est.)	69.4 (est.)	247,382 (est.)

Source: Budget of the United States, Historical Tables.

Table 2-5 Our Growing Dependency on Foreign Capital (dollar figures in billions)

	Total Public debt	*Foreign holdings*	*Foreign holdings (%)*	*Interest paid*
1969	$ 278.1	$ 10.3	3.7	$ 0.7
1970	283.2	14.0	5.0	0.8
1971	303.0	31.8	10.5	1.3
1972	322.4	49.2	15.2	2.4
1973	340.9	59.4	17.4	3.2
1974	343.7	56.8	16.5	4.1
1975	394.7	66.0	16.7	4.5
1976	477.4	69.8	14.6	4.4
1977	549.1	95.5	17.4	5.1
1978	607.1	121.0	19.9	7.9
1979	640.3	120.3	18.8	10.7
1980	709.8	121.7	17.1	11.0
1981	785.3	130.7	16.6	16.4
1982	919.8	140.6	15.3	18.7
1983	1,131.6	160.1	14.1	19.2
1984	1,300.5	175.5	13.5	20.3
1985	1,499.9	222.9	14.9	23.0
1986	1,736.7	265.5	15.3	24.2
1987	1,888.7	279.5	14.8	25.7
1988	2,050.8	345.9	16.9	29.9
1989	2,189.9	394.9	18.0	37.1
1990	2,410.7	440.3	18.3	40.3
1991	2,688.1	477.3	17.8	42.0
1992	2,998.8	535.2	17.8	40.5
1993	3,247.5	591.3	18.2	41.1
1994	3,432.1	655.8	19.1	44.5
1995	3,603.4	848.4	23.5	58.3
1996	3,733.0	1,027.7	27.5	67.7

Source: Budget of the United States Government, 1998, Analytical Perspectives.

foreign investment in debt securities is by foreign central banks, the rest by private investors.

Though our dependency on foreign capital carries some risks, the funds have eased the strain on United States credit markets caused by financing the debt.

(See 129 Is a credit crunch good or bad? 516 What is a stabilization crisis?)

Q 137. What is the difference between public debt and agency debt?

A Public and agency debt are the two basic components of the total national debt (also called gross debt). The lion's share of the total debt is public debt, money the U.S. Treasury has borrowed. Agency debt is the money federal agencies and enterprises, like the U.S. Post Office, have borrowed. Agency debt usually amounts to only about 1 percent of the total debt.

Q 138. What are marketable and non-marketable issues?

A Some of the notes and treasury bills the U.S. Treasury sells to the public to finance the national debt are traded on the securities markets. These are marketable issues. Non-marketable issues, such as U.S. savings bonds, cannot be traded on the market.

(See 128 Where does the government get the money it borrows?)

Q 139. Who holds special issues?

A Special issues are U.S. Treasury notes that can only be held by government agencies and trust funds, such as the Social Security trust fund. Agencies and trust funds also hold marketable Treasury securities, however.

(See 128 Where does the government get the money it borrows?)

III
WHAT THE MONEY IS SPENT ON

IN GENERAL

Q **140. What did the government spend in its first year of operation?**

A Spending by the newly created federal government amounted to only $639,000 in 1789. With spending in the 1990s about $1.6 trillion a year, the government now pays out that $639,000 every thirteen seconds.

(See 147 Who got what in a recent budget?)

Q **141. When did federal spending reach $1 billion a year? $1 trillion?**

A During the first decades of its existence the federal government spent relatively modest sums, in part because most Americans were against the idea of a powerful central government. Spending was generally limited to such basic concerns as providing for the national defense, operating the three branches of government, and maintaining the nation's monetary system. Over seventy-five years passed before federal outlays finally topped the $1 billion mark, and then only during the final year of the Civil War, 1865.

Annual spending fell back the very next year and remained under $1 billion until World War I. Significant, sustained increases in federal spending did not finally begin until the 1930s when the Great Depression changed attitudes about expanding the federal government's role in society. New Deal programs designed to help people make it through the depression gave the government a much larger social role, sharply increased spending, and ushered in an era of almost constant deficits.

But even the mammoth federal outlays for World War II ($92.7 billion in 1945) failed to push spending over $100 billion. That finally happened in 1962 during President John F. Kennedy's administration, and the pace of federal spending picked up quickly afterward. Helped along by President Lyndon Johnson's costly Great Society social programs and a decade of high inflation, it took just another twenty-five years for federal spending to top $1 trillion (in 1987, during President Ronald Reagan's administration).

(See 83 When did federal revenues top $100 billion a year? A trillion? 130 When did the federal debt top $1 trillion? $3 trillion?)

Q 142. How does federal spending affect me?

A Just about everyone is affected directly or indirectly by federal spending. Millions of retired Americans, for example, receive direct benefits and would probably be in serious financial trouble without their monthly Social Security checks, not to mention help from Medicare. Working Americans who at one time or another have been out of work have also relied on the federally supported, state-run unemployment insurance program.

We all feel the bite directly whenever the federal government increases taxes to cover the cost of these and many other spending programs. The more the government takes from us in taxes, the less we have to spend on other things. On the other hand, when the government decides to give tax breaks for specific expenses, such as interest on home mortgages, it can influence how we spend our money.

In addition to providing benefits and creating jobs, federal spending also has indirect effects on us through the economy. Increased spending can help dampen the affects of a recession, and at other times it has been blamed for over-stimulating the economy and pushing up inflation (as in the 1960s and 1970s). The government's tax and monetary policies also influence the economy, which may make it easier—or harder—for us to land a job, to win a promotion, or even to get a loan at affordable interest rates.

(See 24 How does the economy affect me? 37 Do federal regulations affect the economy? 60 Do entitlement programs help dampen recessions? 65 What is fiscal policy? 147 Who got what in a recent budget? 171 Why has social spending risen so dramatically?)

Q 143. How has the government gotten bigger over the years?

A The federal government has grown enormously since the early days of the New Deal, both in terms of its responsibilities and its sheer size. After President Franklin D. Roosevelt committed the government to promoting the economic and social well-being of Americans who were suffering during the depression, the government vastly expanded its efforts to reform and remake society. The federal government, particularly its military arm, underwent another big growth spurt during a second national emergency, World War II. Since that time efforts to enlarge the government's role in society led to still more expansion.

The size of the government workforce has grown enormously since 1933, when there were just under 604,000 civilian employees. By 1990 federal employees numbered 2.25 million, the post–Vietnam War high. (Cutbacks since have pulled the number below 2 million.)

By far the clearest signs of the federal government's growth are economic—federal spending and tax revenues have undergone phenomenal growth since the 1930s—even allowing for inflation. The government took in just under $2 billion in revenue during 1933, President Roosevelt's first year in office, and spent $4.6 billion. By 1996 federal revenues had topped $1.45 trillion, and spending was even higher, $1.56 trillion (for budget growth data, see Figure 3-1). So, too, were the deficits, though—$2.6 billion in 1933 against $107 billion in 1996. (Even as a percentage of GDP, spending and revenues showed impressive growth, from 7.4 percent and 3.4 percent, respectively, in 1933 to 20.8 percent and 19.4 percent in 1996).

The spending has not been without rewards, though. The United States has grown into the world's most powerful nation and ranks among the most highly developed, thanks in part to federal spending. Americans also enjoy an especially high standard of living, and through a variety of health, education, and income safety net pro-

Figure 3-1 Annual Federal Budget Growth, 1960–1997 (by percentage of inflation-adjusted dollars)

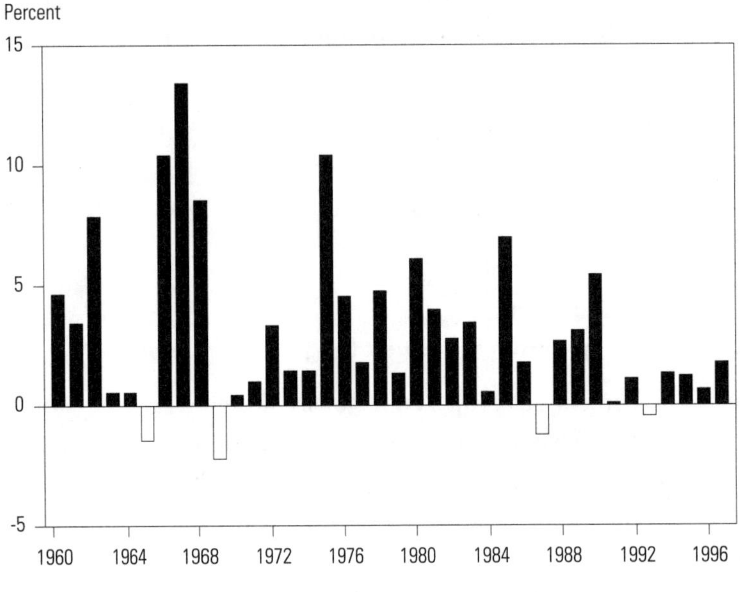

Source: Budget of the United States, 1998, Historical Tables.

Note: Percentages for 1996 and 1997 are estimates.

grams, the federal government today provides security and benefits to tens of millions of Americans.

(See 83 How have federal revenue and outlays grown over the years? 161 How many people receive federal benefits? 398 What was the classical view of the economy? 400 What effect did the 1930s depression have on the fundamental philosophy behind federal spending?)

▶ What has federal spending been year by year? *See 83 How have federal revenue and outlays grown over the years?* ◀

Q 144. Which federal agency gets the biggest slice of the federal budget?

A The Social Security Administration has had that distinction since 1991, when defense spending dropped off following the close of the Cold War. At that point Social Security accounted for 21.6 percent of the budget, and defense, about 19.8 percent. Since then the Treasury and Health and Human Services have rivaled Social Security in spending but have not topped it.

(See 147 Who got what in a recent budget? 200 When did Social Security spending top 20 percent of the federal budget?)

Q 145. When did the federal government post its first deficit?

A In just the fourth year of its existence, 1792, the federal government posted its first deficit of $1.4 million. But between 1789 and 1849 the government managed to come out ahead and actually reduced the national debt to $64 million, a drop of $13 million from $77 million. (The federal government assumed an existing debt, mainly for costs of the Revolutionary War, when it was formed in 1789). During the Civil War, relatively huge deficits ($963.8 million in 1865 being the largest) pushed the debt up over $2.7 billion. But budget surpluses for twenty-eight consecutive years cut it back to $961 million by 1893. A series of deficits followed from 1894 to 1899, though, and by 1900 the national debt stood at about $1.3 billion.

(See 11 Is there a difference between the budget deficit and the debt? 13 Why does the government spend more than it takes in? 14 Why doesn't the government just keep raising taxes to meet its expenses? 16 What is the longest period of consecutive budget deficits? 17 How big is the national debt? 20 Should the budget be balanced? 167 What has the deficit been, year by year since 1901?)

Q 146. How have federal spending patterns changed since 1960?

A The most obvious change is that total spending has shot up from billions to trillions, but an equally dramatic shift took place in where the money is being spent. Over 52.2 percent of the total budget went for defense in 1960, while 26.2 percent was spent for direct payments to individuals in federal (and federal-state) entitlement programs such as Social Security and welfare. By 1996, though, the situation had completely reversed. Federal payments to individuals for all entitlement programs claimed a whopping 57.6 percent of the budget—and that amount is expected to continue growing. Meanwhile the budget share for defense spending, which has been shrinking since 1960 (notwithstanding the uptick for a defense buildup during the Reagan administration in the 1980s), amounted to just 16.2 percent of the total 1996 budget (see Table 3-1).

The change reflected a striking shift in federal priorities toward social spending, as well as some unexpected consequences of that shift, that resulted in skyrocketing costs. The turning point came with the Great Society programs of the 1960s, when Congress and the president created new entitlement programs, such as Medicaid (medical care for the indigent), and greatly expanded the benefits of existing ones. These programs helped the needy and made the lives of many Americans more secure, but they also made controlling federal expenditures much more difficult. That is because spending for these entitlement programs is mandatory—if someone is eligible, the government must pay them benefits no matter how much has been budgeted.

Table 3-1 New Directions For Federal Spending

Category	*% in 1960*	*% in 1996*
Defense	52.2	17.0
Payments for individuals	26.2	58.3
All other grants	4.9	5.1
Net interest	7.5	15.5
All other federal spending	14.4	6.5
Offsetting receipts (subtracted from total)	–5.2	–2.4
	100%	100%*

* Total here includes some small amounts of direct payments to individuals and state and local government grants.

Source: Budget of the United States, 1998: Historical Tables.

Few people anticipated how expensive these entitlement programs would become. Congress greatly expanded benefits without raising taxes enough to cover new expenses, while inflation, abuse, and fraud also helped drive up costs. Now that the general population is getting older and more people are becoming eligible for Social Security and other benefits, costs threaten to rise even faster. Since the 1970s ever-expanding social spending has become the single largest factor pushing up deficits and the debt. The rising debt in turn has contributed to the doubling of another budget expense, net interest costs, from 7.5 percent in 1960 to 15.9 percent in 1996.

(See 171 Why has social spending risen so much? 437 What did President Lyndon Johnson's Great Society program attempt to do? 439 Did defense spending or social spending post the biggest increases during the Johnson years? 461 Why were deficits so high during the Carter years? 475 Why were deficits so high during the Reagan years?)

Q 147. Who got what in a recent budget?

A The major players in the annual competition for federal tax dollars are grouped into two major categories, executive departments and major agencies, and ranked according to what they spent. The following figures are for actual spending in fiscal 1996. (For information on how the federal government dollar is spent, see Figure 3-2.)

Executive department	*Spending (in billions)*
Treasury	$365.0
Health and Human Services (including Medicaid, Medicare)	320.0
Defense—military	253.0
Agriculture	54.0
Transportation	39.0
Veterans Affairs	37.0
Labor	32.0
Education	30.0
Housing and Urban Development	26.0
Energy	16.0
Justice	12.0
Interior	7.0
State	5.0
Commerce	4.0

(Continued on next page)

Executive department	*Spending (in billions)*
Major agencies	
Social Security Administration	$375.0
Office of Personnel Management	43.0
Corps of Engineers, military retirement, and other defense	33.0
NASA	14.0
Funds appropriated to the president	10.0
Environmental Protection Agency	6.0
The Judiciary	3.0
Legislative branch	2.0
Small Business Administration	1.0
General Services Administration	1.0
Executive Office of the President	0.2
All other agencies	9.0
Undistributed offsetting receipts (money collected by the government)	–135.0
Total	$1,560.30*

*Slight difference in total due to rounding.
Source: Budget of the United States, 1998: Historical Tables.

(See 4 How much does the government spend in a year? 13 Why does the government spend more than it takes in? 73 What are the government's major revenue sources?)

Q 148. Why was Treasury Department spending so high?

A The $365 billion Treasury spent was the second largest expenditure in the 1996 budget, and the department's outlays are expected to hit $400 billion by the year 2000. Why? Because Treasury is responsible for paying interest on the national debt, which amounted to $344 billion in 1996. The tab for interest could reach $374 billion by 2000, unless deficits become a thing of the past before then.

(See 3 Who actually spends the money? 232 What does the Treasury Department spend its money on?)

Figure 3-2 The Federal Government Dollar—Where It Goes

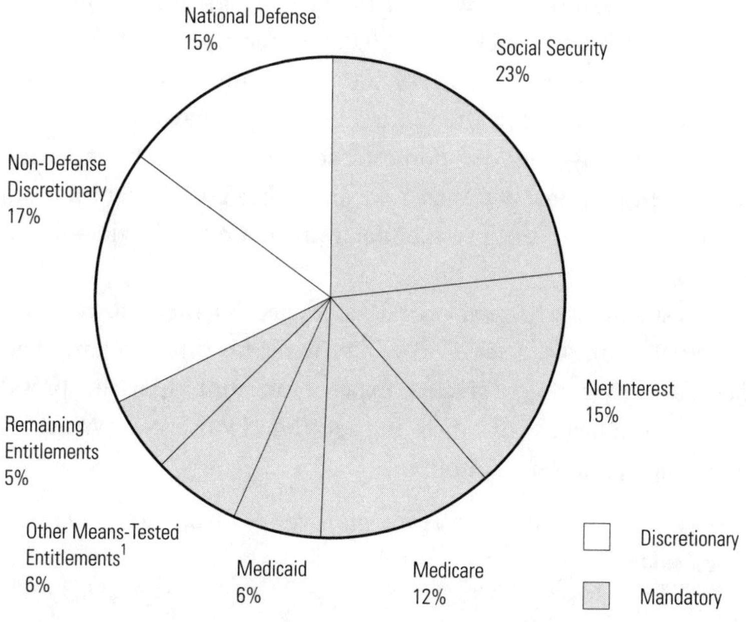

Note: Numbers do not add due to rounding.

[1] Means-tested entitlements are those for which eligibility is based on income. The Medicaid program is also a means-tested entitlement.

Q 149. Will Social Security be the single largest federal expenditure in years to come?

A For the foreseeable future, yes, but Health and Human Services spending, now the third largest spending category, is growing faster. It is expected to close the gap and move up to the number two slot in the government's spending parade within the next few years, because it handles funding for the two big hospital insurance programs, Medicaid and Medicare. By the year 2000 Social Security spending will be $454 billion, Health and Human Services $414 billion, and Treasury $400 billion.

(See 171 Why has social spending risen by so much? 194 Why was Social Security established? 204 Will the Social Security program actually go bankrupt? Why?)

150. What do we pay the president and vice president?

The president earns $200,000 a year and the vice president $171,500, as of the mid-1990s. The president's perks include a $50,000 expense account, $100,000 allowance for travel and other expenses, and a $19,000 entertainment allowance. The president and first family live rent-free in the White House (they pay for their own food), and the government not only pays for a domestic staff but also covers expenses for all official White House functions. *Air Force One* and other government aircraft are at the president's disposal, as is the presidential retreat, Camp David, in the Maryland mountains.

The vice president has had an official residence on the U.S. Naval Observatory grounds since 1977 and has use of *Air Force Two* as his official plane. The vice president makes do with a much smaller expense account than the president's—just $10,000 a year—and has use of offices in the White House West Wing, in the Executive Office Building, and on Capitol Hill.

(See 155 What do senators and representatives get paid? 157 What is a Supreme Court justice's salary?)

151. How much does it cost to run the White House?

The White House, a national treasure as well as the president's official residence, cost about $8 million to operate in 1996, or about $60,000 for each of its 132 rooms. The $8 million pays for a domestic staff of thirty-six and all expenses for official White House functions. The president and first family live there rent-free, but must pay for meals and other incidental expenses.

The White House has been reimbursed $1.75 million for political events held there from 1993 to 1997, including President Bill Clinton's fund-raising coffees, receptions for top-ranking Democrats, and similar partisan political activities.

152. What does the budget for the Executive Office of the President include?

The $202 million spent in 1996 on the Executive Office of the President included salaries of the president and 1,015 staffers, operating expenses for the White House and vice presidential residence, and money for the various councils and offices attached to the president's executive office (such as the Office of Management and Budget). It does not include billions of dollars in funds appropriated to the president (see next question), nor the vast sums Congress allocates to the various departments and agencies responsible in some way to the executive branch. In 1997 President Bill

Clinton abandoned his earlier pledge to cut the White House staff by 25 percent, citing new staffing needs in both the counsel's office and drug control office. The 1996 budgets for major councils and offices within the executive office are listed below.

	Spending (in millions)
Office of Management and Budget	$56
Office of Administration	31
Office of National Drug Control Policy	25
Office of the U.S. Trade Representative	21
National Security Council	6
Office of Science and Technology Policy	5
Special assistance to the president and vice presidential residence	4
Council of Economic Advisers	3

Q 153. What are "Funds Appropriated to the President"?

A Congress appropriates about $10 billion annually to the president for a variety of domestic and international programs. These funds are accounted separately from the Executive Office in the budget and include such programs as:

	1996 Spending (in millions)
International Security Assistance (including peacekeeping and counter-terrorism)	$4,302
Agency for International Development	3,058
International development assistance	1,470
International monetary programs	694
Peace Corps	213
Federal drug control programs	48
Inter-American Foundation	19

Q 154. How does Congress spend the money it gets?

A The $2.3 billion allotted Congress in the 1996 budget was spent for salaries of members of Congress and their staffs, committee operations, security and other housekeeping expenses, and for various agencies that fall under jurisdiction of Congress.

Salaries for the 100 senators cost $16 million, while their staff and office expense account was $205 million. The Senate spent a total of $420 million during 1996.

The 435 House members received $74 million in salaries and other expenses and spent a total of $741 million for the year. Joint House-Senate committees accounted for another $78 million. Among the agencies under direct control of Congress and included in its 1996 budget are:

	Spending (in millions)
Congressional Budget Office	$ 22
Architect of the Capitol	147
Library of Congress	327
Government Printing Office	105
General Accounting Office	399

Q 155. What do senators and representatives get paid?

A Both senators and members of the House of Representatives have the same salary, $133,600, as of the mid-1990s. Members of both houses are entitled to automatic cost-of-living increases and also rate a number of perks, including free postage for official correspondence (the franking privilege), an office and a staff allowance, and health and retirement plans.

(See 150 What are the salaries of the president and vice president? 157 What is a Supreme Court justice's salary?)

Q 156. What does the judicial branch do with its $3 billion?

A Salaries and expenses for members of the Supreme Court ($25 million), U.S. Court of Appeals for the Federal Circuit ($14 million), and U.S. Court of International Trade ($10 million) accounted for only a small part of the judiciary's 1996 budget. Instead, the bulk of spending went for salaries and expenses in the far more numerous lower federal courts (appeals and district courts), which accounted for almost $2.5 billion in 1996. The federal court system also spent $277 million on legal defender services and $65 million on fees for jurors and commissioners. Administrative and staff expenses for the judiciary were $52 million, and the government contributed $33 million to the judicial retirement fund. Violent crime reduction programs accounted for another $30 million in 1996.

(See 241 How much does federal law enforcement cost?)

Q 157. What is a Supreme Court justice's salary?

A The associate justices on the Court earn $164,100 a year and the chief justice gets slightly more, $171,500. Justices also enjoy fringe benefits, not the least of which is job security—their appointments to the Supreme Court are for life. The Court budget also pays for the justices' staffs. Associate justices get four law clerks, two secretaries, and a messenger, and the chief justice is allowed an additional secretary.

(150 What do we pay the president and vice president of the United States? 155 What do senators and representatives earn?)

Q 158. Has excessive spending eroded the public's confidence in government?

A A 1997 public opinion survey by the nonpartisan Council for Excellence in Government revealed the leading cause of low public confidence in the federal government is wasteful spending. Fully 76 percent of those responding to the poll believed it was a major cause. Those polled also blamed other contributing factors, including self-interested politicians (mentioned by 63 percent of people responding); unkept promises (63 percent); and crime, poverty, and drugs (62 percent). About 50 percent also said special interest influence was an important reason behind the public's lack of confidence in government.

The poll found only 22 percent had a great deal of confidence in the federal government generally, up somewhat from a poll taken two years earlier. That was behind local government (in which 38 percent had a great deal of confidence) and state government (32 percent) but ahead of Congress (21 percent) and the national news media (20 percent).

On the question of what government could do to improve itself, 79 percent of respondents suggested balancing the budget. Enacting campaign finance reform was the second-leading choice (76 percent), followed by basing salaries of government workers on performance (72 percent), forming more public-private partnerships (70 percent), and giving states and localities control of some federal programs (67 percent).

(See 13 Why does the government spend more than it takes in? 169 What were the Golden Fleece Awards? 285 How has Congress's control over the way federal agencies spend money changed over past years? 287 How do interest groups influence the budget process? 323 What is the largest single spending bill Congress has ever passed? 359 What is pork-barrel spending?)

Q 159. How many people work for the federal government?

A As of 1996, the government employed 2.9 million civilian employees (not counting the Postal Service, which is now an independent government corporation). That was down from a high of 3.31 million civilian employees in 1990, and a thirty-year low for the government workforce. The Department of Defense (768,000) and Department of Veterans Affairs (251,000) employed the biggest share of civilian workers. Most employees worked in the executive branch (2.8 million), while only about 61,000 worked for the legislative and judicial branches.

Meanwhile downsizing the military has greatly reduced the number of soldiers in uniform. Military personnel in 1996 numbered 1.5 million, less than half the Vietnam War–era high of almost 3.6 million (reached in 1968).

(See 143 How has the government gotten bigger over the years? 393 What cuts in the federal government has President Bill Clinton made?)

Q 160. What are entitlement programs?

A Entitlement programs guarantee benefits to any recipient who meets the eligibility requirements. Social Security, Medicare, and food stamps are all entitlement programs that provide benefits to individuals, but in some programs organizations and even government agencies may be eligible. The government is obligated by law to provide as much money as is needed for entitlement programs, no matter how many eligible recipients apply for benefits. Congress can change that, of course, but only by passing a new law ordering cutbacks or other changes.

(See 93 What are the social insurance taxes? 171 Why has social spending risen by so much? 172 Can entitlement programs be changed? 181 Does social spending really help ease poverty? 197 Why is Social Security called the "third rail" of American politics?)

Q 161. How many people receive federal benefits?

A Tens of millions of Americans receive direct payments or government-financed services through dozens of entitlement programs offered by the federal government (or federal-state partnerships). Some people, of course, get benefits from more than one program, especially where programs are interrelated or directed toward helping a particular group, such as disabled or blind people. Many millions of other Americans also receive benefits indirectly, through tax breaks (such as the interest deduction for home mortgages) and services the government provides free. The current number of people receiving direct benefits or services through major federal (and federal-state) entitlement programs are as follows:

Social Security: 43 million retired and disabled workers, dependents, and survivors

Medicare: 33 million elderly and disabled persons

Medicaid (federal-state): 38 million needy persons, elderly persons in nursing homes, and disabled persons

Welfare: 12 million needy persons

Rent subsidies: 4.8 million low-income households

Food stamps: 25.5 million low-income persons

School lunch program (including meals at day care centers): 28.5 million children

Earned Income Credit (tax break or outright refund): 40 million low-income people

Unemployment insurance benefits (federal-state program): 8.5 million workers who lost their jobs

College student loans, grants, and work study programs: 7.5 million low- and middle-income college students

Veterans' disability compensation: 2.6 million veterans and their survivors

Montgomery G.I. Bill (education benefits): 430,000 veterans, and active and reserve military personnel

Housing assistance (direct and guaranteed loans): 1.43 million households (low-income and first-time buyers) and small businesses

(See 146 How have federal spending patterns changed since 1960? 174 What percentage of the budget goes for social spending? 179 How much does the government pay to individuals, program by program? 213 How many of those below the poverty line do not collect any benefits?)

Q 162. Is there a difference between discretionary and mandatory spending?

A *Discretionary spending* is spending Congress has control over; funding levels can be raised or lowered during the annual appropriations process. For the most part discretionary spending provides money for defense, agency operating expenses, and grants to state and local governments.

Mandatory spending is open-ended. So long as certain criteria are met, the money must be paid, no matter how much is spent in a given year. For example, anyone who is eligible will get their medical bills paid under the Medicaid plan, even if Medicaid expenditures are already billions over budget. Most, but not all, mandatory spending is for entitlement programs like Social Security, Medicare, and Medicaid. (Congress made spending for interest on the public debt mandatory in the 1800s.)

Mandatory spending has mushroomed from just 30 percent of the federal budget in 1963 to over 65 percent in 1996, making it extremely difficult for Congress to control spending and balance the budget. Congress must actually pass laws in order to make any changes to mandatory spending programs. Nearly all the mandatory spending growth stems from legislation passed prior to 1980.

(See 13 Why does the government spend more than it takes in? 165 What is "backdoor spending"? 170 Why spend tax dollars on social programs? 171 Why has social spending risen by so much? 172 Can entitlement programs be changed? 174 What percentage of the budget goes for social spending? 176 Could entitlement caps control spending? 362 What does PAYGO mean? 377 What are debt ceilings?)

Q 163. How have federal grants to state and local governments changed over the years?

A The federal government provides funds directly to state and local governments by way of grants for such things as mass transit, highway construction, sewage treatment plants, community development, education, job training, housing, and welfare programs. Grants represented just 7.6 percent of the federal budget in fiscal 1960 (about $7.1 billion in grants), and at that time capital investment grants for projects such as mass transit and highways amounted to about half of the grant money.

Though total state and local grants grew steadily as a percentage of the federal budget (14.6 percent, or $227.8 billion in 1996), most of that increase paid expenses for Medicaid and social programs. Capital spending grants for things like highways held steady at 3.6 percent of total federal spending throughout the 1960s and into the 1970s. But during the Reagan-Bush years cutbacks trimmed capital spending down to a low of 2.1 percent (in 1991). Under President Bill Clinton capital spending rose to 2.6 percent of the total 1996 budget.

(See 448 What was revenue sharing?)

Q 164. What is "corporate welfare"?

A Federal subsidies and tax loopholes that benefit corporations are called corporate welfare by critics in Congress who oppose them as unfair and wasteful. A privately funded study by a Washington think tank estimated federal subsidies that benefit business were worth about $60 billion a year, and tax breaks for big corporations cost the government another $30 billion annually. Among the subsidy programs critics have taken aim at are the Overseas Private Investment Corporation ($281 million in loans and loan guarantees to corporations investing overseas), federally funded fossil energy research ($1.37 billion for researching coal, oil, and gas as energy sources), the International Monetary Fund General Agreements to Borrow ($3.5 billion, which often benefits American banks by helping debtor nations pay off loans), and highway demonstration projects ($4 billion, which benefits contractors but does little to improve local economies). President Bill Clinton's original 1998 budget package included proposals to close some corporate tax loopholes as part of the effort to achieve a balanced budget.

(See 89 What are the major tax expenditures and how much revenue is lost through them? 120 Why have corporate tax revenues declined over the years?)

Q 165. What is "backdoor spending?"

A Backdoor spending is budget terminology for spending that is outside the annual appropriations process. It is also called uncontrollable or mandatory spending. Backdoor spending accounts for about three-quarters of all federal outlays and includes money for Social Security and other entitlement program benefits.

Laws setting up backdoor spending programs were deliberately written to insulate the programs from political or fiscal considerations for various reasons. Payment of interest on the federal debt was made mandatory, for example, in order to guarantee the government's credit rating. And with Social Security and other mandatory "safety net" entitlement programs, Congress sought to create a social insurance system that would guarantee benefits to all who were eligible, whenever they needed them. That meant preventing future Congresses from cutting spending in any given year, even though costs might rise far above what had been expected because more people became eligible.

There are drawbacks to making spending mandatory, though, which did not become apparent until Congress began to make serious efforts at getting federal spending under control. Because Congress has resorted to backdoor spending for so many programs, mandatory spending now accounts for the majority of the budget. With so much of the spending required by law, there is much less that Congress can cut—at least not without a politically costly fight to change laws governing the entitlement programs.

The various ways Congress has set up backdoor spending programs are as follows:

* Set up the program as an entitlement, such as Social Security or Medicare, which requires the government to make direct payments to all qualified recipients, no matter how many may be eligible or in what year they apply. Entitlement programs account for the largest part of backdoor spending.
* Make the appropriation open-ended and permanent. An example is the law requiring payment of all interest on the national debt whenever it comes due.
* Give agencies the authority to enter contracts, borrow money, or guarantee loans that the government will ultimately have to pay back.

For certain programs, particularly social programs benefiting mainly people in urban areas, legislators sometimes used backdoor spending devices to get around conservative opposition in appropriations committees. Senior members of Congress representing rural areas once dominated appropriations committees in the House and Senate and generally viewed such spending unfavorably. By including backdoor spending mechanisms in the original authorization bill, legislators could shortcut the normal two-step authorization/appropriations procedure. That allowed them to bypass appropriations committees altogether, but it also eliminated congressional control over the spending.

(See 146 How have federal spending patterns changed since 1960? 170 Why spend tax dollars on social programs? 171 Why has social spending risen by so much? 172 Can entitlement programs be changed? 279 Does the budget include all government spending? 348 How did the "two-step" authorization-appropriations process evolve?)

Q 166. How do "iron triangles" work to increase spending?

A The term iron triangle refers to the relationship between lobbyists, heads of federal agencies, and congressional committees that fund the agencies. Federal spending has created huge special interest groups made up of voters who benefit one way or another from certain government programs. The elderly, teachers, social workers, welfare recipients, businesses that receive government contracts, even state and local officials—all have a vested interest in maintaining or even increasing federal spending that benefits them. As one historian described it, "We have, in effect, created a special interest group that includes a majority of the population."

Groups of voters as large as these have political clout Congress cannot ignore. They also have organizations, such as the American Association of Retired Persons and the American Federation of Teachers, which protect their interests and lobby for favorable legislation. As one corner of the "iron triangle," the lobbyists for special interest groups work with heads of federal agencies (the second corner), who actually run the programs and spend the money. That only strengthens the lobbyists' influence when they deal with congressional committees (the third corner), which fund and monitor programs benefiting special interest groups. In this way lobbyists are ideally positioned to protect things like entitlement benefits and to push for increased spending.

(See 13 Why does the government spend more than it takes in? 287 How do interest groups influence the budget process?)

Q **167. What has the deficit been, year by year since 1901?**

A Between 1900 and 1997 the government has posted annual deficits seventy times (see Table 3-2). Overspending of revenues did not become a chronic problem until World War II, though, when annual deficits skyrocketed to the $50 billion range. Deficits of a few billion remained the norm in following years until the 1970s, when rising costs for social programs pushed deficits in dollar terms above World War II levels and beyond. Since 1930, the highest deficit in terms of percentage of GDP was posted in 1943—30.3 percent.

(See 11 Is there a difference between the budget deficit and the debt? 12 When did the government post the largest deficit in its history? 83 How have federal revenues and outlays grown over the years?)

Q **168. Have there been important disagreements over Congress's spending powers?**

A The Constitution gives Congress clear control over deciding how to spend money but is less specific about what the money can be spent on. By authorizing Congress to establish armed forces, courts, roads, and post offices, for example, the Constitution specifically grants Congress power to spend money on them. More generally, though, a clause in Article I, Section 8, states Congress has the power to collect taxes "to pay the debts and provide for the common defence and general welfare of the United States. . . ."

Table 3-2 The Deficit's Upward March (in millions)

	Receipts	*Outlays*	*Deficit (–) or surplus*	*Percent of GDP*
1901	$588	$525	$63	—
1902	562	485	77	—
1903	562	517	45	—
1904	541	584	–43	
1905	544	567	–23	—
1906	595	570	25	—
1907	666	579	87	—
1908	602	659	–57	—
1909	604	694	–89	—
1910	676	694	–18	—
1911	702	691	11	—
1912	693	690	3	—
1913	714	715	–*	—
1914	725	726	–*	—
1915	683	746	–63	—
1916	761	713	48	—
1917	1,101	1,954	–853	—
1918	3,645	12,677	–9,032	—
1919	5,130	18,493	–13,363	—
1920	6,649	6,358	291	—
1921	5,571	5,062	509	—
1922	4,026	3,289	736	—
1923	3,853	3,140	713	—
1924	3,871	2,908	963	—
1925	3,641	2,924	717	—
1926	3,795	2,930	865	—
1927	4,013	2,857	1,155	—
1928	3,900	2,961	939	—
1929	3,862	3,127	734	—

Table 3-2 *(Continued)*

	Receipts	*Outlays*	*Deficit (–) or surplus*	*Percent of GDP*
1930	4,058	3,320	738	0.7
1931	3,116	3,577	–462	–0.5
1932	1,924	4,659	–2,735	–4.0
1933	1,997	4,598	–2,602	–4.5
1934	2,955	6,541	–3,586	–5.8
1935	3,609	6,412	–2,803	–4.0
1936	3,923	8,228	–4,304	–5.4
1937	5,387	7,580	–2,193	–2.5
1938	6,751	6,840	–89	–0.1
1939	6,295	9,141	–2,846	–3.2
1940	6,548	9,468	–2,920	–3.0
1941	8,712	13,653	–4,941	–4.3
1942	14,634	35,137	–20,503	–14.1
1943	24,001	78,555	–54,554	–30.3
1944	43,747	91,304	–47,557	–23.0
1945	45,159	92,712	–47,553	–21.9
1946	39,296	55,232	–15,936	–7.3
1947	38,514	34,496	4,018	1.8
1948	41,560	29,764	11,796	4.7
1949	39,415	38,835	580	0.2
1950	39,443	42,562	–3,119	–1.1
1951	51,616	45,514	6,102	1.9
1952	66,167	67,686	–1,519	–0.4
1953	69,608	76,101	–6,493	–1.7
1954	69,701	70,855	–1,154	–0.3
1955	65,451	68,444	–2,993	–0.8
1956	74,587	70,640	3,947	0.9
1957	79,990	76,578	3,412	0.8

(Continued on next page)

Table 3-2 *(Continued)*

	Receipts	*Outlays*	*Deficit (–) or surplus*	*Percent of GDP*
1958	79,636	82,405	–2,769	–0.6
1959	79,249	92,098	–12,849	–2.6
1960	92,492	92,191	301	0.1
1961	94,388	97,723	–3,335	–0.6
1962	99,676	106,821	–7,146	–1.3
1963	106,560	111,316	–4,756	–0.8
1964	112,613	118,528	–5,915	–0.9
1965	116,817	118,228	–1,411	–0.2
1966	130,835	134,532	–3,698	–0.5
1967	148,822	157,464	–8,643	–1.1
1968	152,973	178,134	–25,161	–2.9
1969	186,882	183,640	3,242	0.3
1970	192,807	195,649	–2,842	–0.3
1971	187,139	210,172	–23,033	–2.1
1972	207,309	230,681	–23,373	–2.0
1973	230,799	245,707	–14,908	–1.1
1974	263,224	269,359	–6,135	–0.4
1975	279,090	332,332	–53,242	–3.4
1976	298,060	371,792	–73,732	–4.3
1977	355,559	409,218	–53,659	–2.7
1978	399,561	458,746	–59,186	–2.7
1979	463,302	504,032	–40,729	–1.6
1980	517,122	590,947	–73,835	–2.7
1981	599,272	678,249	–78,976	–2.6
1982	617,766	745,755	–127,989	–4.0
1983	600,562	808,380	–207,818	–6.1
1984	666,499	851,888	–185,388	–4.9
1985	734,165	946,499	–212,334	–5.2
1986	769,260	990,505	–221,245	–5.1

Table 3-2 *(Continued)*

	Receipts	*Outlays*	*Deficit (–) or surplus*	*Percent of GDP*
1987	854,396	1,004,164	–149,769	–3.3
1988	909,303	1,064,489	–155,187	–3.1
1989	991,190	1,143,671	–152,481	–2.8
1990	1,031,969	1,252,705	–221,194	–3.9
1991	1,055,041	1,324,400	–269,359	–4.6
1992	1,091,279	1,381,681	–290,402	–4.7
1993	1,154,401	1,409,414	–255,013	–3.9
1994	1,258,627	1,461,731	–203,104	–3.0
1995	1,351,830	1,515,729	–163,899	–2.3
1996	1,453,062	1,560,330	–107,268	–1.4

* $500,000 or less.
Source: Budget of the United States, 1998: Historical Tables.

That expression "general welfare" became the focal point of disagreement even before the Constitution had been ratified. One side believed it should be interpreted strictly and wanted spending limited to only those purposes specifically stated in the Constitution. The other side interpreted "general welfare" more loosely, saying it gave the government powers beyond those explicitly named in the Constitution.

The disagreement persisted into the twentieth century, but the looser interpretation was finally confirmed by Supreme Court decisions on New Deal legislation in the 1930s, notably *United States v. Butler* (1936). In *Butler* the Court ruled that spending was constitutional "so long as the welfare at which it is aimed can be plausibly represented as national rather than local."

(See 3 Who actually spends the money? 78 What articles of the Constitution grant the power to tax and spend? 80 Why was the 16th Amendment necessary? 146 How have federal spending patterns changed since 1960? 321 What did the Supreme Court ruling in United States v. Butler *do? 381 Which president resorted to impoundment to cut federal spending? 400 What effect did the 1930s depression have on the fundamental philosophy behind federal spending? 455 What were the battle lines in Congress over the Congressional Budget and Impoundment Control Act?)*

Q 169. What were the Golden Fleece awards?

A The brainchild of Sen. William Proxmire (D-Wis.), the monthly Golden Fleece awards were designed to publicize wasteful or questionable spending of taxpayer dollars by federal agencies. The first was awarded in March 1975 for an $84,000 National Science Foundation study into "Why people fall in love." Proxmire and his staff continued issuing the humorously worded and highly publicized awards nearly every month for the next fourteen years until his retirement. Defense Department spending was frequently a target—for example, Proxmire lambasted the Pentagon's $162-million budget for periodicals as "evidence of the Pentagon's new motto: Better read than dead."

(See 359 What is pork-barrel spending? 361 What were the Grace Commission findings on government waste?)

SOCIAL SPENDING

Q 170. Why spend tax dollars on social programs?

A The lives of many Americans would be much less secure without federal entitlement programs like food stamps, Medicare, Medicaid, unemployment insurance, and Social Security. Among other things, these programs provide a cushion against emergencies that could happen to most anyone, such as losing a job, suffering a severe medical illness, or being disabled by an accident on the job. Then, too, Social Security and military and civil service pension plans ease the anxieties of old age by providing a stable income for millions of elderly Americans. Moreover, millions of families would fall below the poverty line without the federal benefits they receive; millions of others would have no income at all, no food, and no shelter.

Supporters of social programs argue that in a country as wealthy as the United States, the federal government should do all it can to help those in need. But there is more to their arguments than compassion. Entitlement programs also can help people become productive citizens again through job training and placement services, can provide a more stable home environment for raising children and to prevent crime, and can even help meet basic nutritional needs to prevent serious illness due to malnutrition.

These programs are expensive. Waste, inefficiency, and outright abuse are of course a factor. But the main reason costs are so high for the biggest entitlement programs is that tens of millions of Americans have come to rely on them.

(See 181 Does social spending really help ease poverty?)

Q 171. Why has social spending risen by so much?

A Social spending, mainly for entitlement programs, has increased dramatically since the late 1960s. In 1962 outlays for entitlements totaled just $27.9 billion. Annual spending jumped to $61.1 billion by 1970, quadrupled to $262.3 billion by 1980, and more than doubled to $568.5 billion by 1990. Unless Congress enacts significant changes, that impressive growth rate will not slow much in the near future. According to current estimates, entitlements will top the $1 trillion a year mark by the year 2000 (see Figure 3-3).

Much of that increase stems from the fact that during the 1960s Congress decided to aggressively expand the government's responsibility for social welfare. President Lyndon Johnson's Great Society program created or enlarged scores of federal entitlement programs, making millions more people eligible for federally funded benefits. Too often, though, in their zeal to reform society, legislators either badly underestimated future costs or did not even consider them. Then, during the 1970s, Congress substantially enlarged entitlement spending again by making more people eligible for programs and by increasing benefits.

Another major change that contributed to rising costs was indexing of entitlement benefits for inflation. This system automatically increased benefits in step with rises in the Consumer Price Index. Indexation of individual entitlement programs began in the early 1960s with civil service and military retirement benefits (Social Security was indexed from 1975). Virtually all major entitlement programs had been indexed by 1979, locking in substantial social spending increases whenever inflation was high.

Population changes have also driven up costs for Social Security, civil service, and military retirement programs. The percentage of the population reaching retirement age has been increasing steadily since the 1950s. In 1955, for example, about 4.8 percent of the population was receiving Social Security benefits. By 1978 that figure had tripled to 15.8 percent.

(See 181 Does social spending really help ease poverty? 185 Why have health care costs been rising so rapidly? 204 Will the Social Security program actually go bankrupt? Why? 450 What changes in Social Security benefits did Congress make in 1972?)

Q 172. Can entitlement programs be changed?

A Technically speaking, Congress can change entitlement programs any way it wants to—so long as enough members in both houses are willing to vote for it. But as a practical matter Congress has been able to do little without broad-based public support. The major entitlement programs like Social Security and Medicare provide benefits to

Figure 3-3 Growth in Entitlement Spending

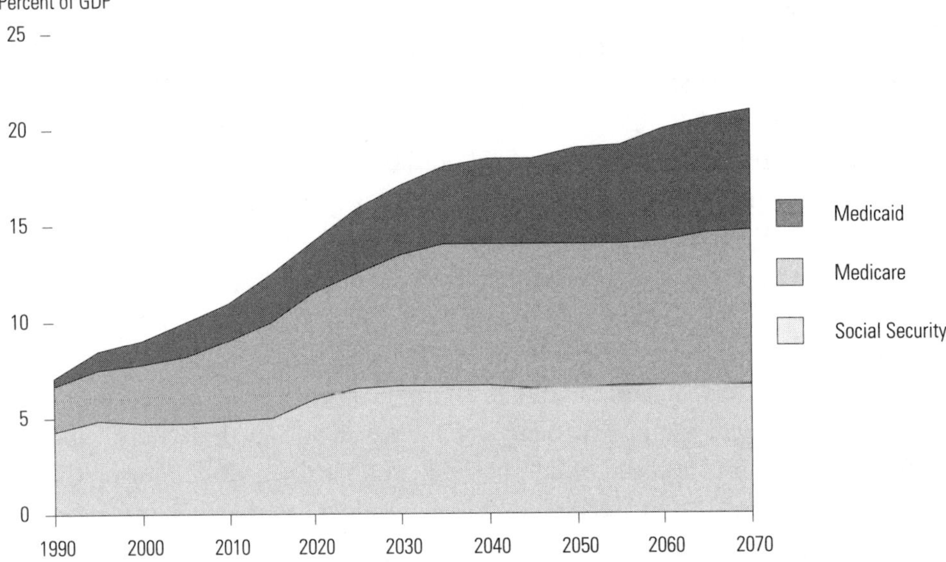

Sources: Social Security Administration, Department of Health and Human Services, Office of Management and Budget, and Council of Economic Advisers.

Note: Medicaid expenditures after 2050 are projected by the Council of Economic Advisers.

many millions of Americans and so are very popular. Every member of Congress ultimately has to answer to voters back home, and even talk of tinkering with these programs has provoked a major public outcry in the past.

The Reagan administration sparked a firestorm of criticism during the early 1980s by suggesting adjustments to Social Security. The idea was quickly abandoned, but there remained the problem of fixing entitlement programs, which continued pushing up the deficit and the debt. These mushrooming costs and the impending bankruptcy of Social Security and Medicare trust funds eventually forced Congress to act on entitlement reforms, though it has dared to consider major changes only recently.

(See 171 Why has social spending risen by so much? 191 What changes in Medicare did the 1997 balanced budget deal make? 197 Why is Social Security called the "third rail" of American politics? 397 What was the 1997 balanced budget agreement? 488 What did the 1997 balanced budget agreement do to cut taxes?)

Q 173. What does the public think about cutting entitlement programs?

A A recent poll showed most people are against cutting benefits for Social Security and Medicare to balance the budget. Instead, they believe these programs can be kept from going broke in the next century by eliminating wasteful spending, abuse, and fraud. Over 75 percent of those responding were convinced a balanced budget can be achieved without changing the benefits.

But the survey also found most people do not realize that entitlements now account for over 60 percent of federal spending and that balancing the budget will be virtually impossible without making adjustments to the programs. Only 27 percent of those polled knew how much of the budget goes for Social Security, and just 28 percent were aware that most retirees actually get more money out of Social Security than they paid in.

Those polled generally opposed remedies like a payroll tax hike (to increase Social Security revenues), an across-the-board benefit cut, or an increase in the retirement age. But they did approve cutting benefits for upper-income retirees.

(See 171 Why has social spending risen by so much? 181 Does social spending really help ease poverty? 188 How has Medicare spending grown as a percentage of the budget over past years? 197 Why is Social Security called the "third rail" of American politics? 198 Do retirees take more out of the Social Security system than they put in?)

Q 174. What percentage of the budget goes for social spending?

A About 62 percent of the budget—some $969 billion—was allocated to social spending in fiscal 1996. Among the programs funded are Social Security, Medicare, Medicaid, various other health programs, education and training, social services, veterans' programs, unemployment insurance, and welfare.

(See 83 How have federal spending patterns changed since 1960? 131 When did social spending actually begin to mushroom? 147 Who got what in a recent budget? 170 Why spend tax dollars on social programs? 171 Why has social spending risen by so much?)

Q 175. Which social spending programs currently command the largest share of federal spending?

A Social Security is the single largest expenditure in the federal budget and the largest of all categories of social spending. About twenty-three cents of every dollar the government spends goes to the Social Security program, but the government also funds scores of other social programs. Spending (by category) for the various social programs is as follows:

	Social Spending in 1996 (in billions)
Social Security	$350
Income security	226
Medicare	174
Health	119
Education, training, employment and social service	52
Veterans' benefits	37
Community and regional development	11
Total	969

(See 147 Who got what in a recent budget? 161 How many people receive federal benefits? 171 Why has social spending risen by so much? 185 Why have health care costs been rising so rapidly? 194 Why was Social Security established? 199 How many people are receiving Social Security benefits and how much do they depend on them? 201 What are the two largest Social security programs and what purposes do they serve?)

Q 176. Could entitlement caps control spending?

A Spending caps are high on the list of possible entitlement reforms, but just how to arrange the mechanics of the caps is still an open question. Total entitlement spending could come under a single cap, or caps could be set for specific programs. Cuts to enforce the spending caps could be automatic—and so less difficult politically for Congress to handle. But a more flexible approach would require a decision by Congress on whether to allow excess spending (because, for example, the country is in a recession) or to stay within the cap by cutting spending.

Then there is the problem of how to make the cuts:

* Cuts could be across-the-board, affecting all entitlement programs, or in just those programs where spending has exceeded the limit.
* Offsetting cuts might be required to make up only part of the overage, or they might be spread over several years.

* For cuts within a program, they might be arranged to effect only recipients above a set income level, fees for certain services might be increased, or all the program's recipients might have their benefits cut equally.

(See 162 Is there a difference between discretionary and mandatory spending? 394 What did Executive Order 12857 do?)

Q 177. What is a transfer payment?

A *Transfer payment* is a budget term for direct payment of benefits to individuals who qualify for federal entitlement programs. The weekly check an unemployed person receives is a transfer payment and so is a retired person's monthly Social Security check. Federal outlays to doctors for treating Medicare patients are also counted as transfer payments.

Economists do not count transfer payments when they calculate the Gross Domestic Product (GDP) because the money (a considerable amount) has nothing to do with current production of goods and services in the economy.

(See 29 What exactly is Gross Domestic Product? 160 What are entitlement programs?)

Q 178. What federal programs make transfer payments?

A Scores of federal programs make direct payments of benefits to eligible individuals. Generally speaking, the programs provide people with a social safety net, offering income security for the aged (and others), basic insurance against accidents and ill-health, opportunities for advancement through training and education, and assistance with taking care of such basic needs as food and housing. Specific programs include the Social Security retirement and survivor benefits program, Social Security disability compensation, federal employee retirement programs, unemployment compensation, Medicare, Medicaid, welfare, job training programs, food stamps, subsidized school lunches, and rent and housing subsidies.

(See 146 How have federal spending patterns changed since 1960? 170 Why spend tax dollars on social programs? 171 Why has social spending risen by so much?)

Q 179. How much does the government pay to individuals, program by program?

A The federal government paid out about $909 billion in direct payments and grants to individuals in 1996. The following figures are the latest available estimates of the final 1996 spending totals:

	Spending (in millions)
Social Security and railroad retirement	
Social Security—old age and survivors insurance	$303,539
Social Security—disability insurance	43,281
Railroad retirement	4,598
Federal employee retirement and insurance	
Civil service retirement	39,670
Military retirement	28,831
Veterans' service connected compensation	14,222
Other	1,338
Unemployment compensation	22,958
Health care	
Medicare (Parts A and B)	191,265
Medicaid	91,990
Veterans' medical care	16,736
Other	8,003
Income assistance and allied programs	
Supplemental Security Income program (SSI)	22,938
Welfare (grants to states)	16,670
Low-income home energy assistance	1,067
Earned income tax credit	19,159
Legal services	282
Daycare assistance (grants to states)	933
Veterans' pensions (non-service connected)	2,834

	Spending (in millions)
Food and nutrition assistance	
Food stamps	25,422
Child nutrition and special milk programs	7,875
Supplemental feeding programs	3,678
Commodity donations and other	851
Housing assistance	24,498
Assistance to students	
Student assistance	11,407
Veterans' education benefits	1,427
Other	
Coal miners' and black lung benefits	1,212
Veterans' insurance and burial benefits	114
Payments to Japanese American WWII internees	6
Refugee assistance and other	2,619

Source: Budget of the United States, 1998: Historical Tables.

(See 161 How many people receive federal benefits? 174 What percentage of the budget goes for social spending?)

Q 180. What are block grants?

A Block grants are lump sum payments for grants-in-aid to states. (A grant-in-aid is money the federal government gives states to help pay for public services and other public assistance programs.) Republicans have championed the idea of converting federal payments to states into block grants as a means of giving states more control over entitlement spending. The welfare reform act, for example, changed federal welfare benefit payments into block grants that allow states to decide how best to spend the money, within general guidelines. In the past, funds had been paid to states according to how many residents were actually on welfare. Federal regulations also spelled out exactly how the money was to be spent.

(See 163 How have federal grants to state and local governments changed over the years? 209 How did the 1996 welfare reform act change the welfare system?)

Q 181. Does social spending really help ease poverty?

A President Bill Clinton's proposed 1998 budget estimated that about 57.6 million people would have been poor in 1995 without some form of government aid. About 27 percent were elderly, 43 percent were aged eighteen to sixty-four, and 30 percent were children under age eighteen. Government spending for income support and other social programs cut the number of people living below the poverty line in 1995 by 47 percent, so that the actual number of people classified as poor was 30.3 million. (The poverty line is the level of income below which the government designates individuals as poor.)

* Social insurance programs lifted the largest number of people above the poverty line, about 67 percent of them. This group included 93 percent of the elderly who would have been among the poor without social spending programs.
* Means-tested benefit programs (recipients must have incomes below a certain level) kept another 28 percent out of poverty, including 60 percent of the children who would otherwise have been classified as poor.
* Tax breaks for the poor lifted the remaining 5 percent above the poverty line. One important low-income tax benefit is the Earned Income Tax Credit (see next question).

(See 20 Should the budget be balanced? 143 How has government gotten bigger over the years? 165 What is "backdoor spending"? 170 Why spend tax dollars on social programs? 171 Why has social spending risen by so much? 210 What are the main welfare programs and how many recipients were there in a recent year? 211 What percent of the population is below the poverty line?)

Q 182. What is the Earned Income Tax Credit?

A The Earned Income Tax Credit (EITC) is a tax credit for low-income families that sometimes includes a cash refund. Sen. Russell Long (D-La.) was instrumental in adding the EITC program to the tax code to offset the regressive effects of a payroll tax hike on the working poor. About 20 million workers and their families benefited from EITC in 1996, receiving an average credit of about $1,400. Overall the program cost the government about $24.3 billion in lost tax revenues and outright refunds.

EITC benefits are set up to give workers a positive rather than negative incentive to increase their income up to the program's phase-out level. But the program's rules are complicated, and a 1990 IRS check of EITC compliance found nearly 40 percent of the benefits went to people who were not even eligible. Nevertheless, that same year Congress voted to expand the EITC program.

(See 101 What is a negative income tax? 333 Who is Russell Long and what is he remembered for?)

Q 183. How many people are not covered by health insurance?

A As of the mid-1990s, about 40 million of the 265 million Americans did not have health insurance, either because they could not afford it, could not get insurance in the first place, or did not qualify for a federal health care program. Young adults and children of uninsured parents make up the bulk of the uninsured. Most people who do have insurance get it through group plans offered at their workplace.

(See 192 What Medicaid reforms did the 1997 balanced budget deal make?)

Q 184. What has the government been spending on health care programs?

A Federal spending on health care has been rising steadily as a percentage of total expenditures since the 1960s. It trebled from 2.1 percent of all federal spending in 1962 to 7.1 percent in 1970, and continued expanding during the 1970s and 1980s. By 1991 it had reached 15.3 percent of total spending. During the Clinton administration, federal health care spending shot up again, topping 20.9 percent of federal spending in 1996. Government spending for health care now amounts to 4.4 percent of GDP.

Q 185. Why have health care costs been rising so rapidly?

A Hospital and other medical costs generally have increased faster than inflation for a number of years, and this has made health care more expensive for everyone, not just those who rely on help from Medicare or Medicaid. But there are some specific reasons why spending for the two federal programs has shot up eleven-fold over the past twenty years (see previous question).

* The number of people eligible for Medicare—those over age sixty-five—has been rising, up from just over 20 million in 1960 to just over 30 million in 1990. People today are living longer (thanks in part to advances in our health care system), and the population generally will only continue getting older as the baby boomer generation ages. By 2020 almost 55 million Americans will be over sixty-five.

* Expensive new medications and treatments, such as organ transplants, have been developed in recent years. While they save lives, they have helped drive costs to the breaking point for Medicare and Medicaid.
* Lax control over payments for treating Medicare and Medicaid patients has led to abuse and outright fraud by some health care providers. Overcharging for patient care, charges for unnecessary treatments, and fraudulent billing for treatments never provided have cost the government many millions over the years.

(See 170 Why spend tax dollars on social programs? 171 Why has social spending risen by so much?)

Q 186. What made passage of Medicare in 1965 such a notable event?

A Medicare was probably the most important welfare legislation passed since enactment of the Social Security system in 1935, and it did much to ease the suffering and financial hardships of the elderly. Liberals had been trying to win enactment of a national health care program for the aged since the 1940s, and this long-delayed victory marked a major advance in their drive to expand the federal government's social responsibilities.

The Medicare bill President Lyndon Johnson signed into law, a centerpiece of his Great Society program, was much more sweeping, and costly, than anything liberals had previously proposed, however. The Medicare act established both a basic health plan covering (then) some 19 million elderly persons, and a supplementary plan for millions of others. But it went beyond Medicare to increase Social Security retirement benefits by 7 percent and boost federal funding for child health care. Funding for these initiatives was to come from payroll taxes and general revenues.

(See 170 Why spend tax dollars on social programs? 181 Does social spending really help ease poverty? 190 When will Medicare funds run out? 204 Will the Social Security program actually go bankrupt? Why?)

Q 187. What is the difference between Medicare and Medicaid?

A *Medicare* is a part of the Social Security program. It pays medical expenses for elderly people over the age of sixty-five and disabled persons who qualify for Social Security. The program is divided into two parts—Medicare Part A, the hospital insurance program financed by a payroll tax, and Medicare Part B, the supplementary medical insurance, which is partly financed by premiums. *Medicaid* covers medical expenses of the needy, no matter what their age. The program is not connected with Social Security and is actually administered by the states, but the federal government pays over half the program costs, about 57 percent in 1995.

Q 188. How has Medicare spending grown as a percentage of the budget over past years?

A The budget for fiscal 1967, the first year with Medicare in full operation, shows the program cost about $2.7 billion, or just under 2 percent of total federal spending. Medicare rose about a billion a year thereafter until the mid-1970s, when the program accounted for 4 percent of federal spending, and costs suddenly began moving upward at a faster pace. By 1980 Medicare accounted for $32 billion (almost 5½ percent of the budget), but that was just the beginning—Medicare spending exploded during the 1980s. The 1985 budget saw it double to $65 billion, and in 1990 Medicare topped $98 billion, amounting to about 8 percent of the budget. By 1996 Medicare accounted for about 11 percent of all federal spending and cost $171 billion for the year. It was expected to consume 12 percent of the budget by 1998.

(See 170 Why spend tax dollars on social programs? 171 Why has social spending risen by so much? 185 Why have health care costs been rising so rapidly?)

Q 189. What about Medicaid spending?

A Even though the federal government pays only about half of the costs, the bill for Medicaid has grown so rapidly it now amounts to almost 6 percent of the annual budget. The federal share of Medicaid expenses stood at just $2.7 billion in 1970, but by 1980 it had quadrupled to $14 billion. Medicaid payments nearly tripled during the 1980s, topping $41 billion in 1990, and will more than triple again by 2002 unless Congress takes steps to curb spending. Medicaid spending in 1996 was $92 billion.

The bulk of Medicaid spending goes to the elderly and disabled (about 61 percent). As of 1996, at least half of all adults with AIDS and up to 90 percent of all children with AIDS were receiving Medicaid benefits.

Q 190. When will Medicare funds run out?

A Claims against the Medicare trust first overtook annual revenues from payroll taxes in 1996. According to Congressional Budget Office estimates, claims will continue to outstrip revenue, even when reforms approved as part of the 1997 balanced budget package are factored in. Unless Congress enacts further reforms, the Medicare trust will go bankrupt in 2007.

(See 170 Why spend tax dollars on social programs? 171 Why has social spending risen by so much? 183 How many people are not covered by health insurance? 185 Why have health care costs been rising so dramatically? 204 Will the Social Security program actually go bankrupt? Why?)

Q 191. What changes in Medicare did the 1997 balanced budget agreement make?

A Most of the spending cuts in the balanced budget deal were realized by reducing the growth of Medicare costs—savings will amount to $115 billion over five years for a net reduction of 12 percent of the projected cost growth. Changes in payments to health care providers will be a big part of that savings: growth of the basic rate to hospitals will be capped at 1.8 percent per year from 2000 onward, and fee schedules for doctors, nursing homes, and other health care providers will also be adjusted.

Among the other Medicare reforms was the transfer of payments for home health services from Medicare Part A to Part B. That helped put off the bankruptcy of the Medicare trust fund from 2001 to 2007, because patient premiums and the federal government pay the costs of Medicare Part B health care services. Payroll taxes alone finance Part A services covered by the trust fund. Medicare Part B premiums will rise to $67 a month by 2002, $15.50 more than originally projected.

Reforms also allow Medicare recipients to take advantage of HMOs, add $4 billion in spending for screening for cancer and disorders, and set up an experimental medical savings account program. In addition, the budget deal set up the National Bipartisan Commission on the Future of Medicare to study further Medicare reforms.

(See 208 Will current reform proposals do away with Social Security as we know it? 397 What was the 1997 balanced budget agreement?)

Q 192. What Medicaid reforms did the 1997 balanced budget agreement make?

A The balanced budget agreement adjusted the Medicaid program, giving states greater control over rates paid to health care providers and allowing them to take advantage of managed care and other options. In addition, it set up a new $23.4 billion program that will provide health insurance to about 3.4 million children (partly paid for by an increase in the cigarette tax). It reduced the federal "disproportionate share" payments to states with large numbers of poor and uninsured people, but added $1.5 billion for a Medicaid program that pays Medicare Part B premiums for eligible low-income recipients. Overall, the balanced budget agreement cut Medicaid spending by about $10.4 billion over five years.

(See 397 What was the 1997 balanced budget agreement?)

Q 193. Do HMOs offer any advantages?

A Health Maintenance Organizations, HMOs, have emerged as an important way to save money on medical costs. They have already proved themselves a popular alternative to more expensive health insurance plans, and some political leaders think encouraging more people to join HMOs will help lower health care costs generally.

HMOs save their clients money by requiring them to see affiliated doctors within the area and to see general practitioners first, before seeking treatment from more expensive specialists. Some critics have raised concerns that the emphasis HMOs place on keeping costs down may prevent patients from getting specialized treatments they need. Other practices coming under fire include rules mandating shortened hospital stays and refusing to reimburse patients for emergency room visits when no actual medical emergency is involved.

Q 194. Why was Social Security established?

A Part of President Franklin Roosevelt's depression-era New Deal, Social Security was created in 1935 so that the elderly would always have enough to live on. Up until that time people working in factories and other low-paying jobs had only what little they could save to cover their retirement. When they became too old to work, many were forced to rely on their children or the charity of others for support until they died.

The basic Social Security program gives everyone who works a guaranteed minimum income for their old age, and also provides the disabled with an income safety net.

Q 195. Was the United States the first country to enact a Social Security System?

A No, in fact it was the last major industrial nation to do so. By 1935, when Social Security was established here, twenty-two European nations and six other countries around the world had comprehensive benefit programs covering sizable portions of their populations. German chancellor Otto von Bismarck is said to have established the first old age pension system in 1875. During the late 1800s Germany created other new social security programs providing sickness, maternity, disability, and old age benefits. Britain adopted its own social security system, including disability benefits, health care, and unemployment insurance between 1908 and 1925. France did so between 1905 and 1928.

Q 196. How does the Social Security program work?

A The Social Security system was set up as a huge national pension system that was to be self-supporting through payroll taxes. Workers and their employers each pay half of the tax, which is based on the worker's wages. Self-employed persons pay the full amount of the tax themselves, based on their income. Payroll taxes are deposited in the Social Security trust fund, which by law can only invest the money in risk-free federal government securities.

The system is self-supporting, but not in the way many people think. Payroll taxes workers pay now do not go into an account to pay for their retirement. Instead the taxes pay for benefits of those who are already retired. When people who are working now retire, someone else's taxes will be covering their benefits. That is part of the reason the system is in trouble. As things stand now, it takes contributions from more than two workers to support benefits for one retiree, and when the baby boomer generation reaches retirement age early in the next century, there will be a flood of new retirees. Meanwhile, the decline in the birthrate means there will soon not be enough new workers paying into the system.

To become eligible for retirement benefits, people must work and pay the payroll tax over a minimum number of years and be anywhere from sixty-five to sixty-seven years old (depending on their date of birth). Monthly benefits range from a minimum to a maximum depending on how much the worker has contributed over the years. The average payment for a retired male worker is about $759, and for a retired female worker, about $548. Congress has increased monthly payments substantially over the years and since 1975 automatic cost of living increases, or COLAs, have helped Social Security recipients keep pace with inflation. They have also added to the financial strain on the Social Security fund, however.

(See 41 What impact does the inflated CPI have? 204 Will the Social Security program actually go bankrupt? Why? 205 What is the dependency ratio? 208 Will current reform proposals do away with Social Security as we know it?)

Q 197. Why is Social Security called the "third rail" of American politics?

A Political leaders have found that attempts to reform the Social Security system can provoke a major outcry from voters, even if they involve only relatively minor reductions in benefits. For that reason, politicians regard Social Security with the same caution people have for the high-voltage third rail found on electrified commuter railroads. They usually just want to leave it alone.

Social Security is an extremely sensitive issue with voters because so many of them depend on it for retirement or disability income—about 46 million voters in all. And tens of millions of others are now paying into the system with the expectation of receiving benefits when they retire. Naturally they are concerned about any change in a program that is so important to them. But the public response is also magnified by the powerful lobbying groups that monitor the Social Security program.

President Ronald Reagan discovered in 1981 just how dangerous tampering with Social Security could be. One budget-cutting measure the administration put before Congress that year called for eliminating the $122 monthly minimum Social Security benefit. About 2.7 million people received the benefit, and the administration claimed most were federal retirees, who already had substantial federal pension income and so did not need the Social Security payment. Congress initially approved the cut, but the public outcry proved so forceful that it hastily reversed itself.

Q 198. Do retirees take more out of the Social Security system than they put in?

A Officials at Social Security call this a "money's worth" question, and for a variety of reasons it is much easier to answer based on generational groups than for any specific individual. For example, people who retired in the past received much more in benefits than they paid in taxes, because they paid taxes for fewer years (Social Security did not begin operations until 1937).

But as people pay over a longer period, the benefit to tax ratio declines. Still, for workers retiring in the mid-1990s, the ratio remains in their favor because tax rates were much lower until as recently as the late 1970s. Surprisingly, even new workers just entering the labor force in the mid-1990s are expected to break even as a group, getting back almost exactly what they and their employers paid in payroll taxes.

(See 121 How has the tax rate for the employer's share of the payroll tax increased over the years?)

199. How many people receive Social Security benefits and how much do they depend on them?

About 46 million or so people benefited from payments made under one or another of the various Social Security programs in a recent year (see Figure 3-4). For about 60 percent of all recipients those payments amount to 50 percent or more of their annual income. For about 25 percent, the payments represent about 90 percent or more of income (see Figure 3-5).

The number of Americans over age sixty-five (making them eligible for Social Security) has been rising steadily over the past thirty years. They were 30 million strong in 1990, and as baby boomers reach retirement age the number of people relying on Social Security benefits will mushroom. Current estimates predict about 55 million people will be over sixty-five in the year 2020.

(See 161 How many people receive federal benefits? 204 Will the Social Security program actually go bankrupt? Why?)

200. When did Social Security spending top 20 percent of the federal budget?

The Social Security Administration budget remained fairly stable through the 1960s, finishing the decade at $27.3 billion, or 14.8 percent of the total federal budget for

Figure 3-4 Composition of Social Security Recipients

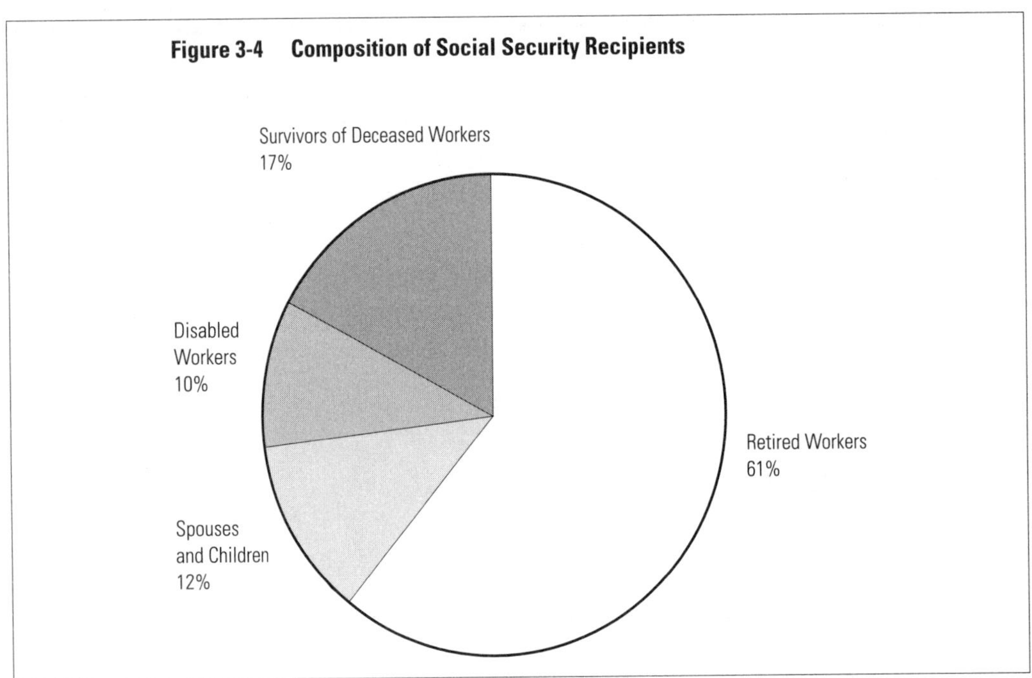

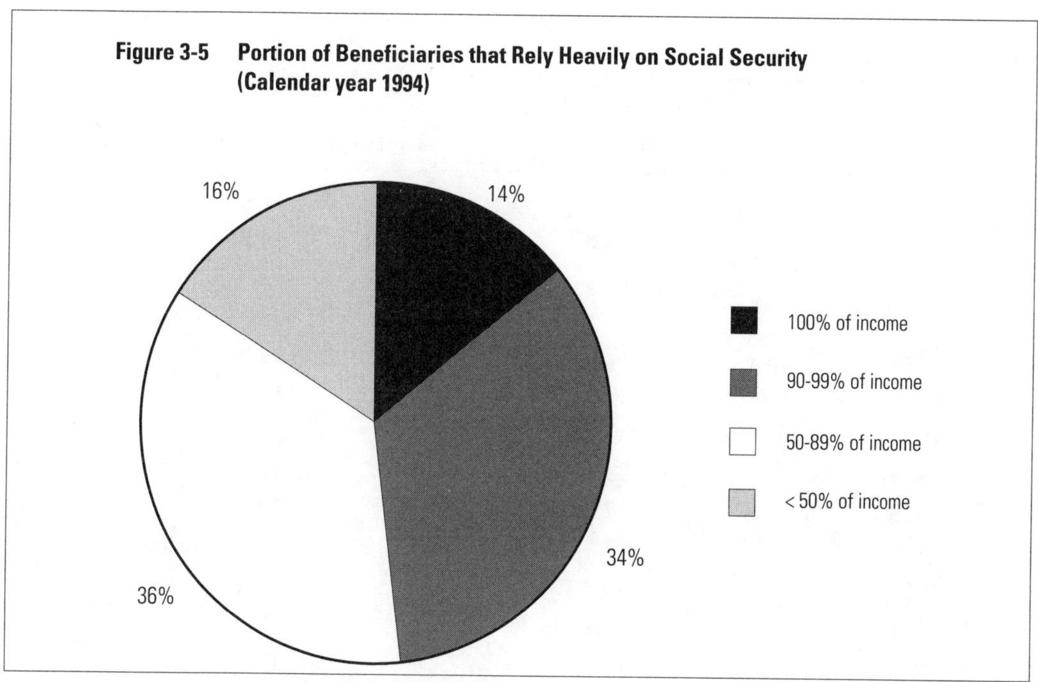

Figure 3-5 Portion of Beneficiaries that Rely Heavily on Social Security (Calendar year 1994)

1969. During the late 1960s and early 1970s, however, Congresses approved benefit increases, eased eligibility standards, and authorized automatic cost-of-living increases for the Social Security program.

Spending began rising rapidly, soon outpacing even the increased payroll taxes imposed to cover the benefit increases. By 1973 spending had nearly doubled, and the Social Security Administration accounted for just over 20 percent of the federal budget. By 1978 Social Security's budget topped $100 billion, and the decade closed with spending quadruple what it had been in 1970. Social Security doubled again during the 1980s to an impressive $247.1 billion (1989) and was expected to top $395 billion in 1997 (see Table 3-3). If government estimates are correct, Social Security alone will consume 25 percent of the federal budget by the year 2000.

(See 144 Which federal agency gets the biggest slice of the budget?)

Q 201. What are the two largest Social Security programs and what purposes do they serve?

A The Old Age, Survivors, and Disability Insurance (OASDI) and Supplemental Security Income (SSI) are the two programs that benefit the largest number of people. OASDI provides retired workers over age sixty-five with a guaranteed minimum income and makes payments for their spouses and children. The program includes Medicare and pays benefits to survivors of deceased workers as well.

Table 3-3 The Rising Cost of Social Security

	Spending by the SSA (in billions)	*Percent of total budget*
1962	$14.4	13.4
1963	15.8	14.2
1964	16.2	14.0
1965	17.5	14.8
1966	20.7	15.4
1967	21.7	13.8
1968	23.8	13.4
1969	27.3	14.8
1970	30.3	15.4
1971	36.2	17.2
1972	40.5	17.6
1973	50.1	20.4
1974	59.1	22.0
1975	70.4	21.2
1976	80.0	21.5
1977	91.3	22.3
1978	100.7	22.0
1979	110.5	21.9
1980	126.0	21.3
1981	147.9	21.8
1982	164.7	22.1
1983	181.7	22.4
1984	189.9	22.3
1985	201.3	21.3
1986	211.0	21.4
1987	219.9	21.9
1988	233.5	21.9
1989	247.1	21.6

Table 3-3 *(Continued)*

	Spending by the SSA (in billions)	*Percent of total budget*
1990	263.1	21.0
1991	286.3	21.6
1992	307.2	22.3
1993	327.3	23.3
1994	345.8	23.7
1995	362.1	23.9
1996	375.2	24.0
1997	395.9	24.3

Source: Budget of the United States, 1998: Historical Tables.

SSI guarantees a minimum monthly income to the disabled and income support to people who are both elderly and very poor.

Q 202. How many people receive OASDI and SSI?

A About 40 million people received OASDI benefits as of the mid-1990s. About 62 percent are retired workers, 12 percent are dependents of retired workers, and 17 percent are survivors of workers who have died. Workers who have been disabled account for the other 9 percent.

SSI provides benefits to about 7 million recipients, of which 75 percent are disabled. Twenty-five percent are elderly people who are very poor.

(See 161 How many people receive federal benefits?)

Q 203. What did the GAO find was wrong with SSI?

A According to a 1997 GAO study, poor management of the Supplemental Security Income (SSI) program has cost millions of tax dollars and leaves the program vulnerable to fraud and abuse. Longstanding problems include overpayments (about $2.3 billion in 1996), thousands of checks sent to ineligible recipients (including prisoners and nursing home patients), and a major backlog of case reviews to determine if recipients are still eligible for SSI. In addition, the GAO reported people have been illegally divesting themselves of assets in order to meet SSI income limits. In an effort to curtail other abuses of SSI, Congress halted payments to alcoholics and drug addicts in 1996.

(See 171 Why has social spending risen by so much? 172 Can entitlement programs be changed?)

Q 204. Will the Social Security program actually go bankrupt? Why?

A Unless something is done, bankruptcy is possible. The Social Security trustees reported in 1996 that the combined Old Age, Survivors, and Disability Insurance (OASDI) funds will be insolvent in 2029 unless some action is taken. The disability insurance fund will actually become insolvent first, in 2015, according to their projections.

Part of the problem lies in the Social Security system itself. Retirees and others are not supported by the payments they made, but by payroll taxes paid by those who are working now. So long as enough people are working and paying into the system it stays afloat, but that is the problem. The birth rate has been declining, and there will eventually be fewer people working to pay for Social Security benefits. Meanwhile, the number of retirees and others receiving the benefits has been increasing sharply, because people are living longer and retiring earlier these days. Unless something is done, the system will go bankrupt when the baby boom generation finally starts retiring in the next century.

(See 198 Do retirees take more out of the Social Security system than they put in? 200 When did Social Security spending top 20 percent of the federal budget? 462 What did the first Social Security rescue plan do? 474 What did the 1983 Social Security rescue plan do?)

Q 205. What is the dependency ratio?

A The dependency ratio is the number of workers paying into the Social Security account, versus the number drawing out benefits. The ratio has been decreasing over the years, posing a long-range threat to the solvency of the Social Security system. During the 1940s when Social Security was starting up, about ten workers were paying into the system for every retiree drawing benefits. By 1980 the dependency ratio was down to three to one, and in 2010 when the baby boomer generation begins retiring, the ratio will have dropped to two workers for each retiree.

Q **206. Do tax breaks on Social Security income actually cost the government money?**

A Retirees, the disabled, and others who receive Social Security payments do not have to pay taxes on their benefits so long as their total income (including Social Security) does not go above a certain level. While that provides welcome tax relief to those receiving Social Security, the federal government lost over $22 billion in tax revenues for 1996 because of it. Revenue losses between 1998 and 2002 are expected to amount to $138 billion for this tax break alone.

(See 88 How do "tax expenditures" affect revenues? 89 What are the major tax expenditures and how much revenue is lost through them?)

Q **207. Has the government been using funds from Social Security for other purposes?**

A This question ranks high among the "hot button" issues today, and many people have been frightened by charges that the federal government has drained all the money out of the Social Security trust fund, leaving nothing but an empty bank account. In fact, there is little or no cash in the trust fund for the same reason people put their cash into savings bonds, money market funds, and other low-risk investments—to earn more money, if only to stay ahead of inflation. Cash sitting idle in a vault actually loses value over the years because inflation makes it worth less.

By law the Department of the Treasury, which manages the Social Security trust funds, can only invest in government securities—considered the safest of all investments. Most trust fund assets have been invested in *special issues*, which are government notes issued only to trust funds. A small amount has been put into Treasury bonds, bills, and notes, which are classified as *public issues* because they can be purchased by the public (see Table 3-4). So, rather than a vault filled with idle cash, the Social Security trust fund has an impressive stack of interest-bearing notes and bonds, which it cashes in whenever it comes time to pay benefits.

Meanwhile, the federal government can and does use for other purposes the cash it gets by issuing the interest-bearing notes to trust funds. You would expect to do the same thing, if you had borrowed money and agreed to pay interest on it.

So is there any reason to worry about what might happen to the trust fund money in the years ahead? Probably not, but there is one potential problem that may present itself in the next century when the baby boom generation begins retiring in large numbers. At that point the Social Security trust fund will begin cashing in many

Table 3-4 Where the Money Is—Social Security Trust Fund Investments (in millions, as of the mid-1990s)

Type of note	*Total invested (in millions)*	*Interest rate earned (%)*
Special issue	$ 14,896	7.875
Certificates of indebtedness	35,477	8.000
Special issue bonds	60,921	6.250
	78,812	7.250
	60,589	7.375
	53,906	8.125
	3,937	8.375
	11,483	8.625
	84,435	8.750
	21,595	9.250
	4,318	10.375
	3,067	10.750
	2,901	13.750
Public issue bonds	5	3.500
	10	7.625
	26	8.000
	4	8.250
	30	11.750
Total invested	$436,412	

Source: Social Security Administration (in *OASIS Magazine,* October 1995).

billions in notes to pay for additional benefits. If the government is still running large deficits at that time, it will likely face serious problems refinancing so much debt in a short span of time.

▶ When was the last major increase in Social Security benefits? *See 450 What change in Social Security benefits did Congress make in 1972?* ◀

Q 208. Will current reform proposals do away with Social Security as we know it?

A The Social Security advisory council, convened to study Social Security reforms, proposed three controversial plans for changing the current system. The plan with the widest support on the council would make some small changes in benefits and raise some taxes other than the payroll tax, leaving the system essentially unchanged. Still more money would be needed, however, and Congress would have to choose between investing part of Social Security trust funds in the stock market (to earn a higher return) and raising payroll taxes. Currently Social Security funds can only be invested in risk-free government securities, which pay just slightly more than inflation.

The two other proposed plans featured more radical changes that would privatize the system to one degree or another. One would hike payroll taxes 1.6 percent and cut benefits sharply. The extra tax money would go into personal retirement accounts, much like 401(k) personal investment accounts, controlled by the worker. The other plan would essentially privatize the Social Security system. It would increase payroll taxes by 1.52 percent and turn over 80 percent of the total payroll tax to the worker for investing in personal investment accounts.

Critics pointed to a number of weaknesses in the basic idea of relying on stock market investments to save Social Security, not to mention the problems of relying on people to invest wisely and to resist the temptation to use the money for other purposes.

Other alternative reforms, while not politically popular, may eventually supply at least part of the solution. These include some combination of reduced benefits (across the board or for future retirees) and increased payroll taxes, postponed benefits and increased penalties for early retirement, cuts in cost of living adjustments (COLAS), and benefit cuts for wealthy retirees.

(See 144 Which federal agency gets the biggest slice of the federal budget? 197 Why is Social Security called the "third rail" of American politics? 200 When did Social Security spending top 20 percent of the federal budget? 204 Will the Social Security program actually go bankrupt? Why?)

Q 209. How did the 1996 welfare reform bill change the welfare system?

A The Personal Responsibility and Work Opportunity Act of 1996 made fundamental changes to the sixty-year-old welfare system. One of the most important is a five-year limit on receiving benefits. In the past, recipients had only to be eligible for benefits (based on financial need) to receive them indefinitely, a situation that led to widespread abuse. In addition, welfare recipients who are able to work are now required by law to do so, the idea here being to move people off welfare and into jobs.

The new law also limits food stamp benefits to just three months in any three-year period for adults who have no children and are able to work, but do not have jobs. (The requirement does not apply to adults over age fifty.)

The method by which the federal government pays its share to states changed as well. States now get a lump sum payment each year (a block grant based on estimates of the state's caseload). The block grant allows states greater flexibility in tailoring their welfare programs to specific needs.

Q 210. What are the main welfare programs and how many recipients were there in a recent year?

A As recently as 1993 there were about 14.1 million people receiving benefits of about $22.3 billion under the country's main welfare program, Aid to Families with Dependent Children (AFDC). An improving economy and publicity surrounding welfare reform combined to reduce the welfare rolls to 12 million by the time welfare reform was passed in mid-1996. Under the new program, Temporary Assistance for Needy Families (TANF), that number was expected to decline even further as recipients move off welfare and into jobs.

Food stamps and other nutritional programs, housing assistance, and child care services are among the other programs available to welfare recipients, as well as other needy people who are not necessarily on welfare. Of these, the food stamp program is the largest and best-known—as many as 28 million people were receiving food stamps in 1993 at a cost of about $25 billion. An improving economy helped reduce recipients to 25 million in 1996, when eligibility rules were tightened. Public housing and housing subsidies for welfare recipients (and other low-income families) are another major welfare expenditure, about $24.5 billion in 1996.

(See 181 Does social spending really help ease poverty?)

Q 211. What percent of the population is below the poverty line?

A Some 36 million people, about 13.7 percent of the population, are poor by current standards. In all, about 8 million households, 10.8 percent of all U.S. households, are getting by with less than $15,000 in annual income, the level of the poverty line. Single mothers head 52 percent of the households in poverty.

The percentage of people below the poverty line has been rising since the early 1970s, largely because the economy has been growing more slowly since then. The low was recorded in 1973 when about 11.1 percent of the population fell below the poverty line.

Q 212. Is race a factor?

A Most poor people are white, accounting for about 67 percent of those below the poverty line. But blacks make up about 29 percent of the poor, a disproportionately high number when you consider that just 13 percent of the population as a whole is black.

Q 213. How many of those below the poverty line do not collect any benefits?

A As of the mid-1990s, about 25 percent of the poor were not receiving any form of federal benefits. Just over half of the poor are not getting welfare (Aid to Families with Dependent Children), and over 80 percent do not live in subsidized or public housing.

Q 214. How many people receive food stamps?

A About 25.5 million people received food stamps in 1996, costing the government a total of about $23 billion. Recipients included people on welfare, disabled persons, the homeless, and people without jobs.

Tighter eligibility rules set by the 1996 welfare reform act were expected to cut off food stamps to about a million recipients in 1997. People between eighteen and fifty years old, who are able to work but have no job, now can receive food stamps for only three months during a three-year period. With average benefits amounting to $120 a month for a single adult, the federal government expects to save about $27 billion over the next five years.

(See 181 Does social spending really help ease poverty? 209 How did the 1996 welfare reform bill change the welfare system?)

Q 215. What has been the change in welfare expenditures over the years?

A For decades the country's main welfare program has been the cash-benefit program, Aid to Families with Dependent Children (AFDC). But since the 1960s, expansion of existing programs and the addition of others (Supplemental Security Income (SSI), food stamps, and so on) have significantly increased the overall cost of the welfare system. Spending totals for AFDC and the more recent SSI are included below:

The Rising Cost of Welfare (in millions)

	AFDC	SSI
1940	$279	—
1941	330	—
1942	376	—
1943	395	—
1944	430	—
1945	401	—
1946	421	—
1947	644	—
1948	732	—
1949	921	—
1950	1,123	—
1951	1,186	—
1952	1,178	—
1953	1,130	—
1954	1,438	—
1955	1,427	—
1956	1,455	—
1957	1,556	—
1958	1,795	—
1959	1,966	—
1960	2,059	—
1961	2,144	—
1962	2,329	—
1963	2,572	—
1964	2,734	—
1965	2,787	—
1966	2,758	—
1967	2,720	—
1968	3,166	—
1969	3,618	—
1970	4,142	—

(Continued)

	AFDC	SSI
1971	5,486	—
1972	6,559	—
1973	5,922	—
1974	5,423	$1,954
1975	5,121	4,320
1976	5,753	4,573
1977	6,165	4,772
1978	6,393	5,280
1979	6,358	4,865
1980	6,924	5,716
1981	7,736	6,467
1982	7,530	6,864
1983	7,875	7,894
1984	8,346	7,633
1985	8,625	8,654
1986	9,877	9,323
1987	10,540	9,933
1988	10,764	11,370
1989	11,166	11,503
1990	12,246	11,493
1991	13,520	14,668
1992	15,103	17,239
1993	15,628	20,343
1994	16,508	23,700
1995	17,133	23,583
1996	16,670	22,938

Source: Budget of the United States, 1998: Historical Tables.

(See 171 Why has social spending risen by so much? 210 What are the main welfare programs and how many recipients were there in a recent year?)

Q 216. Does the government subsidize housing?

A Yes, in a variety of ways and not always for low-income families. In 1996 over 1.3 million families, many of them first-time home buyers, lived in homes purchased with mortgages arranged through the Federal Housing Administration, the Veterans Administration home loan guarantee program, or the Agriculture Department's Rural Housing Service. More generally, the government also gives home owners a tax break through the mortgage interest deduction.

The Housing and Urban Development Department (HUD) provided rent subsidies for more than 4.8 million low-income families in 1996. About 1.4 million families lived in public housing projects, 1.8 million got subsidies for rent in privately owned multifamily houses, and another 1.6 million received vouchers for rent. The government also spent about $1.13 billion to help the homeless through grants to emergency shelters and permanent housing.

Q 217. Why is the government's Section 8 housing subsidy program in trouble?

A Conceived in the 1970s, the Section 8 program encouraged developers to build low-income housing units by guaranteeing long-term rent subsidies. The program offered an alternative to costly public housing projects built by the government. The result was that hundreds of thousands of poor, elderly, and disabled people got "affordable" housing in privately-owned apartment complexes, while developers took the risks and received rent subsidy contracts from the federal government.

Unfortunately, though, Section 8 housing has turned out to be far more expensive than originally expected, throwing the entire program into jeopardy. Inflation clauses in the subsidy contracts have pushed rents (plus the federal subsidy) to an average 130 percent of fair market rates in these apartment complexes. Now the government must decide whether to renew rent subsidy contracts, most of which will end by the year 2000. The alternative is to let billions worth of low-income apartment buildings (and their government-backed mortgages) go into foreclosure.

The current Clinton administration plan focuses on about 500,000 units with rents well above market levels (up to double). It proposes renewing contracts at market level rents (tenant's rent plus subsidy) in return for negotiating a reduction in the developer's mortgage on the apartments (construction expenses were high because of federal standards imposed on builders). The reduced debt would lower mortgage payments and offset the developer's lost income from reduced rents.

As of late 1997, Congress appeared likely to pass a bill lowering rents on Section 8 housing to market rates and restructuring some $125 billion in mortgages for about 8,500 housing projects.

Q 218. Who are Ginnie Mae, Freddie Mac, and Fannie Mae?

A These are nicknames for corporations organized by the government to help finance the home mortgage market. *Ginnie Mae* (Government National Mortgage Association) was created in 1968 to sell securities based on pools of home mortgages financed by the Federal Housing Administration, Veterans Administration, and the Agriculture Department's Rural Housing Service. The securities are sold in what is called the secondary mortgage market and help raise new capital for mortgage loans. Since 1968 Ginnie Mae has originated over $1 trillion in securities and helped finance over 19 million homes for low- and middle-income families. *Fannie Mae* (Federal National Mortgage Association) and *Freddie Mac* (Federal Home Loan Mortgage Corporation) are government-sponsored enterprises wholly owned by shareholders. They also trade in mortgage-backed securities to help expand the home mortgage market. The two corporations held $1.4 trillion in purchased or guaranteed mortgages in 1996. Another government-sponsored enterprise, the Federal Home Loan Bank System, specializes in making collateralized loans to mortgage lenders. It had $153 billion in loans outstanding in 1996.

(See 256 What does the Department of Housing and Urban Development spend? 294 What are government-owned corporations and how are they budgeted?)

Q 219. How much do we spend on education?

A Combined federal, state, and local spending for education is about $500 billion a year. State and local governments foot most of the bill. The federal government's share is only about 6 percent of the overall total, but federal loans and other aid programs help over half of all students pay for college. The Department of Education, which handles federal spending for elementary, secondary, vocational, and higher education spent about $29 billion in 1996 and 1997. The education budget has been rising under President Bill Clinton, however, and he proposed increasing the department's funding for fiscal 1998 by another $10 billion.

(See 221 How big is the federal student loan program?)

Q 220. Has spending per pupil changed in recent years?

A Per pupil spending by federal, state, and local governments combined has almost tripled since 1970, when spending was just over $2,000 a student in public schools. The total rose to $3,000 a student in 1980, over $4,000 in 1990, and about $6,000 per student by 1997. Despite the increases, though, academic achievement by American elementary and high school students consistently lags behind that of students in many other developed countries, including Japan, Germany, and France.

Q 221. How big is the federal student loan program?

A Federally guaranteed educational loans totaled about $19.8 billion in 1996. The direct student loan program dispensed about $9.1 billion in loans that same year. Overall about 7.2 million students from low- and middle-income families benefited from federal loans, grants, and work-study programs in 1996.

The government paid out about $4 billion to banks and companies that service college loans, and $3 billion to subsidize interest on the loans while students are attending college. The government also paid out about $2.8 billion for defaulted student loans.

(See 161 How many people receive federal benefits?)

DEFENSE SPENDING

Q 222. Where has defense usually ranked as a spending priority?

A Defense has traditionally been regarded as one of the federal government's basic responsibilities. Except for a few periods in our history, defense spending has either been the top spending priority or one of the leading expenditures. Needless to say, defense spending rises dramatically during wartime—the $83 billion for defense in 1945 was a stunning 89.5 percent of the federal budget. Defense was the single largest budget expense every year between 1941, when our military buildup for World War II began in earnest, and 1991, when Social Security finally moved into the top spot. Even though the cold war has ended, defense spending remains a leading priority. Actual spending for 1996 was $265.7 billion, and the defense budget is expected to remain in the $260 million to $270 million range into the next century.

(See 144 Which federal agency gets the biggest slice of the federal budget?)

Q 223. What was the biggest defense budget ever?

A By sheer volume of dollars, fiscal 1989's $294.9 billion Defense Department budget was the largest. The 1989 budget came in President George Bush's first year in office but represented the culmination of the Reagan administration's program to build up the military. President Ronald Reagan pushed through defense spending hikes every year he was in office, raising the defense budget from $153.9 billion in fiscal 1981 to the $294.9 billion for fiscal 1989 (the budget having been set during his last year office). Overall, defense spending went up from 22.7 percent of the budget in 1981 to 25.8 percent in 1989. President Bush cut back military spending somewhat but was never far below Reagan's high-water mark.

In terms of percentage of the total federal budget, the 1945 defense budget ($83 billion) still holds the record. Defense spending that year swallowed up 89.5 percent of the federal budget. No other defense budget since World War II has been that high, though spending during the Korean War came close—69.5 percent. The Vietnam War era defense budget never got higher than 46 percent (1968), and percentagewise President Reagan's highest defense budget was only 27.3 percent of all federal spending (1987).

Q 224. How did the Department of Defense spend its budget appropriation in a recent year?

A Of its $253 billion in spending money for 1996, the Department of Defense (DOD) put the largest single chunk of it—$93.6 billion—toward operation and maintenance expenses for the various military branches (active and reserve). Pay for soldiers and officers accounted for another $70 billion, and purchases of weapons and supplies about $42 billion. Expenditures for weapons purchases are expected to rise sharply in the next few years, to an estimated $68 billion by 2002, as the military seeks to modernize weaponry. Other major DOD expenditures include research and development ($36.6 billion), military construction ($6.7 billion), and family housing expenditures ($3.8 billion). The Army National Guard and Air National Guard got a combined total of $10.5 billion. The Department of Energy spent almost $12 billion on defense-related atomic energy programs.

Q 225. Which military branch gets the most money?

A The navy won out in the 1996 budget, but not by a great deal. Funds specifically earmarked and spent for the navy, naval reserve, and marine corps amounted to $75.8 billion, just over $5 billion more than those designated for the air force. The $8.7 billion budgeted for the marine corps, which is part of the navy, more than made up the difference. The navy's big-ticket items included spending for operations and maintenance ($20 billion), officer and enlisted paychecks ($17.9 billion), purchases of ships, munitions, and other weaponry ($15.2 billion total, $7.3 for ships), and research and development ($9 billion).

Q 226. What did the air force spend its money on?

A Of the $70.2 billion the air force got in 1996, the biggest single expense was for operations and maintenance—about $20.6 billion in all. Purchases of planes and other materiel ranked second at about $17.4 billion ($7.9 billion for new aircraft). Paychecks for active and reserve personnel was a close third at about $17.1 billion. The air force spent almost $13.1 billion on research and development and $1.1 billion on family housing for officers and enlisted personnel.

Q 227. What was the army's share of the budget?

A The army's budget was the smallest of the military's three main branches in 1996, amounting to about $55.6 billion. Paychecks represented the single largest expenditure—$21.2 billion—followed by funding for operations and maintenance, at $20.2 billion. Purchases of weapons, ammunition, and other materiel cost $7.1 billion. The army spent another $4.9 billion on research and development.

Though it is called the Army Corps of Engineers, this civil engineering unit has a budget ($3.6 billion) that is handled separately within the Department of Defense.

Q 228. How has the size of the military changed since the end of the cold war?

A At the close of the cold war in 1990, the United States had just over 2 million active soldiers in uniform. The air force had 24 fighter wings and the navy, 546 ships (15 of them aircraft carriers and 31 submarines carrying nuclear missiles). The U.S. strategic nuclear arsenal contained almost 1,600 ICBMs and ballistic missiles carrying nuclear warheads.

Once the Soviet Union collapsed and presented no further serious threat, the government began downsizing the military, cutting costs and reducing overall troop strength to about 1.4 million. Sizable force reductions in every branch were scheduled to be complete or nearly complete by fiscal 1998. The army was to be reduced to 10 active divisions, while the air force trimmed down to 13 fighter wings and 87 heavy bombers. The navy retired 200 ships (including 4 aircraft carriers and 13 subs with nuclear missiles), and our nuclear arsenal was cut to about 980 missiles. Only the marine corps remained at its 1990 force levels—3 divisions and 3 aircraft wings.

(See 222 Where has defense usually ranked as a spending priority? 230 What was the "peace dividend"?)

Q 229. Will all those base closings over the past few years really save any money?

A Yes, the four Base Closure and Realignment Commissions since 1988 have recommended closing ninety-seven big bases and two hundred smaller ones. When all of them have been shut down (by 2001), the government will save an estimated $5.6 billion a year.

Q 230. What was the "peace dividend"?

A When the Soviet Union collapsed and the cold war ended in 1991, there was considerable speculation about what to do with the "peace dividend," the federal money that many supposed would be freed up because defense needs would be far lower. In fact, defense spending did decline over the next few years but only to the $250 billion to $255 billion range, where it is expected to be in the year 2000. That represents a savings, but hardly a massive windfall, and the growth of social spending has already more than offset that amount.

(See 171 Why has social spending risen by so much? 223 What was the biggest defense budget ever? 453 Why did federal spending fail to drop after the Vietnam War, as it had after past wars?)

Q 231. Do we still need new billion-dollar weapons systems?

A The Defense Department thinks so. Even though the cold war is over, the United States still must be able to respond when its interests are threatened. And if we want to keep our position as the world's leading military power, which in itself helps discourage attacks, experts generally agree we have to continue investing in advanced weapons technologies like cruise missiles and Stealth bombers. Among the current new weapons purchases being considered by the Pentagon is a new fighter for the air force, the F-22. Estimates for producing 438 of the radar-evading fighters vary considerably, however, from a low of $48 billion to more than $64 billion.

Q 232. What does the Treasury Department spend its money on?

A Eliminate the $344 billion Treasury paid out for interest on the national debt and the department's budget becomes much more down to earth. When you factor in fees and other money the department collected (about $15.9 billion), Treasury had about $36 billion to carry out its various duties, including $6.7 billion for the Financial Management Service (FMS), which issues all government checks and handles other chores. Other agencies and bureaus funded through the Treasury Department are:

	1996 Spending (in millions)
Internal Revenue Service	$28,593
U.S. Customs Service	1,835
Bureau of Alcohol, Tobacco and Firearms	617
U.S. Secret Service	555
Bureau of the Public Debt	296
Bureau of Engraving and Printing	20
U.S. Mint	−644

Note: A minus sign means fees collected outstripped agency expenses for the year by the amount indicated.

(See 3 Who actually spends the money? 109 Does it really cost $28.6 billion just to collect the taxes? 148 Why was Treasury Department spending so high?)

Q 233. What does the State Department budget cover?

A The $4.95 billion spent in 1996 includes about $2.8 billion for the foreign diplomatic corps itself, including expenses for more than 250 U.S. embassies in foreign countries. Security and maintenance of the embassies themselves cost $496 million; diplomats' salaries and expenses, $339 million; and spending for diplomatic and consular programs, $1.7 billion. State's budget also includes about $1.1 billion for U.S. contributions to the United Nations and other international organizations and conferences. About $190 million of that went for our share of UN peacekeeping operations. Assistance to refugees cost another $607 million.

Q 234. Is the United States behind on payments to the UN?

A Congress has refused to fully fund assessments owed to the UN and other international organizations in years past because of strong disagreement with their policies. As of early 1997, the United States was $1 billion behind in payments to the UN (mainly for peacekeeping operations) and some $850 million in arrears for contributions to international financial organizations to which it belongs.

Q 235. When did spending for the Commerce Department peak?

A Spending by Commerce more than doubled under President Jimmy Carter to hit its highest level to date in 1978—$4.7 billion, up from about $2 billion in 1977. By 1980, however, the Carter administration had trimmed that back to about $3.1 billion. The Reagan administration cut the Commerce budget further still, holding it at about $2 billion for the next eight years. Under President Bill Clinton, spending by Commerce began rising again and in 1996 reached $3.7 billion.

Among the various tasks the Commerce Department performs are promoting overseas trade, negotiating trade agreements, and promoting the development of technology. One agency within Commerce, the National Technical Information Service, is completely self-supporting; its $42 million in expenditures was completely offset by fees. The department also oversees the Census Bureau and the Patent and Trademark Office.

Q 236. How much will the census in the year 2000 cost?

A The Constitution requires that a census be taken every ten years to provide population figures for reapportioning seats in the U.S. House of Representatives. Census data also is used for redrawing state legislative districts and for distributing billions in federal and state funds. While the Census Bureau also provides interim analyses of census data and projections of demographic trends, its main job is actually counting the 265 million or so Americans, and the budget for the year 2000 will jump accordingly. From estimated spending of $603 million in 1998, the projected Census Bureau budget will rise to just over $1 billion in 1999, the year before the census, and more than double to $2.7 billion in 2000, when the census will actually be taken. Spending will plummet back to $536 million the following year.

Q 237. Do patent and trademark fees help offset Patent Office spending?

A Yes. The Patent and Trademark Office issues over 100,000 patents a year and also works to protect U.S. intellectual property rights worldwide. Actual spending for these activities in 1996 was $581 million, but fees collected during the year amounted to $549 million. The government made up the $32 million difference in 1996, but fees were expected to exceed spending in 1997 and subsequent years.

(See 122 How have revenues from "user charges" changed over the years?)

Q 238. If we spend less, will weather forecasts be wrong more often?

A The American Meteorological Society apparently thinks so. The group strongly opposed budget cuts for the National Weather Service (NWS) in fiscal 1998, warning of "potentially tragic consequences." NWS provides daily weather forecasts and also tracks potentially dangerous storms, such as hurricanes, tornadoes, thunderstorms, and blizzards. The agency spends about $400 million annually and had its budget cut by $27.5 million for fiscal 1997. Proposed cuts amounting to another $40 million for fiscal 1998 forced the agency to plan staff reductions at the National Hurricane Center, the National Storm Prediction Center, and the Aviation (weather) Prediction Center. Although opponents of the cuts worried that NWS might be unable to issue timely warnings about hazardous weather, government officials noted that most staff cuts involved clerical workers and short term would not affect forecasting. Over the long term, however, officials predicted stormier times, saying they needed about $11 million restored to their budget to avoid laying off critical personnel.

Q 239. What is the biggest single expenditure in the Agriculture Department budget?

A Food stamps. Almost half the $54.3 billion the department received in 1996 went to the federal food stamp program, one of the most widely used social spending programs. In addition to the $25.4 billion for food stamps, the Agriculture Department's Food and Consumer Service also funded child nutrition programs ($7.9 billion) and the Women, Infants, and Children (WIC) supplemental nutrition programs ($3.7 billion). Together these social spending programs amounted to $37.4 billion in 1996, swallowing up almost 69 percent of the department's budget.

Of the department's other functions, the agricultural extension service (now called the Cooperative State Research, Education, and Extension Service) received $851 million. The department also funds the Animal and Plant Health Inspection Service ($481 million), the Food Safety and Inspection Service ($533 million), and the Agricultural Marketing Service ($450 million). The department's Risk Management agency spent about $1.8 billion through the federal crop insurance program in 1996. Another $5.2 billion was funneled through the Commodity Credit Corporation, which helps support farm income and crop prices through direct subsidies to farmers. The Forest Service spent nearly $3 billion, including $130 million in payments to states for the northern spotted owl guarantee program.

Q 240. How have farm subsidies changed over the years?

A Farm subsidies were first enacted during the Great Depression, when about 25 percent of the population lived on some 6 million farms. At that time farmers struggled to get by on about half the income of the average nonfarm family. The New Deal subsidy program began in 1933 with the Agricultural Adjustment Act, which was designed to help raise farm income by propping up prices for various crops and to stabilize the market by paying farmers to produce less.

Like other New Deal programs, farm subsidies proved so popular they were continued—and expanded—after the depression ended. In addition, the nature of farming changed. Today farming is big business, dominated by fewer, larger operations, and the export market has become far more important than it once was. Only about 2 percent of the population lives on farms now, and most are only part-time farmers. Yet farm subsidies hit record levels during the 1980s, and costs have remained high in the 1990s. (Price supports shot up tenfold between 1980 and 1986, when the Commodity Credit Corporation paid out a record $25.8 billion.)

Efforts to substantially change the farm subsidy program regularly met with failure until 1996. At that time Congress passed a Republican-backed farm bill that ends federal controls over what crops farmers plant and phases out price controls over several years. The bill was designed to end farmers' dependence on subsidies and move agriculture back to a free-market system. Farm production was expected to increase as a result of the reforms, which will lower consumer prices and boost U.S. agricultural exports. Critics worried that prices would fluctuate erratically as farmers shifted from one crop to another.

(See 413 What did President Franklin Roosevelt's New Deal do to cure the Great Depression?)

241. How much does federal law enforcement cost?

The Justice Department, which spent $11.9 billion in 1996, oversees federal law enforcement activities, including the FBI ($2.3 billion), the Drug Enforcement Administration ($749 million), and the Immigration and Naturalization Service ($2.6 billion). The department's legal activities—including the antitrust division, salaries for U.S. attorneys and U.S. marshals—amounted to $2.7 billion in 1996. Operating the federal prison system accounted for another $3 billion.

The Justice Department was also responsible for the radiation exposure compensation program, which spent $22 million in 1996.

(See 269 What does the government spend for the War on Drugs?)

242. What about the Environmental Protection Agency?

Of the $6 billion allotted to the Environmental Protection Agency (EPA) in 1996, the largest single expenditure—$2.6 billion—was for EPA grants to states and Native American tribes. The EPA spent another $1.7 billion on various environmental programs and management, and paid out $1.7 billion from the hazardous waste superfund. It recovered $267 million from polluters in 1996 as part of the superfund program. The price tag for oil spill cleanups was $22 million.

243. Have we grounded the space program?

Well not quite, but the National Aeronautics and Space Administration (NASA), which administers the space program, has been getting by on a budget that is a mere shadow of its former self. Back in the glory days of the 1960s, when beating the Russians in the "space race" and getting a man to the moon were national priorities, NASA's budget hit a high of $5.9 billion.

That may not sound like much now, but those were 1966 dollars, and the total amounted to 4.4 percent of the entire U.S. budget for the year. Even before astronaut Neil Armstrong actually set foot on the moon in 1969, though, the trajectory of NASA's budget had begun dropping, both in dollar amounts and as a percentage of the budget. At the time, the Vietnam War was draining the budget and many people had begun to question spending such vast sums on space exploration when there were so many problems at home.

By the mid-1970s NASA's budget was stuck in the $3 billion to $4 billion range. The dollar amounts of NASA's budget rose during the Reagan administration, hitting

$9.1 billion in 1988, but NASA actually lost ground in terms of the overall budget. It hit an all-time low of 0.7 percent in 1986. The Bush administration pushed NASA spending up to 1 percent of the budget, while President Bill Clinton trimmed it back to 0.9 percent.

Q 244. By what factor has Transportation Department spending increased since the 1960s?

A Almost nine and a half times. Transportation, which oversees such agencies as the Federal Highway Administration, the Federal Aviation Administration, and the Coast Guard, spent just $4.1 billion in 1962. The department's budget began growing by a billion or two a year from the mid-1970s, reaching $19.2 billion by 1980 and $28.6 billion by 1990. Another growth spurt during the Clinton administration pushed Transportation spending up to $38.8 billion by 1996. The department's 1996 budget, including funding for the following agencies, was:

	Spending (in millions)
Federal Highway Administration (including highway trust funds)	$19,749
Federal Transit Administration	4,372
Coast Guard	3,529
Federal Aviation Administration	2,223
Federal Railroad Administration	1,006
Maritime Administration	310
National Highway Traffic Safety Administration	243
Saint Lawrence Seaway Development Corporation	10
Board of Transportation Statistics	2

Q 245. What does the Department of Energy (DOE) do?

A The Department of Energy's atomic energy–related activities include overseeing production and handling of the nation's uranium stocks, handling and storing nuclear wastes, and cleaning up contaminated federal and privately owned facilities that produced uranium and thorium from the 1950s to the 1970s. During 1996 the DOE spent $11.6 billion of its $16.2 billion budget for these activities alone.

DOE agencies also regulate the electric power industry and produce power as well. Among other things, the DOE's Power Marketing Administration operates 129 hydroelectric power dams and 33,000 miles of electric power transmission lines, which account for 6 percent of electric power generation nationwide. Because the agency sells the power, offsetting receipts reduced its expenditures to just $188 million for 1996. The DOE also oversees various research programs, including development of energy conservation technology and basic energy research.

Though many of its programs already existed (in various other cabinet departments), the government organized DOE in 1977 in response to the energy crisis. Funding remained in the $6 billion to $7 billion range until 1981, when it jumped to $11.7 billion. During the Reagan administration, funding continued at the $10 billion to $11 billion level. Spending in 1996 was $16.2 billion.

Q 246. Why do we have a Strategic Petroleum Reserve and how expensive is it?

A During the 1970s, oil embargoes by Arab states caused serious interruptions in our oil supply. The Strategic Petroleum Reserve (SPR) was created in 1975 to ensure emergency oil reserves for military needs and to help dampen effects of sudden interruptions in supplies of imported oil. Administered by the DOE, the SPR has 563 million barrels of oil stored in underground salt caverns along the Gulf Coast.

SPR oil was released into the nation's oil supply system in 1991 during the Persian Gulf War emergency. The extra oil, and the quick American victory, helped push down crude oil prices by $10 a barrel.

The SPR contains enough oil to last about two months in the event of a complete stoppage of all oil imports. The program cost about $236 million to run in 1996.

Q 247. Has the government gone cold on fusion?

A Apparently so. Cuts in federal funds forced the shutdown of Princeton University's Tokamak Fusion Test Reactor in 1997. For half a century scientists have been trying to develop a fusion reactor, which produces energy in the same way the sun does, and have spent $8.2 billion in the process. Scientists at Princeton set a fusion power record by generating enough energy with Tokamak to power some 10,000 houses, but only for one second. A practical fusion-powered generating plant is still decades away.

Proposed federal financing of the research for fiscal 1998 was down to $52 million, less than half that of previous years and only enough to continue theoretical research.

Q 248. What is the Office of Personnel Management (OPM) and why does it spend $42.9 billion?

A The OPM is the federal government's personnel office. It oversees the federal civil service merit system, recruits new government employees, oversees the promotions system, and develops new personnel policies for the government. It does not pay government workers their salaries, but like the personnel office in a private company, it does handle federal employee retirement, health benefit, and life insurance programs. That is where most of OPM's $42.9 billion in spending goes.

Q 249. What does the Department of Veterans Affairs spend?

A Rising about $3 billion a year through the early 1990s, the budget for Veterans Affairs (VA) reached an estimated $39.6 billion in 1997 and was expected to remain in the $40 billion to $43 billion range through 2002. About 250,000 people work for the VA, most of them in the VA hospital network, which treats about 2.9 million veterans. The Veterans Health Administration spent $16.5 billion on health care in 1996.

Meanwhile, veterans also receive various benefits, including disability benefits, rehabilitation programs, insurance, education benefits, VA housing loans, military retirement pay, tax breaks, and burial in the national cemetery system. The 1996 budget for the Veterans Benefits Administration was $18.5 billion.

Q 250. How big is the National Cemetery System?

A As of 1996 about 70,000 veterans (and family members) were buried in the one hundred national cemeteries run by the VA. The cemeteries cost $71 million to operate in 1996, though rising expenses will push that up to $84 million by 1998.

Q 251. What do we spend on the national park system?

A About 280 million people visited the 374 national parks in 1996, but even factoring in entrance fees paid by all those people, overall operating costs still totaled $1.58 billion for the year. Administered by the National Park Service, the system includes such popular vacation attractions as Grand Canyon National Park, Yellowstone National Park, Gettysburg National Military Park, and Everglades National Park. The park service has been taking steps to increase revenues by raising user fees and reforming policies for park concessions contracts.

Q 252. Does the government do anything to help Native Americans?

A Yes, the Bureau of Indian Affairs operates various programs to help tribes and individual Native Americans, including financial assistance, loans and grants, and technical assistance. The government also holds 54 million acres of land in trust for Native Americans and offers technical assistance in managing 16 million acres of forest land. Spending for the Bureau of Indian Affairs was about $2 billion in 1996. Another agency, the National Indian Gaming Commission, spent about $2 million, but that expense was completely offset by fees the government collected.

Q 253. Why did the Department of the Interior spend $6.7 billion in 1996?

A About a third of continental United States, some 700 million acres, is either government property or managed by the government. The Interior Department manages a large part of these federal lands and collects about $2.7 billion a year in royalties for oil, gas, timber, and mineral resources extracted from them. The department's Bureau of Land Management oversees 264 million acres in the West, while the National Park Service, also an Interior Department agency, runs the extensive national park system. Among the department's other agencies are the Bureau of Indian Affairs, the Fish and Wildlife Service, which helps protect endangered species, and Insular Affairs, which provides assistance to U.S. territories, including the Trust Territory of the Pacific Islands.

Q 254. What about the Department of Labor?

A The Labor Department spent almost $32.5 billion in 1996 on a variety of programs, ranging from unemployment insurance to the Bureau of Labor Statistics. The biggest single expenditure was for unemployment compensation payments—about $22.6 billion—along with another $2.3 billion in administrative expenses needed to run the program. (The government took in $28.5 billion in payroll tax contributions earmarked for the unemployment compensation trust fund, however.) The department's Employment and Training Division also runs job training and referral programs, which cost $5.2 billion in 1996. OSHA (Occupational Safety and Health Administration) and the Bureau of Labor Statistics are two other well-known agencies within the department. They spent $287 million and $281 million, respectively, in 1996.

(See 93 What are the social insurance taxes? 95 What are the major federal trust funds and how much do they take in?)

Q 255. Why is spending by the Department of Health and Human Services skyrocketing?

A At $320 billion, Health and Human Services (HHS) spending ranked third highest of the federal agencies, trailing only the Social Security Administration and the Treasury Department in 1996. By the year 2000—just four years later—the HHS budget is expected to jump nearly $100 billion higher to $414 billion, moving the department's spending to second highest in the federal government after the Social Security Administration.

The reason the department's budget is expected to grow so rapidly is that it oversees two fast growing entitlement programs, Medicare and Medicaid. In his 1998 budget, President Bill Clinton estimated that unless there are changes, Medicare spending alone will increase 54 percent between 1997 and 2002, from $192 billion to $295 billion. Medicaid spending is expected to grow by 36 percent, from $98 billion to $133 billion. Together those two programs account for 18 percent of total federal spending.

(See 185 Why have health care costs been rising so rapidly? 187 What is the difference between Medicare and Medicaid? 190 When will Medicare funds run out? 192 What Medicaid reforms did the 1997 balanced budget deal make?)

Q 256. What does the Department of Housing and Urban Development (HUD) spend?

A Spending by the department dipped to $25.5 billion in 1996, down slightly from the previous year's $29 billion. Current projections forecast a rise in spending—about $4 billion in 1997 and another $3.5 billion in 1998—so that by the year 2000 HUD will have outlays of about $32.4 billion.

HUD is responsible for the government's public housing programs ($23.4 billion in 1996) and community planning and development programs. About $284 million of the community development funding went for emergency shelters and housing assistance for the homeless. HUD also oversees two major mortgage loan programs, the Federal Housing Authority (FHA) and the Government National Mortgage Association (Ginnie Mae). Although both these programs made substantial outlays in 1996, offsetting collections produced surpluses for each ($2.6 billion and $563 million, respectively).

(See 218 Who are Ginnie Mae, Freddie Mac, and Fannie Mae?)

Q 257. How much money goes into the presidential election fund each year?

A Over 16 million taxpayers in a recent year indicated they wanted tax dollars set aside for the Presidential Election Campaign Fund, and just under $70 million in tax dollars was earmarked for the fund. Since 1972 over $760 million has gone into the campaign fund.

Q 258. Does PBS still receive federal funding?

A The Public Broadcasting Service (PBS) provides commercial-free educational television programming on designated PBS channels in areas throughout the country. Part of the money PBS needs to operate comes from the federal government by way of the Corporation for Public Broadcasting, which distributes government money to PBS, National Public Radio, 352 public TV stations, and 692 radio stations. The money covers costs for acquiring and producing programming and for various system-wide activities.

During the 1995–1996 budget debates, Republican budget cutters sought to eliminate federal funding for the Corporation for Public Broadcasting. PBS's high-profile counterattack against Republican budget cutters succeeded in largely preserving federal funding, however. Federal spending for the Corporation for Public Broadcasting was $275 million in 1996, and President Bill Clinton's 1998 budget proposed only slightly less, $250 million.

Q 259. What happened to federal funding for the National Endowments? Other cultural activities?

A Republican budget cutters set their sights on eliminating altogether the National Endowment for the Arts (NEA) and the National Endowment for the Humanities (NEH) during budget battles with President Bill Clinton. The two groups provide grants to individuals and groups in support of literature and the arts. Spending in fiscal 1996 was cut by about 40 percent for NEA and 36 percent for NEH, but when the dust settled the two programs were otherwise intact. For fiscal 1997 NEA's budget was $99.5 million, and NEH's, $110 million, though actual spending will be higher because of ongoing payments for grants approved in previous years. (Estimated total spending in 1997 was $128 million for NEA, $130 million for NEH.) President Clinton's 1998 budget proposed increasing spending for both programs to $136 million.

260. How much does the Small Business Administration (SBA) lend businesses?

SBA business loans amounted to $522 million in 1996, and the agency lent another $434 million through its disaster loan program. Taking into account other expenses and receipts for loan payments, SBA spending for 1996 amounted to $873 million. The agency's outlays were expected to drop to just $137 million in 1998, before beginning to rise again.

261. Is the Central Intelligence Agency's budget a secret?

Yes, it was. The amount spent for the CIA does not appear in the budget as a separate item, but a Freedom of Information Act suit forced the CIA to reveal that 1996 spending for all U.S. intelligence activities was $26.6 billion. The 1997 disclosure was the first time since the CIA was founded in 1947 that the government revealed spending for intelligence activities. Spending by agency was not released, but an earlier Clinton administration estimate indicated the 1996 CIA budget was about $3.1 billion.

The House and Senate Select Intelligence Committees approve spending authorizations for the CIA, Defense Intelligence Agency, and eleven other intelligence groups but did not release the figures to the public for security reasons. Some CIA funds are included in the Defense Department spending totals. One item relating to the CIA does appear in the annual budget, however. Spending for the CIA retirement and disability fund amounted to $214 million in 1996.

262. Why is the Nuclear Regulatory Commission's spending so low?

Salaries and expenses for the Nuclear Regulatory Commission (NRC) in 1996 amounted to $507 million, yet total outlays for the year were just $57 million. In future years that total was expected to drop even lower, to around $20 million. The NRC is not doing less, it is simply collecting more in fees from the nuclear facilities it oversees, to offset nearly all the cost of salaries and expenses. The change came as a part of the government's policy of increasing fees for government services to cover operating expenses of the agency.

(See 122 How have revenues from "user charges" changed over the years?)

Q 263. What do other federal commissions spend?

A Other federal commissions (and their spending for 1996) included:

	Spending (in millions)
Commission on Civil Rights	$ 9
Commission on National and Community Service	6
Commodity Futures Trading Commission	50
Consumer Product Safety Commission	42
Equal Employment Opportunity Commission	225
Federal Communications Commission	967
Federal Election Commission	26
Federal Maritime Commission	16
Federal Mine Safety and Health Review Commission	6
Federal Trade Commission	35
International Trade Commission	39
Interstate Commerce Commission	8
Japan-United States Friendship Commission	2
Marine Mammal Commission	1
Occupational Health and Safety Review Commission	7
Panama Canal Commission	−36*
River Basins Commission	2
Securities and Exchange Commission	41

*Negative sign indicates a surplus.

(See 259 What happened to federal funding for the National Endowments? Other cultural activities?)

Q 264. How much did the savings and loan crisis finally cost us?

A As of the mid-1990s, nearly all the direct and current indirect (interest) costs of the savings and loan crisis had been tallied and funded—a total of $160.1 billion (since 1986). Of that taxpayers paid 83 percent, or $132 billion; the banking industry, $28 billion.

Both taxpayers and the banking industry will be paying interest costs associated with financing the S & L bailout for years to come. Bonds sold to raise money for the bailout will ultimately cost a total of $111.8 billion in interest ($20.4 billion paid just to the end of 1995). The matter of what interest the federal government will pay for the many billions it has appropriated to cover bailout costs is more difficult to estimate. That money could be paid immediately from tax revenues, or could be counted as part of the funds the government borrows to meet the deficit. But assuming the entire amount is financed for thirty years (as opposed to being paid immediately with tax revenues), the total could be as much as $209 billion in interest expenses ($33 billion of that would already have been paid out by the end of 1995).

(See 500 When did Congress deregulate the banking industry?)

Q 265. What in the world does the Ounce of Prevention Council prevent?

A Violent crime. Chaired by Vice President Al Gore, the council was set up to coordinate programs organized under the 1994 Violent Crime Control and Law Enforcement Act. The council helps local officials get information about violent crime prevention and awards grants to communities for programs aimed at reducing violent crime. Various cabinet secretaries, the attorney general, and director of the Office of National Drug Control Policy are all members of the Ounce of Prevention Council, which spent an estimated $1 million in 1997.

(See 241 How much does federal law enforcement cost?)

Q 266. Does the government still subsidize the U.S. Post Office?

A Though the U.S. Postal Service still receives some funds from the federal government, it has been an independent government corporation since 1970. The federal funds the Postal Service gets are reimbursements for government use of the mail system and outright appropriations from Congress. The amount of federal subsidies has been steadily reduced since 1970 as the government has turned over more and more of the responsibility for employee retirement, health, and other fringe benefits.

The Postal Service collected $56.8 billion in revenues during 1996, about $1.2 billion of which came from the federal government (reimbursements and the subsidy). Operating expenses for the year were just under that, producing a surplus of $626 million for 1996. Deficits of $1.98 billion and $4.1 billion are expected for 1997 and 1998. The Postal Service is expected to return to profitable operations in the year 2000.

Q 267. What did the government's plan to rescue the District of Columbia do?

A Included in the 1997 balanced budget agreement, a "D.C. rescue plan" provided new federal funding for the city in exchange for the city government's loss of control over a substantial part of its operations. "Home rule" (self-government) for the District of Columbia, in effect since 1973, had come under fire in recent years because of highly publicized charges of corruption and waste in the city's bureaucracy, as well as deterioration of basic city services. Under the rescue plan, home rule would be suspended for at least four years, and the D.C. financial control board would oversee virtually all the city's major departments.

The federal government would then assume responsibility for a city pension fund for police, firefighters, and teachers (now $5 billion in the red), loan D.C. $300 million, make a final $190 million annual payment to the city for 1998 (the 1997 annual payment had been $660 million), assume an extra 20 percent of the D.C. Medicaid program costs (bringing federal contributions to 70 percent), take over prison administration, and set up an economic incentive program to encourage business investment and home buying in impoverished areas of the District.

(See 397 What was the 1997 balanced budget agreement? 488 What did the 1997 balanced budget agreement do to cut taxes?)

Q 268. How much does the United States spend annually on foreign aid?

A The United States uses foreign aid spending to improve national security interests abroad, help promote economic growth in underdeveloped countries, and provide humanitarian aid. Though critics charge that foreign aid programs cost too much, the government actually spends less than 1 percent of its annual budget on international affairs. In 1996 that amounted to about $13.5 billion, and estimates for coming years run in the $14 billion to $15 billion range.

The Agency for International Development (AID) oversees a sizable portion of foreign aid spending, including developmental funds and other economic assistance to dozens of nations (for example, states once part of the Soviet Union). Other foreign aid expenses include money for the United Nations, the International Monetary Fund, and humanitarian programs like Food for Peace (about $1 billion annually).

(See 233 What does the State department budget cover? 234 Is the United States behind on payments to the UN?)

Q 269. What does the government spend for the War on Drugs?

A Federal spending for drug control includes funds for prosecution, treatment, prevention, and research. Total spending for all these activities in 1996 was $13.4 billion, and for fiscal 1997 Congress enacted increases amounting to another $1.7 billion. Virtually every federal department is in some way involved in the effort to control substance abuse. The Defense Department spent $822 million on drug control programs in 1996, for example, the Interior Department's National Park Service $9 million, the State Department's International Narcotics Control Program $115 million, the Transportation Department's U.S. Coast Guard $323 million, Treasury's Customs Service $531 million, and the Veterans Affairs Department $1.1 billion. The Justice Department spent $6.3 billion, including $867 million for the Drug Enforcement Administration (DEA) and $695 million for the FBI. The Office of National Drug Control Policy spent $130 million.

(See 265 What in the world does the Ounce of Prevention Council prevent?)

Q 270. Have we closed the book on the JFK assassination?

A Barring any further outbreaks of media speculation, the Clinton administration apparently thinks so. The JFK Assassination Records Review Board spent $2 million in 1996 and about $3 million in 1997, but President Bill Clinton's latest proposed budget included no further money for the board in 1998 or following years.

IV
THE BUDGETING PROCESS

IN GENERAL

Q 271. How is Uncle Sam's budget different from mine?

A Your budget and the federal government's are alike in some fundamental ways. You have a certain amount of income each year, and you must pay for basic needs like food, clothing, and rent or mortgage payments, as well as for taking a vacation and other things you may want. If you stay within your budget, what you spend will probably be about what you earn in the year. Federal budget writers also try to match the government's spending with income for the year.

Of course, the federal budget is many times larger and more complex than the average family budget. And there are some important other differences as well. For one thing, the federal budget is so large and affects so many people that any major change in spending or revenue can have an impact on the nation's economy. For another, the federal government can raise taxes or borrow almost as much money as it wants. Instead of cutting back expenses or passing unpopular tax hikes when revenues are less than needed for the year, the government has usually found it easier to just borrow the money. That in turn has swelled the national debt.

Another important difference is that instead of just one person—you—deciding what budget choices to make, there are literally thousands of people who influence the process, from agency staffers and presidential advisers to members of Congress, their staffs, and the many lobbyists and special interest groups. All of them represent competing interests for what today are limited federal dollars in the budget. Because of the nature of representative government, Congress usually must piece together suitable compromises to accommodate these varied, often opposing interests. The compromises, however, do not always make the best budget policy.

(See 1 What is the budget? 322 Why is it that Congress has so much trouble keeping spending within a budget?)

Q 272. How is the budget prepared?

A Federal agencies, like the Department of Energy, begin the process by preparing budget requests, which eventually are submitted to the Office of Management and Budget (OMB). Under the direction of the president, the OMB assesses the requests and uses them to prepare a proposed budget for the coming fiscal year. The president submits his proposed budget to Congress in February, about eight months before the fiscal year starts (October 1).

After receiving the president's budget proposal, the House and Senate must agree on a budget resolution, which sets guidelines for spending and estimates revenue for the coming fiscal year. House appropriations committees begin work on specific appropriations, while keeping within guidelines set by the budget resolution. Each year, thirteen major appropriations bills—funding everything from Agriculture to Veterans Affairs—must be passed to complete the budget and keep the government running.

Ideally, House and Senate conferees will resolve differences between versions of these bills during the summer and early fall, and by October 1 the president will have signed all thirteen appropriations bills. But controversy stalls the process, and as has been the case in recent years, passage of annual appropriations bills may be delayed well into the fiscal year. When that happens Congress passes *continuing resolutions* to keep affected agencies running until their annual appropriations have been passed and signed into law.

(See 276 When does the groundwork on future budgets actually begin? 299 Why is the president's annual budget proposal important? 371 Are annual appropriations necessary? 383 What is a budget resolution? 473 When was the first government shutdown and why did it happen? 485 What effect did the 1995–1996 government shutdown have on the budget debate?)

Q 273. What are the thirteen annual appropriations Congress must pass each year?

A Congress funds the operations of government agencies by passing thirteen major appropriations bills each year. If any of the thirteen has not been enacted by the start of the fiscal year on October 1, Congress must pass a continuing resolution or other temporary appropriations measure to keep the affected agencies operating. The thirteen "regular" appropriations are:

1. Agriculture, rural development, and related agencies
2. Commerce, Justice, State, the judiciary, and related agencies

3. Defense
4. District of Columbia
5. Energy and water development
6. Foreign assistance and related programs
7. Interior and related agencies
8. Labor, Health and Human Services, and Education
9. Legislative branch
10. Military construction
11. Transportation and related agencies
12. Treasury, Postal Service, and general government
13. Veterans Affairs, Housing and Urban Development, and independent agencies

Q **274. Are authorization and appropriations bills the same?**

A No, *authorization bills* are written by legislative committees to establish or continue a federal program. The bill usually specifies the time period (a year, multi-year, or indefinite) and sets an upper limit on spending. *Appropriations bills* allow the program to actually spend the money, or enter into contracts that obligate the funds. By custom the House originates appropriations bills and the Senate usually confines itself to revising the House version. Congress must pass thirteen regular appropriations bills each year to keep the various government agencies operating.

(See 273 What are the thirteen annual appropriations Congress must pass each year? 331 What does the Senate Finance Committee do? 337 How are the House and Senate Appropriations committees organized? 350 What happens to appropriations bills in the House and Senate? 352 How do authorization, appropriations, and budget committees interact? 353 How do regular and supplemental appropriations differ? 354 What are general and special appropriation bills? 371 Are annual appropriations necessary?)

Q **275. When does the president submit his budget requests for the upcoming fiscal year?**

A The president's annual budget proposal is supposed to be presented to Congress by the first Monday in February. President Bill Clinton missed that deadline in 1997, however, when he delivered his proposed budget for fiscal 1998 a few days late.

(See 299 Why is the president's annual budget message important? 300 What must be included in the president's budget?)

Q 276. When does the groundwork on future budgets actually begin?

A Because of the enormous detail involved, preparing the budget takes many months and begins well before Congress even begins considering it. Agencies usually start work on their future budget requests in the spring, about nine months before the president submits his proposed budget to Congress. That is about one and a half years before the start of the fiscal year for which the budget is being written.

Working this far in advance creates considerable uncertainty in the budgeting process. When agencies began preparing the 1999 budget in the spring of 1997, they did not even have final spending and revenue totals for fiscal 1997 (which ends that September 30), much less totals for the upcoming fiscal 1998. In addition, it is impossible to guess what policy shifts and unexpected emergencies will occur in the intervening one and a half years.

(See 272 How is the budget prepared?)

Q 277. What is the timetable for writing the budget?

A The president's submission of his proposed budget is a pivotal event in the budgeting process, but budget writers are at work well before and long after the budget proposal has been delivered. The budget cycle in the following timetable for the fiscal 1999 budget could apply to any year, but it represents only an ideal schedule. Delays and missed deadlines occur frequently in the budget process, and the actual timetable for any budget, including fiscal 1999, can vary considerably.

	1997
Spring	Agencies begin preparing budget requests for fiscal 1999.
Summer	Agencies finalize their budget requests and submit them to the OMB.
Fall	OMB reviews agency budget requests and decides on changes; agency appeals on changes are made to OMB or the president.
December	President and staff finalize president's proposed budget.

1998

January	President's budget proposal for fiscal 1999 is printed by the Government Printing Office.
February	Budget proposal is delivered to Congress (by first Monday in February) and released to public.
March 15	Budget committees receive "views and estimates" on spending levels from relevant committees.
April 15	Congress adopts its annual budget resolution for fiscal 1999.
May 15	House may begin floor action on annual appropriations for fiscal 1999, even if the budget resolution has been delayed beyond this time.
June 30	House passes last of annual appropriations bills.
July–September	Senate passes annual appropriations bills; House-Senate conferences work to resolve differences between versions as necessary.
October 1	Fiscal 1999 begins. Congress passes continuing resolutions as needed for annual appropriations not yet enacted. Agencies begin operating under fiscal 1999 appropriations.

1999

January–September	Supplemental appropriations are passed as needed for the current fiscal year.
October 1	Fiscal 2000 starts.

Q **278. What happens after the fiscal year ends?**

A When the fiscal year ends September 30th, the process of closing out the books on the previous year begins. OMB, the Treasury Department, and individual agencies compile final spending and revenue figures, which will be included in the next proposed budget submitted to Congress, the following February. Meanwhile, from the following January onward agencies also compile financial statements on the past fiscal year and conduct evaluations and audits as well.

Q **279. Does the budget include all government spending?**

A Technically, no. Congress has specifically excluded the Social Security trust fund and the Postal Service from the budget. Both were given *off-budget* status to prevent diversion of their assets to other purposes, such as deficit reduction. But in 1968 the government adopted the principle of a "unified" budget, which includes all spending and revenue—both *on-budget* and off-budget—to make the budget more useful in formulating economic policy. So while the formal budget includes only on-budget accounts, the unified (or consolidated) budget totals up on and off-budget accounts. Thus, the government can report two different deficit figures, for example, and both will be correct. The deficit usually reported is the unified budget deficit, however.

Q 280. What are baseline projections?

A When Congress considers spending or revenue legislation, it consults baseline projections to see what impact the bill might have. These projections are estimates of what government spending and revenue would be for the next five years (or other time period) if current federal laws and policies remained unchanged. Once the baseline figures have been established, the cost of a new program or change to an existing one can be calculated.

Baselines, which are routinely prepared by the Congressional Budget Office and Office of Management and Budget (OMB), must take into account a wide variety of factors, such as demographic trends, income levels, participation in entitlement programs, unemployment rates, and inflation. Many of them are difficult to predict beyond the short-term, and government programs and policies also do not remain static. For these reasons baseline projections are at best only rough estimates of what will happen five years into the future. They have become the subject of heated controversy from time to time, especially when the OMB and CBO have produced different estimates.

Nevertheless, Congress needs some idea of what proposed legislation might cost the government before the bill is passed, and estimates using baseline projections offer at least a partial answer. The projections can be used for both spending and revenue legislation.

Q 281. Are the government's budget projections accurate?

A Recent budget battles between Congressional Republicans and Democratic president Bill Clinton have highlighted the importance, and the uncertainty, of estimates the government uses to predict federal revenue and spending. The business of estimating economic trends over even a year's time can be very difficult, and small miscalculations sometimes create a wide discrepancy between the original estimate and the actual figure. Often several factors combine to create the difference—for example, unanticipated changes in federal policy, unforeseen additional expenses (or revenue), or a better (or worse) than expected economy.

The 1996 budget provided examples of various ways estimates can go wrong, though this time the story had a happier ending—the budget deficit turned out to be over $93 billion less than expected. Key comparisons of estimated and actual totals for 1996 are:

—Actual revenues for 1996 were $1,453.1 billion, or $33.6 billion higher than estimated in the president's budget proposal, issued well before the fiscal year began in February 1995. A better than expected economy added most of this money—largely through increased individual and corporate income taxes ($29.5 billion and $14.7 billion, respectively). Collections of excise taxes, customs duties, and miscellaneous receipts were all less than expected, though (over $11 billion less).

—Actual spending for 1996 was $1,560.3 billion, $59.7 billion less than estimated in the president's budget proposal. Government policy changes accounted for $10.5 billion of the decrease, and a better economy, $24.1 billion. Other technical factors accounted for $24.1 billion and included such things as fewer than expected entitlement program beneficiaries, decreases in agricultural price support programs, and fewer bank failures.

—The resulting actual deficit for 1996 was $107.3 billion, $93.3 billion less than the $200.6 billion estimated in the president's budget proposal.

Q 282. Has the government ever run out of money?

A Several times during battles over the rising debt in the 1980s, the government's ability to borrow money it needed was nearly cut off because the national debt had reached the statutory limit. (The total amount the government can borrow, the statutory limit, can only be changed by passing a law.) Usually these near crises lasted only a few days before Congress raised the debt limit again, so that the government did not actually run out of money. But in October and November 1985, thanks to the bitter debate over the Gramm-Rudman-Hollings amendment, which was attached to a bill raising the debt limit, the unthinkable did happen.

The Treasury suddenly found itself strapped for cash in October and had no authority to borrow more. So it arranged to swap about $15 billion in government securities between federal agencies. When the budget debate dragged on into November, Treasury Secretary James A. Baker III turned to more desperate measures: "disinvesting" (literally temporarily taking back) securities in Social Security and other retirement funds. That lowered the government's indebtedness, allowing it to then raise cash by selling Treasury bonds to the public. Once the debt limit was raised, Treasury returned the disinvested securities, with full interest, to Social Security and other funds. It was later revealed that the Treasury had also disinvested securities from the Social Security trust fund in September and October of 1984 to cover borrowing shortfalls.

(See 377 What are debt ceilings? 378 How is the debt ceiling changed? 497 What did Treasury Secretary Rubin do to stave off default during the 1995–1996 budget debate?)

Q 283. What did the 1921 Budget and Accounting Act do?

A This act set up the federal government's first formal budget writing process. Before 1921, Congress wrote tax bills and funded government operations in a haphazard way that made establishing budget policy all but impossible. Agencies simply compiled their annual budget requests and submitted them to Congress in what was called the "Book of Estimates." Congress then passed the necessary legislation to approve funding for the coming year. This system worked so long as revenues generally remained above spending and the government kept spending at a fairly low rate. But after World War I pushed annual spending to billions of dollars a year, Congress at last decided to establish a formal budget.

The 1921 Budget and Accounting Act brought the president into the budget process for the first time—the president was charged with preparing an annual budget proposal. The president's budget was to include proposed revenue and spending for the coming year, as well as actual revenue and spending amounts from the previous year. Congress would then consider the president's recommendations and after adjusting them as it saw fit, pass the necessary legislation. The act created the Budget Bureau to help the president manage the budget process more closely. Congress also set up the Government Accounting Office to better monitor federal spending.

(See 299 Why is the president's annual budget proposal so important? 311 What was the Bureau of the Budget? 342 What does the General Accounting Office (GAO) do? 382 What did the Congressional Budget Control and Impoundment Act of 1972 accomplish?)

Q 284. What have been the major turning points in the history of federal budgeting?

A The most important innovations in the budget process during the 1800s dealt with establishing the committee structure for handling budget matters in Congress.

During the first half of the twentieth century, the government finally adopted a formal budget, and changes in the budgeting procedures within the executive branch were put into place. Since the late 1960s, the effort to find a workable system of spending controls has dominated the debate over federal budgeting.

* The Constitution in 1789 established the government and gave Congress the power to tax and spend. (*See* 320 What is "the power of the purse"?)
* The House established its Ways and Means Committee in 1802. For a time Ways and Means handled all taxing and spending bills for the House. (*See* 334 What does the House Ways and Means Committee do in connection with taxes and the budget?)
* Senate established its Finance Committee in 1816 to handle taxing and spending bills. (*See* 331 What does the Senate Finance Committee do?)
* Congress formed appropriations committees to oversee spending bills (House, 1837; Senate, 1850). (*See* 338 When were the House and Senate Appropriations Committees organized?)
* Two-step authorization/appropriations process to provide funding for federal programs was firmly established in the mid-1800s by congressional rules. It had been a matter of custom until this time. (*See* 348 How did the "two-step" authorization-appropriations process evolve?)
* Taft Commission on Economy and Efficiency recommended in 1910 that Congress's haphazard system of handling the budget be reformed.
* The Budget and Accounting Act of 1921 set up the system of proposed budgets submitted by the president, directly involving the president in the budget system for the first time. It also established support organizations—the General Accounting Office and the Bureau of the Budget. (*See* 283 What did the 1921 Budget and Accounting Act do?)
* President Franklin Roosevelt's Reorganization Plan No. 1 moved the Bureau of the Budget from the Treasury to the newly established Executive Office of the President (1939). (*See* 415 What did President Roosevelt do to change the budget process in the executive branch?)
* Trust funds were included in the budget under a "unified" budget system, adopted in 1967. (*See* 441 What did the President's Commission on Budget Concepts do?)
* Congressional Budget and Impoundment Control Act of 1974 was passed to establish procedures for control of total spending and to curb impoundment of appropriated funds. (*See* 382 What did the Congressional Budget and Impoundment Control Act of 1974 accomplish?)

* Reconciliation process was used to make program cuts for the first time in 1980. (*See* 464 When did Congress first use the budget reconciliation process to cut back expenditures for ongoing programs?)
* Gramm-Rudman-Hollings Act of 1985 established mandatory deficit reduction targets and an automatic procedure to make spending cuts, if needed (sequestration). The act was modified in 1987. (*See* 388 What was the Gramm-Rudman-Hollings Act all about and what happened to it?)
* First budget "summit" was held in 1987. It resulted in a multiyear agreement on budget policy. (*See* 476 What were the budget summits all about?)
* Budget Enforcement Act of 1990 abandoned fixed deficit reduction targets, created PAYGO rules for direct spending programs and revenue measures, and imposed caps on discretionary spending. (*See* 390 What changes in the budget process did the Budget Enforcement Act of 1990 make?)
* Chief Financial Officers Act of 1990 created the post of financial manager for each major agency. (*See* 315 What did the 1990 Chief Financial Officers Act do?)
* Executive Order 12857 was issued, marking an important first step toward controlling entitlement spending. (*See* 394 What did Executive Order 12857 do?)
* Balanced budget agreement was concluded between Democratic president Bill Clinton and leaders of the Republican majority in Congress. It would produce a balanced budget by 2002 or sooner, if estimates were correct [and if thirteen appropriations bills were passed by the full Congress as negotiated].

Q 285. How has Congress's control over the way federal agencies spend money changed over past years?

A When Congress passes a bill funding an agency, it does not just hand over the money and let the agency managers spend as they see fit. Instead, Congress keeps some control by including certain instructions in the bill (or in committee reports), telling the agency how to spend the money or restricting what agency managers can do. The more control Congress keeps, however, the less agency managers have to run their programs, and this sometimes leads to less efficient operations.

The question of how much control Congress should keep has been the focus of an ongoing tug-of-war between Congress and the executive branch. During the 1800s Congress dominated the struggle and wrote appropriations with detailed spending instructions. That changed during the New Deal, however, as the executive branch gained the upper hand. For decades afterward Congress delegated much more spending authority to agencies and passed spending bills with large, lump sum payments. But the upheavals of the Vietnam War and the Watergate scandal turned the tables against the executive branch.

During the 1970s and 1980s, Congress again wrote detailed spending instructions for agencies and restricted what they could do. This finally led to criticism that Congress was micromanaging, with the result that Congress has eased some spending controls.

Q 286. How much of the budget is now subject to annual approval by Congress?

A As of 1996 only about 34 percent of total federal spending was discretionary, that is, subject to the annual approval process. The other two-thirds of the budget went for mandatory spending, including entitlement programs like Social Security, Medicare, and interest payments on the national debt. The rapid growth of both entitlement spending and interest on the debt has steadily eroded the amount of discretionary funds Congress has at its disposal. In 1962, for example, discretionary spending amounted to 67.5 percent of federal spending.

The mushrooming of mandatory spending has had an important impact on efforts to balance the federal budget. Congress must actually pass laws to make any changes to entitlement and other mandatory spending programs, a process that can be difficult and politically costly. But mandatory spending now takes up so much of the budget, there is little else left for making the substantial cuts needed to balance it. By the 1990s Congress was forced to seriously consider cuts in popular entitlement programs such as Medicare, Medicaid, and Social Security.

(See 127 When did Congress make an open-ended commitment to pay interest on the debt? 146 How have federal spending patterns changed since 1960? 162 Is there a difference between discretionary and mandatory spending? 171 Why has social spending risen by so much? 174 What percentage of the budget goes for social spending? 397 What was the 1997 balanced budget agreement? 488 What did the 1997 balanced budget agreement do to cut taxes?)

Q 287. How do interest groups influence the budget process?

A Both the president and members of Congress must keep in mind what voters want if they expect to be reelected to another term (or if their party is to continue in power). Decisions on budget policy—including both spending priorities and taxing measures—can affect whole segments of American society. Depending on what is finally decided, the decision could win the favor of millions of voters or arouse their anger.

Some 43 million Americans receive Social Security retirement benefits, for example, and any decision to cut the federal deficit by reducing Social Security benefits would impact a huge segment of American voters. These voters can and do let their elected officials know individually how they feel about legislation that threatens their interests. But they are also represented in Washington by powerful lobbying groups, which can either reward elected officials with generous campaign contributions or pressure them with threats of a grass-roots movement among their members. Senior citizens, teachers, doctors and other professionals, business and industry, labor unions, farmers, minorities, environmentalists, and many other activist groups all have lobbyists in Washington.

These interest groups and their lobbyists compete for whatever federal money is available in the budget, often in the form of spending increases or tax breaks that will benefit their members. Both the president and Congress have had difficulty resisting pressures of special interest groups in the past, and compromises with these groups on spending and tax matters have helped inflate the budget deficit.

(See 166 How do "iron triangles" work to increase spending?)

Q 288. What is an obligations-based budget system?

A This is a system of budgeting based on the commitment of funds to various purposes, rather than on the actual payment of the money (cash-based system). It is the budgeting system used by the federal government.

In the obligations-based system, funds are assigned to an agency or program at the beginning of the fiscal year for things like paying employee salaries, purchasing supplies, and entering into contracts for everything from leases on office space to developing new weapons systems. Money will eventually have to be paid out for all these expenses. But for budgetary purposes what matters most is that the agency can obligate only a set amount of money for a given purpose. Adding up all the obligations authorized for agencies and programs tells budget writers how much money will be needed to cover obligations for the current year. Actual spending for those obligations, though, will be spread out over the year, or sometimes over several years.

Congress controls federal spending indirectly through this obligations-based budgeting system. The appropriations acts it passes do not give agencies and programs cash to pay the bills. Instead, the acts give them budget authority—the right to obligate a certain amount of money for the stated purposes.

Q 289. What is budget authority?

A The amount of money Congress has appropriated to an agency or program to spend is called budget authority. The time period is often for the fiscal year, but Congress may decide to grant budget authority for a multiyear or even an indefinite period. Budget authority may take the form of an outright appropriation, may authorize the agency to borrow money (*borrowing authority*), or may allow it to enter into contracts that will lead to actual cash outlays (*contract authority*).

Budget authority balances are unspent funds from budget authority granted in previous fiscal years. Agencies lose this money when the budget authority is for only one year and the money has not been obligated. The same is true for multiyear budget authority when the term has expired. When funds for a contract, grant, or other arrangement must be paid out in chunks over a period of years, the money is classified as an *obligated balance.* Agencies usually do not lose budget authority for obligated balances at the end of the fiscal year.

Q 290. What are outlays?

A Outlay is a budget term for a payment made by the government, such as employee paychecks, payments for office supplies, or even money for block grants to states. It differs from budget authority in that an outlay is money the government actually spends, not the amount Congress has appropriated. For that reason, the federal budget lists both budget authority and outlays for agencies and programs. In any given year outlays are usually, but not always, somewhat less than budget authority Congress grants.

▶ What are discretionary and mandatory spending? *See 162 Is there a difference between discretionary and mandatory spending?* ◀

Q 291. How are offsetting receipts treated in the budget?

A Offsetting receipts are funds the government collects, but for budget purposes does not count as revenue. This money, from such things as the sale of oil leases, Medicare premiums, and park entrance fees, is treated as a "negative" outlay in the budget. In many cases offsetting receipts are deducted directly from outlays in the budget of the agency that collects them. That makes the agency's total spending for the fiscal year appear smaller than it actually is.

Other receipts are classified as "undistributed" offsetting receipts, however. These are deducted from total federal outlays just before the bottom line of the annual budget and so are not counted against any particular agency's balance.

(See 122 How have revenues from "user charges" changed over the years?)

Q 292. What are functions?

A Functions (or functional categories) are the broad categories budget writers use when classifying federal spending by purpose (such as international affairs, energy, and national defense). Because the categories pull together all budget accounts related to the purpose, it helps officials map out spending plans for the coming fiscal year. Functions and their respective funding allocations are listed in the annual congressional budget resolution.

Functions are divided into subfunctions, and the amount of money allotted to a function (say national defense) usually differs from the budget for a related agency (like the Defense Department). That is because all spending connected with national defense is included in the function total, not just what has been authorized for the Defense Department. The nineteen functional categories and their code numbers (for the 1998 budget) are listed below.

050 National defense
150 International affairs
250 General science, space, and technology
270 Energy
300 Natural resources and environment
350 Agriculture
370 Commerce and housing credit
400 Transportation
450 Community and regional development
500 Education, training, employment, and social services
550 Health
570 Medicare
600 Income security
650 Social Security
700 Veterans benefits and services
750 Administration of justice
800 General government
900 Net interest
950 Undistributed offsetting receipts

293. How do transfer payments affect the budget process?

From a budgeting perspective, transfer payments have a life of their own. Annual spending on Medicaid payments, for example, depends on how many eligible recipients get benefits in a year, not how much Congress wants to budget for it. Social Security, unemployment insurance, Medicare, and other entitlement programs also require the government to make transfer payments to all individuals who are eligible—as defined by law—no matter what the cost.

That was not a problem in the early 1960s when transfer payments amounted to only $29.5 billion, or less than a third of the total federal budget. But by fiscal 1997 transfer payments had mushroomed to over $960 billion—59 percent of total federal spending—and were expected to top $1 trillion in 1998. Because this spending is mandatory, and because it consumes such a large part of the budget, it makes balancing the budget extremely difficult.

(See 160 What are entitlement programs? 161 How many people receive federal benefits? 165 What is "backdoor spending"? 166 How do "iron triangles" work to increase spending? 170 Why spend tax dollars on social programs? 172 Can entitlement programs be changed? 176 Could entitlement caps control spending? 177 What is a transfer payment? 178 What federal programs make transfer payments? 181 Does social spending really help ease poverty?)

294. What are government-owned corporations and how are they budgeted?

Government-owned corporations are business operations in which the federal government has complete or partial ownership. The corporation may not be under direct government control—the Postal Service, for example, is a quasi-independent corporation. Among the other government-owned corporations are the Pension Benefit Guaranty Corporation, the Overseas Private Investment Corporation, and the Government National Mortgage Association. The federal budget includes only the corporation's net profit or loss for the fiscal year (as added or lost revenue).

The government has also spawned about a dozen government-sponsored enterprises (GSEs), which are involved in the credit and finance markets. They finance education, housing, and other activities by borrowing in the capital market. Though the GSEs have the backing of government credit, the money actually comes from private investors. For budgetary purposes they are considered private corporations. GSEs include the Student Loan Marketing Association (Sallie Mae), Federal Home Loan Mortgage Corporation (Freddie Mac), federal home loan banks, and farm credit banks.

(See 218 Who are Ginnie Mae, Freddie Mac, and Fannie Mae? 266 Does the government still subsidize the U.S. Post Office?)

▶ Do tax breaks affect the budget? *See 88 How do "tax expenditures" affect revenues?* ◀

EXECUTIVE BRANCH

Q 295. Do we look to Congress or the president for leadership on economic issues?

A Most people think of the president as the leader on economic matters, even though the Constitution grants Congress the lion's share of economic powers and the Federal Reserve System also has extraordinary influence over the economy. The presidency is the country's most visible political office, and rightly or wrongly we have come to expect that our presidents will keep the economy running smoothly.

Some of the president's current sway in economic matters stems from legislation Congress passed to expand the president's budgetary powers, in part because managing the federal budget had grown increasingly complex. Until passage of the 1921 Budget Act, for example, the president had virtually no say in the budgeting process, but his annual budget proposal now helps determine fiscal policy goals and the means to achieve them. The government's role in maintaining the country's economic and social well-being has also changed. Ever since the depression of the 1930s, the public has come to believe that the federal government in general—and the president in particular—should actively work to solve economic problems like unemployment, inflation, and recession through fiscal policy.

Presidents have also helped raise our expectations about their ability to produce a prosperous economy. Presidential candidates regularly promise voters they will produce a better economy if elected. Once in office they almost always claim credit for a good economy, but in fairness it should be remembered they also receive the blame for bad economic news, whether they deserve it or not.

(See 43 Do Americans vote their pocket books? 62 Does "laissez-faire" mean more or less government intervention in the economy? 65 What is fiscal policy? 283 What did the 1921 Budget and Accounting Act do? 375 What can presidents do to control spending? 398 What was the "classical" view of the economy? 490 How does the Federal Reserve affect the economy?)

Our "Manager of Profsperity"

"The people of this country are no longer content to let disaster fall upon them unopposed. They now expect their government, under the direct leadership of the president, to prevent a depression or panic and not simply wait until one has developed before putting it to rout. Thus the President has a new function which is still taking shape, that of Manager of Prosperity."

—Political scientist Clinton Rossiter, in *The American Presidency* (1960).

Q 296. What was the first source presidents had for economic advice?

A The Treasury Department was the first agency within the executive branch responsible for giving economic advice to the president. The treasury secretary remains one of the president's chief economic advisers today, and the department continues to play a key role in the government's finances, including collecting federal revenue and managing the currency.

(See 232 What does the Treasury Department spend its money on?)

Q 297. Who advises the president on economic issues now?

A The president's chief economic advisers are the secretary of the treasury, the chairman of the Council of Economic Advisers, and the director of the Office of Management and Budget. The organizations they head serve as an important source of basic economic information, estimates of future economic performance, and the impact of policy decisions on government finances and the economy generally. To one degree or another, however, all other cabinet secretaries and White House political advisers may also influence the president's thinking on economic matters.

(See 232 What does the Treasury Department spend its money on? 305 What does the Office of Management and Budget do? 307 What does the Council of Economic Advisers (CEA) do?)

▶ What limits the president's power to control the economy? *See 65 What is fiscal policy? 66 Do big deficits limit fiscal policy options?* ◀

Q 298. What have been the successes and failures of past fiscal policy?

A Probably the biggest success of postwar fiscal policy has been the moderating of the business cycle. In fact, economic expansions were on average longer (forty-nine months) and recessions on average shorter (ten months) between 1945 and 1975, when the government pursued an activist, recession-fighting policy. By comparison, expansions during the period from 1854 to 1937 lasted on average only twenty-six months, and recessions lasted twenty-two months.

The downfall of postwar fiscal policy was inflation. Prices had remained astonishingly stable up to 1940. (Consumer prices in 1940 were about what they had been in 1778.) But the gradual rise in inflation from 1940 to the mid-1960s, and the explosive growth of inflation through the 1970s, pushed prices up by 400 percent by 1980—a matter of just forty years.

The failure to keep inflation in check resulted in part from the general emphasis on policies aimed at fighting unemployment. But other factors contributed as well—the reluctance of political leaders to implement tough measures to curb inflation, the unpopularity of these measures with the public, and the ongoing struggle between liberals and conservatives over what fiscal policy measures to use (tax hikes or spending cuts), not to mention bitter divisions over what the fiscal policy priorities should be.

(See 49 What causes inflation? 64 What is "stabilization policy"? 65 What is fiscal policy? 68 Can we fine-tune the economy? 435 What were the economic policy successes and failures of the 1960s?)

Q 299. Why is the president's annual budget proposal important?

A The budget proposal is important because it reflects the president's spending priorities, which over time are likely to affect how the government and the nation as a whole will develop. The priorities range from fiscal concerns like lowering unemployment and raising economic growth to choices between specific programs, social programs vs. defense spending, and advancing the president's political agenda. Congress, of course, does not have to accept the proposed budget as is, and when the president and Congress are at odds, the final budget may be substantially different. But at the very least the president's budget proposal becomes a position around which budget battles can be fought—and compromises can be formed. And in less contentious times Congress has often contented itself with making only small ("incremental") adjustments to the president's budget proposal.

Q 300. What must be included in the president's budget?

A Along with the proposed spending and revenue figures for the fiscal year, the president's budget must include five-year spending projections and a review of mandatory spending cuts that would have to be made if the deficit rises above levels specified in the 1991 reconciliation act.

The president's budget must also supply *current services estimates* for revenue, spending, budget authority, and deficits. Experts compile these estimates by projecting what spending, revenue, deficits, and the like would be over the next five years—if existing programs and revenues remained unchanged during that time. The estimates provide a baseline that Congress can use to compare against the president's estimates of costs for new programs, changes to existing programs, and new revenue proposals. Current services estimates also can warn of future problems with spending or revenue collections.

(See 21 Where can I find information on the current year's budget? 280 What are baseline projections?)

Q 301. Which recent presidents have been actively involved in the budgetary process?

A Presidents Richard Nixon and Ronald Reagan both campaigned actively against federal spending, rising deficits, and other budget concerns, but confined themselves to broad policy decisions when it came to preparing the annual budget itself. President George Bush also delegated most of the actual work on the budget to his OMB director and others, while largely concerning himself with overall policy matters.

Presidents Gerald Ford and Jimmy Carter took a "hands on" approach to the details of budget writing and devoted considerable energy toward managing the process.

Q 302. Which presidents gave high priority to tax changes?

A President John F. Kennedy and Ronald Reagan put tax legislation high on their domestic agendas. Both presidents sought major tax cuts during their administrations as a way to stimulate the economy. President Kennedy's was not enacted until after his death, but it eventually provided the stimulus for the strong economic growth of the 1960s. President Reagan's tax cut was larger but less successful short term in stimulating the economy. As it happened, the economy entered a recession just as the tax cut was enacted. Congress soon became worried about the combined effects of the tax cut and the recession on revenues, and so passed a tax hike that undid some of the Reagan tax cut. Nevertheless, the tax cut spurred strong economic (and revenue) growth during the 1980s, though some question how much. Critics also argue the tax cut created larger deficits, but tend to ignore huge increases in federal spending during the 1980s (social spending *and* defense).

President Reagan also made tax reform one of his top priorities, and his 1986 Tax Reform Act substantially changed the tax code.

(See 119 When was the last major overhaul of the tax code and what changed? 468 What did the Reagan tax cut and budget reduction package do? 470 What was the 1982 tax hike?)

Q 303. What is the Statement of Administration Policy (SAP)?

A SAPs outline in writing any concerns the administration may have about changes made to an appropriations bill or any other legislation as it moves through the House and Senate. The administration can issue several statements on a specific bill, each focusing on proposed changes at the current stage in the legislative process. Statements are carefully written to express administration objections and to identify which changes could lead to a presidential veto.

SAPs are an outgrowth of the protracted budget battles of the 1980s, and today provide talking points when presidential aides and members of appropriations committees must negotiate differences over a particular bill. The administration normally writes SAPs at the following stages in the legislative process: (in the House) during appropriations subcommittee and committee markup sessions and during floor action; (in the Senate) during appropriations subcommittee and committee markup sessions and during floor action; and before the House-Senate conference to resolve differences between bills passed by the two houses.

(See 272 How is the budget prepared?)

Q 304. What role does a presidential veto play in the budget process?

A The veto, or the threat of a veto, can be a potent weapon for the president in budget battles with Congress. Many times the president can win concessions just by threatening a veto. But if the president does veto an appropriations bill, for example, the move effectively cuts off funding and could force affected federal agencies to shut down. This happened in late 1995 when sharp disagreements between the Republican Congress and Democratic president Bill Clinton resulted in Clinton vetoes of continuing resolutions (temporary funding bills), which then caused a government shutdown. Ultimately the public and press blamed Republicans in Congress for the shutdown, forcing them to back down from their budget demands.

Under most circumstances, though, there are limitations to the president's veto power. Ultimately appropriations have to be made, and both the president and members of Congress know differences eventually will have to be worked out at the bargaining table. Also, appropriations bills often pass the House and Senate by margins wide enough to override a presidential veto. In those cases, a veto threat carries far less weight, and the president usually will have to sign the appropriations bill even though he objects to parts of it.

(See 318 What is a line-item veto? 369 What is a continuing resolution? 375 What can presidents do to control spending? 473 When was the first government shut-down and why did it happen?)

Q 305. What does the Office of Management and Budget do?

A The Office of Management and Budget (OMB) is the president's clearinghouse for budget requests submitted by federal agencies. The OMB estimates revenues, overall spending, and deficits and decides where funding should be cut or expanded to conform with the president's budget plan. It passes along budget recommendations to the president, compiles the president's annual budget proposal, and monitors congressional action on appropriations. The OMB director ranks among the president's most important advisers on budgetary and economic matters. The OMB also is responsible for reviewing federal regulations in terms of costs and benefits, checking on the effectiveness of federal programs, and monitoring the efficiency of executive branch organization and management procedures.

President Richard Nixon created the OMB in 1970 by reorganizing and expanding the Bureau of the Budget. The OMB director is appointed by the president, subject to Senate confirmation. The director's budget recommendations can have a significant impact on the president's domestic policy.

(See 311 What was the Bureau of the Budget?)

Q 306. Who is David Stockman and what is he remembered for?

A President Ronald Reagan's first OMB director, Stockman is generally credited with being the main architect of the administration's 1981 plan to cut taxes and the federal budget in an effort to control inflation, promote economic growth, and ultimately eliminate deficits. As OMB director from 1981, Stockman had broad powers to propose spending cuts and was frequently in the public eye as an administration spokesman. Probably the most famous of all budget directors, he quickly became a

Clear-eyed vision:

The budget "isn't something you reconstruct each year. The budget is a sort of rolling history of decisions. All kinds of decisions made five, ten, fifteen years ago, are coming back to bite us unexpectedly. There, in my judgment, it will take three or four or five years to subdue it. Whether anyone can maintain the political momentum to fight the beast for that long, I don't know."

—David Stockman, OMB director and President Reagan's chief budget architect, in *Atlantic Monthly* article (December 1981).

symbol of the Reagan administration's aggressive program to reduce federal spending and cut the deficit. But by late 1981 he had begun having doubts and publicly questioned the wisdom of the massive tax cut the administration had just pushed through Congress. Stockman remained as OMB director until 1985, by which time deficits had mushroomed into the $150 billion to $200 billion range. His resignation over policy differences embarrassed the Reagan administration. Administration policies, Stockman believed, were adding to the deficit, not reducing it.

(See 131 When did the federal debt actually begin to mushroom? 375 What can presidents do to control spending? 391 Did President Ronald Reagan cut the size of government? 466 What was President Reagan's economic record? 475 Why were deficits so high during the Reagan years?)

Q 307. What does the Council of Economic Advisers (CEA) do?

A The CEA provides the president with expert advice on economic matters. Made up of three top-notch economists and a small staff, the CEA has primarily been concerned with advising the president on ways to promote economic growth, lower inflation, and keep the unemployment rate down.

The CEA chairman reports directly to the president, though his or her working relationship with the president often has determined how much influence over policy making the CEA actually has. The chair and the two other council members are appointed by the president and confirmed by the Senate.

(See 65 What is fiscal policy? 297 Who advises the president on economic matters now?)

Q 308. Why does the Treasury Department have so much influence in economic policy making?

A In the first place, the Treasury Department is by its very nature deeply involved in economic matters. Its primary jobs are to manage the country's monetary resources and to collect federal revenue. The Treasury regulates the national banks, pays the government's bills, oversees the national debt, conducts research into domestic and international economic concerns, and develops international economic policy. The treasury secretary, usually among the president's closest advisers, is officially the second-ranking cabinet member because of these extensive responsibilities for the nation's finances. All that combines to give the treasury secretary considerable clout when it comes to economic policy making.

(See 296 What was the first source presidents had for economic advice? 297 Who advises the president on economic issues now? 499 What does the Monthly Treasury Statement cover?)

Q 309. Who has served as treasury secretary?

A There have been seventy treasury secretaries since the Constitution went into effect (see below). Alexander Hamilton was the first, and he played a crucial role in establishing the new government's finances. Hugh McCulloch and William Windom are the only treasury secretaries to have held the post twice (1865–1869, 1884–1885; 1881, 1889–1891). Robert E. Rubin was treasury secretary as of mid-1997.

Secretary	*Years served*
Alexander Hamilton	1789–1795
Oliver Wolcott Jr.	1795–1800
Samuel Dexter	1801
Albert Gallatin	1801–1814
George Washington Campbell	1814
Alexander James Dallas	1814–1816
William Harris Crawford	1816–1825
Richard Rush	1825–1829
Samuel Delucenna Ingham	1829–1831
Louis McLane	1831–1833
William John Duane	1833
Roger Brooke Taney	1833–1834

Secretary	*Years served*
Levi Woodbury	1834–1841
Thomas Ewing	1841
Walter Forward	1841–1843
John Canfield Spencer	1843–1844
George Mortimer Bibb	1844–1845
Robert John Walker	1845–1849
William Morris Meredith	1849–1850
Thomas Corwin	1850–1853
James Guthrie	1853–1857
Howell Cobb	1857–1860
Philip Francis Thomas	1860–1861
John Adams Dix	1861
Salmon Portland Chase	1861–1864
William Pitt Fessenden	1864–1865
Hugh McCulloch	1865–1869
George Sewel Boutwell	1869–1873
William Adams Richardson	1873–1874
Benjamin Helm Bristow	1874–1876
Lot Myrick Morrill	1876–1877
John Sherman	1877–1881
William Windom	1881
Charles James Folger	1881–1884
Walter Quintin Gresham	1884
Hugh McCulloch	1884–1885
Daniel Manning	1885–1887
Charles Stebbins Fairchild	1887–1889
William Windom	1889–1891
Charles Foster	1891–1893
John Griffin Carlisle	1893–1897
Lyman Judson Gage	1897–1902
Leslie Mortier Shaw	1902–1907
George Bruce Cortelyou	1907–1909
Franklin MacVeagh	1909–1913
William Gibbs McAdoo	1913–1918
Carter Glass	1918–1920
David Franklin Houston	1920–1921
Andrew William Mellon	1921–1932

Secretary	*Years served*
Ogden Livingston Mills	1932–1933
William Hartman Woodin	1933
Henry Morgenthau Jr.	1934–1945
Frederick Moore Vinson	1945–1946
John Wesley Snyder	1946–1953
George Magoffin Humphrey	1953–1957
Robert Bernard Anderson	1957–1961
Clarence Douglas Dillon	1961–1965
Henry Hamill Fowler	1965–1968
Joseph Walker Barr	1968–1969
David M. Kennedy	1969–1971
John Bowden Connally	1971–1972
George Pratt Shultz	1972–1974
William Edward Simon	1974–1977
Werner Michael Blumenthal	1977–1979
George William Miller	1979–1981
Donald T. Regan	1981–1985
James A. Baker III	1985–1988
Nicholas Frederick Brady	1988–1993
Lloyd Bentsen	1993–1995
Robert E. Rubin	1995–

(See 69 What is monetary policy? 492 Who is Alan Greenspan and why is he so powerful?)

Q 310. Is the president's budget the only source of information on the current budget?

A Though the president's budget is the most comprehensive single source for budget information, more detailed coverage of specific agency and program budgets does exist. These sources include *press briefings on agency finances,* which are released by major agencies soon after the president's budget is made public. Appropriations committees also publish *justification material,* made up of detailed treatments of agency and program spending needs used during committee hearings. Publication is generally some months after hearings have ended, however. Agencies also prepare *internal budgets* and update them during the year, but these usually are not released.

(See 21 Where can I find information on the current year's budget?)

Q 311. What was the Bureau of the Budget?

A Created by the 1921 Budget Act, the Bureau of the Budget became the clearinghouse for budget requests submitted to the president by federal agencies. It operated until 1970, when President Richard Nixon created the Office of Management and Budget.

The bureau was nominally part of the Treasury Department, but the president supervised its activities. Among other duties, the bureau examined agency budget requests in terms of the president's spending priorities. (Budget requests cannot be forwarded to Congress without the president's approval.)

President Franklin D. Roosevelt further enlarged presidential controls in 1935 by requiring that agency requests for legislation also be cleared by the bureau before being presented to Congress. Then in 1939 he transferred the bureau from the Treasury to the Executive Office of the President. Both Roosevelt and later presidents strengthened the bureau's role as a legislative clearinghouse.

Q 312. What attempts to reform the budget process in the executive branch have been made?

A A frequent criticism of the executive branch budget process is that agency budgets overemphasize operating costs and other inputs, instead of focusing on performance ("outputs") and program goals. Various attempts to revamp budgeting procedures to those ends have been made: the 1950s saw performance budgeting; the 1960s, program budgeting and the planning-programming-budgeting system; the 1970s, management by objective and zero-based budgeting; and the 1990s, the performance and results system. Reforms prior to the 1990s proved unsuccessful, though each effort left its mark on the budget process.

Q 313. What did the National Performance Review recommend?

A The 1993 National Performance Review (NPR), a survey of the federal government headed by Vice President Al Gore, found that the federal budget process fails to emphasize program performance and goals. Government managers, the report found, had too little flexibility because of extensive spending controls, many of which were imposed by Congress. The NPR report recommended loosening those controls to encourage more efficient use of federal money. It also suggested various procedural reforms aimed at reorienting the budget writing process toward program performance and objectives. Among the specific suggestions were:

—The president should provide agencies with budget policy guidance early in the budget writing process, rather than making policy decisions after agency requests have been submitted to the OMB.

—More discretion should be given to federal managers, including less earmarking of funds by Congress, control over staffing levels, simplified financial reports, and authority to carry over unspent funds to the next fiscal year.

—The president should negotiate performance agreements with heads of federal agencies in order to set long-term performance goals.

—Biennial (two-year) budgeting should be introduced to free agencies from the annual cycle of budget deadlines. This would allow agencies more time to focus on long-term goals, instead of day-to-day operating expenses.

(See 360 What is earmarking? 371 Are annual appropriations necessary?)

Q 314. How did the Government Performance and Results Act of 1993 propose to reform the budget process?

A The Government Performance and Results Act seeks to reorient the budget process by putting greater emphasis on performance and goals and giving federal managers greater flexibility. It mandates pilot tests that will run from 1993 to 2001 at a minimum of ten agencies. The pilot tests are of three different types, one designed to test performance budgeting, another for performance plans and reports, and the third for expanded flexibility and accountability for program managers.

Q 315. What did the 1990 Chief Financial Officers Act do?

A This act was written to strengthen the government's financial management system and to establish a link between federal budgeting and federal accounting systems. The law created the new Office of Federal Financial Management and the position of deputy director for management, all within the OMB. In addition, the position of chief financial officer (CFO) was created for each of twenty-three major federal agencies. CFOs were charged with responsibility for most all the agency financial matters. The OMB deputy director for management functions as the federal government's CFO.

Q 316. What are bottom-up and incremental budgeting?

A *Bottom-up budgeting* refers to the tendency to begin compiling expenses and other data for a future agency budget request at the agency's lower levels first. The budget request then gradually works its way up through the organization until all administrative units have been included and reviewed. The agency's budget is then sent to the OMB for review.

The system is especially time consuming and tends to emphasize costs (wages, equipment, supplies, and the like) in great detail, instead of focusing on program performance. Also, the many months of preparation required force agencies to begin the process even before they know what their final spending will be for the current year.

Incremental budgeting helps agencies deal with the uncertainties of the budget process. In the past, when economic growth and a steadily expanding federal budget were the norm, agencies tended to request more money for the upcoming year than they had for the previous year—year after year. These "incremental" increases varied in size depending on such things as the agency's clout with Congress, how much its budget had grown in past years, and how tight the budget was for a given year. One problem with emphasizing incremental budget growth is that it diverts attention from needed review of existing programs. Another is that the increments almost always increase and so there is a built-in bias toward spending growth. Ever since the 1970s, when economic growth began lagging, the government has had to fund that incremental growth by borrowing ever larger sums.

(See 272 How is the budget prepared? 276 When does the groundwork on future budgets actually begin? 277 What is the timetable for preparing the budget?)

Q **317. What is reprogramming?**

A When Congress appropriates funding for an agency, it often specifies lump sums for groups of specific projects or activities within the agency's budget. The lump sums are called appropriations accounts, and when an agency shifts money from one project or activity within the same appropriations account it is called *reprogramming.* Agencies usually consult with Congress before shifting the funds, and frequently must either give official notice or get formal approval from the appropriate congressional committee before reprogramming the funds.

Q **318. What is a line-item veto?**

A The Constitution gives presidents the power to veto only an entire bill, not specific parts of it. The *line-item veto,* on the other hand, allows the president to veto the objectionable parts and sign the rest of the bill into law.

The pros and cons of a presidential line-item veto had been debated for well over a century, and in recent years Republican Presidents Ronald Reagan and George Bush championed the idea as a way to cut wasteful spending from the budget. The Republican-controlled 104th Congress did finally enact a limited line-item veto in 1996, and Democratic president Bill Clinton signed it into law. The Supreme Court turned away an initial legal challenge to the law on technical grounds in 1997, and President Clinton began using the line-item veto to strike provisions from legislation in August of that year.

Even though the president's power to use the line-item veto is sharply limited, supporters of the law believe it has clear advantages over allowing vetoes of only an entire bill. In the past, for example, presidents have objected to certain specific spending provisions tucked into a bill, but have had to sign the measure anyway because it was either very popular or urgently needed. In fact, Congress frequently has added controversial items—and pork-barrel spending—to such measures just to avoid a presidential veto.

While experts generally agree the line-item veto will give the president greater power in dealing with Congress, many have argued it will actually have little impact on overall federal spending.

(See 304 What role does a presidential veto play in the budget process? 359 What is pork-barrel spending?)

Q 319. Who was the first president to call for a line-item veto?

A President Ulysses S. Grant was the first to ask for a presidential line-item veto, in 1873. Congress considered (and rejected) the first legislation calling for the line-item veto in 1876. Similar measures had come before Congress over 150 times before the line-item veto was finally enacted in 1996. Along the way, both Republican and Democratic presidents supported the idea (among them Woodrow Wilson, Franklin D. Roosevelt, Harry S. Truman, Dwight D. Eisenhower, Gerald Ford, Ronald Reagan, and George Bush).

CONGRESS

Q 320. What is "the power of the purse"?

A Congress's power to tax, spend, and borrow are often referred to collectively as its "power of the purse." The Constitution specifically grants these powers to Congress, and control of funding gives the legislative branch enormous influence over the policies and development of government, not to mention the well-being of the nation. Through its taxing and spending powers, Congress in this century has vastly increased the size of the federal government, given government far greater control of the economy, and made it responsible for the social and economic well-being of millions of individual Americans and the country as a whole.

While Congress has succeeded in using the power of the purse to advance these broad policy concerns, establishing an effective budget policy has proved far more difficult. Much of what it has achieved since the 1930s has come with a price tag—budget deficits year after year and a mounting federal debt that now exceeds $5 trillion.

Budget battles with the president and the rising debt during the 1970s finally forced Congress to begin getting federal spending under control. Two decades have passed since, and Congress is only now beginning to reestablish control over the purse strings.

(See 2 Who actually approves the budget? 13 Why does the government spend more than it takes in? 20 Should the budget be balanced? 23 What impact does the government have on the economy? 45 What did President Bill Clinton mean when he said the era of big government is over? 65 What is fiscal policy? 67 What role does Congress play in setting fiscal policy? 78 What articles of the Constitution grant Congress the power to tax and spend? 124 Where does Congress get the authority to borrow money? 284 What have been the major turning points in the history of budgeting?)

Q 321. What did the Supreme Court ruling in *United States* v. *Butler* do?

A By this 1935 ruling, the Supreme Court struck down a New Deal law aimed at helping farmers—the Agricultural Adjustment Act of 1933. While the Court opposed the law on technical grounds, the ruling was important because it favored the broad interpretation of Congress's spending powers and provided a test for determining the constitutionality of a spending program.

The Constitution had left open the general question of what Congress could and could not spend money on—in that regard it authorized Congress to "provide for the common defense and general welfare of the United States." Those who favored a stricter interpretation believed spending by Congress should be limited to only those functions specifically mentioned by the Constitution, such as establishing roads, post offices, and the armed forces. By the twentieth century, however, the broader interpretation based on the concept of spending to provide for the "general welfare" was widely accepted.

In ruling on *Butler*, the Court decided that congressional spending was constitutional "so long as the welfare at which it is aimed can be plausibly represented as national rather than local." Later decisions also upheld Congress's use of its taxing powers to provide for the general welfare.

(See 2 Who actually approves the budget?)

Q 322. Why is it that Congress has so much trouble keeping spending within a budget?

A Congress has been spending more than the government collects in revenues for decades now, creating an unbroken string of deficits and a mountain of federal debt that can no longer be safely ignored. Part of the overspending problem has been the systems Congress uses to write the budget. Control was once so diffused among the various committees that making centralized budget decisions was all but impossible. Until 1975 Congress did not even have a way to set overall spending targets for the annual budget, and concerted efforts at enforcing budget targets did not begin until the 1980s.

Another side of the problem was the lawmakers' unwillingness to make hard spending and revenue choices needed to keep deficits and the debt from piling up. For some, it was a matter of protecting cherished programs or caving in to pressure from special interest groups. In other cases, it was the fear that cutting spending for popular programs or raising taxes to fully fund them would anger voters. For many years members of Congress found it easier to avoid the problem by letting the deficit, and the debt, grow. And we voters bear some blame, too, for electing members of Congress who would let that happen, and for believing we could somehow have the federal benefits without paying for them.

Past spending decisions have also come back to haunt Congress. Expansion of Social Security and other entitlement programs during the 1960s and 1970s, for example, increased benefits—and costs—well beyond the taxes imposed to cover them. That has contributed substantially to the deficit since the 1970s. And these decisions, made twenty-five to thirty years ago, now dictate how the government will spend about three-quarters of the entire annual budget. Entitlement programs cannot be changed except by passing laws, which now make it difficult for Congress to make cuts needed to reduce the deficit and balance the budget.

Economic problems—such as inflation and slow growth in the 1970s, the savings and loan bailout, and the stock market crash of the 1980s—also contributed to Congress's budget woes. A sluggish economy cuts federal revenues, and unexpected crises add expenses, both of which put more pressure on Congress to cut spending if it wants to keep the deficit down.

(See 13 Why does the government spend more than it takes in? 19 Can't we just ignore the debt? 20 Should the budget be balanced? 171 Why has social spending risen by so much?)

Q 323. What is the largest single spending bill Congress has ever passed?

A An omnibus bill containing six of the annual appropriations bills for fiscal 1997 is the largest. The bill HR 3610 contained over $610 billion in appropriations ($380 billion in discretionary spending, the rest for mandatory programs) and cleared Congress September 30, 1996, just hours before the start of fiscal 1997.

Previously the largest bill was a $576 billion continuing resolution (H.J. Res. 738 (P.L. 99-491)), which Congress passed October 17, 1986. With the budget process in disarray that year, Congress had not passed a single one of the thirteen annual appropriations bills by the start of fiscal 1987. Instead of passing a temporary continuing resolution and then returning to work on individual appropriations bills, Congress put all thirteen bills into the continuing resolution and made the resolution effective for the entire fiscal year (1987).

Congress sought to avoid this slap-dash approach in 1988, and members of both parties met with the Reagan administration in a budget summit before beginning work on the fiscal 1989 budget. Agreements hammered out at the summit made it possible for Congress to pass all thirteen appropriations bills for fiscal 1989 before the start of the fiscal year in October. The last time that had happened was 1977.

Q 324. Who are the Blue Dogs?

A Organized during the budget battles of 1995, the Blue Dogs are a small group of conservative Democrats in the House of Representatives who offered a Democratic plan to balance the budget in seven years. Rep. Charles W. Stenholm (D-Texas) and Bill Orton (D-Utah) lead the group, which is composed mainly of conservative Democrats from the South and West. Their budget proposal attracted a sizable bloc of Democratic votes in the House, and Blue Dogs figured in budget negotiations during 1996 and 1997.

The Blue Dog plan differed significantly from both Republican and Clinton administration plans as they stood in late 1995. Blue Dogs, for example, had no tax cut in their plan, while Republican and administration budget proposals did ($245 billion and $105 billion, respectively). Their proposed cuts for Medicaid and Medicare were substantially lower than the Republicans' and well above Clinton's. Also, Blue Dogs favored a half percentage point reduction in the Consumer Price Index, more than the two-tenths suggested by Republicans. Another major difference lies in the Blue Dogs' proposed $69 billion discretionary spending cut. That was about half what Republicans envisioned and far deeper than administration officials wanted.

(See 41 What impact does the inflated CPI have? 397 What was the 1997 balanced budget agreement? 488 What did the 1997 balanced budget agreement do to cut taxes?)

Q 325. What are the tax-writing committees in the House and Senate?

A The House Ways and Means Committee and the Senate Finance Committee are the two chief tax-writing committees in Congress. Since the Constitution gives power to originate revenue bills to the House, the Ways and Means Committee takes the lead on most tax legislation. The Senate Finance Committee usually then responds to the House-passed measure, and differences are ironed out in conference.

(See 331 What does the Senate Finance Committee do? 334 What does the Ways and Means Committee do in connection with taxes and the budget? 335 Who has chaired Ways and Means?)

Q 326. What purpose does the Joint Taxation Committee serve?

A This committee's main role is providing expert advice on tax matters for both the House Ways and Means Committee and the Senate Finance Committee. Reflecting its nonpartisan nature, the joint committee is made up of five members each of the House and Senate. It has a staff of over sixty tax specialists, including accountants, lawyers, and economists, who provide advice to the congressional committees. The Joint Taxation Committee itself meets only rarely. Among the committee's other responsibilities are conducting investigations—such as the one President Richard Nixon requested of his own returns—and reviewing tax refunds of over $200,000. Rarely in the limelight, the committee and its staff wield enormous influence on tax and revenue issues, even though the committee has no authority to draft legislation.

Q 327. What are the House and Senate Budget Committees?

A These two committees were created by the Congressional Budget and Impoundment Control Act of 1974 to focus on broad questions about federal spending and revenue. The committees review and recommend changes in the president's annual budget proposal and draft the annual budget resolutions for their respective houses, before the appropriations process begins. Once House and Senate committees begin actual work on authorization and appropriations bills, the budget committees will try to keep them within spending targets set by the budget resolution. But budget committee powers to enforce decisions are limited.

The House committee has been less successful than its Senate counterpart in shaping the budget debate in years past, but neither committee proved able to halt the tide of rising deficits during the 1980s. The 1990 budget deal struck between Congress and Republican President George Bush effectively bypassed the budget committees by making many of the broad budget decisions for them. The five-year, $500 billion agreement allowed the deficit to keep growing while also establishing spending limits and imposing PAYGO rules for mandatory spending (increases must be offset by cuts elsewhere).

(See 272 How is the budget prepared? 362 What does PAYGO mean?)

Q 328. Who has chaired these committees?

A Some notable political figures have served as chair of the Budget Committee. Leon Panetta (D-Calif.), later President Bill Clinton's first OMB director, served as House Budget Committee chairman in the early 1990s. Sen. Edmund Muskie (D-Maine) was first chairman of the Senate Budget Committee. Sen. Pete Domenici (R-N.M.) is the current chairman (as of mid-1997) and a longtime ranking Republican member of the committee.

	Chair, House Budget Committee
1975–1977	Brock Adams (D-Wash.)
1977–1981	Robert N. Giaimo (D-Conn.)
1981–1985	James R. Jones (D-Okla.)
1985–1989	William H. Gray III (D-Pa.)
1989–1993	Leon Panetta (D-Calif.)
1993–1995	Martin Sabo (D-Minn.)
1995–	John R. Kasich (R-Ohio)

	Chair, Senate Budget Committee
1975–1979	Edmund Muskie (D-Maine)
1979–1981	Ernest F. Hollings (D-S.C.)
1981–1987	Pete V. Domenici (R-N.M.)
1987–1989	Lawton Chiles Jr. (D-Fla.)
1989–1995	Jim Sasser (D-Tenn.)
1995–	Pete V. Domenici (R-N.M.)

Q 329. Who is Rep. John Kasich?

A A member of Newt Gingrich's inner circle, Rep. John Kasich (R-Ohio) joined the House Budget Committee in 1989 and became the committee's ranking Republican in 1992, despite his lack of seniority. He has been committee chairman since 1995, when he took over the responsibility for delivering on Republican promises to enact both a balanced budget and substantial tax cuts.

Though he opposes deep cuts in defense, Kasich was the leading Republican opponent of the B-2 stealth bomber program and in 1989 helped force big cuts in Pentagon requests for more of the planes. As the Budget Committee's ranking Republican, he helped lead the fight against President Bill Clinton's economic stimulus package in 1993, and at various times prepared alternative budgets calling for deeper cuts to balance the budget. He has supported the balanced budget amendment and promoted various reforms—including the $500-per-child tax credit—that eventually became part of the Republican Contract With America.

Q 330. What has been Sen. Pete Domenici's top budget priority?

A As Senate Budget Committee chairman from 1981 to 1987 and from 1995 to the present, Sen. Pete Domenici (R-N.M.) has consistently favored deficit reduction, even at the expense of Republican plans for tax cuts. Appalled at the big deficits of the 1980s and 1990s, Domenici has actively supported deep cuts in entitlements and tax increases as a way to eliminate the deficit. In 1985 he and Sen. Bob Dole (R-Kan.) pushed a freeze on Social Security cost-of-living adjustments (COLAs) through the Senate to help cut federal spending, but the plan was dropped by President Ronald Reagan during budget negotiations with Democrats later that year.

Domenici backed Gramm-Rudman and the 1990 budget summit, and in the mid-1990s floated a plan to balance the budget in ten years through tax increases, spending cuts, and a shift from the income tax to a consumption-based tax. His insistence on eliminating the deficit first—before tax cuts—put him at odds with House Republicans supporting the Contract with America during the 1995–1996 budget debates.

(See 484 What did the Republican Contract with America try to do?)

Q 331. What does the Senate Finance Committee do?

A Among the first committees formed within the Senate, the Finance Committee has jurisdiction over almost half of all federal spending (including Social Security, welfare, and health care) and over all legislation dealing with federal taxation. The committee also is responsible for tariffs.

Though the House has the power to originate revenue bills, procedures for writing and amending the legislation are strict. The Senate Finance Committee, on the other hand, has been much more open to amendments that accommodate committee members' interests. For that reason, rider amendments on tax bills have been much more common in the Senate. The committee has a long history of being the focus of lobbying for special tax breaks, and members regularly are at the top of the list for campaign donations.

Because of the committee's wide-ranging power over federal finances, the Senate Finance Committee chair ranks among the most powerful individuals in the Senate. Committee chairmen who have served since 1947 are:

1947–1949	Eugene D. Milikin (R-Colo.)
1949–1953	Walter F. George (D-Ga.)
1953–1955	Eugene D. Milikin (R-Colo.)
1955–1965	Harry Flood Byrd (D-Va.)
1965–1981	Russell B. Long (D-La.)
1981–1985	Robert Dole (R-Kan.)
1985–1987	Bob Packwood (R-Ore.)
1987–1993	Lloyd Bentsen (D-Texas)
1993–1995	Daniel Patrick Moynihan (D-N.Y.)
1995–	William V. Roth Jr. (R-Del.)

Q **332. What is one thing Sen. Robert Byrd is noted for?**

A When he became Appropriations Committee chairman in 1989, Democratic Senator Robert C. Byrd vowed to channel over $1 billion worth of federal spending into his home state of West Virginia—within five years. Byrd met the goal within three, steering to West Virginia an FBI complex, new CIA office complexes, defense installations, and a host of other highway, flood control, research, and education projects. Other senators put up little opposition to his federal spending spree, largely because as chairman Byrd could block funding for federal projects in their home states. Meanwhile, Byrd strongly defended his actions on behalf of West Virginia.

(See 359 What is pork-barrel spending? 360 What is earmarking?)

Q 333. Who was Russell Long and what is he remembered for?

A The Senate Finance Committee chairman for sixteen years and a committee member for thirty-five years, Russell Long made himself a master of the federal tax code. He was deeply involved in revising the code's complex rules and regulations during his tenure. But his tax bills were also known for the various unrelated special interest amendments he attached—especially those amendments favoring oil, gas, and other businesses in his home state of Louisiana.

The son of the notorious Sen. Huey P. Long, Russell Long entered the Senate as a Democrat in 1948. He joined the Senate Finance Committee in 1953 and served as its chair from 1965 to 1981. As chairman, Long used the reward system to garner backing for his bills. Members who supported the measures were allowed to add amendments benefiting their home states. Long retired from the Senate in 1987.

Q 334. What does the House Ways and Means Committee do in connection with taxes and the budget?

A One of the most powerful House committees, Ways and Means originates virtually all tax and tariff bills and oversees almost half of all government outlays, including those for Social Security, health insurance, and unemployment benefits.

Ways and Means has greatest control over taxes, the government's main source of revenue. The committee provides the first draft of tax legislation and so has had a large part in constructing the complex system of tax laws and tax breaks. Virtually everyone in the country is touched in some way by tax code provisions, and that is a major reason why the committee wields so much influence. Even a slight wording change in a tax provision can save businesses or the members of special interest groups millions of dollars in taxes.

Since World War II, Ways and Means probably was at the height of its power during the tenure of Wilbur D. Mills, an Arkansas Democrat who served as chairman from 1957 to 1974. Mills, who invariably sought the committee's consensus, became legendary for his skill in writing complex tax measures and guiding them through the legislative process. Reforms imposed by House Democrats in the 1970s significantly weakened the Ways and Means Committee, but it remains one of the most powerful committees in Congress.

(See 356 Are there differences in House and Senate procedures for tax legislation? 365 Does the Senate ever originate tax bills?)

335. Who has chaired Ways and Means?

Chairs of the Ways and Means Committee since 1947 are:

1947–1949	Harold Knutson (R-Minn.)
1949–1953	Robert L. Doughton (D-N.C.)
1953–1955	Daniel A. Reed (R-N.Y.)
1955–1957	Jere Cooper (D-Tenn.)
1958–1975	Wilbur D. Mills (D-Ark.)
1975–1981	Al Ullman (D-Ore.)
1981–1994	Dan Rostenkowski (D-Ill.)
1994–1995	Sam M. Gibbons (D-Fla.)
1995–	Bill Archer (R-Texas)

Q 336. Who is considered the most powerful Ways and Means chairman of recent times?

A Wilbur D. Mills (D-Ark.), who served 1958 to 1974, not only ranks as the committee's most powerful chairman, he was also among the most powerful House members in his time. His position as chairman of the Ways and Means Committee gave him considerable clout to start with. The committee was responsible for writing all revenue legislation, as well as spending bills for welfare, unemployment insurance, Medicare, Medicaid, and Social Security—about 45 percent of all federal spending. In addition, Mills also served as chairman of the Democratic Committee on Committees, which gave him control over all the party's committee assignments.

Mills kept a tight rein over his committee. He controlled the committee staff and allowed no subcommittees—preventing opponents on the committee from getting assistance needed to prepare alternative bills. Mills also maintained close relations with the committee's Republican minority leader to further cement his control over the committee. Then, too, he invariably sent his bills to the House floor under a closed rule, which barred amendments.

For seventeen years he remained one of the most politically savvy members of Congress. His ability to speak without notes on complex tax issues inspired awe, and his bills regularly passed by comfortable margins in the House. Part of that was his ability to judge shifts in the political winds—an opponent of Medicare, he supported creation of the program after President Lyndon Johnson's reelection landslide in 1964. By 1974, however, Mills had become a target of liberal Democrats. After highly publicized incidents with a striptease dancer, Mills sought treatment for alcoholism and resigned his chairmanship.

Q 337. How are the House and Senate Appropriations Committees organized?

A Appropriations committees in both chambers consist of a full committee and thirteen subcommittees. The thirteen subcommittees correspond to the thirteen regular appropriations bills Congress must pass each year. Each subcommittee has jurisdiction over one of the appropriations bills and wields considerable power over spending bills it drafts.

Much of the work, and the influence, has fallen to the subcommittees rather than the full appropriations committees. Subcommittees operate as independent kingdoms within their jurisdictions. Subcommittee chairs are often referred to as "cardinals" by other members of Congress because of their power. In the House, where appropriations bills originate, the Appropriations Committee ranks among the powerful and prestigious committees.

(See 350 What happens to appropriations bills in the House and Senate?)

▶ How do the various committees handle overlapping budget responsibilities? *See 352 How do the authorization, appropriations, and budget committees interact?* ◀

Q 338. When were the House and Senate Appropriations Committees formed?

A Both the House and Senate formed their appropriations committees at the end of the Civil War. By this time the job of handling both taxing and spending legislation had become too much for the House Ways and Means Committee, and the House formed its Appropriations Committee in 1865. The Senate followed suit in 1867.

During the 1870s and 1880s the House and Senate reacted to the excessive power wielded by appropriations committees and transferred control of about half the annual spending bills to other committees. This solution fragmented the budgeting process, though, and as federal finances became more complex early in the twentieth century, the House and Senate were forced to restore sole appropriations authority to their respective appropriations committees (1920, 1922). At the same time, however, Congress also gave the executive branch a much larger role in the budgeting process.

(See 283 What did the 1921 Budget and Accounting Act do?)

Q 339. Who has chaired these committees?

A Chairs of the House and Senate Appropriations Committees since 1947 are as follows:

	House
1947–1949	John Taber (R-N.Y.)
1949–1953	Clarence Cannon (D-Mo.)
1953–1955	John Taber (R-N.Y.)
1955–1964	Clarence Cannon (D-Mo.)
1964–1979	George H. Mahon (D-Texas)
1979–1993	Jamie L. Whitten (D-Miss.)
1993–1994	William H. Natcher (D-Ky.)
1994–1995	David R. Obey (D-Wis.)
1995–	Bob Livingston (R-La.)

	Senate
1947–1949	Styles Bridges (R-N.H.)
1949–1953	Kenneth McKellar (D-Tenn.)
1953–1955	Styles Bridges (R-N.H.)
1955–1969	Carl Hayden (D-Ariz.)
1969–1971	Richard B. Russell (D-Ga.)
1971–1972	Allen J. Ellender (D-La.)
1972–1977	John L. McClellan (D-Ark.)
1978–1981	Warren G. Magnuson (D-Wash.)
1981–1987	Mark O. Hatfield (R-Ore.)
1987–1989	John C. Stennis (D-Miss.)
1989–1995	Robert C. Byrd (D-W.Va.)
1995–1997	Mark O. Hatfield (R-Ore.)
1997–	Ted Stevens (R-Alaska)

Q **340. What is Jamie L. Whitten remembered for?**

A Apart from holding the record as the longest-serving member of Congress (fifty-three years and two months at his retirement in 1995), Jamie L. Whitten (D-Miss.) was also the last of the conservative southern Democrats who once ruled Congress as powerful committee chairmen. From 1979 to 1993, Whitten was chairman of the Appropriations Committee, which oversees all spending bills in the House. But he also spent over four decades as chairman of the Appropriations Agriculture Subcommittee, where he fought for such programs as soil conservation, crop subsidies, rural home loans, and rural electrification.

Whitten's power as committee chairman has been diluted in recent years by budget control measures, which impose strict limits on what the Appropriations Committee can spend. And the thirteen subcommittee chairmen—dubbed the College of Car-

"When you handle money, you're in the strongest position you can be in, in Congress."

—Jamie L. Whitten (D-Miss.), former House Appropriations Committee chairman.

dinals—operate more or less independently on legislation within their jurisdictions. But as chairman, Whitten was responsible for midyear supplemental appropriations (extra funding for programs that have run out of money), disaster-aid bills, and continuing resolutions.

To some degree all of these bills are "must pass" emergency measures, providing Whitten with ample opportunity to slip in various amendments for pork-barrel projects. Over the years Whitten earned a reputation as a shrewd trader in appropriations pork, and as he once put it, "I've never seen a disaster that wasn't an opportunity."

Q 341. What role does the Congressional Budget Office play?

A Staffed by budget experts and economists, the Congressional Budget Office (CBO) provides Congress with nonpartisan economic forecasts, budget analyses, and policy options. It estimates costs over five years for proposed bills and also handles legislative scorekeeping.

Created by the Congressional Budget and Impoundment Control Act of 1974, the CBO helps Congress consider broad budget policy matters and assess the mass of information in the president's proposed budget. It is the congressional equivalent of the president's Office of Management and Budget (OMB). Differing estimates prepared by the two offices have fueled debates between Congress and the president from time to time.

Although CBO services are available to all congressional committees, it has close ties with the House and Senate Budget Committees. The CBO director is appointed by the House Speaker and Senate president pro tem to a four-year term. A succession of able and respected directors has helped increase the CBO's prestige and influence.

(See 305 What does the Office of Management and Budget do? 367 What is scorekeeping?)

Q 342. What does the General Accounting Office (GAO) do?

A The congressional watchdog for federal spending, the GAO has wide-ranging power to audit spending by government agencies and to conduct special investigations involving the misuse of public funds. Congress has also charged the agency with making recommendations for reducing wasteful spending and achieving greater efficiency in government operations. The GAO reports its findings to Congress annually and employs a staff of five thousand, making it the largest agency supporting Congress.

The president appoints a comptroller general to head the GAO for a fifteen-year term, with confirmation by the Senate. The comptroller is directly responsible to Congress, however, and can only be removed by a joint resolution. Either a congressional committee or an individual member of Congress can request a special GAO investigation. GAO findings have often significantly affected public policy.

Q 343. Who gets GAO reports on audits and investigations?

A The GAO sends both its annual report and findings from special investigations to the House and Senate Government Operations Committees, not to the White House or other executive branch agency.

Q 344. Does the trend toward annual authorizations of programs have any effect on Congress?

A Congress has favored annual authorizations over multiyear or permanent measures since the 1950s. At the same time, though, federal programs have become far more complex and have increased sharply in number, making the annual review of program needs much more time consuming. As a result, the trend toward reauthorizing programs each year has helped slow the budget writing process, but it does increase congressional spending control. Within Congress, annual reauthorizations also increase the power of authorization committees at the expense of appropriations committees.

(See 371 Are annual appropriations necessary?)

Q 345. How often has Congress passed the budget on time?

A Since the early 1970s Congress has managed to enact all thirteen annual appropriations before the start of the fiscal year (October 1) just four times—fiscal 1976, 1988, 1994, and 1997.

Q 346. Does Congress have to pass legislation before it can spend money?

A Congress does not actually spend the money, it only appropriates money for spending by government agencies and programs. And to do that Congress must pass legislation in accordance with Article I, Section 9, of the Constitution, which specifies, "No money shall be drawn from the Treasury, but in consequence of appropriations made by law. . . ." In fact, passing the annual appropriations bills needed to fund federal government operations is one of the most important tasks Congress completes each year.

(See 2 Who actually approves the budget? 3 Who actually spends the money? 273 What are the thirteen annual appropriations bills Congress must pass each year?)

► What is the difference between appropriations and authorization bills? *See 274 Are authorization and appropriations bills the same?* ◄

Q 347. Can Congress pass an appropriations bill before the president has signed the authorizing bill for a program?

A Both the House and Senate have procedural rules against considering an appropriation until the president has signed the authorization bill for the program. Congress has generally abided by this "two-step" procedure. One of the few exceptions is the part of annual military appropriations authorized by the Constitution. Occasionally Congress has ignored the two-step rule for this appropriation. The House may also waive the two-step rule by voting a "special rule." Senate rules also allow exceptions and generally are more lenient.

Q 348. How did the "two-step" authorization-appropriations process evolve?

A The two-step process of passing authorizing legislation first and then passing an appropriations bill to provide funding actually predates Congress. The first Congress employed the method in setting up the War Department. Subsequent Congresses generally followed the practice, even though neither the House nor Senate had written rules to that effect. During the 1800s, though, increasing efforts to attach substantive amendments to appropriations bills finally forced the House to include a written distinction between authorization and appropriations measures. The House adopted its measure in 1837, and the Senate followed suit with its own rule some years later.

> ***"Appropriators are the car mechanics of Congress. They lie there on their backs looking into the engine of government with grease up to their elbows. It's boring, grubby work. But one reason they're so successful is that so few people take the time to know how the engine runs."***
>
> —Anonymous Capitol Hill veteran, quoted in Brian Kelly's *Adventures in Porkland*

(See 274 Are authorization and appropriations bills the same? 346 Does Congress have to pass legislation before it can spend money?)

Q 349. Which house originates tax bills, appropriations bills, and authorization bills?

A The Constitution specifically grants the House the power to originate all revenue bills. By custom the House also originates all appropriations bills. Though there is no basis for this practice in the Constitution, the House has been quick to defend it against any infringement by the Senate. Little wonder. Because it drafts both spending and revenue bills, the House exercises considerable control over federal finances. The Senate, of course, has the power to amend both types of bills in any way it sees fit. Also, there are no restrictions on which house may originate authorization bills, another important facet of the federal spending process.

(See 365 Does the Senate ever originate tax bills?)

Q 350. What happens to appropriations bills in the House and Senate?

A The process of drafting appropriations bills in Congress begins with overview hearings before the House and Senate Appropriations Committees. The OMB director and others discuss the president's budget priorities for the upcoming fiscal year at these hearings. Then the thirteen appropriations subcommittees in each chamber conduct their own hearings. Representatives of federal agencies within the subcommittee's jurisdiction discuss funding needs with the subcommittee.

The House Appropriations subcommittees do the work of drafting, or marking up, the thirteen regular appropriations bills. Marking up begins after subcommittees receive their spending allocations for the upcoming fiscal year (specified in the budget resolution). Each subcommittee must tailor its appropriations bill so that spending is within its overall allocation.

Once an appropriations bill has been drafted by the appropriate House subcommittee, it is marked up by the full committee and reported to the full House. After floor debate, the full House votes on the measure.

The Senate Appropriations Committee, which also has thirteen subcommittees, then refers the House-passed bill to the subcommittee with the appropriate jurisdiction. The Senate subcommittee reviews hearings the House held on the bill and marks up the House bill, adjusting funding for the various programs in its jurisdiction as it sees fit. But ideally the subcommittee keeps the overall spending total within its funding allocation. The full Appropriations Committee then marks up this Senate version of the bill and reports it to the Senate for floor action.

Once both houses of Congress have passed their own versions of the appropriations bill, any differences must be resolved in conference. The agreed-upon revisions must be approved by the House and Senate, before the appropriations bill can be sent to the president for his signature. This process must, of course, be carried out for all of the thirteen regular appropriations bills Congress passes each year.

(See 273 What are the thirteen annual appropriations Congress must pass each year? 362 What does PAYGO mean? 363 How does a conference committee alter tax and spending bills? 367 What is scorekeeping? 371 Are annual appropriations necessary? 383 What is a budget resolution?)

Q 351. Can appropriations bills be amended once they have cleared the House Appropriations Committee?

A Appropriations bills can be amended, but in the past, amendments from the House floor that make major changes have been relatively infrequent. The power and prestige of the Appropriations Committee has helped keep challenges to the committee's spending decisions to a minimum. The House did use floor amendments at times during the 1980s to impose across-the-board spending cuts of a percent or two. These amendments did not target individual agencies or programs, however.

Q 352. How do the authorization, appropriations, and budget committees interact?

A Generally speaking, authorization committees set policy, appropriations committees provide funding, and budget committees try to control overall federal spending. There has always been a tension between authorization and appropriations committees, with each sometimes writing legislation that oversteps the boundary between setting policy and funding. The creation of budget committees in the 1970s to oversee the budget making process in Congress has added a new dimension to relations between these committees.

Budget committees and authorization committees tend to work at cross-purposes and so are likely to have strained relations. That is because budget committees use the reconciliation process to force authorization committees to make cuts in specific legislation, so that spending will fall within overall budget targets. This infringes on the authorizing committee's policy making powers. The reconciliation procedure can also be used to block funding for programs the authorization committee wants.

Budget committees and appropriations committees, on the other hand, have tended to have closer working relationships.

Q 353. How do regular and supplemental appropriations differ?

A Any of the thirteen annual appropriations passed by Congress are called *regular appropriations.* Should budget authority provided by the regular appropriation run out before the end of the fiscal year, Congress must pass a *supplemental appropriation* to provide added funds. Otherwise, the affected agencies or programs would have to shut down for lack of money.

(See 273 What are the thirteen appropriation bills Congress must pass each year?)

Q 354. What are general and special appropriations bills?

A *General appropriation bill* refers to both regular and supplementary appropriation bills funding more than one agency or program. *Special appropriation bills* are measures that fund only one agency or apply to a single purpose. The distinction is important because special appropriation bills are not subject to rules of the two-step authorization-appropriation process (other unauthorized appropriations can be added to special appropriations bills). The House classifies continuing resolutions as special appropriations, the Senate, as general.

Q 355. How did the Legislative Reform Act of 1970 change the appropriations process in the House?

A The first major procedural reform passed by Congress since 1946, the Legislative Reform Act of 1970 generally opened up congressional legislative activity to greater public scrutiny. This affected the appropriations subcommittees, which had previously done their work behind closed doors. (The closed sessions meant other members of Congress had little opportunity to get information they needed to challenge appropriations bills until just before floor action began.) The 1970 reform called for open subcommittee and committee hearings unless a majority voted against it, but today key bill-drafting sessions of subcommittees are still closed.

Democrats, who were in the majority, pushed through subsequent reforms in the 1970s that affected appropriations committees, including: making it possible to challenge the seniority system for selecting subcommittee and committee chairs; providing for election of committee chairs by all House Democrats in a secret ballot; barring House members from serving on more than two appropriations subcommittees.

Q 356. Are there differences in House and Senate procedures for tax legislation?

A The Constitution specifies that the House must originate revenue legislation, and most of these bills are drafted by the House Ways and Means Committee. The full committee, rather than a subcommittee, holds hearings and drafts tax bills. The House usually considers tax bills under a limited or closed rule, which either restricts or bars altogether any amendments from the floor.

The Senate usually begins work on tax bills after the House has passed its version. Tax bills fall within the jurisdiction of the powerful Senate Finance Committee, which "marks up" the bill. The Senate has fewer restrictions than the House for adding amendments to tax bills, both in committee and from the floor.

Before budget rules were adopted, the Senate sometimes attached so many amendments providing for new spending (called "Christmas treeing" a bill) that the "tax" bill wound up costing the government more money than it generated in the new tax. Budget rules now bar amendments that would push up the deficit, but on balance the Senate still adds more amendments than the House.

The House and Senate frequently pass very different versions of the same tax bill, which means the measure is often rewritten by the conference committee. At times the actual work of drafting the compromise measure is left to the chairs of the Senate Finance and House Ways and Means Committees. The full conference committee then votes to approve the revised bill.

(See 365 Does the Senate ever originate tax bills?)

Q 357. What purpose do "limitations" and "appropriations committee reports" serve?

A Appropriations committees often use these devices to control how funds are to be spent. *Limitations* are included in the spending bill itself and may simply specify an upper limit for spending on a particular activity. Often, however, limitations are used by appropriations committees to set policy—usually the responsibility of the autho-

Perspectives on Congress and pork-barrel spending

"A billion here and a billion there [for pork-barrel spending] and pretty soon you're talking about real money."

—Sen. Everett Dirksen, as quoted in Brian Kelly's *Adventures in Porkland*

rizing committee. Phrases like "provided none of the funds shall be used for. . ." in an appropriations bill provide explicit directions on how funds can be spent. At times, limitations have imposed important policy changes, ranging from interstate highway speed limits to weapons systems deployment.

Appropriations committee reports accompany appropriations bills but do not have the force of law. They explain what the committee intended to do in the bill, however, and provide detailed recommendations on how agencies should spend the money. As a rule, agencies follow the guidelines. Congress often uses committee reports to earmark money for special interest programs it wants funded. Committee reports are also used to highlight differences with the executive branch over the amount of spending for programs covered in the appropriations bill.

(See 274 Are authorization and appropriations bills the same? 359 What is pork-barrel spending? 360 What is earmarking?)

Q 358. How does "logrolling" figure in the legislative process?

A Logrolling is a practice of trading votes that dates back at least to the early days of Congress. Individual senators, House members, or groups of them try to win support for their bill by promising to support current or future legislation of members whose votes they are courting. Though logrolling is often associated with bills benefiting a member's home state or district, it did also figure in efforts to cut the budget deficit during the 1980s. Here, instead of sharing rewards, members of Congress used logrolling tactics to divvy up the burden of budget cuts.

Q 359. What is pork-barrel spending?

A Pork has been described as "federal spending with a ZIP code attached"—spending for federal projects that benefit a single state, locality, or group and the member of Congress who represents them. In fact, members of Congress are sent to Washington to look after the interests of constituents back home, as well as to take care of

"... All congressmen would score pork if they had the power. But the big guys eat first, then toss leftover scraps to those they favor. And because everyone else wants it, a sort of balance of terror emerges where no one will challenge the porkers because they want theirs someday. You'd be making a mistake if you thought of this [pork-barrel spending] as petty. There's big stakes here."

—Anonymous former White House aide

"What would you be willing to do without if you knew you had to pay for it out of your own pocket? Because, of course, all spending in Washington comes out of the same pocket. Taxpayers just don't see it that way. They think they're getting something for nothing. That's the big inside joke in Washington."

—James Dale Davidson, National Taxpayer's Union
[both quotes from Kelly, *Adventures in Porkland.*]

national concerns. Those who do a good job of "bringing home the bacon" are usually rewarded when elections roll around.

By definition, pork is a form of wasteful spending, but identifying it is not always easy. First of all, one taxpayer's waste may be another's salvation. Pink bollworm research might look like a federal grant giveaway, but to California cotton growers it resulted in a big drop in pesticides needed to get their crops to market. Also, projects located in a particular city do not always benefit only local residents. Often they serve a clear national interest and so do not qualify as pork. But if the member of Congress wins a number of these projects for his or her home state through political clout, they may fall into the pork-barrel category.

The difficulty in identifying pork-barrel spending just makes it easier for members of Congress to give in to the temptation of sending some federal spending to their own districts. So does the fact that it is virtually a way of life in Congress. Nearly all members of Congress engage in pork-barrel spending from time to time.

(See 169 What were the Golden Fleece awards?)

Q 360. What is earmarking?

A When funds are specifically directed to a particular purpose or account, they are said to be earmarked. Some federal revenues are earmarked for a particular trust fund (such as the Social Security trust) and cannot be used for any other purpose. Funds

Figure 4-1 Growth of Academic Earmarks (dollars, 1980–1992)

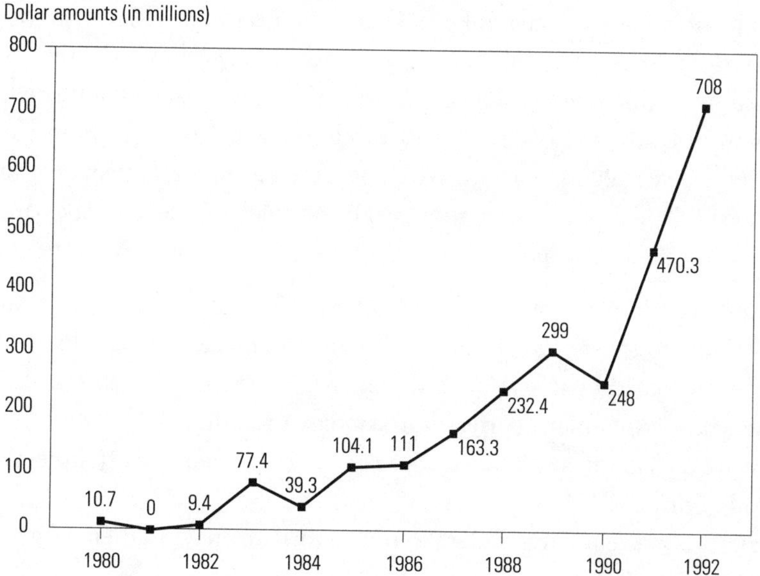

in authorization and appropriations bills may be earmarked for a particular purpose, when committee members want to be sure an agency spends a set amount of money for it. Earmarking funds sometimes has been a source of contention between authorization and appropriations committees, because both want control of funding and may have very different ideas about how the money should be spent. Also, the president and agencies receiving the funds would prefer to have the flexibility to spend the money according to their own priorities.

Earmarking figures in pork-barrel spending as well. Members of appropriations committees and others in Congress who want money for projects in their home states will try to get part of the money in an appropriations bill earmarked for their projects. This, of course, guarantees the members' support for the bill, a device that has helped win passage of many spending bills. It has also kept the practice of earmarking alive, despite criticism from reformers (see Figure 4-1).

Earmarking money for these special projects is often done in committee reports, not in the appropriations bills themselves. Among the various annual appropriations bills, the defense bill has been a frequent target for earmarking associated with pork-barrel spending.

(See 169 What were the Golden Fleece Awards? 359 What is pork-barrel spending?)

Q 361. What were the Grace Commission findings on government waste?

A Headed by business executive J. Peter Grace, the President's Private Sector Survey on Cost Control (the Grace Commission) reported a staggering 2,478 recommendations to reduce government waste. The commission estimated that enacting its recommendations would save $424 billion over three years and would eliminate the federal deficit by the year 2000, without harming defense or social programs and without raising taxes. The report noted about 100 examples of wasteful spending for which Congress was directly responsible. Among the commission's recommendations were:

* Limit benefit payments for food stamps, Medicare, and other social welfare programs to those who really need them (three-year savings, $59 billion).
* Reduce bloated civil service and military retirement benefits to bring them in line with private plans (three-year savings, $61 billion).
* Privatize federal electric power generating agencies (three-year savings, $20 billion).
* Repeal laws requiring federal contractors to pay higher wages (three-year savings, $5 billion).
* Close unnecessary military bases (annual savings, $2 billion).
* End federal subsidies for military commissaries (annual savings, $758 million).

(See 229 Will all those base closings over the past few years really save any money? 475 Why were deficits so high during the Reagan administration?)

Q 362. What does PAYGO mean?

A Pay-As-You-Go, or PAYGO, is a rule established by the Budget Enforcement Act of 1990. It applies to mandatory spending programs and bars Congress from making any changes to mandatory spending programs that would increase the budget deficit. If, for example, Congress passes a bill reducing revenues for entitlements (such as a payroll tax cut) or increasing entitlement spending, it must make up the lost revenue by increasing other taxes or by cutting the budget of another mandatory spending program.

No offsetting cuts are required when an economic slump or costs of an existing program push up the deficit. But if Congress fails to cut enough to offset increased spending for new tax and mandatory spending laws, the president must actually "sequester" the additional money to keep the deficit from rising (*see* 389 What are automatic spending cuts?). PAYGO rules can be suspended if economic or other circumstances warrant.

While PAYGO helps control mandatory spending, it does not impose a fixed cap on it. True, new entitlement legislation cannot raise spending. But costs of existing programs can rise significantly from year to year as a result of cost-of-living adjustments and increased enrollment of eligible recipients.

(See 160 What are entitlement programs? 162 Is there a difference between discretionary and mandatory spending? 176 Could entitlement caps control spending? 289 What is budget authority?)

Q 363. How does a conference committee alter tax and spending bills?

A House and Senate versions of appropriations and tax bills are no different than other important legislative measures. By the time they have passed their respective houses the versions usually contain substantial differences (especially tax bills, to which the Senate often adds rider amendments). The differences must be resolved before the bill can be sent to the president for his signature, however, and the task of ironing them out usually falls to a conference committee.

Largely made up of members of committees in both houses that originally handled the bill (other involved members may be included), the conference committee is supposed to confine itself to only those parts of the bill that are in disagreement. In addition, no new provisions are to be added. But in practice, appropriations and tax bills may be almost completely rewritten in conference. Sometimes, when tax or spending bills are highly complex, are urgently needed, or the committee chairs are especially powerful, the House and Senate committee chairs may meet alone to work out differences between the two versions. Their version of the bill is then submitted to the full conference committee for approval.

Once the conference committee has approved a compromise version, it sends a conference report to both houses. The House and Senate must then approve the new version before it can be sent on to the president.

Q 364. What does "too big to butcher" mean?

A Members of Congress sometimes use this expression to describe programs that have already cost so much money that it would seem wasteful to halt further funding. A program to develop a new weapons system might become "too big to butcher" after $10 billion has been sunk into it, for example, especially if enough progress has been made to show Congress there might eventually be a return on the investment. Nevertheless, in these times of tight budgets big programs do sometimes get cut even though large sums already have been committed to them. For example, the government's $8.2 billion program to build a huge particle accelerator in Texas was shut down recently in a cost-cutting move, even though a considerable amount of work on it had been completed.

Q 365. Does the Senate ever originate tax bills?

A The Constitution grants the power to originate revenue bills to the House, and normally these measures begin in the House Ways and Means Committee. The Senate Finance Committee usually begins Senate consideration of revenue measures once the bills have passed the House and routinely adds amendments to them.

There are some exceptions, though. The Senate Finance Committee sometimes begins work on revenue bills before the House has completed its work. Or the Senate may use its amendment power to create what is essentially a new bill. That happened in 1982, when the Senate originated the largest peacetime tax increase in U.S. history by adding amendments to a minor tax bill passed by the House.

Also, the Senate may originate the annual budget resolution, including revenue figures for upcoming years. But the resolution has no legal authority and does not actually raise any revenue.

Q 366. Who defends the president's budget in Congress?

A Representatives from federal agencies bear the brunt of defending the president's budget recommendations at appropriations committee hearings. They are supposed to support the president's spending decisions for individual agencies no matter what funding levels their agencies originally requested, although they usually can make their positions known through informal contacts with members of Congress. Presidential advisers and OMB officials testify before Congress on broad economic issues related to the budget and on the president's overall budget policy. OMB monitors testimony and other submissions to Congress to ensure they are consistent with the president's budget policy.

(See 272 How is the budget prepared? 299 Why is the president's annual budget proposal important?)

Q 367. What is scorekeeping?

A The Congressional Budget Office monitors legislation moving through Congress by providing estimates of what each bill will cost and how it will impact the overall budget for the year. These *scorekeeping reports,* as they are called, are issued by the House and Senate Budget Committees.

The reports show in detail how congressional action on individual bills will affect federal receipts, spending limits, the deficit, and the debt. That way members of Congress can see what must be done to make a particular bill fall within budget limits, and also can keep track of the cumulative effect of other measures that have already been approved. Scorekeeping was introduced by the Congressional Budget Control and Impoundment Act of 1974.

The CBO produces scorekeeping reports by tallying the estimated costs of pending and approved legislation against targets set by the annual budget resolution for spending, revenue, deficit, and debt levels. Budget resolution targets are enforced by procedural rules in the House and Senate. If pending legislation threatens to push spending beyond what was allocated to a committee, for example, the bill becomes subject to points of order, which may make passage difficult.

(See 322 Why is it that Congress has so much trouble keeping spending within a budget? 372 What did the Congressional Budget Control and Impoundment Act of 1974 accomplish? 383 What is a budget resolution?)

Q 368. What is reconciliation?

A Reconciliation is the name for the procedure Congress uses to change existing revenue and spending laws. The process was set up by the Congressional Budget Control and Impoundment Act of 1974 and comes into play in those years when Congress must adjust total revenue and spending to bring them into line with targets set by the annual budget resolution.

The process begins with *reconciliation instructions,* which are included in the annual budget resolution. The instructions name specific committees and say how much overall revenue or spending must be changed for agencies within the committee's jurisdiction. The committees themselves then decide what programs must be changed and by what dollar amounts to meet the targets.

Bills the committees finally write to specify the revenue or spending changes are combined into a *reconciliation bill.* The reconciliation bill must then pass both houses and be signed into law.

In the past, reconciliation instructions have largely been issued to those committees overseeing revenues and mandatory spending programs. Discretionary spending by authorization and appropriations committees is usually controlled through the annual appropriations process.

(See 162 Is there a difference between discretionary and mandatory spending? 383 What is a budget resolution? 464 When did Congress first use the budget reconciliation process to cut back expenditures for ongoing programs?)

▶ How does Congress raise the debt ceiling? *See 378 How is the debt ceiling changed?* ◀

Q 369. What is a continuing resolution?

A When Congress needs emergency funding to keep government agencies operating, it can pass a continuing resolution, or CR. Congress has resorted to this stopgap measure from time to time for over a century, but since the 1950s CRs have been a regular feature of the appropriations process. Congress's annual task of passing the thirteen regular appropriations bills that keep the government operating has become steadily more time consuming, because the government has grown in size and complexity. If any one of those regular appropriations bills has not been passed by the start of the fiscal year on October 1, the affected agencies run out of money and must shut down—unless Congress passes a continuing resolution.

Congress was forced to pass at least one continuing resolution a year between 1954 and 1991, except for 1988. Most were short-term measures, but since the 1970s Congress has steadily increased their scope. In 1986 Congress actually passed a continuing resolution that included all thirteen regular appropriations bills and made it effective for the whole fiscal year. Congress passed another omnibus CR in 1987, but since then has returned to using CRs as a temporary stopgap.

CRs are often used to pass unrelated but controversial measures, which are attached as amendments. Because the funding is urgently needed to keep the government operating, members of Congress and the president must weigh the political cost of delaying the CR against the worth of fighting the controversial amendments.

(See 273 What are the thirteen regular appropriations bills Congress must pass each year? 323 What is the largest single spending bill Congress has ever passed? 473 When was the first government shutdown and why did it happen?)

Q 370. For which fiscal year did Congress pass the most continuing resolutions?

A Congress was forced to fall back on a record thirteen continuing resolutions before passing the last appropriations bill for fiscal 1996. Wrangling between Republican conservatives and Democratic President Bill Clinton over budget priorities had continued through much of 1995 and well into 1996, delaying completion of the fiscal

1996 budget until April 1996. Because fiscal 1996 had begun October 1, 1995, Congress resorted to continuing resolutions to keep the government running.

The previous record was set in 1990, when the Democrats controlled Congress and Republican president George Bush was in the White House. Congress passed five continuing resolutions before completing the fiscal 1991 budget.

Q 371. Are annual appropriations necessary?

A Congress has appropriated at least some funds on a yearly basis since its very first session, even though the Constitution does not require it. But passing the thirteen regular appropriations bills each year has become an increasingly complex and time-consuming process, prompting some reformers to call for biennial appropriations—making appropriations every two years. Congress could pass supplementary spending bills as necessary during the two years.

Ideally, Congress would be able to focus on passing authorization bills in the first year of the biennial cycle, and then turn to appropriations bills in the next. The system would loosen congressional controls over spending. But by eliminating the yearly crush of budget work, it would allow Congress to focus on program performance, budget priorities, and long-term policy.

The 1993 National Performance Review supported biennial budgeting, but critics argue that about two-thirds of the budget is already obligated to mandatory spending and so would not fall within the new budget process.

(See 286 How much of the budget is now subject to annual approval by Congress? 344 Does the trend toward annual authorization of programs have any effect on Congress? 350 What happens to appropriations bills in the House and Senate?)

SPENDING CONTROL AND BUDGET CUTTING

Q 372. What are the pros and cons of stricter budget control?

A Over the years Republicans and Democrats alike have advanced sound reasons for spending federal dollars on various priorities (defense, Medicare, education, scientific research, and so on). But chronic deficits and the mushrooming federal debt finally forced Congress to confront the budgetary consequences of all these spending decisions and to examine the system it uses to write the budget itself.

An easy solution to the deficit problem would be to simply raise taxes, and in recent years liberals have favored tax hikes to help cut the deficit. But as politicians have long known, tax increases are not popular with voters—especially if Congress only creates new deficits by spending more once the tax has been passed. Another "after the fact" method to fix the budget is to cut spending. Conservatives found out in the mid-1990s, however, that voters want many of the entitlement programs targeted for deficit reduction.

Congress has been struggling with another approach for decades—how to control federal spending before the money is committed to agencies and programs. But the budgeting process is so complex and filled with so much uncertainty that the task at times has seemed almost impossible.

A system that imposed very strict controls on annual spending, for example, could prevent the government from responding to disasters or other unexpected emergencies for lack of money (an argument raised against the balanced budget amendment). And tight controls over spending do not sit well with congressional committees, which measure their power by how much spending *they* control. On the other hand, if spending controls are loose and without any real means of enforcement (as they were), spending and deficits will almost certainly rise (as they have). Time and again Congress has been unable to muster the political will to keep spending under control without some procedural mechanism to fall back on. The decades-long search for that mechanism has produced the budget resolution, reconciliation, scorekeeping, spending caps, and other devices, but only recently have serious efforts at controlling spending begun to bear fruit.

(See 387 What is a balanced budget amendment?)

Q 373. What one year between 1956 and the present did federal spending actually decline?

A The only year the government posted a decline in spending was during the Johnson administration—1965. Federal spending, which had been increasing because of Vietnam War costs, actually was $300 million lower in 1965, down from $118.5 billion in 1964. The combined spending of the war and President Lyndon Johnson's newly created Great Society programs produced a spending growth spurt of $16.3 billion the following year, however, and federal spending has not stopped growing since.

The spending rise in itself would probably not be an issue if it were matched by an equal rise in revenues. But Congress has been consistently spending more than it collects in revenue for decades. That in turn swelled the national debt—and interest payments—to a point where they raised serious concerns about getting federal spending under control.

> ***"The concept of budget control violates the second rule of congressional life: what is good for the member is not necessarily good for the institution. Enacting truly effective budget reform would require members to sacrifice much of their power within the institution. Authorization and appropriations subcommittee chairs would have to defer to the dictates of the budget committees or perhaps the party leadership on budgetary matters. Would voters be understanding if their members of Congress could no longer deliver the benefits of pork-barrel spending or prevent tax increases?"***
>
> —Daniel P. Franklin, *Making Ends Meet: Congressional Budgeting in the Age of Deficits* (1993)

(See 4 How much does the government spend in a year? 83 How have federal revenue and outlays grown over the years?)

Q 374. When did efforts to control spending begin in Congress?

A Congress has been trying to control its habit of overspending revenues since the end of World War II. The Legislative Reorganization Act of 1946 set up budget procedures in which a resolution of Congress would set maximum spending for the coming year. But the experiment proved a failure after just three years. In 1950 Congress had more success with an omnibus appropriations bill (instead of thirteen separate appropriations bills), but in 1951 returned to the system of separate appropriations. Later reform proposals during the 1950s and 1960s—such as forming a Joint Budget Committee, mandating a balanced budget, imposing spending ceilings, and so forth—all failed to win approval of both houses.

Then in the early 1970s, with deficits and the debt rising sharply because of Great Society programs and costs of the Vietnam War, President Richard Nixon fought a pitched political battle with Congress over his refusal to spend money it had appropriated. That finally forced Congress to act, and the result was the Congressional Budget Control and Impoundment Act of 1974. It provided the basis for Congress's first sustained effort to assert control over spending, though more than two decades later the problem has yet to be fully resolved.

(See 381 Which president resorted to impoundment to cut federal spending? 382 What did the Congressional Budget and Impoundment Control Act of 1974 accomplish?)

Q **375. What can presidents do to control spending?**

A Ever since 1921, when Congress made the president responsible for preparing the annual budget proposal, presidents have had some measure of control over federal spending, and the budget generally. Congress still has the ultimate authority over budget matters, though, limiting the president's power to raise or lower federal spending. This is especially true when the president belongs to one party and Congress is dominated by the other, which has often been the case in recent decades.

When the president wants to limit spending by Congress—or, as is the case with President Bill Clinton, to limit spending cuts by Congress—he has several options:

—Deliver a proposed budget to Congress that limits or increases spending to levels the president wants, either overall or in programs the president feels have greatest priority. A hostile Congress may well ignore the budget proposals, though.

—Veto spending measures the president deems too high or too low. Republican presidents Richard Nixon, Gerald Ford, Ronald Reagan, and George Bush all vetoed measures in their efforts to limit spending. Democratic president Bill Clinton has used his veto power to prevent Congress from making cuts in social spending he believed were too deep. In any case, a veto is only effective if Congress does not have the votes to override it.

—Refuse to spend money appropriated by Congress. President Richard Nixon used this technique to cut federal spending, but Congress has since made this device—called impoundment—all but impossible without congressional approval.

—Compromise. Go along with some high-spending programs favored by Congress in an effort to win cutbacks in others, or vice versa. Every president has engaged in the give-and-take process with Congress on budget matters. Congress has the upper hand, however, and if enough members are willing to vote for it, the budget will be larger or smaller accordingly.

—Go public. Every Republican president since Richard Nixon has complained about "big spending" liberals and otherwise railed against overspending by Congress. President Clinton has likewise gone public in recent budget battles with the Republican-controlled Congress, but his effort was mainly to limit spending cuts and tax cuts.

(See 295 Do we look to Congress or the President for leadership on economic issues? 299 Why is the president's annual budget proposal so important? 304 What role does the presidential veto play in the budget process? 381 Which president resorted to impoundment to cut federal spending?)

Q 376. What might happen if the government cut back spending too quickly?

A A sudden cut in federal spending, especially if it is large enough, could depress the economy and cause a recession. Toward the end of World War II, for example, many economists worried that the sudden drop in defense spending after the war might throw the economy into a major recession. In fact, federal spending plummeted from $90 billion in 1945 to $30 billion in 1948, and there was a recession, but it was short-lived. There was, as it turned out, considerable pent-up consumer demand that helped pave the way to a peacetime economy in which government spending was considerably less. Countries ravaged by World War II added to the demand for goods produced in the United States, and so helped to offset the loss of federal spending to the domestic economy.

Even smaller cutbacks that occur over a longer time period can have an impact on a specific industry or locale. The recent wave of military base closings, for example, posed serious economic hardships for the cities and towns that had come to depend on them for jobs and revenue. Defense cutbacks, and the earlier cuts in spending for space exploration, hit high-tech and aerospace industries hard, forcing layoffs of thousands of people.

Q 377. What are debt ceilings?

A At one time Congress authorized a specific amount of debt each time the Treasury issued securities to raise money. Beginning in 1917, though, the nature of statutory limits on government debt began to change, and since 1941 the debt limit has been a fixed ceiling on the total amount the federal government can borrow. The debt ceiling has not been an effective method of preventing overspending by the government, because every time deficits push the national debt up against the limit, Congress simply raises it. Since 1960 alone Congress has acted sixty-seven times to raise the limit, pass a temporary increase, or otherwise tinker with the debt limit.

Q 378. How is the debt ceiling changed?

A Congress can change the debt limit in two ways. One is to pass legislation specifying a new debt ceiling. The other is through a joint resolution setting the debt limit at the level specified in the budget resolution for the fiscal year. The main purpose of the budget resolution is to help Congress set overall spending goals, but it also specifies the debt limit.

By the rules of the House, once both the House and Senate have adopted the annual budget resolution, the approval of a separate joint resolution for the new debt ceiling is deemed automatic. The Senate can vote to change the limit, but once the amended joint resolution passes both houses, it is sent to the president for his signature. The debt ceiling has been raised many times by both methods.

(See 383 What is a budget resolution? 463 How did the Gephardt Rule sidestep the problem of raising the debt limit in the House?)

Q 379. In which year did Congress raise the debt ceiling the most times?

A The record stands at seven times, in 1990. Between August and October 1990, Congress passed six temporary measurers raising the debt limit from $3.12 trillion to $3.195 trillion. Finally, on November 5, it enacted the seventh bill, this time permanently raising the debt limit to $4.14 trillion.

Q 380. Have spending limits worked any better than debt ceilings?

A No, during the 1960s and early 1970s Congress consistently accepted and then sidestepped spending limits. With federal spending already beginning to rise rapidly in 1966, due to spending for the Vietnam War and Great Society programs, House Republicans tried unsuccessfully to cut a number of regular appropriations bills by 5 percent. Conservatives won a $4 billion cut the following year, though rises in mandatory spending forced a net increase of $1 billion in federal outlays. Congress passed spending ceilings for 1968, 1969, 1970, and 1971, only to raise them when spending threatened to exceed the limits. Though Presidents Richard Nixon and Gerald Ford called for spending limits each year from 1972 to 1976, Congress failed to pass any further annual spending limits. Instead it tried a new system based on the annual budget resolution, enacted in the Congressional Budget Control and Impoundment Act of 1974.

(See 284 What have been the major turning points in the history of federal budgeting? 382 What did the Congressional Budget Control and Impoundment Act accomplish?)

Q 381. Which president resorted to impoundment to cut federal spending?

A Because the Constitution does not specify whether presidents must spend money appropriated by Congress, it was possible for presidents to impound (refuse to spend) the money. Though presidents as far back as Thomas Jefferson had impounded funds from time to time, President Richard M. Nixon used impoundments so extensively he finally brought both the impoundment issue and Congress's lack of spending control to a head.

While President Nixon, a Republican, was in office, spending for Great Society social programs and the Vietnam War were rapidly increasing budget deficits. Democrats, who controlled Congress, rebuffed President Nixon's efforts at cutting back spending, but he retaliated by impounding funds he considered wasteful. By 1973 President Nixon's impoundments totaled more than $20 billion, and critics charged he was using them to curb or eliminate programs supported by Democrats. Congress finally became so irritated with the impoundments it effectively eliminated them by passing the 1974 Congressional Budget and Impoundment Control Act. But President Nixon had made his point. The act also set up a new budget process aimed at helping Congress get federal spending under control.

(See 382 What did the Congressional Budget and Impoundment Control Act of 1974 accomplish?)

Q 382. What did the Congressional Budget Control and Impoundment Act of 1974 accomplish?

A This act finally established the mechanism, the budget resolution, by which Congress could set overall budget priorities for the coming fiscal year, before actually starting work on the individual appropriations bills. It also set up new procedures making it all but impossible for presidents to impound appropriated funds without permission from Congress.

The new budget rules set up a budget committee in the House and Senate and established the Congressional Budget Office to provide nonpartisan budgetary analysis. The budget committees were given responsibility for reviewing the president's annual budget proposal, receiving budget recommendations from congressional committees, and making overall recommendations to Congress on budget policy.

Under the new budget procedure, Congress each year passes a budget resolution stating its budget priorities and setting spending and revenue targets. Then work on the thirteen annual appropriations bills begins. Individual committees must tailor revenue and spending bills under their jurisdiction to targets set for them in the annual budget resolution, a process called reconciliation. Once this work is done, the thirteen annual appropriations bills can then be considered and enacted by Congress.

New impoundment procedures contained in the act require the president to notify Congress before canceling spending for a program (called a rescission). The spending cannot be canceled, however, unless Congress approves it within forty-five days. Presidents are allowed to temporarily delay spending (called a deferral) for various reasons, unless Congress votes against it.

The new budget system nearly foundered in the 1970s and early 1980s. Congress regularly missed deadlines and failed to muster the resolve to curb spending until budget deficits passed the $200 billion mark in the mid-1980s. That finally prompted passage of a new budget reform measure, the Balanced Budget and Emergency Deficit Act of 1985. (See 388 What was the Gramm-Rudman-Hollings Act all about and what happened to it?)

(See 368 What is reconciliation? 384 What is a rescission? 455 What were the battle lines in Congress over the Congressional Budget and Impoundment Act?)

Q 383. What is a budget resolution?

A A budget resolution lays out the spending and revenue goals Congress wants to achieve in the budget for the upcoming fiscal year. It is a concurrent resolution of Congress and so does not have the force of law. But it does set binding totals for spending and revenues that Congress will later incorporate into laws actually appropriating funds.

The budget resolution contains both overall budget goals and specific targets set for budget categories (called functions). The overall budget goals include total revenue for the fiscal year, total spending (including loan obligations and guarantees), the projected deficit, and the debt limit. The specific targets apportion specific amounts of the spending total to the budget categories. Authorization and appropriations committees with jurisdiction over programs in the budget categories must tailor legislation to meet these targets. Budget resolutions may also include reconciliation instructions to committees with jurisdiction over certain programs.

Congress is supposed to pass the budget resolution by April 15 to allow time for passing the regular appropriations bills before the fiscal year starts on October 1. It has met the deadline only rarely, even when it was May 15 (until fiscal 1987).

(See 292 What are functions? 368 What is reconciliation? 457 When did Congress pass its first budget resolution?)

Q 384. What is a rescission?

A When the president wants to cut back spending previously approved by Congress for an agency or program, he submits a rescission request to Congress. The request specifies the amount of the cut and estimates the impact. Congress then has forty-five days to pass a bill approving the spending cut, all or in part. If Congress takes no action within the forty-five days, the rescission request is refused and the president must allow the money to be spent.

The rescission mechanism was set up by the Congressional Budget and Impoundment Control Act of 1974. Rescissions replaced impoundments, a procedure by which presidents could refuse to spend money without consulting Congress. President Richard Nixon's extensive use of impoundments to cut spending finally provoked Congress to sharply limit the practice. Generally speaking, Congress has not responded favorably to rescission requests.

Q 385. Which president made the most rescission requests?

A President Ronald Reagan is far and away the leader in this category. During his eight years in office he sent 602 rescission requests to Congress, asking for over $43 billion in spending cuts to programs. Congress approved just $15.6 billion of the rescission requests, $10.8 billion of it during President Reagan's first year in office, 1981.

President George Bush was a distant second with 169 rescission requests for $13.3 billion. Congress approved just 34 for about $2.4 billion. Presidents Gerald Ford and Jimmy Carter also submitted numerous requests (152 and 122, respectively) and both fared about as well as other presidents with Congress. President Bill Clinton proposed 125 rescissions (through 1996), of which Congress approved 82 for a total of $3.3 billion in cuts.

Q 386. What role did Speaker Tip O'Neill play in the budget debates of the 1980s?

A An old school ward politician, House Speaker Tip O'Neill became the Democratic party's standard bearer after President Jimmy Carter failed to win reelection in 1980. President Ronald Reagan's overwhelming popularity and the stronger Republican minority swept into the House on his coattails left Speaker O'Neill and his party on the defensive during Reagan's first year. President Reagan won big cuts in spending and a massive tax cut as well in 1981, but a recession in 1981–1982 tipped the balance on budget matters back in O'Neill's favor (conservative southern Democrats refused to back further Reagan budget initiatives).

After that, Speaker O'Neill led the successful liberal Democratic opposition to President Reagan's efforts to further cut social spending programs. A fiercely partisan politician, O'Neill worked to pack committees with loyal liberal Democrats and

"I've been one of the great spenders of all time. . .I admit it."

—Speaker Tip O'Neill Jr. (D-Mass.), speaking in 1981 on his record as a liberal politician

refused to allow Republicans committee seats in proportion to their numbers. From 1983 onward, budget battles between President Reagan and Democrats led by Speaker O'Neill brought the budget process to a virtual standstill, contributing to the gridlock and huge deficits of the 1980s.

▶ How did the government shutdowns figure in the budget debate? *See 473 When was the first government shutdown and why did it happen?* ◀

Q 387. What is a balanced budget amendment?

A A balanced budget amendment is a proposed constitutional amendment that proponents believe would be an effective way to control federal spending. If passed by Congress and ratified by the states, the amendment would require that annual federal spending be kept at or below revenue collected during the year. The most recent version, which failed in the Senate by one vote in 1997, called for balancing the budget by 2002. Every year after that the budget would have to be balanced, unless three-fifths majorities in both houses of Congress voted to waive the requirement.

The balanced budget amendment has been a leading issue for conservative Republicans since the late 1970s, and conservative Democrats in Congress who support efforts to rein in federal spending have voted for balanced budget amendments in the past. Democrats led by President Bill Clinton opposed the amendment in 1997, however, gathering support for its defeat by saying the amendment might threaten Social Security benefits and claiming the president's balanced budget plan would make the amendment unnecessary. Critics also worried that such an amendment might force the government to make unnecessarily deep spending cuts and/or encourage the use of bookkeeping tricks to meet rigid budget goals. The 1997 balanced budget deal struck between the Republican-controlled Congress and President Clinton further undermined support for a constitutional amendment.

A nearly successful movement to adopt a balanced budget amendment began in the states during the 1970s. By 1984 thirty-two state legislatures had adopted resolutions calling for a constitutional convention to draft the amendment, and only two more states were needed. But the movement faltered soon after, and some states rescinded their resolutions.

Meanwhile, the balanced budget amendment became a rallying cry of the conservative movement led by Ronald Reagan in the late 1970s and the 1980s. During

Reagan's presidency and that of fellow Republican president George Bush, bills for balanced budget amendments passed one house but were defeated in the other (1982, 1986, 1990). President Clinton also led successful Democratic opposition to Republican-backed balanced budget amendments in Congress during 1995 and 1996.

(See 13 Why does the government spend more than it takes in? 14 Why doesn't the government just keep raising taxes to meet its expenses? 20 Should the budget be balanced? 320 What is "the power of the purse"? 322 Why is it that Congress has so much trouble keeping spending within the budget?)

Q 388. What was the Gramm-Rudman-Hollings Act all about and what happened to it?

A Responding to the $200 billion deficits of the mid 1980s, budget reformers in Congress pushed through a radical budget cutting measure called the Balanced Budget and Emergency Deficit Control Act of 1985—more familiarly known as the Gramm-Rudman-Hollings Act, after its three principal sponsors in Congress.

The act set annual targets for the deficit, reducing it in steps to bring the budget into balance in five years (by 1991). It also installed a new feature in the budget process—sequestration, or automatic spending cuts (see next question). These cuts would be activated if Congress passed a budget with a deficit over the target level.

The plan appeared to be working in 1986 when the first round of mandatory cuts ($11.7 billion) was ordered. The Supreme Court created a temporary snag, however, when it ruled part of the plan unconstitutional. It said using the Government Accounting Office (GAO)—a part of Congress—to ratify the amount of the automatic spending cuts violated the separation of powers doctrine. But budget reformers soon fixed that problem by having the OMB—part of the executive branch—ratify the cuts.

Automatic spending cuts of $23 billion were scheduled for October 1987, at least until the stock market crash of 1987 sent shock waves throughout the financial world. Fears about a major financial panic, or, worse, a depression, forced President Reagan and Congress to try to restore public confidence. As part of that effort, they held the 1987 budget summit to hammer out an agreement on the deficit. The agreement put together $76 billion in cuts over two years (1988 and 1989) and rendered Gramm-Rudman automatic cuts unnecessary.

The Gramm-Rudman act was soon to be completely overtaken by events. Budget battles between President George Bush and Congress in 1989 had dragged out approval of the 1990 budget, and serious problems loomed ahead for the 1991

Speaking of the Gramm-Rudman-Hollings Act, one of its chief sponsors, Sen. Phil Gramm (R-Tex.), once described it as the "worst way of doing budgets except for all the other ways we've tried."

budget. The massive cost of the savings and loan bailout and the 1990 recession combined to make meeting the Gramm-Rudman deficit target of $64 billion all but impossible. The OMB had projected the deficit would exceed $169 billion. Congress had no choice but to scrap Gramm-Rudman in favor of a new budget control plan, the Budget Enforcement Act of 1990.

Q 389. What are automatic spending cuts?

A Automatic spending cuts were the "teeth" in the Gramm-Rudman-Hollings Act. If members of Congress failed to make the tough spending and revenue decisions needed to reduce the deficit to the required level, the act mandated automatic spending cuts (called *sequestration* of funds) to do it for them. Half the cuts would come from defense and half from nondefense programs, and the cuts were to be spread evenly across all affected programs. No cuts were permitted for Social Security, programs for the poor (such as food stamps), interest on the debt, and veterans' benefits. Cuts were limited for Medicaid and the student loan program.

The OMB and CBO got the job of monitoring federal spending, revenue, and the size of the deficit. The OMB also projected the size of automatic spending cuts needed to meet deficit targets. The OMB then notified the president if automatic spending cuts were needed. It was the president's job to issue a sequestration order in August, putting a temporary hold on spending. A second order in mid-October then made the cuts permanent.

Q 390. What changes in the budget process did the Budget Enforcement Act of 1990 make?

A The rigid Gramm-Rudman timetable for deficit reduction had not taken into account unforeseen economic problems (a recession and the savings and loan bailout). By 1990 it had become clear that meeting the 1991 deficit target of $64 billion would be virtually impossible, forcing Congress to scrap the rigid deficit targets and modify the system of automatic cuts. These changes were made in the Budget Enforcement Act of 1990 (BEA), which itself was part of the 1990 deficit reduction package passed by Congress.

BEA set *adjustable* deficit targets that allowed for unexpected economic changes and unforeseen rises in entitlement program costs. For fiscal 1991 to 1993, BEA imposed separate spending caps for defense, domestic, and international programs. Funds are automatically sequestered if spending exceeds one of these caps, but cuts are limited to only those programs within the cap. The president can authorize spending above the cap in times of war or disaster without triggering automatic cuts (as President George Bush did during the 1991 Persian Gulf War).

The act targets discretionary spending and does nothing to control costs of existing entitlement programs. If spending increases because more people become eligible for Social Security benefits, for example, BEA does not compensate by enforcing cuts elsewhere. But it did set up the PAYGO system to control any new or expanded benefits of entitlement programs. New spending for entitlement benefits, or any revenue loss, must be offset by cuts in another entitlement program or by revenue gains elsewhere.

The three separate spending caps were replaced by a single cap on discretionary spending for fiscal 1994 and 1995. BEA rules have since been extended to 1998.

(See 362 What does PAYGO mean? 367 What is scorekeeping? 476 What were the budget summits all about? 480 What price did President Bush pay for going back on his campaign pledge, "Read my lips, no new taxes"?)

Q 391. Did President Ronald Reagan cut the size of government?

A No. Though he campaigned hard against the Democratic opposition in Congress for spending cuts and smaller government, President Reagan's two terms actually brought increases in federal spending and the size of government. Annual federal spending rose $386 billion, from $678 billion in 1981 to $1.06 trillion in 1988, President Reagan's last full year in office. The federal deficit more than doubled from almost $79 billion to $155 billion, and total federal civilian employment went up as well, from about 2.16 million in 1981 to 2.22 million in 1988.

What President Reagan did accomplish, however, was to force budget issues into the national arena and to begin making the public aware that a balanced budget was possible. Furthermore, he promoted the ideas that reducing the size of government and the amount it spends were ways to solve the deficit problem. In that regard, he set the stage for all the efforts at downsizing and spending control that followed, both during his two terms and after. His introduction of income tax indexation (to adjust for inflation) and budget summitry also had far-reaching impact on the budget debate.

"A true economic policy revolution means risky and mortal combat with all the mass constituencies of Washington's largesse—Social Security recipients, veterans, farmers, educators, state and local officials, the housing industry and many more."

—David Stockman, former director of the Office and Management and Budget under President Reagan
[as quoted in Brian Kelly's *Adventures in Porkland*]

Needless to say, it would have been better to have made the point without the large deficits of the 1980s, but President Reagan was far from solely responsible for them. Part of the spending increase during the Reagan years did stem from the president's pledge to rebuild U.S. military forces. That raised defense spending by about 5 percent of annual federal outlays. But the larger part of the overall spending increase during his term came from the skyrocketing costs of entitlement programs such as Medicaid, Medicare, and Social Security, which liberals in Congress adamantly defended and the president could not control.

Reagan's defense budget increases, about $10 billion to $25 billion a year, wound up adding some $150 billion a year to defense spending by 1988. Meanwhile, annual spending for social programs (discretionary and entitlement) increased by $171 billion by 1988.

President Reagan did manage to trim 29,000 federal employees from civilian agencies, but by 1988 federal employment showed a net increase because the civilian workforce at the Department of Defense had grown.

(See 12 When did the government post the largest deficit in its history? 45 What did President Bill Clinton mean when he said the era of big government is over? 143 How has the government gotten bigger over the years? 466 What was President Reagan's economic record? 468 What did the Reagan tax cut and budget reduction package do?)

Q 392. What is downsizing?

A Downsizing is a term that first appeared in the mid-1970s and refers to permanent reductions in the workforce of a company, organization, and, more recently, the federal government. Hiring freezes, early retirement packages, and layoffs all have been used to make the personnel reductions. The idea is to reduce costs and create a leaner, more efficient operation. Downsizing does force greater efficiency, but by placing a greater workload on the remaining staff it can also result in delays and outright cuts in services. Another danger of excessive downsizing is that when longtime employees are lost, valuable work experience goes with them.

Figure 4-2 Executive Branch Civilian Employment, 1965–1996 (excluding Postal Service)

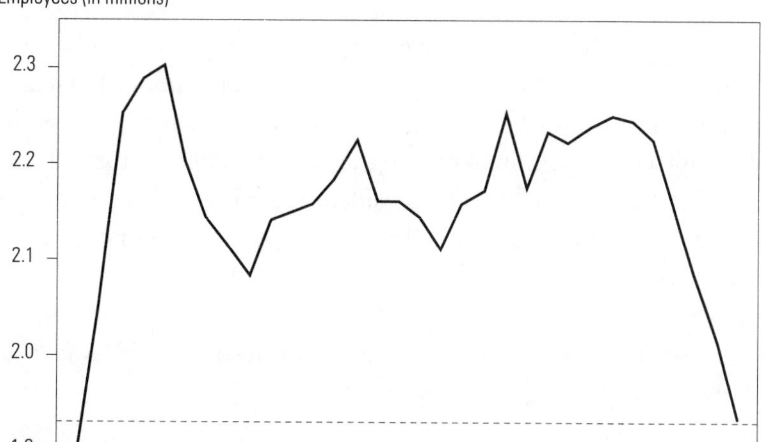

Note: Data is end-of-year count.

Q 393. What cuts in the federal government has President Bill Clinton made?

A While resisting big cuts in social spending, where spending growth is highest, President Bill Clinton has nevertheless managed to cut the deficit sharply (from $255 billion in 1993 to an estimated $70 billion or so in 1997). He has done it with tax increases, caps on discretionary spending, and smaller cutbacks to reduce waste and inefficiency (for example, he eliminated two hundred programs and closed two thousand obsolete field offices). Clinton had considerable help from the economy, however. Better-than-expected economic growth kept federal revenues expanding while the president chipped away at the spending side of the budget.

An important part of President Clinton's cutbacks was downsizing the government workforce (see Figure 4-2). By the beginning of his second term he had eliminated over 250,000 positions through normal attrition and early retirement packages. At about 1.9 million employees, the federal civilian workforce in 1997 was at its lowest level in thirty years.

Q 394. What did Executive Order 12857 do?

A Issued by President Bill Clinton, this executive order marked a tentative first step toward controlling spending on mandatory entitlement programs. The cost of entitlement programs has been mushrooming, and because anyone who qualifies for benefits is entitled to them by law, keeping spending under control has been extremely difficult.

Clinton's executive order set annual spending targets for total mandatory spending from 1994 to 1997. Only federal deposit insurance and interest payments (also mandatory) were not included, and targets are adjusted each year according to the number of recipients in entitlement programs and other factors. If mandatory spending is higher than the targets, the president must inform Congress, which then may decide to decrease direct spending, increase revenues, or do nothing at all.

One problem with this system is that it has no teeth. Congress need do nothing at all if spending exceeds targets. Another is that adjustments are only required when the number of beneficiaries goes up. The target is not lowered if fewer people than expected receive benefits.

(See 170 Why spend tax dollars on social programs? 171 Why has social spending risen by so much? 172 Can entitlement programs be changed?)

Q 395. How has Speaker Newt Gingrich influenced the budget debates of the 1990s?

A Combative and possessed of boundless confidence, House Speaker Newt Gingrich (R-Ga.) was the architect of the conservative Republican resurgence in the mid-1990s that finally pushed Congress over the last hurdles to a balanced budget. Convinced that "politics matters," Gingrich has been promoting conservative Republican ideas—and fearlessly attacking Democrats—ever since arriving in the House of Representatives in 1978. But it was his strategy of using the much-maligned Contract with America to nationalize congressional races in 1994 that won a Republican majority in the House for the first time in forty years.

The victory thrust Gingrich into national prominence and the House speakership. He delivered on his campaign pledge to push the conservative agenda through the House in the first one hundred days of the 104th Congress, but his combative style during the government shutdowns over budget issues in late 1995 nearly proved his undoing. While substantial public support for balancing the budget remained, Gingrich's intransigence sent his popularity rating into a tailspin. The Speaker all but disappeared from public view, at least until conservatives showed they could hold onto Republican majorities in both houses of Congress during the 1996 elections.

Meanwhile, in a considerably more low-key fashion, Republican conservatives continued along the path set by Gingrich, scoring long-sought victories on welfare reform, the line-item veto, downsizing of liberal "big government," domestic spending cuts, and finally, in 1997, the elusive balanced budget deal with President Bill Clinton.

(See 397 What was the 1997 balanced budget agreement? 483 How did the Republican sweep in the 1994 congressional elections change the budget debate? 484 What did the Republican Contract with America try to do? 485 What effect did the 1995–1996 government shutdowns have on the budget debate? 488 What did the 1997 balanced budget agreement do to cut taxes?)

Q 396. If we are downsizing the government and cutting the deficit, why is federal spending still growing?

A Federal spending was expected to grow by some $254 billion between 1996 and the year 2000, despite all budget cutting efforts up to the beginning of fiscal 1998. That was still more than the government expected to collect in revenues for the period, but budget cutters could claim a partial victory—spending *growth* has declined.

Part of the problem with reining in federal spending is that *mandatory spending*—including entitlement programs and interest on the debt—accounts for about 66 percent of the budget. Entitlement programs must be fully funded each year unless Congress changes laws governing these programs, and until the 1990s Congress was reluctant to do so because the programs were so popular. So in the past, budget cutters were only able to focus on the remaining 34 percent of the budget, the so-called *discretionary spending,* which pays for such things as defense and operating the government.

The fact that entitlements are the fastest growing sector of federal spending has further complicated spending control. The total growth of annual discretionary spending was expected to be just $29.5 billion between 1996 and 2000, while annual mandatory spending will mushroom by $224.5 billion. More people are becoming eligible for entitlement programs like Social Security and Medicare, and Medicaid costs have continued to rise as well. Social Security, for example, will account for $70 billion more in federal spending by 2000.

Q 397. What was the 1997 balanced budget agreement?

A Culminating over two years of intense wrangling between the Republican-controlled Congress and President Bill Clinton, Congress finally enacted legislation to balance the budget in five years. As outlined in May 1997 and confirmed by budget reconciliation bills passed in August, the budget agreement will achieve a small projected surplus in fiscal 2002 and will yield additional surpluses between 2002 and 2007.

Three views of the balanced budget agreement:

"[This is] the dawning of a new era, an era where we recognize the limits of government."

—House Budget Committee chairman John R. Kasich (R-Ohio)

"It is a quick fix for the next few years, not a reliable blueprint for our nation's future."

—House minority leader Richard Gephardt (D-Mo.)

"The true hero is this stupendous economy. . . . The economy has done more to reduce the deficit than the politicians have."

—Concord Coalition director Martha Phillips

The budget agreement included spending cuts and other savings (about $263 billion), tax cuts ($95 billion net), and new spending (some $30 billion)—all tallied over the next five years. Spending cuts ranged from $115 billion in Medicare and $10.5 billion in Medicaid to $77 billion in defense and $61 billion in other discretionary spending. The budget agreement embraced a wide range of tax cuts (*see* 488 What did the 1997 balanced budget agreement do to cut taxes?), established a new program to provide health care to poor children (*see* 192 What Medicaid reforms did the 1997 balanced budget deal make?), provided a quick-fix for Medicare (*see* 191 What changes in Medicare did the 1997 balanced budget deal make?), and increased federal aid to the District of Columbia (*see* 267 What did the government's plan to rescue the District of Columbia do?). The new spending sought by Democrats included billions for additional Pell grants for college students, increased health care for children in low-income families, and welfare benefits for legal immigrants.

While the budget deal reached a goal long-sought by Republicans—a balanced budget—it left a considerable amount of work to be done on some of the most pressing long-term budget issues, especially problems with controlling costs of Social Security, Medicare, Medicaid, and other entitlement programs. There was also the nagging problem of whether current projections—on which the formula for balancing the budget is based—are correct. Among the most critical assumptions budget planners made was that there would be no recession between now and 2002.

(See 171 Why has social spending risen by so much? 191 What changes in Medicare did the 1997 balanced budget deal make? 192 What Medicaid reforms did the 1997 budget agreement make? 267 What did the government's plan to rescue the District of Columbia do? 395 How has Speaker Newt Gingrich influenced the budget debates of the 1990s? 488 What did the 1997 balanced budget agreement do to cut taxes?)

V

BUDGET TIME LINE—HIGHLIGHTS FROM THE PAST 65 YEARS

IN GENERAL

Q 398. What was the "classical" view of the economy?

A Classical theory remained the dominant economic theory until the depression shattered the economy in the 1930s. This theory described the economy as a naturally self-adjusting mechanism that worked so long as things like supply and demand, wages and prices, and savings and investment were allowed to balance themselves against each other without interference. Classical economists thought wages and prices, for example, balanced supply and demand.

Too much demand for available goods, according to classical theory, pushed prices up (and thus slowed demand) until demand finally came into balance with supply. Too little demand caused prices to fall. The free-market balancing mechanism was also supposed to automatically eliminate unemployment: If there were too many workers for the existing demand, classical theorists insisted, wages would fall until employers could afford to hire more workers.

Prolonged double-digit unemployment during the 1930s shook the long-held belief that wages and prices in a free market would adjust naturally and keep workers employed. The realization ushered in the era of Keynesian economics and the federal government's efforts to stabilize economic ups and downs through fiscal policy (federal taxing and spending policies).

(See 26 Who or what determines supply and demand? 55 What is a recession? A depression? 62 Does "laissez-faire" mean more or less government intervention in the economy? 63 What exactly is Keynesian economics? 64 What is "stabilization policy"? 68 Can we "fine tune" the economy? 69 What is monetary policy? 298 What have been the successes and failures of past fiscal policy?)

Q 399. How have fundamental attitudes about federal budget policy changed since the country was formed?

A During the first decades after the Constitution was adopted, most people believed the government should strive for a balanced budget (during peacetime), should keep federal spending to a minimum, and should work toward eliminating the national debt altogether. The federal government was supposed to play only a limited role in society, one focused on such basic "public good" functions as operating the executive, legislative, and judicial branches, providing for the national defense, and overseeing the country's monetary system.

The Civil War ushered in greater tolerance for a continuing national debt, though, and the debt rose from $90.6 million in 1861 to $2.8 billion by 1866. After the war the government continued trying to balance the budget and reduce the debt. But there was a new emphasis on servicing the debt, as opposed to eliminating it. In fact, Congress had already passed—in 1847—a permanent, open-ended authorization for paying all interest on the national debt as it came due.

The government did pay down the debt, which hit a post–Civil War low of $961 million in 1893 and then hovered in the $1.1 billion to $1.2 billion range until the United States entered World War I. Wartime spending pushed the debt to a new peak of $25.5 billion by 1919.

During the early 1900s there remained a strong commitment to minimizing federal spending, balancing the budget, and reducing—if not eliminating—the national debt. Between 1919 and 1930 the federal government orchestrated surpluses that actually reduced the national debt to a post–World War I low of $16.2 billion in 1930. But the shock of the Great Depression soon brought a sea change in fundamental attitudes about budget policy. (See next question.)

(See 62 Does "laissez-faire" mean more or less government intervention in the economy? 127 When did Congress make an open-ended commitment to pay interest on the debt? 133 What has the federal debt been over the years?)

Q 400. What effect did the 1930s depression have on the fundamental philosophy behind federal spending?

A Sentiment for a stronger federal role in economic and social matters already existed in the early 1900s. But the turning point did not come until the country experienced the devastating economic collapse of the Great Depression in the 1930s. Unemployment jumped to 24.9 percent by 1933, and millions struggled just to feed themselves

> ***"The programs inaugurated during the last four years to combat the depression and to initiate many needed reforms have cost large sums of money, but the benefits obtained from them are far outweighing their costs. We shall soon be reaping the full benefits of those programs and shall have at the same time a balanced budget that will also include provision for reduction of the public debt."***
>
> —President Franklin Roosevelt, 1937

and their families. People desperately needed help, and only the federal government seemed capable of pulling the economy, and the country, out of the depression.

From that time forward, federal spending has been a basic tool of the government's fiscal and social policy, both to provide for the immediate needs of the disadvantaged and to stimulate the economy generally. Support for keeping spending within the limits of revenues—a balanced budget—did not disappear altogether. But accepted federal policy now included deficit spending during economic emergencies and to promote the social welfare, as well as to defend the country during wartime.

Although federal spending by itself did not cure the depression, it did ease suffering during the crisis and helped keep the economy going until the recovery.

(See 412 What caused the Great Depression? 413 What did President Franklin Roosevelt's New Deal do to cure the Great Depression?)

Q 401. What was the impact of the new federal spending policy?

A Few would question that the conservative balanced budget policy had to be abandoned during the Great Depression and World War II. But by the time these emergencies had passed, considerable public support existed for expanding the federal government's role in society even further. On the one hand, there were real social and economic needs public officials felt the government should address, and on the other, Keynesian economists actually supported increased federal spending during nonemergencies as a way to stimulate the economy.

But with the passing of the "outdated" balanced budget policy, Congress and the president no longer had a yardstick by which to judge how many new programs the government, and the economy supporting it, could afford. Who was to say that school lunches for needy children were more important than job training programs for their jobless parents?

Deficit spending, once an emergency measure, handed the government a way to undertake more and more of these new programs, while temporarily avoiding the higher taxes needed to pay for them. Over the next decades this unleashing of federal spending led to a phenomenal expansion of the government, its budgets (and deficits), and the national debt. Congress has mounted serious efforts to restore some control over federal spending only since the 1980s.

(See 372 What are the pros and cons of stricter spending control?)

▶ How has the budget process changed over the years? *See 284 What have been the major turning points in the history of federal budgeting? 286 How much of the budget is now subject to annual approval by Congress?*

Is the debt getting larger or smaller? *See 134 Has the national debt ever gone down in recent years? 373 What one year between 1956 and the present did the budget actually decline?* ◀

Q 402. Which presidents substantially expanded the social "safety net" programs?

A Presidents Franklin Roosevelt and Lyndon Johnson are probably best known for expanding the social safety net programs during their administrations. President Franklin Roosevelt, of course, created the foundation for these programs in response to the Great Depression of the 1930s.

Among the many programs established by President Roosevelt's New Deal are Social Security and the federal unemployment insurance program. President Johnson's Great Society program expanded existing programs like Social Security and also created new ones to improve civil rights, health care, education, housing, and other aspects of American life. Among President Johnson's most notable new programs were Medicare and Medicaid.

(See 143 How has the government gotten bigger over the years? 414 What were the most important new social spending programs enacted during President Franklin Roosevelt's New Deal? 437 What did President Lyndon Johnson's Great Society program attempt to do?)

Q 403. What percentage of GDP did federal spending amount to in 1930? In 1996?

A Federal spending amounted to just 3.3 percent of GDP in 1930, and reflected traditional attitudes toward government's limited role in society. Spending began rising under President Herbert Hoover in response to the widening depression though (6.8 percent in 1932), and reached its high for the 1930s under President Franklin Roosevelt—10.6 percent in 1934. The World War II years saw federal spending at its highest in relation to GDP this century—44.2 percent of GDP in 1944.

Federal government expansion, and growth of federal benefits to individuals, has pushed spending well above New Deal era levels, and since 1952 federal outlays have never dipped below 17 percent of GDP.

Spending has remained above 20 percent of GDP since 1975, though by 1996 it was falling (back to 20.8 percent of GDP). The postwar highwater mark for federal spending relative to GDP occurred during Reagan's term—23.6 percent in 1983.

(See 28 How fast has the economy been growing over the years? 83 How have federal revenue and outlays grown over the years? 143 How has the government gotten bigger over the years? 161 How many people receive federal benefits?)

Q 404. How strong has economic growth been since World War II?

A Economists use the annual increase in GDP as their measure of economic growth. (GDP is the total output of goods and services during a given year.) From the end of World War II to the mid-1990s, the economy grew at an average rate of about 3 percent a year. But postwar growth proceeded in three distinct phases.

* The first phase saw a 0.2 percent per year average between 1946 and 1951. The average is deceptively low because of a big drop caused by demobilization after World War II.
* The second phase was characterized by a 3.4 percent a year average (moderate-to-high growth) between 1952 and 1969. During the Eisenhower administration GDP increased on average 2.3 percent a year. The Kennedy-Johnson years posted high growth rates, with GDP increasing over 5 percent during four years (1962, 1964, 1965, 1966).
* The third period was one of moderating growth, about 2.5 percent on average, stretching from 1970 to the mid-1990s and including six recessions.

The first phase includes the largest postwar GDP drop, 20.6 percent in 1946, because of demobilization, and the largest postwar GDP growth, 9.9 percent in 1951, because of the Korean War buildup. The uninterrupted growth between 1959 and 1969 was the longest postwar economic expansion. The Reagan-Bush era economic expansion lasting from 1983 to 1990 was the second-longest postwar growth spurt.

(See 28 How fast has the economy been growing over the years?)

Q 405. Under which president was economic growth the highest?

A President John F. Kennedy's three years in office saw the highest average GDP growth rate, 4.8 percent. Interestingly, President Gerald Ford had the second highest rate, 4.6 percent. President George Bush, whose only term coincided with a recession and weak economic recovery, had the lowest average growth rate, 1.5 percent.

(See 64 What is stabilization policy? 65 What is fiscal policy? 295 Do we look to Congress or the president for leadership on economic issues? 298 What have been the successes and failures of past fiscal policy?)

Q 406. How has unemployment changed over the years?

A The unemployment rate is the percentage of the workforce that is jobless and actively seeking work. It tends to rise during recessions and fall once the economy begins recovering. Unemployment is politically a very sensitive issue, and since the 1940s the government has been committed to keeping unemployment as low as possible. Nevertheless, the average unemployment rate for any given year tends to be slightly higher in more recent decades than in the 1940s and 1950s. That is true because a higher percentage of the population is working (up from 55.8 percent in 1946 to 66.2 percent in the mid-1990s). The overall average unemployment rate since World War II is about 5.8 percent. Major ups and downs in the rate include:

* Average unemployment during the Truman years was largely at or below 4 percent (1949–1950 excepted), but it crept upward during the Eisenhower years to 5.4 percent.
* The Kennedy-Johnson years brought declining unemployment, from over 6 percent in 1961 to 3.5 percent in 1969.
* The recessions of the 1970s (1970, 1975) and the influx of baby boomers and women into the workforce pushed the average rate back up into the 6 percent range for much of the decade (it topped 8 percent during the 1975 recession).
* Recessions in 1980 and 1981–1982 pushed unemployment to new highs before the Reagan economic expansion pulled the average unemployment rate down to 5.3 percent.
* Unemployment again rose for a time because of the 1990–1991 recession.

(See 32 How many people are working in the United States? 33 Does full employment help or hurt the economy? 422 Why did Congress pass the Employment Act of 1946?)

Q 407. Which postwar president posted the lowest and highest average unemployment rates?

A Though presidents are largely captives of economic conditions during their terms of office, their economic policies can certainly influence the unemployment rate.

Among the postwar presidents, Lyndon Johnson enjoyed the lowest average unemployment rate, 3.8 percent. President Harry Truman did second best, with 4 percent for his eight years in office. President Gerald Ford had the worst record, though his 7.4 percent average unemployment was for less than one term (1974–1977) and included the 1975 recession.

President Ronald Reagan's 7.2 percent average unemployment rate was second-to-last, though the 1982 recession skewed his average. The 9.7 percent average unemployment for 1982 was a postwar high for any given year. But because the strong economic recovery began in 1983, Reagan also posted a larger reduction in average unemployment than any other postwar president—2.3 percent.

(See 32 How many people are working in the United States? 43 Do Americans vote their pocketbooks?)

Q 408. How have tax revenues as a share of GDP changed since World War II?

A Surprisingly, though actual revenue from taxes has risen consistently over the years, tax revenues as a share of GDP have remained within a fairly narrow range, fluctuating for the most part between 16 percent and 19.5 percent of GDP. It has been higher or lower for only a very few years since World War II. The all-time low of 14.8 percent was reached in 1950, and the high of 20.2 percent was recorded twice, in 1969 and 1981. In all, taxes as a share of GDP rose above 19 percent on four occasions, 1952–1953 (the Korean War), 1959–1970 (the Vietnam War), 1979–1982 (inflation-induced bracket creep), and 1987–1989 (following the 1986 tax reform).

The average share since World War II has been about 18.2 percent, although Presidents Harry Truman, Dwight Eisenhower, John F. Kennedy, and Gerald Ford all had lower averages.

(See 83 How have federal revenues and outlays grown over the years?)

Q 409. Under which president have average tax revenues been lowest? Highest?

A Tax revenues as a percent of GDP were on average lowest during President Harry Truman's term of office (1945–1953). Tax revenues under Truman averaged 17.2 percent of GDP, but the difference between lowest and highest averages was not especially wide, just 2.2 percent. Still, that 2 percent difference amounts to considerable revenue, somewhere between $120 billion and $180 billion in a $6 trillion economy.

President Jimmy Carter had the highest average, 19.4 percent of GDP, in part because of "bracket creep" caused by inflation. Interestingly, President Ronald Reagan had the second highest average, 18.7 percent of GDP, even though he pushed through a major tax cut early in his first term.

Of course, presidents alone do not set tax policy—ultimately Congress and the president share the responsibility. Also remember that tax rates are sometimes used to stimulate or restrain the economy.

Q 410. Under which presidents did we have the largest personal income tax cuts? Tax increases?

A Traditional party labels blur somewhat when you look at changes in personal income tax revenues. These revenues registered their largest postwar decline during the Nixon years, when they dropped by 2.8 percent of total tax revenues. Presidents Ronald Reagan, John F. Kennedy, and George Bush also reduced personal income taxes as a share of total tax revenues (−2.7 percent, −0.6 percent, −0.5 percent). Given the oft-repeated criticism that Republicans favor business, it is interesting that three of the four administrations that had reductions in personal income tax revenues should be Republican.

The two largest increases in the share of personal income tax revenues came during the Johnson and Carter administrations (3.44 percent, 3.38 percent), both Democratic.

(See 75 When did our income taxes become the government's main revenue source? 115 Has the mix of federal tax revenues changed over the years? 116 When have personal income tax revenues been at their lowest? 119 When was the last major overhaul of the tax code and what changed? 120 Why have corporate taxes declined over past decades? 302 Which presidents gave high priority to tax changes?)

Q 411. What happened with corporate and social insurance tax revenues?

A Two Republicans, Presidents Dwight Eisenhower and Richard Nixon, both reduced corporate tax receipts as a share of total tax revenues (−8.3 percent , −5.1 percent). Three Democratic presidents were among the top five who also posted reductions in the corporate share (Carter, −5.2 percent; Kennedy, −1.3 percent; Johnson, −1.24 percent). The Reagan administration saw an increase in the corporate share of tax revenues, up by 0.2 percent. But by the time Reagan took office, the corporate share had reached an unusually low level.

Social insurance tax revenues have increased as a percentage of total tax revenues in every administration since Truman's. They saw their biggest jumps during three Republican administrations—the Nixon, Eisenhower, and Reagan presidencies (9.4 percent, 7.6 percent, and 5.8 percent, respectively). Presidents Ford, Carter, Johnson, and Bush posted the lowest postwar increases in social insurance taxes (in that order). President George Bush, who went back on his "no new taxes" pledge, presided over a 1.5 percent increase.

(See 115 Has the mix of federal tax revenues changed over the years? 120 Why have corporate tax revenues declined over past decades? 121 How has the tax rate for the employer's share of the payroll tax increased over the years? 302 Which presidents gave high priority to tax changes?)

ROOSEVELT ADMINISTRATION (1933–1945)

President Franklin Roosevelt was the first Democratic president to be elected since Woodrow Wilson. With Republican policies thoroughly discredited by the ravages of the Great Depression, which began during President Herbert Hoover's administration, Democrats also gained control of both houses of Congress for the first time since 1919. Democrats retained strong majorities in both houses of Congress throughout the Roosevelt administration.

Q 412. What caused the Great Depression?

A Economists have proposed several theories to answer this question, but probably the most widely accepted explanation puts much of the blame on the government's overly restrictive monetary and fiscal policies. In fact, the Federal Reserve's tight money policy during the Hoover administration did reduce the nation's money supply (M-1) by 25 percent between 1929, the year the stock market crashed, and 1933, the year President Franklin Roosevelt took office. That probably caused the 8 percent-a-year deflation that marked the economic collapse, and also drove up real interest rates, which further depressed the economy. (Today, a tight money policy is exactly the opposite of what would be recommended to counter an economic downturn. But the effects of monetary policy were not fully understood in the early 1930s.)

The government's fiscal policy was also counterproductive. Both President Herbert Hoover and President Franklin Roosevelt worried about deficits during the depression, and this lingering concern for balancing the budget tended to hold down federal spending when it was most needed. Even with President Roosevelt's New Deal spending programs, which aided millions of jobless Americans, federal outlays remained about 9 percent to 10 percent of GDP. That was not enough to pull the economy out of the deep depression and far less than wartime levels—over 40 percent of GDP—which finally did. Tax hikes passed under both Hoover (1932) and Roosevelt (1936) further depressed the economy and probably helped prolong the depression. (Here again, the economic effects of raising and lowering taxes were not fully understood.)

(See 55 What is a recession? A depression? 62 Does "laissez-faire" mean more or less government intervention in the economy? 63 What exactly is Keynesian economics? 65 What is fiscal policy? 69 What is monetary policy? 489 What is the Federal Reserve? 490 How does the Federal Reserve effect the economy? 493 What is the money supply? 507 Why is money sometimes "tight" and sometimes "loose"?)

Q 413. What did President Franklin Roosevelt's New Deal do to cure the Great Depression?

A When President Roosevelt took office, the nation was in the depths of the Great Depression. Some 15 million people were jobless, industrial production had been cut in half, and a wave of bank failures was sweeping the nation. To be sure, Roosevelt's New Deal programs addressed many of the basic needs of millions of people who had suddenly found themselves without work and without food. But in the midst of this crisis, the New Deal also did much to restore people's confidence and give them hope that things would get better.

The massive programs begun under the New Deal shifted the federal government away from what had been a limited role in the economy and society. Government took on the responsibility for managing the economy as part of the effort to cure the depression and help ease people's suffering. It spent previously unheard of amounts for public assistance. By 1939 federal spending for domestic assistance had reached $7 billion, more than the government was spending for defense at the time. Deficit spending, once condoned only for wartime emergencies, became a more or less accepted feature of the New Deal in light of the domestic emergency. And Roosevelt's New Deal programs also actively sought to redistribute wealth between social groups and regions of the country.

Did the New Deal finally cure the depression? In fact, Roosevelt's programs provided millions with desperately needed emergency relief and addressed a multitude of specific social and economic ills. Many important and lasting social programs also came out of the New Deal, and the economy did improve somewhat after President Roosevelt took office. But an outright cure for the depression eluded the Roosevelt administration throughout the 1930s. The economy did not finally shake off the depression until the early 1940s when military spending for World War II began rising sharply.

Q 414. What were the most important new social spending programs enacted during President Franklin Roosevelt's New Deal?

A Many New Deal programs survived only so long as the emergency of the Great Depression. But a number were either intended as permanent reforms or proved so popular that they survive in some form today. Among these lasting programs created as part of the New Deal are Social Security (the largest and most popular of federal social programs today), unemployment insurance, welfare, farm subsidies, and federal credit assistance for housing, farms, and small businesses.

▶ Why was the farm subsidy program created? *See 240 How have farm subsidies changed over the years?*

When did Congress enact Social Security? *See 194 Why was Social Security established? 196 How does the Social Security program work?*

Did New Deal spending create the national debt? *See 18 Where did the national debt come from?*

Did Keynesian economics affect federal spending policies? *See 63 What exactly is Keynesian economics? 400 What effect did the 1930s depression have on the fundamental philosophy behind federal spending?* ◀

Q 415. What did President Franklin Roosevelt do to change the budget process in the executive branch?

A As part of his Reorganization Plan Number 1 in 1939, President Roosevelt created the Executive Office of the President and transferred the Budget Bureau from the Treasury Department to it. This move further solidified presidential control of the Budget Bureau, but President Roosevelt went a step further. By presidential directive he made the bureau responsible for clearing all legislation, not just appropriations bills, that Congress sent to the president for signing. Thereafter, the bureau was responsible for coordinating legislation with administration policy and even prepared draft veto messages when it recommended vetoing legislation.

(See 311 What was the Bureau of the Budget?)

▶ Why was *United States v. Butler* so important? *See 168 Have there been important disagreements over Congress's spending powers?* ◀

Q 416. What important change did President Franklin Roosevelt's New Deal policies make in the tax structure?

A The payroll tax, introduced in 1935 to pay for the newly created Social Security system, probably represents the most important change of that era. At the time the tax rate was too small to have any significant impact, but increased "social insurance" benefits and the payroll tax hikes that accompanied them decades later have changed that. Payroll taxes now account for 35 percent of revenues, a major share of federal taxes. Furthermore, payroll taxes are not progressive; that is, they tax everyone at the same level no matter what their income. Expansion of payroll taxes has been a significant factor in undermining the progressivity of the tax system.

(See 73 What are the government's major revenue sources? 84 What is the difference between progressive and regressive taxes? 93 What are the social insurance taxes? 115 Has the mix of federal revenues changed over the years? 171 Why has social spending gotten so high?)

Q 417. How did President Roosevelt's "wealth tax" affect the debate over tax policy?

A While President Roosevelt initially showed some reluctance to become involved in tax policy, his now famous attack on "an unjust concentration of wealth and economic power" in 1935 and following years left little doubt as to where his administration stood. Angered by the fact that some of the wealthy had been avoiding paying taxes, President Roosevelt launched his pointed attack in support of a "wealth tax" bill, which became law later in 1935.

Congress trimmed back provisions of Roosevelt's original wealth tax bill, but nevertheless made the income tax for individuals more progressive, hiked rates, slapped a tax on corporate dividends, raised the top tax rate to 79 percent for those earning over $5 million, and made it harder to avoid paying income taxes. The act also raised corporate tax rates and increased estate and gift taxes as well.

Despite the changes brought by this bill and subsequent tax measures Roosevelt supported during the 1930s, the president's actual influence over tax policy was not that substantial. His attack on the wealthy for avoiding paying taxes struck a nerve, however, and to this day it remains a central issue in the debate over tax fairness and progressivity.

(See 84 What is the difference between progressive and regressive taxes? 85 What is tax fairness?)

Q 418. Did President Roosevelt's policies deepen the 1937–1938 recession?

A During the 1930s President Roosevelt had accepted deficits as the price of emergency relief programs he created to counter the Great Depression. But he retained a lingering concern about large deficits, especially because the depression refused to end. It had been getting better slowly, at least until the Federal Reserve's inflation-fighting efforts sent the economy into a recession in 1937. President Roosevelt initially decided spending cuts were needed to make up for lost revenue and keep the budget closer to balance.

But he soon learned an important lesson about fiscal policy. The cuts quickly deepened the recession, and unemployment shot back up to early depression-era levels. By 1938 President Roosevelt became convinced that increased federal spending was needed to combat the depression. In following years he ignored the deficit and worked to increase government outlays.

(See 65 What is fiscal policy? 490 How does the Federal Reserve affect the economy?)

Q 419. By how much did federal spending rise during World War II, and what did that do to the economy?

A Federal spending increased almost tenfold between 1940 and 1945, mushrooming from $9.5 billion in fiscal 1940 to $92.7 billion in fiscal 1945. By comparison, federal spending in the New Deal era preceding World War II had only trebled, rising from $3.6 billion in 1931 to $9.5 billion in 1940.

The wartime military buildup and enormous outpouring of federal dollars for military supplies at last laid the lingering depression to rest. The long-dormant manufacturing sector finally awoke, and the GNP more than doubled during the war years. Suddenly everyone who wanted to work (and who was not in uniform) had a job, including women in large numbers. Unemployment plummeted from 14.6 percent in 1940 to 1.9 percent in 1943.

Q 420. What changes in taxation did the war bring?

A The federal government financed wartime spending through a combination of borrowing and increased taxes (income and excise). Personal income taxes were hiked to produce 43 percent of all federal revenue by 1945 (up from 20 percent of revenues in 1940). According to estimates, about 46 percent of the cost of World War II was paid for by current taxes (borrowing, especially through bond sales, made up the balance). One major wartime tax innovation that remains with us today is the system of withholding taxes from employee paychecks. It was established by the Revenue Act of 1943.

(See 115 Has the mix of federal revenues changed over the years?)

TRUMAN ADMINISTRATION (1945–1953)

President Harry Truman, a Democrat, succeeded to the presidency on President Franklin Roosevelt's death on April 12, 1945. He went on to win reelection in his own right—surprising many with a dramatic come-from-behind victory. Democrats also continued to enjoy majorities in both houses of Congress, except for the 80th (1947–1949), in which Republicans controlled both houses.

Q 421. What effect did demobilization have on the economy?

A Considering the massive changes, the transition from wartime to peacetime economy was amazingly smooth. For example, federal spending plummeted from a peak of $93 billion in 1945 to $55 billion in 1946, the first year after the war. Spending finally bottomed out in 1948 at $29.7 billion.

Changes of that magnitude should have had a severe impact on the economy. Some experts even feared a return to the depression era because of the sudden drop in demand. But they failed to consider pent-up demand for consumer goods and other items that had become scarce during the war years. There was a recession (in 1948–1949), but it was comparatively mild. Ultimately, rising consumer and business spending after the war made up for about two-thirds of the drop in federal spending. Coupled with foreign demand for American-made goods, the strong private-sector demand prevented a return to the depression.

Another reason why the economy remained healthy was that unemployment stayed surprisingly low. Demobilization released millions of soldiers into the workforce. Meanwhile, though, about 4.3 million workers—many of them women who had started working to help the war effort—left the workforce and so made room for the returning soldiers. Also, the manufacturing and building sectors quickly expanded to meet rising demand, creating millions of new jobs, and a substantial number of ex-soldiers took advantage of the GI bill to go to college.

In fact, the biggest problem associated with demobilization was inflation. Wartime wage and price controls had kept prices artificially low, and when controls were lifted during the late 1940s inflation shot up (from 2.5 percent in 1945 to a high of 14.4 percent in 1947). The recession in 1948–1949 ended this short-lived, postwar inflationary surge, though.

Q 422. Why did Congress pass the Employment Act of 1946?

A World War II had shown that by stimulating the economy, government spending could cut unemployment drastically—joblessness had fallen to a mere 1 percent by 1944. This was essentially what Keynesian economic theory had predicted, and many in Congress believed the government should use spending, even deficit spending when necessary, to hold unemployment to the bare minimum.

To that end the full employment bill was introduced in Congress. It would have made full employment a national goal and would have authorized the government to use deficit spending whenever necessary to achieve it. Conservatives and business leaders opposed the measure on grounds it would lead to excessive government regulation of the economy, as well as budget deficits and inflation. Though President Harry Truman supported the bill, Congress passed a watered down version that set "maximum employment, production and purchasing power" as the government's economic goals (not just full employment). Steps taken to achieve the goals were to be in keeping with the free enterprise system, and the president was to report to Congress on the state of the economy each year. The act also created the Council of Economic Advisers, which reported directly to the president.

Though all references to full employment and deficit spending had been removed, the bill and the debate surrounding it nevertheless established the framework for the government's fiscal policy during the postwar era. The U.S. economy remained a free market system, but the federal government was firmly committed to facilitating (rather than regulating) economic growth. And within that system, efforts to promote maximum employment had to be balanced against the need to promote economic growth as well.

(See 23 What impact does the government have on the economy? 33 Does full employment help or hurt the economy? 64 What is "stabilization policy"? 65 What is fiscal pol-

icy? 406 How has unemployment changed over the years? 407 Which postwar president posted the lowest and highest average unemployment rates?)

Q 423. What were the battle lines on fiscal policy between Democrats and Republicans in the late 1940s?

A Congressional Republicans, after sixteen years as the minority party, finally regained control of both houses for the 80th Congress (1947–1949). They attacked Democrats for high spending and high taxes, and now in control of Congress, pushed through tax cut packages in 1947 and 1948. Led by President Harry Truman, Democrats fought back by accusing Republicans of supporting inflationary policies. They opposed the tax cuts as inflationary—Truman labeled them "the wrong kind of tax reduction at the wrong time"—because wartime spending still had not been cut enough and employment was high. President Truman vetoed two tax cut bills Congress passed in 1947, but his veto of a 1948 tax cut was overridden.

As it happened, the timing of the tax cut was near-perfect. It served as a needed fiscal stimulus as the country slipped into a mild recession in 1948–1949. The recession also forced President Truman to finally abandon his drive for a tax hike to balance the budget in 1949. After three straight years of budget surpluses (1947–1949), the budget returned to a deficit in 1950.

▶ What spending controls did Congress try during the 1940s and 1950s? *See 374 When did efforts to control spending begin in Congress?*

What was notable about income taxes in 1950? *See 116 When have personal income tax revenues been at their lowest?* ◀

Q 424. Why was the Bretton Woods System important?

A With the General Agreement on Tariffs and Trade (GATT) and the Marshall Plan, the Bretton Woods System was one of three agreements that helped establish the postwar international economic system. These agreements made possible the rapid economic growth enjoyed by the United States and other developed countries during the 1950s and 1960s.

The Bretton Woods Agreement, signed in 1945 at Bretton Woods, New Hampshire, established the international system of exchange rates and created the International Monetary Fund (IMF) and the World Bank as well. The agreement sought to establish a stable system of currency exchange based on fixed exchange rates, which would then aid international finance. The IMF was organized to oversee the exchange rate system, while the World Bank was responsible for making loans for reconstruction projects in war-torn Europe and for development projects in third world nations.

(See 503 What is the exchange rate? 504 What proved to be the advantages and disadvantages of pegging the value of foreign currencies on the US dollar?)

Q 425. What was GATT and how did it affect the economy?

A GATT, or the General Agreement on Tariffs and Trade, created a framework for promoting international trade. The initial agreement was signed by the United States and other founding members in 1947 to establish rules of trade within the group, including the use of tariffs rather than quotas or other trade barriers, and to extend "most-favored-nation" status (granting preferential treatment on import duties) and other privileges to all member nations. GATT also provided an organization for resolving trade disputes and for promoting freer trade. GATT played a key role in the postwar expansion of international trade. The trade in turn fueled sustained economic growth in the United States during the 1950s and 1960s, as well as Europe's rapid recovery after the war.

GATT, the Bretton Woods System, and the Marshall Plan were three important agreements that effectively established the international economic system after World War II. GATT was renamed the World Trade Organization in 1993 and at that time included over one hundred member nations.

(See 513 Is trade protectionism good or bad for the economy?)

Q 426. What did the Marshall Plan do?

A The largest American foreign aid plan in the country's history, the Marshall Plan helped countries rebuild after World War II. Between 1948 and 1952, the United States dispensed over $13 billion in aid, mainly to European nations but also to certain Asian countries. The plan helped bring about a swift recovery in Europe and also helped strengthen U.S. allies against the rising cold war threat from the Soviet Union. It was one of the three important agreements that helped establish the international economic order after the war (along with the Bretton Woods System and General Agreement on Tariffs and Trade).

Among the recipients of aid under the Marshall Plan were the United Kingdom ($3.2 billion), France ($2.7 billion), and West Germany ($1.4 billion).

Q 427. What changes to Social Security did Congress make in the 1950s?

A In 1950 Congress increased Social Security benefits by 70 percent in response to changes in the cost of living since the 1930s. At the same time it raised the maximum income subject to payroll tax to $3,600. It also eased eligibility requirements and expanded coverage to include many self-employed persons (professionals and farmers were still excluded) and some 9.2 million state and local government employees. Later in the 1950s, Congress raised both the payroll tax rate and the maximum taxable wage base, and further extended coverage (including self-employed farmers) to provide benefits to about 80 percent of the workforce.

Congress moved a program for the disabled, Aid to the Permanently and Totally Disabled, to the Social Security System in 1956, creating the disability insurance trust fund. The Social Security program was renamed Old Age, Survivors and Disability Insurance (OASDI).

(See 201 What are the two largest Social Security programs and what purposes do they serve?)

Q 428. Did the Korean War affect inflation?

A Both increased defense spending and consumer fears about possible wartime shortages helped push up inflation after the outbreak of the Korean War in 1950. Between late 1950 and 1953 federal spending rose 77 percent, from $43 billion to $76 billion. Factories expanded wartime production, unemployment dropped to just 2.9 percent in 1953, and people rushed to buy consumer goods.

The situation had all the earmarks of Keynesian excess demand, and in 1950 the Consumer Price Index rose 5.8 percent, as if to confirm a new round of inflation was beginning. The Truman administration intervened quickly, though, by imposing controls on wages, prices, and credit and by approving a timely tax increase. As a result, the Consumer Price Index rose by less than 1 percent in 1952 and 1953.

(See 52 What does inflation do to the economy? 64 What is "stabilization policy"? 65 What is fiscal policy?)

Q 429. What did the 1951 accord between the Treasury and the Federal Reserve do?

A This agreement gave the Federal Reserve greater independence in setting interest rates and so became the basis for postwar monetary policies aimed at stabilizing the economy. During World War II the Fed had pegged interest rates on government bonds (at or below 2.5 percent) in order to help keep the cost of servicing the national debt to a minimum. It enforced low interest rates by buying up all bonds on the open market at face value.

Immediately after the war the Treasury department insisted the policy be continued, but the hard-and-fast, low-interest-rates policy aggravated inflation and recessions, both serious problems in the late 1940s. The Treasury finally relented in 1951 after a new round of inflation in 1950. The Fed has since used various means to raise and lower interest rates to keep inflation in check. It has also done so to soften the effects of recessions.

(See 44 What can the economy do to the budget? 48 How does inflation affect my paycheck? 54 Who cured high inflation? 69 What is monetary policy? 489 What is the Federal Reserve? 490 How does the Federal Reserve affect the economy? 493 What is the money supply?)

EISENHOWER ADMINISTRATION (1953–1961)

A Republican and World War II hero, President Dwight Eisenhower served two terms. Republicans held slim majorities in both houses of Congress between 1953 and 1955. From 1955 onward, though, Democrats controlled both houses of Congress.

Q 430. What was President Dwight Eisenhower's fiscal policy record?

A During his eight years in office, President Eisenhower emphasized conservative policies of fighting inflation, balancing the budget, and minimizing government interference in the economy. He tried to reduce federal spending and hold off on tax cuts to fight inflation, which averaged 1.4 percent between 1953 and 1961. His efforts to hold down federal spending and balance the budget resulted in three budget surpluses (1956, 1957, 1960).

President Eisenhower was skeptical of Keynesian economics and used federal fiscal policy tools only sparingly to deal with the ups and downs of the economy. He believed instead that the private sector could produce economic growth and jobs with little or no government interference. Some Democrats attacked President Eisenhower's fiscal restraint as a return to "Hoover economics," and many thought he tolerated higher levels of unemployment than were necessary. But Eisenhower was in fact willing to let the deficit rise during recessionary times (1953–1954, 1957–1958).

(See 404 How strong has economic growth been since World War II? 406 How has unemployment changed over the years? 408 How have tax revenues as a share of GDP changed since World War II? 411 What happened with corporate and social insurance revenues?)

Q 431. How did federal fiscal policy change in the 1950s?

A The federal government's willingness to tolerate deficit spending during a recession was the major fiscal policy change of this decade. Instead of trying to follow a fixed balanced budget policy, the government instead pursued a more flexible approach, letting automatic "stabilizers" like unemployment benefits, tax cuts, and other federal spending help soften the impact of the recession. During both recessions of his administration—1953–1954 and 1957–1958—President Dwight Eisenhower allowed deficits to rise markedly, though after the second recession he cut back spending so sharply that it helped cause a new recession.

(See 55 What is a recession? A depression? 60 Do entitlement programs help dampen recessions? 64 What is "stabilization policy"? 65 What is fiscal policy? 298 What have been the successes and failures of past fiscal policy?)

Q 432. Why did President Eisenhower cut back federal spending so sharply in 1959?

A After the brief recession in 1957–1958, the deficit swelled to $12.9 billion in fiscal 1959, the highest level of President Eisenhower's two terms. Eisenhower reacted by cutting back federal spending sharply, even though a nationwide steel strike had helped throw the economy into a new recession in 1959. Critics attacked the president for having pulled too much federal spending power out of the economy at such an inopportune time, but he defended the move.

In past recessions, wages and prices had fallen as the economy slumped. But during the 1957–1958 downturn, President Eisenhower noted, wages and prices had continued to rise. That ominous trend had necessitated a strong fiscal response. Otherwise, he warned, it might lead to "real inflationary trouble in a time of prosperity." In fact, during the 1970s the economy was plagued by inflationary troubles very much like those described by President Eisenhower, troubles that came to be called "stagflation."

President Eisenhower's spending cuts did produce a budget surplus for fiscal 1960. But the lack of spending stimulus helped prolong the recession into the election season that fall, and the lagging economy contributed to Richard Nixon's loss in the 1960 presidential election.

"We now have many things that need doing. . . . Schools and aid to education, research support and facilities, health facilities, urban rental housing, urban redevelopment, resource development, metropolitan communications, are all deficient or lagging. It would surely be a mistake to talk of tax reduction to make jobs when so many of our schools are dirty, rundown, overcrowded, understaffed, on double shifts, or scheduled to become inadequate when the increase in the school population hits them."

—John Kenneth Galbraith, noted liberal economist, arguing for increased federal spending before a congressional committee in 1958.

(See 43 Do Americans vote their pocketbooks? 52 What does inflation do to the economy? 57 Does disinflation always come with a recession? 58 What is stagflation? 65 What is fiscal policy?)

Q 433. What were the general economic views of liberals and conservatives in the 1950s?

A Conservatives generally believed that business would produce economic prosperity, if only the government would refrain from interfering in the private sector. As to fiscal matters, conservatives cast disagreements with liberals over federal spending as a matter of "savers" versus "spenders."

For their part, liberals believed the government should be expanding its role in the economy, because at bottom they doubted the private sector alone could provide full employment and prosperity for everyone. They blamed sagging economic growth on the "laggard government" of President Dwight Eisenhower and called for increased federal spending to address a multitude of needs. Interestingly, liberals ultimately chose to frame their arguments for bigger government in terms of complicated economic theories, a tack that Republican supply-siders also took two decades later to push for smaller government.

(See 71 What is supply-side economics?)

KENNEDY ADMINISTRATION (1961–1963)

A Democrat, President John F. Kennedy served only part of his term before being killed by an assassin in 1963. During his time in office Democrats held solid majorities in both houses of Congress, but conservative Democrats opposed many of Kennedy's initiatives.

"Our present choice is not between a tax cut and a balanced budget. . . . The choice, rather, is between chronic deficits arising out of a slow rate of economic growth, and temporary deficits stemming from a tax program designed to promote fuller use of our resources and more rapid economic growth. . . . Unless we release the tax brake which is holding back our economy, it is likely to continue to operate below its potential, federal receipts are likely to remain disappointingly low, and budget deficits are likely to persist."

—President John F. Kennedy, speaking in defense of his proposed tax cut. Republican supply-siders used the same arguments two decades later to promote the Reagan tax cuts. The Laffer curve was also based on the premise that higher taxes slowed the economy.

Q 434. How did President John F. Kennedy's fiscal policy differ from President Eisenhower's?

A The Kennedy administration believed the government should stimulate the economy directly to keep it expanding and to achieve full employment. President Kennedy was convinced that increased federal spending, or tax cuts, could be used to achieve those goals. President Dwight Eisenhower, on the other hand, had been reluctant to resort to this type of direct federal government intervention in the economy.

President Kennedy tried to implement his plan by seeking a tax cut when the economy slowed in 1962, but Congress voted against the measure. In 1964, soon after Kennedy's assassination, President Lyndon Johnson did succeed in pushing through the tax reduction package. By this time, however, the economy had picked up steam again.

(See 408 How have tax revenues as a share of GDP changed since World War II? 436 What was unusual about President Johnson's tax cut? 437 What did President Lyndon Johnson's Great Society program attempt to do?)

▶ When did the country's longest economic expansion begin? *See 47 When was the last expansion? The longest?* ◀

JOHNSON ADMINISTRATION (1963–1969)

Democrat Lyndon Johnson succeeded to the presidency on Kennedy's death in 1963 and was elected to office in his own right in 1964. Democrats also retained solid majorities in both houses throughout the Johnson years, and as a former member of both the House and Senate, Johnson had greater success than Kennedy at steering legislation through Congress.

Q 435. What were the economic policy successes and failures of the 1960s?

A Economic policy during the Kennedy-Johnson years posted some stunning successes, beginning with the longest continuous expansion, which lasted from February 1961 to February 1969. GDP nearly doubled from $530 billion to $948 billion, disposable personal income increased by 33 percent, and corporate profits jumped by 100 percent during that time. Meanwhile, the unemployment rate dropped to 3.5 percent by 1969, as the booming economy created a total of about 11 million new jobs.

The monkey wrench in the works, however, was inflation. Consumer prices began increasing in 1966 (up 3.4 percent for the year) and became a serious problem by 1969 at 6.1 percent—by then the country was experiencing the worst inflation since World War II. Among other things, experts believed the government's efforts at stimulating the economy (in other words, the 1964 tax cut) had helped cause the inflation. Though unemployment had dropped sharply from levels experienced in the 1950s, by the mid-1960s the economy was growing too fast. Spending for the Vietnam War only added to the inflationary "excess demand" that was building up.

The Johnson administration recognized too slowly that inflation was getting out of hand, and then implemented a temporary tax surcharge too late to be effective. In fact, the inflation that got started in the 1960s continued to defy fiscal policy remedies throughout the 1970s.

(See 49 What causes inflation? 50 When have there been bouts of inflation since World War II? 65 What is fiscal policy? 298 What have been the successes and failures of past fiscal policy?)

Q 436. What was unusual about President Johnson's tax cut?

A Johnson's 1964 tax cut marked the first time the government intentionally reduced taxes even though the economy was expanding. The results were dramatic. Unemployment fell sharply between 1963 and 1965 (5.7 percent to 4.3 percent), and federal revenue actually increased (even after adjustments for normal growth and inflation). The success of the tax cut convinced the Johnson administration that it could "fine tune" the economy to achieve its goals.

The tax cut was the largest ever up to that time and included across-the-board cuts in the personal income tax rates. It gave considerable relief to wealthy taxpayers by lowering the top (marginal) rate from 91 percent to 70 percent by 1965, and cut the corporate tax rate from 52 percent to 48 percent by 1965. Overall, the tax cuts shifted an estimated $11 billion-plus from the public sector to the private sector. Decades later, supporters of supply-side economics pointed to this tax cut as a justification for the big Reagan tax cut in 1981.

(See 68 Can we "fine tune" the economy? 71 What is supply-side economics?)

▶ In what years did spending and revenues break the $100 billion mark? *See 82 When did federal revenues top $100 billion a year? A trillion? 141 When did federal spending reach $1 billion a year? $1 trillion?* ◀

Q 437. What did President Lyndon Johnson's Great Society program attempt to do?

A The Great Society program was the most sweeping set of social reforms enacted since the New Deal, adding numerous new social programs and greatly enlarging existing ones. Succeeding to the presidency after Kennedy's assassination, President Johnson won passage of the Civil Rights Act of 1964 and a major tax cut, both of which Kennedy had been trying to steer through Congress. But that same year he also announced his plans for the Great Society program, which would fight poverty, disease, and other social ills. Much of the Great Society legislation was approved in 1965, when Democratic majorities in Congress helped pass eighty of the eighty-three measures President Johnson sent to Capitol Hill.

Among the programs President Johnson created for his Great Society were Medicare (health insurance for the aged), Medicaid (health program for the poor), the first comprehensive federal aid program for elementary and secondary education, the Model Cities program, the Community Action Program, job training, and housing programs.

Meanwhile, President Johnson had launched his War on Poverty in 1964 with passage of the Economic Opportunity Act. This program proved to be among his most controversial because of problems with mismanagement and public reaction to riots and crime in inner city neighborhoods, where much of the federal antipoverty effort was being directed.

By 1966 President Johnson's commitment to the Vietnam War had dampened enthusiasm in Congress for further Great Society reforms. While some of Johnson's Great Society programs came under increasing criticism and were eventually terminated, many others proved so beneficial and popular with voters that they remain in operation in the 1990s.

"... We have the opportunity to move not only toward the rich and the powerful society, but upward to the Great Society. The Great Society rests on abundance and liberty for all. It demands an end to poverty and racial injustice, to which we are totally committed in our time. But that is just the beginning. . . . In the remainder of this century urban population will double, city land will double, and we will have to build homes, highways and facilities equal to all those built since the country was first settled. So over the next 40 years we must rebuild the entire urban United States."

—President Lyndon Johnson, speech at the University of Michigan, May 22, 1964

▶ How long had the Medicare program been in the works? *See 186 What made passage of Medicare in 1965 such a notable event?* ◀

Q 438. What new payroll tax did Congress establish in 1965?

A The health insurance payroll tax was enacted in 1965 to finance the Medicare program. A hospital trust fund was set up separate from other Social Security trusts, and both employers and employees were to make equal payments into the trust, based on taxable earnings.

(See 121 How has the tax rate for the employer's share of the payroll tax changed over the years?)

Q 439. Did defense spending or social spending post the biggest increases during the Johnson years?

A President Lyndon Johnson was responsible for big increases in federal spending because he chose to fight the Vietnam War and to establish his Great Society programs at the same time. The cost of the Vietnam War was high enough in monetary terms—between 1964 and 1969 defense spending increased by 50 percent (from $54.7 billion to $82.5 billion). Surprisingly, though, social spending rose even faster, shooting up 88 percent between 1964 and 1969 (from $35.3 billion to $66.4 billion).

Overall, federal spending increased by 55 percent from $118.5 billion to $183.6 billion between 1964 and 1969.

(See 146 How have federal spending patterns changed over since 1960? 171 Why has social spending risen by so much?)

▶ What happened in experiments with the negative income tax? *See 101 What is a negative income tax?*

What efforts were made in Congress to get the deficit under control? *See 374 When did efforts to control spending begin in Congress?*

Which year of Johnson's presidency did federal spending actually decline? *See 373 What one year between 1956 and the present did federal spending actually decline?* ◀

Q 440. Why did Congress pass the foreign investors act?

A Concerned about the declining balance-of-payments during the mid-1960s, Congress passed the foreign investors bill to encourage purchases of U.S. stocks and bonds by foreigners. The act, with later modifications, did gave tax breaks to foreign investors, but it also fixed tax loopholes that had allowed some foreigners to avoid paying U.S. taxes altogether.

(See 136 Have we mortgaged the country to foreign investors?)

Q 441. What did the President's Commission on Budget Concepts do?

A Between the end of World War II and the late 1960s, Congress had excluded an increasing amount of spending from the federal budget to insulate it from political pressures. Trust funds for Social Security, veterans' benefits, and the like were designated as off-budget. Government-backed enterprises, such as the Export-Import Bank and Tennessee Valley Authority, were also excluded, while direct and government-guaranteed loans were not fully reported. In 1967 President Lyndon Johnson's Commission on Budget Concepts recommended adopting a "unified" budget that included all spending and revenue. The change was intended to make the budget more useful in formulating economic policy. President Johnson adopted the "unified" budget approach in his 1968 budget.

(See 279 Does the budget include all government spending?)

Q 442. What did the battle over President Johnson's tax surcharge reveal about the limits of fiscal policy?

A When he finally recognized that the economy was overheating in the mid-1960s, President Lyndon Johnson resisted one important fiscal policy alternative—spending cuts—because the cuts might threaten his Great Society programs. But he was not anxious to ask Congress for the other alternative, a tax hike, which would be unpopular with voters. Meanwhile, there was considerable sentiment in Congress for cutting spending.

In January 1967 President Johnson finally urged a temporary surtax to cool economic growth, but a battle with budget cutters raged in Congress from 1967 to 1968 over whether to raise taxes or cut spending. When President Johnson's temporary 10 percent surtax finally was enacted in mid-1968, three years had passed since the time when many economists believed some type of anti-inflationary action was needed. That long lag time had allowed inflation to accelerate beyond a point where short-term measures would suffice, and many economists believe the surcharge failed because of the delay.

The delay while Congress debated the important fiscal policy questions was a necessary part of the democratic process. But economic conditions are constantly changing, and timing, as happened with the surtax, can make the difference between success and failure. In fact, the lag time in gaining approval for discretionary fiscal measures like tax hikes and spending cuts has proved to be a serious limitation of the government's stabilization policy.

(See 64 What is "stabilization policy"? 65 What is fiscal policy? 68 Can we "fine tune" the economy? 70 Are there political advantages of monetary policy?)

NIXON ADMINISTRATION (1969–1974)

A Republican and former vice president of the United States, Richard Nixon mounted an aggressive campaign to cut federal spending as a means of controlling inflation. Democrats had majorities in both houses of Congress throughout President Nixon's term of office, though, and strenuously opposed his efforts to cut spending, especially for social programs.

Q 443. What change in inflation did economists say occurred in the 1970s?

A Past recessions had almost always pushed up unemployment and caused prices to drop—or price increases to at least slow—thus easing inflation. When the economy expanded, however, the reverse would happen. Inflation would rise and unemployment would decline. This inverse relationship between inflation and unemployment became a cornerstone of federal fiscal policy during the postwar years—stimulating the economy would lower unemployment while increasing inflation. Tax hikes or spending cuts would lower inflation but raise unemployment.

During the recession of 1969–1970, though, inflation continued to rise even though unemployment was going up. The old inflation-unemployment relationship had become unhitched, defying the logic of Keynesian economics and creating what economists called stagflation. The problem of high unemployment and rising inflation plagued the economy throughout the 1970s while the president and Congress tried to find a way to make fiscal measures work. Ultimately, though, the government was forced to rely increasingly on monetary policies to wring inflation out of the economy.

(See 54 Who cured high inflation? 58 What is stagflation? 70 Are there political advantages to monetary policy?)

Q 444. What was President Richard Nixon's initial strategy for fighting inflation?

A When he entered office, President Nixon planned to rely on what he called gradualism, small spending cuts coordinated with a tight money policy to reduce inflation, which had been rising since the late 1960s. As a conservative Republican he also hoped to achieve a balanced budget, and his proposed budget for fiscal 1970 would have produced a small surplus. The heavily Democratic Congress refused to approve most of his spending cuts, however, because many of them targeted social programs Democrats supported. With social spending still rising rapidly (defense spending was declining despite the ongoing Vietnam War), President Nixon countered by vetoing appropriations bills and impounding funds Congress had already appropriated.

While relations between President Nixon and Democrats in Congress grew steadily worse, inflation continued to rise and finally hit 6 percent in 1970. That prompted Congress to pass its own answer to inflation, the Economic Stabilization Act of 1970.

(See 304 What role does a presidential veto play in the budget process? 381 Which president resorted to impoundment to cut federal spending?)

▶ Did President Nixon post the last budget surplus? *See 15 How many times have there been budget surpluses since the depression era?*

What reforms affected the budget process in Congress? *See 355 How did the Legislative Reform Act of 1970 change the appropriations process in the House?* ◀

Q 445. What was the Economic Stabilization Act of 1970?

A With this act, Congress gave President Richard Nixon authority to use wage and price controls to combat rising inflation. As a conservative Republican, President Nixon opposed the controls on grounds they infringed on the rights of American workers and insisted they would only delay a new round of inflation. He signed the act in 1970 but at first refused to impose the controls. Rising unemployment, continued inflation, and an upcoming presidential election combined to force President Nixon to recant his opposition and impose the controls in 1971, however. (See next question.)

Q 446. What did President Nixon's order establishing wage and price controls do?

A With the possibility of the 1970 recession lingering into his reelection campaign, President Nixon abandoned both his gradualism and his conservative approach to fighting inflation when he imposed wage and price controls (his "New Economic Policy") in August 1971. He had already decided the economy needed fiscal stimulus in order to hasten the recovery; freezing wages and prices seemed the only way to prevent a new round of inflation the increased federal spending was likely to bring.

Nixon's controls began with a ninety-day freeze on wages, prices, and rents, followed by a system of guidelines for wage and price increases. The strategy appeared to work early on—the economy picked up, unemployment dropped, inflation remained under control through 1972, and President Nixon was reelected. But inflationary pressures brought on by increased spending, and economic distortions caused by the wage and price controls, soon undermined the controls (for example, a paper shortage arose because manufacturers could get higher prices by exporting it than by selling it at the government-imposed price in the U.S.). Inflation began rising again, and industries were increasingly excluded from the controls. The system was finally abandoned as a failure between 1973 and 1974, unleashing a new round of inflation (up to 11 percent in 1974).

President Nixon's order establishing wage and price controls also dismantled key elements of the Bretton Woods System. It ended the agreement to convert dollars into gold (between 1960 and 1971 38 percent of U.S. gold reserves had been siphoned off because of it). Later, in 1973, an international agreement formally ended the system of fixed exchange rates, which had failed to allow for differences in rates of inflation between countries. Thereafter, the dollar was allowed to "float" against other currencies.

(See 424 Why was the Bretton Woods System important? 503 What is the exchange rate? 504 What proved to be the advantages and disadvantages of pegging foreign currencies on the dollar?)

Q 447. What were the federally backed bailouts of the 1970s?

A Congress authorized financial aid in one form or another in three highly publicized bailouts during the 1970s—Lockheed (1971), New York City (from 1975), and Chrysler (1979). Both the Lockheed and Chrysler bailouts involved federal loan guarantees ($250 million and $1.5 billion, respectively) that helped keep two major U.S. corporations out of bankruptcy and saved the jobs of thousands of workers. The New York City bailout approved in late 1975 provided desperately needed financial aid to keep the city out of bankruptcy. Ultimately, the city got $2.3 billion a year in loans between 1976 and 1978, and in 1978 it got long-term loan guarantees of as much as $1.65 billion.

Q 448. What was revenue-sharing?

A President Nixon at first embraced the idea of revenue-sharing as a way to consolidate federal aid for states into large block grants. Many existing federal programs gave money directly to states for education, community development, and the like. The block grants would eliminate federal guidelines and red tape and help shift the burden of various programs from the federal government to the states.

House Ways and Means chairman Wilbur Mills (D-Ark.) held hearings on revenue-sharing in 1971 because, he said, he wanted to expose the plan's weaknesses. By late 1971, though, Mills had realized revenue-sharing could be arranged to direct most of its funding to urban areas (mostly controlled by liberal Democratic mayors), rather than to state governments (many dominated by more conservative, rural interests). Mills and his committee then wrote a $5.3 billion revenue-sharing plan of its own and organized it to give two-thirds of the money to local governments. The Mills plan was enacted in October 1972 and provided grant money for, among other things, operating and maintenance expenses for public safety, public transportation, health, recreation, libraries, social services, and environmental protection.

The revenue-sharing program continued throughout the 1970s but finally fell victim to budget cutting in the mid-1980s.

(See 163 How have federal grants to state and local governments changed over the years?)

▶ How did President Nixon's Budget Bureau reforms affect budgeting procedures? *See 311 What was the Bureau of the Budget? 305 What does the Office of Management and Budget do?*

Why did spending ceilings fail to control rising expenditures? *See 377 What are debt ceilings? 378 How is the debt ceiling changed?*

Did President Nixon use his veto power to fight spending increases? *See 304 What role does a presidential veto play in the budget process? 375 What can presidents do to control spending?* ◀

Q 449. What spending cuts did President Nixon announce after his reelection in 1972?

A Following his landslide reelection victory over Senator George McGovern, a liberal Democrat who had campaigned on the promise of a guaranteed annual income for all Americans, President Nixon next decided to confront the spending policies of the Democratically controlled Congress. In January 1973 President Nixon delivered a proposed budget for fiscal 1974 that included major spending cutbacks, to be achieved by eliminating or scaling back over one hundred programs. Furthermore, he asked that Congress agree to a $268.7 billion spending ceiling for 1974 (the exact amount he had proposed spending) and even suggested revisions in congressional budget procedures.

Many of the programs President Nixon wanted to cut were popular with constituents and enjoyed strong Democratic support in Congress. But Nixon claimed his landslide reelection victory gave him a mandate for the changes. Reaction by the Democratic leadership was unequivocal. House Speaker Carl Albert (D-Okla.) responded that Congress "will not permit the president to lay waste the great programs . . . which we have developed during the decades past."

(See 381 Which president resorted to impoundment to cut federal spending?)

Q 450. What changes in Social Security benefits did Congress make in 1972?

A Concerned about the effects of inflation on retirees' Social Security benefits, Congress passed (over President Nixon's veto) a 20 percent across-the-board increase that raised average monthly benefits for a retired worker from $129 to $156. The increase was the third in just four years, the others being 15 percent in 1969 and 10 percent in 1971. The latest changes, which were attached to a debt ceiling increase, also indexed Social Security payments for the first time, providing recipients with an automatic increase tied to rises in the Consumer Price Index. Indexing would eventually have a major impact on spending for Social Security and other entitlement programs.

But that was not all. The bill also converted the federal-state Old Age Assistance program to one fully funded by the federal government—the Supplemental Security

Income (SSI) program. This new program only added to the growth of social spending during the 1970s. Later that same year, Congress also passed a bill making numerous changes to Social Security programs, including a benefit increase for widows and widowers, guaranteed a minimum monthly benefit of $170 for everyone paying into the fund for thirty years, and increased benefits for those who delayed retirement past age 65. It also established a federal program for assisting the aged, blind, and disabled (and provided guaranteed income assistance), extended Medicare coverage to 1.7 million disabled Social Security recipients, and extended Medicare coverage to almost all kidney disease patients for hemodialysis or transplants.

The bill imposed modest increases in payroll taxes (a 0.65 percent rate increase and a rise of $3,000 in the maximum taxable income). By the mid-1970s, however, mushrooming costs of the expanded Social Security program were already putting the program in financial jeopardy.

(See 171 Why has social spending risen by so much? 199 How many people receive Social Security benefits and how much do they depend on them? 200 When did Social Security spending top 20 percent of the federal budget? 204 Will the Social Security program actually go bankrupt? Why?)

Q 451. What is the Federal Financing Bank?

A Congress set up the Federal Financing Bank within the Treasury Department in 1973 to help coordinate sales of government securities issued by various government agencies. In the past, agencies like the Export-Import Bank and the Federal National Mortgage Association sold their own securities to the public, competing with each other and with the Treasury for available private investment funds. The Federal Financing Bank was designed to minimize the disruption of financial markets. It bought securities from the government agencies and then sold its own securities to the public to pay for the purchases.

Q 452. How much did the Vietnam War ultimately cost?

A Though U.S. involvement in the Vietnam War had its beginnings in the Eisenhower and Kennedy administrations, it did not become a full-scale war until President Lyndon Johnson committed large numbers of U.S. troops in the mid-1960s.

Then the war and increased defense outlays dragged on into the Nixon administration. A peace treaty finally ended U.S. involvement in 1973, but the cost of the war had been high. Between 1965 and the war's end, over 57,000 American soldiers had been killed and the government had spent about $102 billion.

Q 453. Why did federal spending fail to drop after the Vietnam War, as it had after past wars?

A There was no post–Vietnam War peace "dividend" because the cost of entitlement programs, such as Social Security, Medicaid, and food stamps, was rising so rapidly it absorbed whatever savings could have been realized from defense cutbacks. In fact, defense spending declined $6 billion a year between 1969 and 1973 as President Richard Nixon wound down U.S. involvement in the war. But during the same period, annual mandatory payments for entitlement programs increased by $50 billion. Instead of a drop in federal outlays after the war, spending only continued to rise and deficits began growing ever-larger.

(See 131 When did the budget deficit actually begin to mushroom?)

Q 454. How did the oil shortages and other "supply shocks" affect inflation?

A Until the supply shocks of the 1970s, the prime cause of inflation had been excess demand within the economy. The government's fiscal measures for fighting inflation sought to control this demand without producing high unemployment. But by the early 1970s these remedies for inflation were already proving inadequate. Then came the Arab oil embargo of 1973 and 1974: Arab oil-exporting countries deliberately stopped shipping oil to the United States because it had supported Israel in the 1973 Arab-Israeli War.

The resulting shortage of oil added a massive new inflationary pressure—this time from the supply side of the fundamental supply and demand equation. The price of imported oil tripled during the Arab oil embargo, and that was not the only "supply shock"; poor harvests around the world and rising demand for U.S. food exports created shortages here in the United States. Food prices suddenly jumped 20 percent in the early 1970s. The effects of these higher prices rippled through the economy, pushing up other prices and creating a strong inflationary surge.

The United States was hit with another oil shock in 1979, when the supply of Iranian oil was cut off by the Iranian revolution. The price of oil jumped 15 percent, and there were shortages in various parts of the country for a time, but increased production from other countries soon made up for the loss of Iranian oil.

(See 52 What does inflation do to the economy?)

Q 455. What were the battle lines in Congress over the Congressional Budget and Impoundment Control Act?

A President Nixon's refusal to spend funds appropriated by Congress—a procedure called impoundment—had become a key administration weapon for holding down domestic spending in the early 1970s. But Nixon made such extensive use of impoundments that it angered many in Congress, particularly Democrats, who argued the president was encroaching upon Congress's constitutional authority to spend the money. Democrats, meanwhile, were also determined to protect funding for the Great Society social programs they had established in the previous decade. Nixon's impoundments finally provoked congressional action to limit the president's authority to refuse to spend appropriated funds.

Although the impoundments spurred Congress to action, they ultimately proved to be a secondary consideration. It was also clear that Congress had to reform its budget procedures, but writing the law became an exercise in power brokering. While conservatives backed tighter budget control measures, liberals opposed procedural reforms that might result in funding cuts for social spending programs. At the same time, various committee chairmen maneuvered to protect their authority over spending and taxing decisions against infringements by would-be reformers.

The compromise bill Congress finally enacted introduced the "budget resolution" to the budget process and curbed the president's impoundment powers. (See 382 What did the Congressional Budget Control and Impoundment Act of 1974 accomplish?) Interestingly, Sen. Sam J. Ervin Jr. (D-N.C.) chaired the Senate Operations Committee, which drafted the initial budget and impoundment bill. Ervin later chaired the Senate committee investigating wrongdoing by the Nixon administration in the Watergate scandal.

(See 381 Which president resorted to impoundment to cut federal spending? 383 What is a budget resolution?)

FORD ADMINISTRATION (1974–1977)

Republican president Gerald Ford took office following President Nixon's resignation during the Watergate scandal. Democrats again controlled both houses of Congress.

Q 456. What was President Gerald Ford's economic record?

A When President Ford took office in mid-1974, he planned to fight inflation using the approach Nixon had adopted after wage and price controls failed—moderate fiscal restraint supported by the Federal Reserve's tight money policy. But by late 1974 the economy had slipped into its worst postwar recession up to that time, thanks to a business slowdown brought on by the sudden oil price hikes. With unemployment rising, Ford had no choice but to support a tax cut to stimulate the economy. Democrats in Congress argued for substantially more fiscal stimulus than President Ford wanted, but Congress finally passed a compromise tax cut of $23 billion in March 1975—after the economy had begun to recover.

Throughout his term, President Ford struggled with the Democratic Congress over spending issues. The debate reflected the dilemma brought on by the failure of federal policy to deal with the twin evils of inflation and unemployment. Democrats in Congress favored stimulating the economy to keep people working (see 458 What was the Humphrey-Hawkins full employment bill?)—even though that would increase inflation. President Ford wanted to make fighting inflation the top priority of fiscal policy even if it meant higher unemployment.

Fiscal stimulus packages, rising costs for entitlement programs, and inflation all contributed to the big jump in deficits during the Ford administration. Previous postwar highs for deficits had ranged around $20 billion to $25 billion, but now deficits skyrocketed from $6.1 billion in 1974 to $53.2 billion in 1975. The following year, the deficit hit $73.7 billion, surpassing the World War II high ($54.5 billion) for the first time. Inflation did drop to 4.8 percent in 1976, but unemployment remained high, averaging 8.5 percent for 1975 and 7.7 percent for 1976.

▶ Why were the Golden Fleece awards presented? *See 169 What were the Golden Fleece awards?* ◀

Q 457. When did Congress pass its first budget resolution?

A Congress first tried out the budget process introduced by the Congressional Budget Control and Impoundment Act in 1975. Some deadlines were waived, but in December 1975 Congress finally approved its first budget resolution, which set the overall size of the federal budget (for fiscal 1976). That first year was a trial run, however, and the new system did not go into full effect until fiscal 1977. Sharp debates between liberals and conservatives preceded passage of the budget resolution that year. In fact, budget priorities remained a contentious issue throughout the late 1970s, even though Democrats controlled both the executive branch and Congress. President Jimmy Carter wavered between stimulating the economy to lower unemployment and imposing spending restraints to bring down inflation. Democrats in the House, meanwhile, were badly divided over budget priorities.

(See 382 What did the Congressional Budget Control and Impoundment Act of 1974 accomplish?)

Q 458. What was the Humphrey-Hawkins full employment bill?

A The original Humphrey-Hawkins bill would have committed the federal government to keeping the unemployment rate for adult men at 3 percent or less, with the government providing "last resort" jobs for those needing them. Backed by liberals with the support of organized labor and black leaders, the bill was sponsored by Sen. Hubert H. Humphrey (D-Minn.) and attempted what the original version of the Employment Act of 1946 had tried to do—force the federal government to make low unemployment its top priority. The bill, Humphrey said, would put in place "a new economics that puts all of America's resources back to work."

The bill became enmeshed in the struggle between President Ford and the Democratic Congress over economic policy. But even liberal economists criticized the plan as inflationary and unsound. When Democratic President Jimmy Carter took office, he made lowering unemployment a priority but opposed the idea of setting 3 percent as a fixed goal of federal policy. The watered-down version of the Humphrey-Hawkins bill that finally passed Congress in 1978 (with President Carter's endorsement) was largely a symbolic gesture.

(See 422 Why did Congress pass the Employment Act of 1946? 456 What was President Gerald Ford's economic record?)

▶ When did the government's fiscal year shift to October 1? *See 10 What is a fiscal year and why does it start October 1?*

What new tax credit was added to the tax code in 1975? *See 182 What is the Earned Income Tax Credit?*

How close did states come to forcing adoption of a balanced budget amendment to the Constitution? *See 387 What is a balanced budget amendment?* ◀

CARTER ADMINISTRATION (1977–1981)

A Democrat from Plains, Georgia, President Jimmy Carter had won the election as a populist candidate who was outside the regular Democratic party circle. Democrats controlled Congress during all four years of the Carter administration, but Carter's relations with the regular party, especially the liberal wing, were not the best.

Q 459. What were the new economic realities of the 1970s?

A Behind the government's fiscal policy dilemma of choosing between fighting inflation or reducing unemployment lay structural problems in the economy that had become obvious by the late 1970s. They imposed new limits on the government and the economy, a sharp change from the 1960s when it seemed that anything was possible. The new economic realities were:

* Productivity, which had grown an average 3 percent a year from 1947 to 1965, rose an average of 2.3 percent annually from 1965 to 1973 and averaged just 0.8 percent between 1973 and 1980. The low productivity growth contributed to inflation and also made American goods less competitive relative to foreign producers (because they cost more to make).
* The massive influx of baby-boomers and women into the labor force during the late 1960s and 1970s probably encouraged the government to put too much emphasis on stimulating the job market, instead of holding inflation down. That aggravated inflation. The new workers were inexperienced as well, which added to the decline in productivity growth.
* The jump in energy prices during the 1970s not only added to inflation but also forced fuel conservation measures that reduced productivity. Requiring truckers to keep within a 55-mph speed limit to conserve fuel, for example, added to the time and cost of transporting goods.
* The economics of scarcity emerged as a problem during the 1970s. Fiscal policies based on Keynesian economics sought to stabilize the economy by controlling demand and largely ignored the supply side of the equation. At least part of the inflation during the 1970s was due to insufficient supply, rather than increased demand. The scarcity—of oil and various other items during the 1970s—drove up prices (and so inflation) because demand could not be met. The country's sagging productivity growth and outdated physical plant contributed to the shortages.
* High inflation during the 1970s discouraged savings and investment while encouraging consumer spending. During periods of high inflation there is less incentive to save or invest in future business growth because inflated dollars will be worth less in the future.
* The sharp increase in federal regulations for environmental protection, worker safety, consumer protection, and such fulfilled worthy goals, but taken together they had the impact of slowing down the growth of productivity and adding to inflation.
* Entitlement programs created or expanded in the 1960s (and added to in the 1970s) were now maturing, and in the process were absorbing more and more of

the federal budget. Because payments for these programs were mandatory, the possibility of cutting federal spending to keep deficits down was limited to the shrinking discretionary part of the budget. Neither tax hikes nor deep spending cuts were popular options with the Carter administration (or any other). That virtually assured a growing deficit problem as program costs mounted.

(See 27 Why is productivity important? 58 What is stagflation? 171 Why has social spending risen by so much? 454 How did oil shortages and other "supply shocks" affect inflation?)

Q 460. What was President Carter's economic record?

A President Carter entered office planning to focus on lowering unemployment, while also emphasizing a more limited role for government and making good his promise to eliminate the deficit by 1981. Working with the Democratic-controlled Congress, he won passage of increased spending for jobs and public works. He also promoted a monetary stimulus to the economy between 1977 and 1979, efforts that helped create the biggest three-year money supply expansion since World War II.

With the economy expanding between 1977 and 1979, the deficit remained in the $40 billion to $50 billion range, even though entitlement costs were rising rapidly. Much of that cost increase was hidden by inflation-induced tax bracket "creep," which produced enough new revenue to cover the extra federal spending. (Every 1 percent of inflation automatically adds 1.5 percent to federal revenues.) By 1978 inflation was rising and averaged 9 percent for the year. To make matters worse, the Organization of Petroleum Exporting Countries (OPEC) doubled the price of oil between 1979 and 1980. Inflation then jumped to 13.3 percent in 1979 and to nearly 20 percent in 1980.

Though President Carter resisted tough anti-inflationary measures in 1979 for fear of slowing the economy, he had little choice by early 1980. In March 1980 President Carter authorized the Federal Reserve to restrict consumer credit and orchestrated a policy of fiscal restraint to complement the Fed's anti-inflationary, tight money policy. A recession in 1980 was the result, as Carter administration officials had expected.

Even though he faced reelection that fall, President Carter resisted demands for a tax cut to stimulate the economy because it would have been inflationary. Economist Paul Samuelson warned that Carter's anti-inflation strategy might cause two or three years of economic stagnation and cost him his reelection.

(See 49 What causes inflation? 50 When have there been bouts of inflation since World War II? 51 Under which presidents has average inflation been highest and lowest?

52 What does inflation do to the economy? 114 How has tax indexation changed tax policy?)

Q 461. Why were deficits so high during the Carter years?

A The sharp rise in deficits begun during the Ford administration continued through the Carter years, despite the president's pledge to balance the budget by 1981. Deficits did dip from the record $73.7 billion in 1976, but they never approached the modest deficits of the 1950s and early 1960s. In fact, Carter's deficits failed to drop below $40 billion and by the end of his term topped $73 billion. The upward trajectory of deficits had been clearly established by the close of the 1970s.

These deficits had persisted, despite a drop in defense spending during the 1970s, because entitlement program payments to individuals had been growing at an average of 7.1 percent for the decade. True, the 1974–1975 recession contributed to the problem, but other long-term factors were pushing costs up. Congress had voted three big hikes in Social Security benefits between 1970 and 1972, the number of people taking advantage of federal programs like food stamps and Supplemental Security Income (SSI) had increased sharply, and more people were using Medicare and Medicaid to pay medical bills.

(See 66 Do big deficits limit fiscal policy options? 167 What has the deficit been, year by year, since 1901? 171 Why has social spending risen by so much? 475 Why were deficits so high during the Reagan years?)

Q 462. What did the first Social Security rescue plan do?

A Congress in 1977 passed the largest peacetime tax increase up to that time in order to cover the mushrooming cost of Social Security benefits, which resulted from major expansions of the program in the 1960s and 1970s. Both the payroll tax rate and the maximum taxable earnings were increased beginning in 1979, and the tax increase was expected to produce an additional $227 billion over ten years. Congress did correct one technical problem, which had allowed future retirees to retire with benefits higher than their pre-retirement wages, but it eased other requirements, which would increase Social Security spending.

By 1980 the drain on Social Security trust funds caused by liberalized benefits was threatening to render the system insolvent. President Carter went so far as to recommend cutting "unnecessary" benefits, but all Congress did in 1980 was to adopt stopgap measures.

(See 121 How has the tax rate for employer's share of payroll taxes changed over the years? 171 Why has social spending risen by so much? 188 How has Medicare spending grown as a percentage of the budget over past years? 200 When did Social Security spending top 20 percent of the federal budget? 204 Will the Social Security program actually go bankrupt? Why? 450 What changes in Social Security benefits did Congress make in 1972?)

Q 463. How did the Gephardt Rule sidestep the problem of raising the debt limit in the House?

A Adopted by the House in 1979, the Gephardt Rule allows for an automatic increase in the debt limit when the House passes a budget resolution that pushes federal borrowing beyond the current limit. Once the budget resolution is passed, the rule makes automatic the House approval of the required joint resolution raising the debt limit. The rule was adopted to avoid a separate vote on the debt limit, but delays in adopting the budget resolution have regularly forced the House to adopt short-term debt limit increases anyway.

In the past the House had always passed a separate measure raising the debt limit. But the direct vote made many members politically uncomfortable because debt limit increases were often accompanied by bitter floor fights over the broader issue of federal spending. Also, because passage of bills raising the debt limit are essential to keeping the government operating, House members frequently attached unrelated amendments that might otherwise have provoked a floor fight or presidential veto. The House rule was named after its chief sponsor, Rep. Richard Gephardt (D-Mo.). The Senate has no comparable rule, so that debt limit increases are passed in separate bills, often after long debates.

(See 377 What are debt ceilings? 378 How is the debt ceiling changed? 379 In what year did Congress raise the debt ceiling the most times? 380 Have spending limits worked any better than debt ceilings?)

▶ How did the 1979 oil embargo affect the economy? *See 454 How did the oil shortages and other "supply shocks" affect inflation?*

What did newly appointed Federal Reserve chairman Paul Volcker do to fight inflation? *See 54 Who cured high inflation?*

What was the windfall profits tax? *See 100 Has Congress imposed special taxes on corporate profits?* ◀

464. When did Congress first use the budget reconciliation process to cut back expenditures for ongoing programs?

During the Ford and Carter years, House and Senate Budget Committee leaders had put together budget resolutions by adding up spending needs for the various budget categories and using that total to determine the overall size of the budget. This approach worked well enough so long as the budget continued expanding—there was no need to force committees to compete for available funding.

That practice finally began to change in 1979, when Congress was forced to consider difficult spending cuts to help fight inflation. The budget process nearly failed that year. But the Democratic Congress returned to the task in 1980, mindful that it had yet to deliver on President Carter's promise of a balanced budget by 1981.

The attempt to write a fiscal 1981 budget with a small surplus was torpedoed by the onset of the 1980 recession, but Congress was determined to keep the deficit to a minimum anyway. So in late 1980 Congress used a budget reconciliation bill for the first time to trim the expected deficit by $8.2 billion—by raising revenues and cutting existing programs in education, health, unemployment compensation, transportation, and other areas.

In the end the cuts were little more than a symbolic gesture, though, because the deficit for fiscal 1981 eventually soared to a record $79 billion. But passage of the first reconciliation bill did set the stage for President Ronald Reagan's use of the procedure to make major budget cuts for fiscal 1982.

(See 368 What is reconciliation? 467 How did the Reagan administration win approval for major tax and spending cuts from Congress?)

465. What first appeared in President Carter's annual economic report?

President Carter's annual economic report for 1980 forecast a recession, the first time a recession had been predicted in the thirty years presidents had been submitting the report to Congress. The recession arrived as expected in the second quarter of 1980, even as high inflation and high interest rates continued to plague the economy. The economic ills contributed to the failure of President Carter's reelection bid in the fall of 1980.

(See 43 Do Americans vote their pocketbooks? 59 What is the Misery Index?)

▶ How did the "misery index" affect President Carter's reelection campaign? *See 59 What is the Misery Index?* ◀

REAGAN ADMINISTRATION (1981–1989)

Republican President Ronald Reagan, nicknamed the "great communicator" by his supporters, succeeded in raising budget issues to a national priority through his budget battles with Congress and through the mushrooming deficits that plagued his administration. During his two terms, Democrats retained solid control of the House. Republicans held the majority in the Senate from 1981 to 1987, the Democrats for the remainder of Reagan's second term (and on into the 1990s).

Q 466. What was President Reagan's economic record?

A President Reagan was both the victim and the beneficiary of President Jimmy Carter's decision to appoint Paul Volcker as Federal Reserve chairman in 1979. Volcker's anti-inflation fight largely caused the 1981–1982 recession—the worst downturn since the Great Depression. Because of it Reagan was forced to reverse his supply-side tax cut policy and actually propose a tax increase. But painful as the recession was for the country, it did finally end the chronic high inflation that had plagued the economy during the 1970s. And what followed was the second-longest economic expansion of this century, lasting from December 1982 to July 1990. President Reagan pointed to the boom as a vindication of his economic policies (dubbed "Reaganomics" in the media).

Mushrooming deficits during his two terms clouded President Reagan's economic record and intensified the budget debate in Congress. Like President Carter before him, Reagan had promised to balance the budget (by 1983). But with the recession starting only months after he took office and Democrats in Congress refusing to pass domestic spending cuts (beyond one package of reductions), he was forced to admit balancing the budget would not be possible.

Embarrassed as he was by the rising deficits, President Reagan adamantly opposed undoing any of the big personal income tax cuts he had won from Congress in 1981. He believed a tax hike might slow economic growth and complained that it would have little effect on the deficit, because Congress would only spend the extra revenue anyway. Critics also blamed President Reagan's defense budget increases for pushing up the deficit, but spending for social programs, which Democrats in Congress defended vigorously, went up by even more.

President Reagan's two terms amounted to something of a standoff with Democrats in Congress—both sides refused to give up their cherished priorities and so allowed the deficit and the national debt to grow to new heights.

Strategy for the 1980s?:

"When in office liberals . . . will always spend generously, regardless of budgetary considerations, until the public permits the conservatives an interregnum in which to clean up the mess—but with liberals retaining their status as the activist party, the party of the natural majority. The neo-conservatives have decided that two can play at this game—and must, since it is the only game in town. . . . They vigorously advocate [increased defense spending and] tax cuts, with the budget remaining a secondary consideration."

—Irving Kristol, conservative thinker

(See 66 Do big deficits limit fiscal policy options? 71 What is supply-side economics? 391 Did President Ronald Reagan cut the size of government? 475 Why were deficits so high during the Reagan years?)

Q 467. How did the Reagan administration win approval for major spending cuts from Congress?

A Past efforts at making major cuts in federal spending had foundered because the legislation was sent piecemeal to individual congressional committees. There members of Congress and special interests affected by the cuts usually managed to whittle them down. But President Reagan took a different tack.

Soon after entering office, the president asked Congress to consider making $41.4 billion in spending cuts for over eighty federal programs. In a strategy masterminded by David Stockman, Reagan's OMB director, the Republican-dominated Senate agreed to package all the budget cuts into one reconciliation measure. That forced House and Senate votes on just one measure—not eighty separate bills. The strategy took advantage of the reconciliation procedure created by the Congressional Budget Control and Impoundment Act of 1974.

Liberal Democrats objected to the shortcut procedure, but in the House a coalition of the Republican minority and fiscally conservative Democrats from the South provided the needed votes to pass the reconciliation bill.

(See 13 Why does the government spend more than it takes in? 19 Can't we just ignore the debt? 20 Should the budget be balanced? 322 Why is it that Congress has so much trouble keeping spending within a budget? 368 What is reconciliation?)

"The fact is, we are rolling the dice with the lives of millions of Americans. Whether they are children, the elderly, the poor, or farmers, whether it is rural areas or urban areas, we do not know what we are doing in terms of impacting on those Americans."

—Rep. Leon E. Panetta (D-Calif.), then chairman of the House Budget Committee budget reconciliation task force, on the $35 billion in spending cuts for fiscal 1982 (and $37 billion in tax cuts) being pushed through Congress by the Reagan administration.

Q 468. What did the Reagan tax cut and budget reduction package do?

A Signed into law by President Reagan on August 13, 1981, the budget cut package was the deepest passed by Congress up to that time. It reduced spending for fiscal 1982 by almost $35.2 billion, somewhat less than the president had asked, and would save an estimated $130.6 billion by 1984.

Companion legislation the White House pushed through Congress cut taxes by $37.4 billion, well short of Reagan's $53.9 billion request. Called the Economic Recovery Tax Act of 1981, the tax cut bill reduced individual tax rates by 25 percent in stages over a thirty-three-month period. It also included a fundamental change in the tax system—tax indexation, a mechanism to automatically adjust tax brackets for inflation and largely eliminate "bracket creep."

Substantial as the personal income tax cut was, the first of the staged cuts was almost entirely eaten up by a scheduled hike in the Social Security tax rate (and taxable earnings base) that took effect in early 1982. In fact, by this time over half of all workers paid less in federal income taxes than for Social Security taxes.

The ease with which President Reagan had pushed through the deep cuts at first shook liberal Democrats and then stiffened their resolve. A new round of cuts promoted by the Reagan administration a short time later was stopped in its tracks.

(See 113 How does inflation affect my taxes? 114 How has tax indexation changed tax policy?)

Responding to critics of his spending and tax cut plan, President Reagan asked, "Have they an alternative which offers a greater chance of balancing the budget, reducing and eliminating inflation, stimulating the creation of jobs and reducing the tax burden? And if they haven't, are they suggesting we can continue on the present course without coming to a day of reckoning"?

—President Ronald Reagan, in an address before a joint session of Congress, February 18, 1981.

▶ What happened when Congress voted a cutback in Social Security benefits? *See 96 Can the money in trusts be diverted to other purposes? 172 Can entitlement programs be changed? 173 What does the public think about cutting entitlement programs? 197 Why is Social Security called the "third rail" of American politics?* ◀

Q 469. Was the Reagan tax cut fair?

A During and long after the 1981 debates over the Reagan tax cuts, Democrats vehemently denounced them as "tax cuts for the rich." But according to the *IRS 1985 Statistics of Income Bulletin,* the total share of income tax revenues paid by the wealthy actually increased significantly from 1981 to 1983 (from 15.2 percent to 20 percent), even though their tax rate had been reduced more than those of other groups.

Meanwhile, middle- and low-income earners were the ones who paid less. For example, in 1983 about 70 percent of all taxpayers reported adjusted gross incomes of $25,000 or less. In 1979 this income group had paid 30 percent of total personal income tax revenues collected by the government. In 1983 that share dropped to less than 22 percent. The net effect of the Reagan tax cut had been to shift more of the tax burden to the wealthy, the 1 percent of taxpayers earning more than $100,000.

(See 85 What is tax fairness? 87 What are marginal tax rates?)

Q 470. What was the 1982 tax hike?

A The move in Congress toward the 1982 tax hike, called the Tax Equity and Fiscal Responsibility Act, came soon after the Reagan tax cut was enacted in mid-1981. With signs of a recession already becoming clear in mid-1981, President Reagan himself proposed a $22 billion tax increase and new spending cuts to counter projected increases in the deficit that the worsening economic slump would surely bring. But sentiment in Congress was also mounting to undo the Reagan tax cut of the previous year. It was only by agreeing to a larger tax increase (mainly in corporate taxes) that President Reagan was able to preserve his multi-year personal income tax cut. Ultimately the 1982 tax increase raised federal revenues by an estimated $98.3 billion during the fiscal years 1983 to 1985, and restored about 25 percent of tax revenues foregone in the 1981 tax cut.

(See 365 Does the Senate ever originate tax bills?)

Q 471. What caused the 1981–1982 recession?

A The tight money policy being followed by the Federal Reserve to fight inflation was largely responsible for the recession, the deepest since the Great Depression. It followed a brief recession in 1980, which also has been attributed to the Fed's anti-inflation measures.

Because President Reagan's major tax cut was passed just as the recession was beginning, the economic downturn only magnified the government's revenue losses. Personal, corporate, and other tax revenues normally drop during recessions because less money is being made. What is more, the "automatic stabilizers" (unemployment compensation, welfare, food stamps, and so on) push up federal expenses because more people are out of work. The recession-induced drop in revenues and increased "automatic stabilizer" spending collided with the first stage of the Reagan tax cut—and the ongoing rise in entitlement spending—to produce the first-ever $100-billion-plus deficit. The record deficit was a major embarrassment to the Reagan administration, which had pledged to balance the budget by 1983.

(See 54 Who cured high inflation? 60 Do entitlement programs help dampen recessions? 475 Why were deficits so high during the Reagan years? 490 How does the Federal Reserve affect the economy?)

▶ What caused the savings and loan crisis? *See 500 When did Congress deregulate the banking industry?* ◀

Q 472. How did a strengthened Democratic majority in the House alter the budget debate in 1983 and 1984?

A Democrats gained twenty-six seats in the House during the 1982 congressional elections, firming up their majority in that chamber and allowing them to dominate the budget battles of 1983 and 1984. In 1983 Democrats pushed through budget resolutions for fiscal 1984 mandating restoration of some previously cut funding for social spending, a rollback of defense spending, and passage of new taxes. President Reagan mounted strong opposition, however, and Congress faltered before implementing the necessary reconciliation bills to effect the changes. Congress finally adjourned in late 1983 without having completed the action, leaving the budget debate once again stalemated.

When Congress reconvened in early 1984, the Reagan administration and Republican-controlled Senate forced consideration of deficit reduction legislation based on the reconciliation bills that had not been passed. For that reason Congress got a late start on the budget for fiscal 1985 and did not finally pass the budget resolution until the day the year officially began, October 1, 1984. Meanwhile, Congress was clearly making no headway on the deficits, which in 1983 and 1984 were $208 billion and $185 billion, respectively.

But by 1985 the mushrooming deficits and the budget deadlock did open the way for consideration of new budget control procedures. What finally emerged was the

Balanced Budget and Emergency Deficit Control Act of 1985, better known as Gramm-Rudman-Hollings.

▶ What is the Gramm-Rudman-Hollings Act? *See 388 What was the Gramm-Rudman-Hollings Act all about and what happened to it?* ◀

Q 473. When was the first government shutdown and why did it happen?

A Whenever budget controversies delay passage of the annual appropriations bills needed to fund the government, Congress relies on continuing resolutions, temporary funding measures that keep the government operating until the regular appropriations are passed. Presidents usually are reluctant to veto these measures because doing so might force the government to shut down.

During the 1981 budget battles with Congress, however, President Reagan vetoed a continuing resolution in November because the spending levels Congress had specified were too high. Fiscal 1982 was already one month old and Congress had passed only one regular appropriation bill, so that Reagan's veto effectively cut off funding for all federal agencies except those involved in essential activities. Many government employees left work for part of the day. In the meantime, Congress passed a new continuing resolution that met President Reagan's approval, and most federal employees returned to their jobs the next day.

President Reagan shut down the government for a few hours twice more by vetoing continuing resolutions. President Bush also vetoed a continuing resolution that shut down the government during his term. Two shutdowns also occurred during the pitched budget battle over the 1996 fiscal year budget.

(See 479 Why did the government shut down during the Columbus Day weekend in 1990? 485 What effect did the 1995 government shutdowns have on the budget debate?)

Q 474. What did the 1983 Social Security rescue plan do?

A Estimates on which the first rescue plan in 1977 had been based quickly proved to be overly optimistic. The drain on the Social Security trust fund caused by increased benefits continued for almost seven straight years before Congress acted in 1983 to rescue the system. It moved up scheduled payroll tax increases, delayed cost-of-living adjustments, increased the maximum taxable income, raised the retirement age after the year 2000, and increased taxes paid by the self-employed to the full combined employer/employee amount. By 1985 the Social Security trust fund was rising rapidly, although there remained the question of whether it would stay solvent in the next century when the big baby boom generation reached retirement age.

Meanwhile, Congress also expanded Social Security coverage in the 1983 bill. It voted to include federal civilian workers hired from 1984 onward, which meant that by 1993 130 million workers would be paying Social Security taxes and some 40 million would be receiving benefits.

(See 204 Will the Social Security program actually go bankrupt? Why? 462 What did the first Social Security rescue plan do?)

▶ To what emergency measures did the Treasury resort in 1985 to meet federal financial obligations? *See 282 Has the government ever run out of money?*

When did the movement for a balanced budget amendment peak in Congress? *See 387 What is a balanced budget amendment?*

What did the Tax Reform Act of 1986 do? *See 119 When was the last major overhaul of the tax code and what changed?* ◀

Q 475. Why were deficits so high during the Reagan years?

A Critics of President Reagan variously blamed his economic policies (Reaganomics) and his defense spending increases for the $100 billion to $200 billion deficits posted during his two terms. His "supply-side" tax cut did reduce federal revenues in the short term, but the tax cut certainly also contributed to the economic—and revenue—growth that lasted from 1983 to 1990. Furthermore, the high deficits outlived the Reagan administration, persisting throughout the 1980s and well into the 1990s.

The underlying problem was that federal spending was growing faster than revenues, an imbalance presidents and Congress had been wrestling with for decades. Annual spending rose by $473 billion between 1980, President Carter's last full year in office, and 1988, President Reagan's last full year in office. (By contrast, spending increased $219 billion during President Carter's four years alone.) But because spending outstripped revenue growth, the deficit more than doubled from $73 billion in 1980 to $155 billion in 1988, with deficits in three interim years topping $200 billion (net interest during this period is charted in Figure 5-1).

President Reagan did increase the defense budget significantly, adding $10 billion to $25 billion to it a year until by 1988 defense spending was about $156 billion more a year than it had been in 1980. But the larger part of the total spending increase under President Reagan came from the skyrocketing cost of entitlements and other social spending, such as Medicaid, Medicare, Social Security, and education—all programs that many Democrats in Congress fought to preserve. Between 1980 and 1988 the annual budget for social programs (discretionary and entitlement) increased by

Figure 5-1 Net Interest, 1960–2000

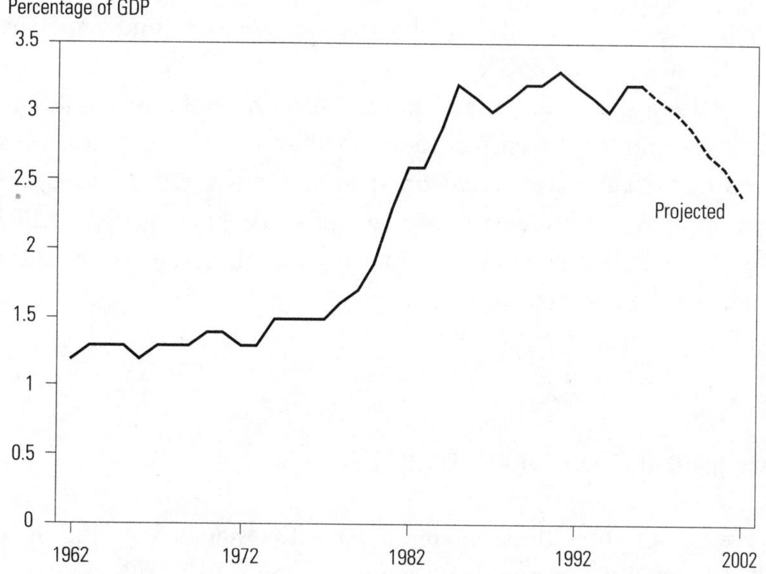

$220 billion. In fact, the sharp rise in social spending that began in the 1970s simply continued into the 1980s and 1990s, along with the deficit.

(See 18 Where did the national debt come from? 66 Do big deficits limit fiscal policy options? 167 What has the deficit been, year by year, since 1901?)

▶ Did interest payments on the national debt also mushroom? *See 132 How much does the interest on the federal debt cost now?*

What caused the savings and loan crisis? *See 264 How much did the savings and loan crisis finally cost us? 500 When did Congress deregulate the banking industry?* ◀

Q 476. What were the budget summits all about?

A The stock market crash on October 19, 1987, was so severe that for a time many people feared a return of the Great Depression. With financial markets here and abroad on edge, President Reagan and Congress decided to avoid the bruising budget struggles of past years and work together on a deficit-cutting package. They did so by hammering out an agreement during the 1987 "budget summit," a new feature of the budget process.

Only a few key members of Congress and the Reagan administration took part in the summit, which led to the chief criticism of the summits—that they shut too many members of Congress out of the process. But the four-week round of negotiations produced a two-year agreement on deficit reduction. After it was enacted by the full Congress, the package cut $76 billion in defense and nondefense spending over two years (fiscal 1988 and 1989).

President George Bush had far less success with budget summitry than Reagan did. The first summit between Bush administration and congressional negotiators in 1989 produced a quick agreement on spending cuts for fiscal 1990, but Congress balked at approving a cut in the capital gains tax. Enactment of $12.3 billion in spending cuts did not come until two months after the fiscal year began. These troubles were but a prelude to the upheavals following the 1990 budget summit, however (see 478 What happened at the 1990 budget summit?).

BUSH ADMINISTRATION (1989–1993)

Republican President George Bush entered office with rising deficits and the mushrooming national debt now a top priority. Democrats controlled both houses of Congress throughout Bush's one term in office.

Q 477. What was President Bush's economic record?

A To some degree, President George Bush found himself in the wrong place at the wrong time. American voters look to the president for leadership on the economy and, characteristically, blame him when the economy slumps, regardless of whether or not he could have prevented it. Unfortunately for President Bush, the long business expansion of the 1980s ground to a halt in 1990. The economy then limped along in a disappointingly weak recovery until the fourth quarter of 1992, when strong growth finally began anew. But that was too late for President Bush, who lost his reelection bid largely because of the weak economy (Democrats pushed the slogan, "It's the economy, stupid").

Part of the problem was that budget cutting and the continuing deficit problem left President Bush little room for fiscal maneuvering to end the recession. The government simply could not afford to increase spending to stimulate the economy. In fact, downsizing of the military following the end of the cold war brought big cuts in defense spending.

The end result was a dismal economic record for the Bush administration. Growth of the economy as measured by GDP averaged an anemic 1.5 percent for 1989 to

1993, the lowest of any post–World War II administration. Because of the recession and weak recovery, average employment growth was also the worst of any postwar administration, just 0.4 percent. Unemployment averaged 6.6 percent, only slightly ahead of the Carter administration average.

(See 43 Do Americans vote their pocketbooks? 66 Do big deficits limit fiscal policy options? 476 What were the budget summits all about?)

▶ Was there anything unusual about President Bush's 1989 defense budget? *See 223 What was the biggest defense budget ever?*

What was the price tag for the government's savings and loan bailout? *See 264 How much did the savings and loan crisis finally cost us?* ◀

Q 478. What happened at the 1990 budget summit?

A Negotiators at the 1990 budget summit faced a nearly impossible task. The deficit was rising rapidly, the savings and loan bailout had added many billions in unexpected federal spending to the budget, and the economy had slipped into a recession. Meanwhile, the OMB estimated the deficit for fiscal 1991 would be a dizzying $105 billion over the Gramm-Rudman target.

The Bush administration had called the bipartisan budget summit in May—and agreed to tax hikes in June—but by mid-September talks with Democrats on a deficit-cutting package had broken down. With the new fiscal year approaching, a "hyper-summit" of eight key congressional and administration negotiators finally struck a deal to cut the deficit by $500 billion over five years. But rank-and-file House members balked at having had so little say in the negotiations. Despite a televised appeal by President Bush, conservative Republicans led by Rep. Newt Gingrich (R-Ga.) teamed up with liberal Democrats to defeat the budget deal in the House.

Democrats then wrote their own $490-billion deficit-reduction plan, which included big defense cuts, smaller Medicare cuts than the summit package, hikes in gasoline taxes and user fees, and added "soak-the-rich" provisions (increasing the top tax rate from 28 to 31 percent, ending some tax deductions, and eliminating a capital gains tax cut). The Democratic plan that Congress finally enacted was called the Omnibus Budget Reconciliation Act of 1990. The act not only provided for the largest deficit reduction package up to that time, it also included the Budget Enforcement Act, which rescinded key features of Gramm-Rudman (see 390 What changes in the budget process did the Budget Enforcement Act of 1990 make?).

Q 479. Why did the government shut down during the Columbus Day weekend in 1990?

A After President Bush's $500 billion deficit-cutting deal was defeated in the House (see question above), the federal government was left without a budget for fiscal 1991. Congress quickly sent President Bush a continuing resolution to fund the entire government, raise the debt limit, and suspend the massive automatic Gramm-Rudman cuts that would have been required. But President Bush, angry and embarrassed by the failure of his budget deal, struck back at Congress by refusing to sign it. That in turn forced the government to shut down over the Columbus Day weekend. Popular tourist attractions like the Smithsonian Institution and the Washington Monument were among the more obvious signs of the shutdown, but passage of a new continuing resolution brought federal employees back to work after the holiday weekend.

(See 369 What is a continuing resolution? 473 When was the first government shutdown and why did it happen? 485 What effect did the 1995 government shutdowns have on the budget debate?)

Q 480. What price did President Bush pay for going back on his campaign pledge, "Read my lips, no new taxes"?

A While running for the presidency in 1988, candidate Bush made a major campaign theme out of his memorable slogan, "Read my lips—no new taxes!" Both Bush and Republicans generally opposed the Democratic plan of raising taxes to cut the deficit, rather than cutting spending. But with the economy heading into a recession (see poverty rate chart, Figure 5-2) and the deficit spinning out of control, President Bush reversed himself during the 1990 budget summit in order to win Democratic support for a budget that would substantially reduce the deficit.

The five-year deal he struck at the summit would have included both spending cuts and revenues from tax increases. But when it came time for Congress to approve the deal, the rank and file rebelled at having been left out of the negotiating process. Democrats then wrote their budget package.

The whole affair turned into a disaster for President Bush. Many conservative Republicans felt the president had betrayed them by agreeing to raise taxes, and said as much. The crisis over the Persian Gulf War in 1991 helped divert media attention from the issue of President Bush's broken promise during following months. But during the 1992 presidential elections, Democrats naturally took every opportunity to remind voters President Bush had gone back on his word.

Figure 5-2 Poverty Rates, 1989–1995

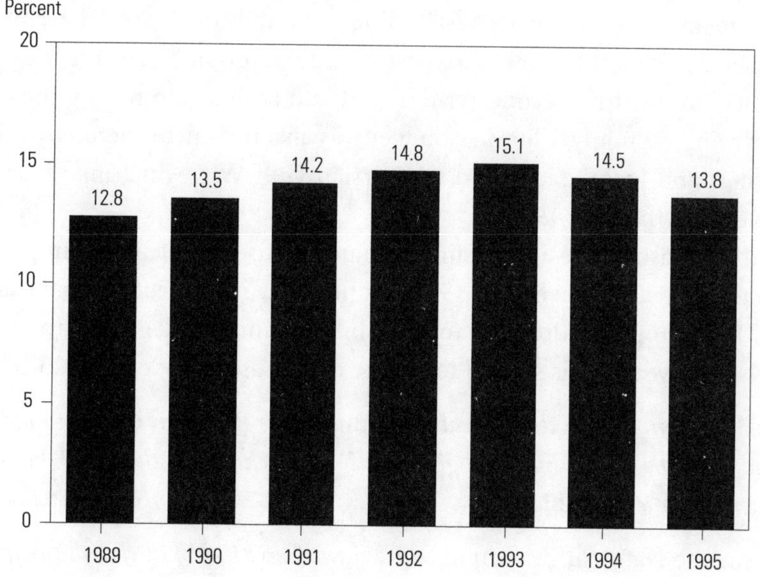

(See 478 What happened at the 1990 budget summit?)

► In which year of Bush's presidency did the debt top $3 trillion? *See 130 When did the federal debt top $1 trillion? $3 trillion?*

Does the Bush administration also hold the record for the biggest deficit ever? *See 12 When did the government post the largest deficit in its history?*

What ever happened to the peace dividend? *See 228 How has the size of the military changed since the end of the cold war? 229 Will all those base closings over the past few years really save any money? 230 What was the "peace dividend"?* ◄

CLINTON ADMINISTRATION (1993–   )

A Democrat from Arkansas, President Bill Clinton won election to two terms. During his first term, he settled on a strategy of steering a middle course between liberals and conservatives on budget matters. Meanwhile, Democrats held majorities in both houses of Congress from 1993 to 1995, but a stunning off-year election victory gave Republicans control of both the House and Senate in 1995, the first time that had happened in decades. Democrats had not lost control of the House in the past forty years.

Q 481. Did the deficit grow smaller during President Clinton's first term?

A Yes. President Clinton's modest spending cuts and 1993 tax hike combined with strengthening economic growth to increase federal revenues, cutting the deficit in half by the beginning of his second term in 1997. In addition to having the advantage of an improving economy, Clinton's budget was also not encumbered by huge costs for the savings and loan bailout and the Persian Gulf War, which had helped drive up deficits during the early 1990s.

For these reasons, President Clinton managed to orchestrate an impressive reduction in the deficit. At the end of 1993, his first year in office, the deficit stood at $255 billion. By 1996 it had dropped to $107 billion, and thanks to a strong economy in 1997, the first year of his second term, the deficit dropped to just $23 billion.

(See 393 What cuts in the federal government has President Clinton made? 397 What was the 1997 balanced budget agreement? 488 What did the 1997 balanced budget agreement do to cut taxes?)

▶ What was the National Performance Review? *See 313 What did the National Performance Review recommend?* ◀

Q 482. What was President Clinton's 1993 tax increase designed to do?

A Early in his first term President Clinton sought to reduce the federal deficit by making modest cuts in spending and by raising taxes, primarily on the rich. The measure was far from popular, even among Democrats. Nevertheless, his tax increase and spending cut package passed the Democratically controlled Congress by the narrowest of margins in both houses (Vice President Al Gore cast the tie-breaking vote in the Senate). Not a single Republican voted for the measure, making it the first time Congress had ever passed a major bill without any votes from the minority party.

The Omnibus Budget Reconciliation Act, as the bill was called, projected a $496 billion cut in the deficit over four years—$241 billion in tax increases and $255 in spending cuts. The act raised the top tax rate to 39.6 percent, increased the taxable portion of Social Security benefits, hiked the corporate tax rate by 1 percent, and added 4.3 cents to the tax on gasoline and other fuels. The act froze discretionary spending at 1993 levels and specified about $25 billion in entitlement spending increases (mainly for the Earned Income Tax Credit).

According to observers, the overall package was remarkably similar to the 1990 budget package.

(See 478 What happened at the 1990 budget summit?)

▶ Did President Clinton try to control entitlement spending? *See 394 What did Executive Order 12857 do?* ◀

Q 483. How did the Republican sweep in the 1994 congressional elections change the budget debate?

A For the first time in decades a Democratic president faced a Congress controlled by Republicans. Since the 1970s Republican Presidents Nixon, Ford, Reagan, and Bush all had to contend with Congresses controlled by Democrats, and this divided government led to protracted struggles and outright deadlock over budget issues. Now the arrangement was completely reversed. A Democrat was in the White House, and Republicans had control of both the House and Senate for the first time since the 80th Congress (1947–1949).

Their stunning victory at the polls gave Republicans the initiative in the budget debate during much of 1995. It also emboldened the newly elected members of Congress, as well as one of the chief organizers of the sweep, Rep. Newt Gingrich (R-Ga.), who became Speaker of the House. Eventually Republicans outlined a plan to both balance the budget in seven years and deliver a hefty tax cut to the American people. But Republican overzealousness, the unpopularity of proposed deep spending cuts in so many federal programs, and determined opposition from President Clinton combined to derail the Republican juggernaut by late 1996.

(See 485 What effect did the 1995 government shutdowns have on the budget debate?)

Q 484. What did the Republican Contract with America try to do?

A A conservative Republican reform agenda promoted by Rep. Newt Gingrich (R-Ga.), the Contract with America included ten major legislative initiatives. The agenda's two main goals were passing tax cuts for individuals and businesses to stimulate the economy, and cutting back the social service and regulatory roles of the federal government. Scaling back "big government" would serve several purposes, such as making a balanced budget feasible by reducing federal spending, reducing regulatory costs to help U.S. businesses meet foreign competition, and promoting a sense of personal responsibility among Americans.

House Speaker Gingrich pushed all the Contract with America measures through the House within the first one hundred days of the 1995 session of Congress. In the early going, the House failed to pass the term-limits bill, while the Senate killed the balanced budget amendment and stalled other measures. The controversy over the

1995–1996 shutdowns shifted attention away from the contract (and Gingrich). But by mid-1996 two important Contract with America bills were among those Congress had enacted, namely welfare reform and the line-item veto. Meanwhile, the Republican agenda also helped push the center of the ongoing debate over spending cuts, tax cuts, and a balanced budget in a distinctly more conservative direction.

President Bill Clinton, and Democrats generally, continued to resist both deep cuts in social spending and rollbacks of environmental and other regulations. But by 1997 President Clinton had adopted such basic Republican goals as balancing the budget by 2002, a major tax cut, reducing government social responsibilities ("the era of big government is over"), and substantial spending cuts. There remained considerable differences between the president and conservative Republicans over how best to reach those goals, however.

(See 45 What did President Bill Clinton mean when he said the era of big government is over? 395 How has Speaker Newt Gingrich influenced the budget debates of the 1990s? 396 If we are downsizing the government and cutting the deficit, why is federal spending still growing? 397 What was the 1997 balanced budget agreement?)

Q 485. What effect did the 1995 government shutdowns have on the budget debate?

A Public reaction against the two shutdowns in late 1995 and early 1996 proved a serious setback for House Speaker Newt Gingrich and the conservative Republican effort to fulfill the Contract of America. Although President Bill Clinton actually precipitated both shutdowns by vetoing bills needed to fund the government, the media and the public blamed Republican intransigence on budget issues for the crisis. President Clinton for the most part stood his ground on his budget priorities and refused to go along with cuts Republicans wanted in various social programs, especially Medicare and Medicaid.

Ultimately the strength of the public outcry over the shutdowns blunted the momentum of the Republican budget-cutting drive and gave President Clinton a far stronger bargaining position than he had had during 1995. Speaker Gingrich, whose popularity ratings sank to subterranean levels during the shutdowns, all but disappeared from public view until after the 1996 presidential elections. He, and his conservative followers, had been chastened by the experience and showed a greater willingness to compromise.

Certainly the reaction against the shutdowns contributed to President Clinton's reelection victory that fall. Republican successes in congressional races left them in control of Congress, though, and President Clinton found himself about where he had been in 1995 and 1996—inching his "centrist" position inexorably rightward in search of a budget deal.

(See 397 What was the 1997 balanced budget agreement? 473 When was the first government shutdown and why did it happen?)

Q 486. What finally happened in the fiscal 1996 budget debate?

A Soon after ending their shutdown strategy, conservative Republicans threw in the towel on a key goal for 1996—an agreement to balance the budget in seven years. Instead, budget conservatives were forced to negotiate a much smaller package of cuts for what they called a "down payment" on a balanced budget. Negotiations on the final bills of fiscal 1996 dragged on until late April 1996, seven months after the start of the fiscal year.

Ultimately both sides gave ground. Republicans walked away with a 9 percent cut in domestic spending, far less than they had originally sought, but a major spending cut on the order of the 1981 Reagan cuts (14 percent). President Bill Clinton meanwhile gained considerable prestige for his tough stand earlier in the budget battle and also protected his priorities in such areas as job training, environmental protection, and education. For 1996 at least, more critical cuts in welfare, Medicare, Medicaid, and other entitlement spending were left undone.

(See 240 How have farm subsidies changed over the years? 323 What is the largest single spending bill Congress has ever passed? 397 What was the 1997 balanced budget agreement?)

Q 487. Was passage of the fiscal 1997 budget any different?

A After the bitter budget battles of 1995, Republicans and Democrats managed to orchestrate a show of bipartisan harmony in 1996. With both parties eyeing the upcoming presidential elections that fall, Congress and President Clinton managed to put aside their differences and pass the budget for fiscal 1997 before the October 1 starting date. The budget has been in place by October 1 only four times since the early 1970s.

As might be expected in an election year, there was a whiff of extra pork-barrel spending in the budget, but in the main budget writers sought to hold the line on spending by making offsetting cuts for new spending programs. Discretionary spending for 1997 was $503 billion, up from $488 billion for 1996 but still less than the $508 billion initially approved for 1995.

(See 323 What is the largest single spending bill Congress has ever passed? 397 What was the 1997 balanced budget agreement?)

▶ When was the line item veto passed? *See 318 What is a line-item veto?*

What changes did the welfare reform package make? *See 209 How did the 1996 welfare reform bill change the welfare system?*

What was the significance of President Clinton's statement, "The era of big government is over?" *See 45 What did President Bill Clinton mean when he said the era of big government is over? 393 What cuts in the federal government has President Bill Clinton made?*

How did President Clinton and Congress finally balance the budget? *See 397 What was the 1997 balanced budget agreement?* ◀

Q 488. What did the 1997 balanced budget agreement do to cut taxes?

A The $95 billion in net tax cuts included in the 1997 balanced budget agreement represented a major victory for conservative Republicans. Both a balanced budget and tax cuts had been high on their agenda since 1995, when Republicans won control of both houses of Congress for the first time in decades. Among the Republican-backed tax reforms in the budget agreement were a $500-per-child tax credit, a cut in the capital gains tax, and a big increase in the estate tax exemption. President Bill Clinton won important tax concessions too, however, including many of the eleven tax incentives for education that he had sought and an extension of the $500-per-child tax credit to low-income workers who owe no income taxes. He also forced Republicans to back down on adjusting capital gains taxes for inflation.

The tax package actually included both tax cuts and increases for a net reduction of $95 billion over five years ($275 billion over ten years). The tax increases, mainly from airline travel taxes and a cigarette tax hike, amounted to $56 billion over five years ($126 billion over ten years). The budget agreement reformed the capital gains tax (see 86 What is the capital gains tax?), increased estate tax exemptions from $600,000 to $1 million by 2006, reduced the alternative minimum tax paid by corporations that owe no taxes, and raised income limits on IRA accounts. Among the education incentives were college tuition tax credits, creation of tax-preferred education savings accounts, and deductions for interest on student loans. (See also 397 What was the 1997 balanced budget agreement?)

The tax cut was the first broad reduction passed by Congress since President Ronald Reagan's big 1981 tax cut, but it added up to only 1 percent of total tax revenues. The 1997 tax cut was only about one-tenth of the Reagan cuts.

(See 14 Why doesn't the government just keep raising taxes to meet its expenses? 85 What is tax fairness? 98 How much revenue do estate and gift taxes produce? 372 What are the pros and cons of stricter budget control? 374 When did efforts to control spending begin in Congress? 395 How has Speaker Newt Gingrich influenced the budget debates of the 1990s? 468 What did the Reagan tax cut and budget reduction package do? 482 What was President Clinton's 1993 tax increase designed to do? 484 What did the Republican Contract with America try to do?)

VI
THE GOVERNMENT IN THE BANKING BUSINESS

IN GENERAL

Q 489. What is the Federal Reserve?

A The Federal Reserve is the nation's central bank. Its primary task is making and carrying out monetary policy, which it does through the Federal Reserve System. The Fed, as it is called informally, also oversees the nation's banking system.

Created in 1914, the Federal Reserve System is made up of twelve regional banks and twenty-five branch banks, a board of governors, and certain advisory groups. The seven members of the board of governors (nominated by the president and confirmed by Congress) are responsible for setting monetary policy and administering the Federal Reserve System. The Fed wields great influence over the American economy because its decisions can generate hundreds of billions of dollars worth of economic growth. Because of that, the chair of the board of governors ranks among the most powerful positions in the federal government.

Fed monetary policy works chiefly through controlling the money supply and certain interest rates.

(See 54 Who cured high inflation? 69 What is monetarism? 70 Are there political advantages to monetary policy? 492 Who is Alan Greenspan and why is he so powerful? 493 What is the money supply? 495 What is the discount rate? 496 Who sets the prime rate?)

Q 490. How does the Federal Reserve affect the economy?

A The Federal Reserve can influence the economy in various ways, but most often it does so by controlling the money supply. Generally it increases growth of the money supply indirectly, by buying back government securities from banks. Banks then have more cash to lend their customers for investment and other spending, which stimulates new economic activity. Or the Fed can reduce money supply growth by selling government securities to the banks at attractive rates, leaving them with less cash to lend to businesses. That drives up interest rates, slows down the economy, and also reduces inflation.

Another way the Federal Reserve controls the money supply is to change the size of reserves banks must hold. By law, banks are required to keep a fraction of their deposits as cash on hand—the reserve—against potential withdrawals by depositors. The rest of the deposits can be used for loans, which earn money for the bank. Raising reserve requirements means banks have less cash to lend, while lowering the requirement frees up more money.

The Fed also can change the rate of interest charged on certain types of loans to banks (the discount rate). Raising the rates tends to slow borrowing (and so economic activity), while lowering them tends to stimulate the economy.

(See 54 Who cured high inflation? 69 What is monetary policy? 459 What were the new economic realities of the 1970s? 493 What is the money supply? 495 What is the discount rate? 496 Who sets the prime rate?)

Q 491. Does the president control the Federal Reserve?

A No, the Federal Reserve is an independent agency that is for the most part outside the control of the president and Congress. The Fed usually does try to accommodate the president's policy aims. But its power over the economy rivals that of the president and at times has been the most important limit on presidential economic policy. (The Fed is self-supporting and so does not even rely on Congress for funding, though Congress could theoretically pass laws limiting its authority.)

Though the president's fiscal policy and Fed monetary policy have been at loggerheads from time to time, the two usually seek to coordinate their efforts to maximize the effect on the economy. Presidents often can influence Fed policy through informal means, and nonbinding policy agreements can be worked out during the monthly meetings between the Treasury secretary, the chair of the Council of Economic Advisers, the president's budget director, and the Fed chair.

(See 489 What is the Federal Reserve?)

Q 492. Who is Alan Greenspan and why is he so powerful?

A To begin with, as the current chairman of the Federal Reserve System, Alan Greenspan occupies one of the most powerful offices in the federal government. Decisions by

Greenspan and the Fed's board of governors can push the economy upward or downward depending on their intent. Power of that magnitude commands near universal respect in the financial world, where billions of dollars are at stake.

Another reason Greenspan is so powerful is that under his leadership inflation has remained in check and the economy has achieved a stable, upward growth rate. That record won him reappointment as Fed chairman by three different presidents—Ronald Reagan, George Bush, and Bill Clinton. Endorsements like those carry considerable weight within the political sphere and give Greenspan even greater influence within the government than he might ordinarily have had.

(See 54 Who cured high inflation?)

Q 493. What is the money supply?

A Generally speaking, the money supply is the total amount of bills and coins in circulation plus the total value of demand deposits held by banks and credit unions. The amount of money available is a crucial factor in the economy because it is used for nearly all economic transactions. When there is plenty of money available, economic activity tends to increase. When there is too little, the lack of money tends to slow the economy. The Federal Reserve uses various tools at its disposal to regulate the growth of the money supply.

Economists measure the money supply in three basic ways—M-1, M-2, and M-3. M-1 is the narrowest measure of the money supply, including just the currency in circulation and bank deposits. M-2 includes M-1 plus savings and time deposits under $100,000, shares of money market mutual funds, and large overnight deposits by corporations, which are called repurchase agreements. M-3 includes M-2, time deposits over $100,000, and long-term repurchase agreements (see Table 6-1).

(See 54 Who cured high inflation? 69 What is monetary policy? 502 Why is money sometimes "tight" and sometimes "loose"?)

Q 494. What is the federal funds rate?

A The federal funds rate is the interest rate banks charge on short-term loans of reserve funds, called *federal funds,* to other banks. Banks that have more than the legal minimum of reserves on deposit with the Federal Reserve can lend the excess to another bank, which needs additional reserves. Loans typically are for one day and are in multiples of a million dollars. When a loan is made, the Federal Reserve simply notes the changes in the banks' reserve accounts; the reserve funds remain on deposit with the Federal Reserve.

Table 6-1 Money Supply Growth (Percentage change, year to year)

	M-1	*M-2*	*M-3*
1959	—	—	—
1960	0.5%	4.9%	5.2%
1961	3.2	7.4	8.1
1962	1.8	8.1	8.9
1963	3.7	8.4	9.3
1964	4.6	8.0	9.0
1965	4.7	8.1	9.0
1966	2.4	4.6	4.8
1967	6.6	9.3	10.4
1968	7.7	8.0	8.8
1969	3.3	3.7	1.4
1970	5.1	6.6	10.0
1971	6.5	13.4	14.6
1972	9.2	13.0	14.2
1973	5.5	6.6	11.2
1974	4.4	5.5	8.6
1975	4.8	12.7	9.5
1976	6.5	13.3	11.9
1977	8.2	10.3	12.2
1978	8.2	7.6	11.8
1979	6.8	7.9	9.7
1980	6.8	8.5	10.3
1981	6.8	9.7	12.5
1982	8.7	8.8	9.0
1983	9.8	11.4	9.9
1984	5.9	8.7	11.0
1985	12.3	8.0	7.3
1986	16.9	9.5	9.0
1987	3.5	3.6	5.4
1988	4.9	5.8	6.5
1989	0.9	5.5	3.9

(Continued on next page)

Table 6-1 *(Continued)*

	M-1	*M-2*	*M-3*
1990	4.0	3.7	1.4
1991	8.6	3.1	1.3
1992	14.2	1.6	0.2
1993	10.2	1.6	1.5
1994	1.8	0.4	1.6
1995	–2.1	4.2	5.9
1996	–4.3	4.6	7.0

Source: Economic Report of the President, 1997.

The interest rate of these federal fund loans usually is lower than the Federal Reserve discount rate (the rate the Fed charges for loans to member banks). The federal funds interest rate tends to rise during times of tight money policy.

Q 495. What is the discount rate?

A When commercial banks must borrow money from a Federal Reserve bank, the interest rate they pay is called the discount rate. The discount rate, or rediscount rate as it is also called, is one way the Federal Reserve controls the money supply, and it is considered a barometer of whether the Fed is trying to expand or tighten the money supply (see Table 6-2).

By raising the discount rate, the Fed makes it more costly for commercial banks to borrow money, and for businesses that borrow from the commercial bank. The extra cost discourages businesses from seeking new loans and so dampens economic activity. When the discount rate comes down, it makes loans cheaper and stimulates business activity.

In practice, however, banks that need to borrow money use the Federal Reserve only as a last resort. That is because the discount rate is usually higher than the interest charged for other sources of funds.

Q 496. Who sets the prime rate?

A The prime rate is the lowest short-term interest rate commercial banks charge their biggest and most creditworthy corporate customers. Commercial banks set the rate

Table 6-2 Key Interest Rates, 1940–1996

	Discount rate (at N.Y. Federal Reserve Bank)	*Federal funds rate*	*Prime rate (charged by banks)*
1940	1.00%	—	1.50%
1941	1.00	—	1.50
1942	1.00	—	1.50
1943	1.00	—	1.50
1944	1.00	—	1.50
1945	1.00	—	1.50
1946	1.00	—	1.50
1947	1.00	—	1.50–1.75
1948	1.34	—	1.75–2.00
1949	1.50	—	2.00
1950	1.59	—	2.07
1951	1.75	—	2.56
1952	1.75	—	3.00
1953	1.99	—	3.17
1954	1.60	—	3.05
1955	1.89	1.78%	3.16
1956	2.77	2.73	3.77
1957	3.12	3.11	4.20
1958	2.15	1.57	3.83
1959	3.36	3.30	4.48
1960	3.53	3.22	4.82
1961	3.00	1.96	4.50
1962	3.00	2.68	4.50
1963	3.23	3.18	4.50
1964	3.55	3.50	4.50
1965	4.04	4.07	4.54
1966	4.50	5.11	5.63
1967	4.19	4.22	5.61
1968	5.16	5.66	6.30
1969	5.87	8.20	7.96

(Continued on next page)

Table 6-2 *(Continued)*

	Discount rate (at N.Y. Federal Reserve Bank)	Federal funds rate	Prime rate (charged by banks)
1970	5.95	7.18	7.91
1971	4.88	4.66	5.72
1972	4.50	4.43	5.25
1973	6.44	8.73	8.03
1974	7.83	10.50	10.81
1975	6.25	5.82	7.86
1976	5.50	5.04	6.84
1977	5.46	5.54	6.83
1978	7.46	7.93	9.06
1979	10.28	11.19	12.67
1980	11.77	13.36	15.27
1981	13.42	16.38	18.87
1982	11.02	12.26	14.86
1983	8.50	9.09	10.79
1984	8.80	10.23	12.04
1985	7.69	8.10	9.93
1986	6.33	6.81	8.33
1987	5.66	6.66	8.21
1988	6.20	7.57	9.32
1989	6.93	9.21	10.87
1990	6.98	8.10	10.01
1991	5.45	5.69	8.46
1992	3.25	3.52	6.25
1993	3.00	3.02	6.00
1994	3.60	4.21	7.15
1995	5.21	5.83	8.83
1996	5.02	5.30	8.27

Source: Economic Report of the President, 1997.

themselves, usually based on a complex formula, and interest rates for loans to all other less-favored customers are proportionately higher. At times major banks may set slightly different prime rates, in which case the prime rate is said to be split. In recent years the prime rate has remained under 10 percent, but at the height of the rise of interest rates in 1981, it topped 20 percent.

▶ What does the Treasury Department do? *See 308 Why does the Treasury Department have so much influence in economic policy making?* ◀

Q 497. What did Treasury Secretary Rubin do to stave off default during the 1995–1996 budget debate?

A Faced with the possibility that the United States might default for the first time ever on interest and principal payments to bondholders, Treasury Secretary Robert E. Rubin resorted to extraordinary but legal financial maneuvers to keep government accounts in the black. In the fall of 1995, urgently needed legislation to raise the debt limit became caught in the crossfire during the fierce budget battle between the Republican-controlled Congress and President Bill Clinton. By mid-November the Treasury was so close to the current $4.9 trillion debt limit that it would have been unable to borrow enough money to meet a $25 billion interest payment.

Rather than allow the government to default, Rubin "disinvested" $61.3 billion in government securities from two civil service retirement funds. Largely a bookkeeping maneuver, it involved replacing the securities with a non-interest-bearing IOU. That technically erased $61.3 billion in bonds from the Treasury's balance sheet, allowing it to raise that amount through the sale of new bonds on the public bond market. (The two civil service funds had provisions allowing such temporary "disinvestment," so long as both the securities and lost interest were restored at a later date.)

(See 207 Has the government been using funds from Social Security for other purposes?)

For the Fed Chairman, It's an Outcry.

"Clearly to default for the first time in the history of this nation is not something anyone should take in a tranquil manner."

—Federal Reserve Chairman Alan Greenspan, from testimony during a Senate Banking Committee hearing, September 22, 1995

Q 498. Why is Treasury's Financial Management Service (FMS) important?

A Whenever the Treasury wants to issue a check or make an electronic transfer, it is the Financial Management Service's job to actually fill out the check and send it out. All the checks and transfers the government makes from the Treasury are handled by FMS, including federal employee paychecks, income tax refunds, Social Security and other benefit checks, and even payments to businesses that provide the services and supplies the government uses. In all, the FMS writes about 500 million checks and handles 250 million electronic transfers each year.

(See 3 Who actually spends the money?)

Q 499. What does the monthly Treasury statement cover?

A The *Monthly Statement of Receipts and Outlays of the United States Government* gives a detailed summary of revenue collections, budget expenditures, and deficits for the fiscal year to date. Also included are statements of activity in trust fund accounts, public debt securities, and public enterprise funds. The Treasury also publishes the *Daily Statement of the Treasury.*

Q 500. When did Congress deregulate the banking industry?

A Congress passed the Depository Institutions Deregulation and Monetary Control Act in 1980. Bank deregulation had been under consideration since the Nixon years, and the 1980 act came in part at the urging of the Carter administration. It eliminated many regulatory distinctions between commercial banks and thrift institutions (savings and loan banks), mutual savings banks, and credit unions, lifted interest rate ceilings on savings accounts, raised the deposit insurance limit from $40,000 to $100,000, and made other changes.

A second, more fateful step in deregulation came when Congress passed the Depository Institutions Act in 1982. This law allowed thrift institutions to make loans in various new markets, with or without security. Previously thrifts had been limited to making loans in strictly defined markets, such as home mortgages, which made it difficult for them to compete with commercial banks. The new law loosened other banking restrictions as well, allowing developers to own savings and loan banks (S & Ls), and even made it possible for S & L owners to lend themselves bank funds. New accounting practices and other changes made it possible for S & Ls to resist government seizure even when they were technically insolvent.

The S & Ls' highly publicized speculation in real estate and other ventures, and their ability to resist being taken over by the government in the event of insolvency were among the factors contributing to the savings and loan crisis of the late 1980s. But the chief cause was one that had troubled the industry for decades—interest rates. Like all other banks, S & Ls make money by loaning out much of the money depositors put into savings accounts. In the case of S & Ls, though, most of the money went into long-term loans at fixed rates (such as thirty-year mortgages).

So long as the interest rate of the loan was greater than the interest the S & L paid depositors, the bank made money. But during the late 1970s and early 1980s especially, short-term interest rates were very high, and the rate S & Ls had to pay to attract depositors soared above what they were getting for the long-term (thirty-year) mortgage loans. S & Ls lost billions as a result, and the prolonged high interest rates finally brought on the S & L crisis.

(See 264 How much did the savings and loan crisis finally costs us?)

Q **501. What purpose do Treasury bills serve?**

A Treasury bills (or T-bills) are the shortest-term notes issued by the federal government. They are sold at a discount on the face value, mature in 91 or 182 days, and because of the government's high credit rating, are considered an attractive short-term investment by banks, foreign central banks, and businesses.

The Federal Reserve uses T-bills extensively in its efforts to stabilize the economy. By buying or selling large blocks of the notes, the Federal Reserve can raise or lower the amount of money in the nation's financial system. T-bills also offer the government a fairly inexpensive way to borrow money.

In addition, the Treasury issues longer-term securities, including Treasury notes with maturities of up to ten years and Treasury bonds that have maturities of up to thirty years (see Table 6-3). The Treasury also issues the familiar U.S. Savings Bonds.

(See 490 How does the Federal Reserve affect the economy?)

Q **502. Why is money sometimes "tight" and sometimes "loose"?**

A These two expressions frequently appear in newspaper and magazine articles referring to the Federal Reserve's monetary policy. An easy (or loose) money policy makes more money available to commercial banks, which then lend the money for business investment and other purposes. The increased flow of money in turn usually produces a rise

Table 6-3 Treasury Bill and Bond Interest Rates, 1940–1996

	3-mo.	*6-mo.*	*3-year*	*10-year*	*30-year*
1940	0.014%	—	—	—	—
1941	0.103	—	—	—	—
1942	0.326	—	—	—	—
1943	0.373	—	—	—	—
1944	0.375	—	—	—	—
1945	0.375	—	—	—	—
1946	0.375	—	—	—	—
1947	0.594	—	—	—	—
1948	1.040	—	—	—	—
1949	1.102	—	—	—	—
1950	1.218	—	—	—	—
1951	1.552	—	—	—	—
1952	1.766	—	—	—	—
1953	1.931	—	2.47%	2.85%	—
1954	0.953	—	1.63	2.40	—
1955	1.753	—	2.47	2.82	—
1956	2.658	—	3.19	3.18	—
1957	3.267	—	3.98	3.65	—
1958	1.839	—	2.84	3.32	—
1959	3.405	3.832%	4.46	4.33	—
1960	2.928	3.247	3.98	4.12	—
1961	2.378	2.605	3.54	3.88	—
1962	2.778	2.908	3.47	3.95	—
1963	3.157	3.253	3.67	4.00	—
1964	3.549	3.686	4.03	4.19	—
1965	3.954	4.055	4.22	4.28	—
1966	4.881	5.082	5.23	4.92	—
1967	4.321	4.630	5.03	5.07	—
1968	5.339	5.470	5.68	5.65	—
1969	6.677	6.853	7.02	6.67	—

Table 6-3 *(Continued)*

	3-mo.	*6-mo.*	*3-year*	*10-year*	*30-year*
1970	6.458	6.562	7.29	7.35	—
1971	4.348	4.511	5.65	6.16	—
1972	4.071	4.466	5.72	6.21	—
1973	7.041	7.178	6.95	6.84	—
1974	7.886	7.926	7.82	7.56	—
1975	5.838	6.122	7.49	7.99	—
1976	4.989	5.266	6.77	7.61	—
1977	5.265	5.510	6.69	7.42	7.750%
1978	7.221	7.572	8.29	8.41	8.490
1979	10.041	10.017	9.71	9.44	9.280
1980	11.506	11.374	11.55	11.46	11.270
1981	14.029	13.776	14.44	13.91	13.450
1982	10.686	11.084	12.92	13.00	12.760
1983	8.63	8.75	10.45	11.10	11.180
1984	9.58	9.80	11.89	12.44	12.410
1985	7.48	7.66	9.64	10.62	10.790
1986	5.98	6.03	7.06	7.68	7.780
1987	5.82	6.05	7.68	8.39	8.590
1988	6.69	6.92	8.26	8.85	8.960
1989	8.12	8.04	8.55	8.49	8.450
1990	7.51	7.47	8.26	8.55	8.610
1991	5.42	5.49	6.82	7.86	8.140
1992	3.45	3.57	5.30	7.01	7.670
1993	3.02	3.14	4.44	5.87	6.590
1994	4.29	4.66	6.27	7.09	7.370
1995	5.51	5.59	6.25	6.57	6.880
1996	5.02	5.09	5.99	6.44	6.710

Source: Economic Report of the President, 1997.

in business activity and an expanding economy. Lower interest rates generally accompany a period of easy money, and this helps stimulate demand for the loans.

Tight money policy tends to restrict the amount of money commercial banks have to lend, and rising interest rates also make loans less attractive because they now cost more. Ultimately this slowing of money supply growth dampens business activity and slows the economy. The Federal Reserve has imposed a tight money policy for much of the 1980s and 1990s as a means of controlling inflation.

(See 49 What causes inflation? 52 What does inflation do to the economy? 490 How does the Federal Reserve affect the economy? 493 What is the money supply?)

BEYOND OUR BORDERS

Q 503. What is the exchange rate?

A If you want to travel to France, for example, you will want to trade some of your dollars for the French currency, the franc. In a recent year you would have gotten about 5.5 francs for every dollar you traded, because the *exchange rate* at that time was 5.5 to 1.

The exchange rate is nothing more than the trading ratio of one currency against another. The rate for dollars varies from one country to the next and also over time as the value of the dollar changes relative to other currencies.

The exchange rate is an essential part of international trade. Goods bought for import usually are paid for in the seller's currency, and the exchange rate provides a convenient way of converting from one currency to another. The rate itself also can affect a country's exports. If the country's currency has a low value (many Japanese yen for one American dollar, for example), its exported goods will be cheaper in foreign markets. On the other hand, a country with a high-value currency will have trouble exporting to foreign markets because its goods will be too expensive.

Some typical exchange rates for one American dollar in a recent year are: 1.36 Canadian dollars, 1.62 German deutsche marks, 242.6 Greek drachmas, 102.2 Japanese yen, 31.3 Indian rupees, 1.5 British pounds, and 0.73 Australian dollars.

(See 510 What happens when the dollar is devalued?)

▶ What did the Bretton Woods Conference do? *See 424 Why was the Bretton Woods System important?* ◀

Q 504. What proved to be the advantages and disadvantages of pegging the value of foreign currencies on the U.S. dollar?

A The Bretton Woods System of fixed exchange rates based on the U.S. dollar helped promote stability in international monetary exchange and so contributed to the sharp increase in world trade after World War II. Unfortunately, that system proved unable to compensate for differences in inflation rates between countries. And a key feature of the system, the agreement by the United States to convert dollars into gold, led to a gold drain. Between 1949 and 1971, U.S. gold reserves dropped from about $23 billion to just $10 billion. That prompted President Richard Nixon's order ending both the agreement to convert dollars into gold and the Bretton Woods System of fixed exchange rates. In the future, currency values were to "float" against one another on the international currency market.

Q 505. How do the United States and other countries control the value of their currencies?

A Though the present system allows currencies to "float" against one another, governments can and do act to raise or lower the value of their currencies. A country's central bank can raise the value of its national currency, for example, by making large purchases on the international currency market. Selling the national currency on the currency market lowers the value.

The United States buys and sells dollars through its central bank, the Federal Reserve System. But even the substantial U.S. reserves alone may not be enough to change the dollar's value by the desired amount. For that reason, the United States and other major countries usually try to coordinate their exchange rate policies and cooperate in efforts to adjust currency levels.

Q 506. Does a strong dollar help the economy?

A A dollar that is too strong in the long run probably would hurt the economy. When the dollar is strong (worth more relative to other currencies), it does make buying imports cheaper and so helps hold down consumer prices. For example, Japanese cars and imported foreign oil are less expensive when the dollar is strong, and generally speaking the lower prices tend to increase imports.

But the strong dollar also makes U.S. goods more expensive on foreign markets, and so cuts into exports. As exports drop off and imports increase, the country will suffer a growing trade deficit. Meanwhile, the declining exports will result in lost jobs and slowed economic growth.

(See 509 Why do we have trade deficits?)

Q 507. What purpose do conferences of G-7 nations serve?

A These annual economic summits, which have been held since 1975, are attended by leaders of nations known as the Group of Seven, or G-7—the United States, Japan, Great Britain, Canada, Germany, France, and Italy. Together these nations control a huge share of the international economy, and the G-7 meetings have increased international economic coordination. Agreements on currency levels and coordinated buying and selling of currencies to maintain the desired currency values are an important part of G-7 negotiations. But the meetings also deal with various other economic concerns, such as promoting freer trade. In this case the summits have provided a forum at which leaders of nations met face-to-face to discuss removing trade barriers.

Q 508. What is the balance of payments?

A The balance of payments is the sum of all money a country collects from foreign trading partners during a year (or other time period) minus all the payments it makes to foreign countries. It includes the *balance of trade* (the difference between receipts from exports and payments for imports), as well as private loans and interest to and from foreign sources, money spent by tourists, government aid and grants to foreign countries, and transfers of gold bullion. If the total value of all these exports is greater than imports, it is called a *trade surplus.* If exports are less than imports, it is a *trade deficit.* A chronic unfavorable balance of payments can have an impact on the stability of the country's currency.

The balance of payments is also referred to as the current account.

Q 509. Why do we have trade deficits?

A The United States posted a small surplus in its balance of payments for most years between 1950 and 1970. The cost of maintaining large contingents of military forces overseas, foreign aid, and investments in Europe by U.S. businesses all helped keep trade surpluses fairly small during that period. During the 1960s and 1970s, however, increased competition from foreign manufacturers and a growing dependence on imported oil began to affect our balance of payments. Under President Richard Nixon, the government even devalued the currency in 1971 and 1973 to promote a better balance of payments. But oil price hikes during the 1970s, the increasing success of foreign goods in the U.S. market, greater reliance on foreign capital to finance the debt, and increased foreign investment in the United States have combined to create major trade deficits year after year since the 1980s (see Table 6-4).

Q 510. What happens when the dollar is devalued?

A Devaluation is reduction in the value of a country's currency relative to that of another country or relative to gold. A country may devalue its currency when the value of its exports is far less than the cost of its imports (a balance of payment problem). By lowering the value of its currency, the country creates more demand for its exported goods—because they are now cheaper in foreign markets—and so raises the volume of exports. Imported goods cost more, however, because the country's currency is worth less, but that, too, helps the country's balance of payments problem by lowering demand for imports.

Because currency values today are allowed to "float" against one another, the dollar's value may rise (a stronger dollar) or fall (a weaker dollar) depending on a variety of economic and other considerations. The government does intervene in currency markets from time to time to raise or lower the dollar's value.

Q 511. With which countries does the United States have large trade deficits?

A As of the mid-1990s, the United States had trade deficits with about twenty countries. Of the deficits, the largest by far was with Japan, which amounted to –$59.3 billion in 1995. Our next largest trade deficit was with China— –$22.7 billion—followed by Canada (–$10.8 billion), Germany (–$9.6 billion), Taiwan (–$8.9 billion), and Italy (–$6.8 billion).

Q 512. Has the trade deficit with Japan been increasing or decreasing?

A Despite the best efforts of the past three presidents, the annual U.S. trade deficit with Japan has remained stuck in the $40 billion to $60 billion range since the mid-1980s (see Table 6-5).

Table 6-4 Balance of Payments—Going Out of Balance

	Surplus or deficit (–) (in billions)		*Surplus or deficit (–) (in billions)*
1950	–1.8	1973	7.1
1951	0.9	1974	2.0
1952	0.6		
1953	–1.3	1975	18.1
1954	0.2	1976	4.3
		1977	–14.4
1955	0.4	1978	–15.1
1956	2.7	1979	–0.2
1957	4.8		
1958	0.8	1980	2.3
1959	–1.3	1981	5.0
		1982	–11.5
1960	2.8	1983	–43.9
1961	3.8	1984	–98.6
1962	3.4		
1963	4.4	1985	–124.2
1964	6.8	1986	–152.1
		1987	–167.4
1965	5.4	1988	–128.4
1966	3.0	1989	–105.6
1967	2.6		
1968	0.6	1990	–94.7
1969	0.4	1991	–9.5
		1992	–62.6
1970	2.3	1993	–100.0
1971	–1.4	1994	–148.4
1972	–5.8		
		1995	–148.1
		1996	–148.1

Source: Economic Report of the President, 1997.

Table 6–5 The High Cost of Trade With Japan (in millions of dollars)

	Trade balance	*Imports from Japan*	*Exports to Japan*
1960	$ 303	$ 1,149	$ 1,452
1965	–330	2,414	2,084
1970	–1,265	5,875	4,610
1975	–2,915	12,336	9,421
1976	–6,892	16,922	10,030
1977	–9,859	20,273	10,414
1978	–13,576	26,461	12,885
1979	–10,588	28,169	17,581
1980	–12,183	32,973	20,790
1981	–18,081	39,904	21,823
1982	–18,966	39,932	20,966
1983	–21,665	43,559	21,894
1984	–33,560	57,135	23,575
1985	–46,152	68,783	22,631
1986	–55,030	81,911	26,882
1987	–56,326	84,575	28,249
1988	–51,794	89,519	37,725
1989	–49,059	93,553	44,494
1990	–41,105	89,684	48,580
1991	–43,385	91,511	48,125
1992	–49,601	97,414	47,813
1993	–59,355	107,246	47,891
1994	–65,668	119,156	53,488
1995	–59,137	123,479	64,343
1996	–47,682	115,218	67,536

Source: Bureau of the Census.

Q 513. Is trade protectionism good or bad for the economy?

A Trade protectionism, in which a country heavily taxes or otherwise limits imports, is generally thought to hamper economic growth. That is because other countries respond with trade barriers of their own and so cut access to foreign markets, markets that could encourage expansion of domestic industries.

The United States maintained protectionist tariffs throughout much of the 1800s and early 1900s. The Republican party strongly supported the high-tariff policy. In the mid-1930s, though, the Democratic-controlled Congress authorized President Franklin Roosevelt to begin negotiating with other nations for mutual tariff reductions. From that time forward, and especially since World War II, the United States has been generally committed to eliminating trade barriers and opening up freer trade, on the principle that it will stimulate economic growth (as in GATT and NAFTA).

At times, however, Congress has enacted tariffs to protect specific industries or to encourage specific foreign countries to open their markets to U.S. goods.

(See 425 What was GATT and how did it affect the economy?)

Q 514. What is NAFTA?

A NAFTA, or the North American Free Trade Agreement, is an international trade pact between the United States, Canada, and Mexico. Approved by the three countries in 1993, NAFTA will eliminate tariffs and other trade barriers between the three countries over a period of fifteen years, creating one of the world's largest free-trade zones. Canada and the United States had already lowered many tariffs on trade between themselves by signing a separate trade agreement in 1989.

NAFTA became an issue in the 1992 presidential campaign when third-party candidate Ross Perot warned of a "giant sucking sound," which he said would follow passage of NAFTA. That sound was to be created by the rush of American manufacturing jobs leaving the country to take advantage of Mexico's low-cost labor. Nevertheless, Congress approved the agreement in 1993, creating a free-trade zone that rivals the newly enlarged European Economic Community.

Q 515. How did devaluation of Mexico's peso affect the dollar?

A The United States has had economic ties with Mexico for many years, and passage of NAFTA in 1993 further increased the economic interdependence. While both parties enjoy advantages in this relationship, there are some disadvantages as well. One of them became all too apparent shortly after Mexico drastically devalued the peso in 1994, precipitating a collapse of that country's economy. As the peso plummeted on world markets, the U.S. dollar began falling with it, because the United States was so heavily invested in Mexico. Nor could the United States allow the economic collapse of a key member of the newly formed trading partnership. In the end the United States helped stabilize Mexico's economy, and its currency, with $12.5 billion in loans, about the same amount the International Monetary Fund lent Mexico during the crisis. Mexico repaid the U.S. loan in full by early 1997. The Treasury Department reported earning about $580 million in interest.

(See 510 What happens when the dollar is devalued?)

Q 516. What is a stabilization crisis?

A Although it is unlikely one would ever occur, a stabilization crisis could arise from the U.S. dependence on foreign capital to finance the national debt. Once held entirely by American investors, the national debt became so large that foreign investors now provide capital for a substantial part of it.

Under most circumstances this is not a problem; in fact, it gives other countries a stake in keeping the U.S. economy growing. But there could be serious repercussions if the foreign investors all suddenly cashed in their securities because, for example, they had lost confidence in the U.S. dollar. The resulting stabilization crisis would push the value of the dollar down sharply and create a credit crunch as the government began drawing up all available capital on the domestic market. Both inflation and interest rates would skyrocket.

(See 19 Can't we just ignore the debt? 128 Where does the government get the money it borrows? 136 Have we mortgaged the country to foreign investors?)

BIBLIOGRAPHY

In addition to books listed below, the reader will find further information in various periodicals, such as the *Washington Post, Congressional Quarterly,* and *Congressional Digest,* by consulting indexes to bound volumes, periodical databases, Web sites, and other information sources.

Ammer, Christine, and Dean S. Ammer. *Dictionary of Business and Economics.* Rev. ed. New York: Free Press, 1986.

Barone, Michael, and Grant Ujifusa. *The Almanac of American Politics 1996.* Washington, D.C.: National Journal, annual.

Boskin, Michael J., ed. *Frontiers of Tax Reform.* Stanford, Calif.: Hoover Institution Press, 1996.

Buchholz, Todd G. *From Here to Economy: A Shortcut to Economic Literacy.* New York: Dutton, 1989.

Bullock, Charles Jesse. *The Finances of the United States from 1775 to 1789, With Especial Reference to the Budget.* Philadelphia: Porcupine Press, 1979.

Bureau of the Census. *Historical Statistics of the United States, 1789–1945: A Supplement to the Historical Abstract of the United States.* Washington, D.C.: Bureau of the Census, 1949.

Calleo, David P. *The Bankrupting of America: Funny Money and the Federal Budget Deficit.* New York: Morrow, 1992.

Carroll, Richard J. *The Economic Record of Presidential Performance: From Truman to Bush.* Westport, Conn.: Greenwood Publishing Group, 1995.

Carruth, Gorton. *The Encyclopedia of American Facts and Dates.* 10th ed. New York: Harper & Row, 1997.

Chernow, Barbara A., and George A. Vallasi, eds. *The Columbia Encyclopedia.* 5th ed. New York: Columbia University Press, 1993.

Cogan, John F. *Federal Budget Deficits: What's Wrong with the Congressional Budget Process.* Stanford, Calif.: Hoover Institution Press, 1992.

Cogan, John F., Timothy J. Muris, and Allen Schick. *The Budget Puzzle: Understanding Federal Spending.* Stanford, Calif.: Stanford University Press, 1994.

Collender, Stanley E. *Guide to the Federal Budget, Fiscal 1998.* Lanham, Md.: University Press of America, 1997.

Congress A to Z: A Ready Reference Encyclopedia. 2d ed. Washington, D.C.: Congressional Quarterly, 1993.

Congressional Quarterly Almanac. Washington, D.C.: Congressional Quarterly, annual.

Congressional Quarterly's Guide to Congress. 4th ed. Washington, D.C.: Congressional Quarterly, 1991.

Cranford, John. *Budgeting for America.* Washington, D.C.: Congressional Quarterly, 1989.

Daniel, Clifton, ed. *Chronicle of the Twentieth Century.* Mount Kisco, N.Y.: Chronicle Publications, 1988.

Derks, Scott, ed. *The Value of a Dollar: Princes and Incomes in the United States 1860–1989.* Detroit: Gale Research, 1994.

Dodd, Donald B., and Wynelle S. Dodd. *Historical Statistics of the United States, 1790–1970.* Tuscaloosa: University of Alabama Press, 1973.

Doty, Roy. *How Much Does America Cost?* Garden City, N.Y.: Doubleday, 1979.

Duncan, Philip D., and Christine C. Lawrence. *Congressional Quarterly's Politics in America.* Washington, D.C.: Congressional Quarterly, annual.

Economic Report of the President. Washington, D.C.: Government Printing Office, annual.

Encyclopedia Americana. Danbury, Conn.: Grolier.

Encyclopedia Britannica. 15th ed. Chicago: Encyclopedia Britannica.

Facts on File Yearbook: The Indexed Record of World Events. New York: Facts on File, annual.

Franklin, Daniel. *Making Ends Meet: Congressional Budgeting in the Age of Deficits.* Washington, D.C.: Congressional Quarterly, 1992.

Galbraith, John Kenneth, and Nicole Salinger. *Almost Everyone's Guide to Economics.* Boston: Houghton Mifflin, 1978.

Gilmour, John B. *Reconcilable Differences? Congress, the Budget Process, and the Deficit.* Berkeley: University of California Press, 1990.

Gordon, John Steele. *Hamilton's Blessing: The Extraordinary Life and Times of Our National Debt.* New York: Walker and Company, 1997.

Government Accounting Office. *Financial Audit, Resolution Trust Corporation's 1995 and 1994 Financial Statements.* Washington, D.C.: Government Accounting Office, 1996.

Greenwald, Douglas. *McGraw-Hill Encyclopedia of Economics.* New York: McGraw-Hill, 1994.

Henderson, David R. *Fortune Encyclopedia of Economics.* New York: Warner Books, 1993.

Ippolito, Dennis. *Uncertain Legacies: Federal Budget Policy from Roosevelt Through Reagan.* Charlottesville: University Press of Virginia, 1990.

James, Simon. *A Dictionary of Economic Quotations.* 2d ed. Lanham, Md.: Littlefield, 1984.

Kasten, Richard. *The Changing Distribution of Federal Taxes, 1975–1990.* Washington, D.C.: Congressional Budget Office, 1987.

Kelly, Brian. *Adventures in Porkland: How Washington Wastes Your Money.* New York: Random House, 1992.

Kravitz, Walter. *Congressional Quarterly's American Congressional Dictionary.* Washington, D.C.: Congressional Quarterly, 1993.

Lee, Susan. *Susan Lee's ABCs of Economics.* New York: Poseidon Press, 1987.

Legler, John B. *Regional Distribution of Federal Receipts and Expenditures in the Nineteenth Century, A Quantitative Study.* New York: Arno Press, 1977.

LeLoup, Lance T. *Budgetary Politics.* 4th ed. Brunswick, Ohio: King's Court Communications, 1988.

Lynch, Thomas D. *Public Budgeting in America.* 4th ed. Englewood Cliffs, N.J.: Prentice Hall, 1994.

Marini, John A. *The Politics of Budget Control: Congress, the Presidency, and the Growth of the Administrative State.* New York: Crane Russak, 1992.

McGraw-Hill Dictionary of Modern Economics. 3d ed. New York: McGraw-Hill, 1984.

Morgan, Iwan W. *Eisenhower versus "the Spenders": The Eisenhower Administration, the Democrats, and the Budget, 1953–1960.* New York: St. Martins, 1990.

Neely, Richard. *Tragedies of Our Own Making: How Private Choices Have Created Public Bankruptcy.* Champaign: University of Illinois Press, 1994.

Nelson, Michael, ed. *Congressional Quarterly's Guide to the Presidency.* Washington, D.C.: Congressional Quarterly, 1996.

Nelson, Michael, ed. *The Presidency A to Z: A Ready Reference Encyclopedia.* Washington, D.C.: Congressional Quarterly, 1994.

Penner, Rudolph G., and Alan J. Abramson. *Broken Purse Strings: Congressional Budgeting, 1974–1988.* Washington, D.C.: Urban Institute Press, 1988.

Rubin, Irene S. *The Politics of Public Budgeting: Getting and Spending, Borrowing and Balancing.* Chatham, N.J.: Chatham House, 1993.

Rutherford, Donald. *Dictionary of Economics.* New York: Routledge, 1992.

Savage, James D. *Balanced Budgets and American Politics.* Ithaca, N.Y.: Cornell University Press, 1988.

Schick, Allen. *Crisis in the Budget Process.* Washington, D.C.: American Enterprise Institute for Public Policy, 1986.

Schick, Allen. *The Capacity to Budget.* Lanham, Md.: Urban Institute Press, 1990.

Schick, Allen. *The Federal Budget: Politics, Policy, Process.* Washington, D.C.: Brookings Institution, 1995.

Schick, Allen. *The Whole and the Parts: Piecemeal and Integrated Approaches to Congressional Budgeting.* Washington, D.C.: Committee on the Budget, U.S. House of Representatives, 1987.

Shuman, Howard E. *Politics and the Budget: The Struggle Between the President and the Congress.* 3d ed. Englewood Cliffs, N.J.: Prentice Hall, 1992.

Solomon, Gerald B. *The Balanced Budget: A Republican Plan.* Stockbridge, Mass.: Berkshire House, 1995.

Statistical Abstract of the United States. Austin, Texas: Reference Press, annual.

Stewart, Charles Haines. *Budget Reform Politics, the Design of the Appropriations Process in the House of Representatives, 1865–1921.* New York: Cambridge University Press, 1989.

U.S. Office of Management and Budget. *Budget of the United States Government, A Citizen's Guide to the Federal Budget.* Washington, D.C.: Government Printing Office, annual.

U.S. Office of Management and Budget. *Budget of the United States Government, Analytical Perspectives.* Washington, D.C.: Government Printing Office, annual.

U.S. Office of Management and Budget. *Budget of the United States Government, Historical Tables.* Washington, D.C.: Government Printing Office, annual.

U.S. Office of Management and Budget. *Budget of the United States Government, the Budget.* Washington, D.C.: Government Printing Office, annual.

Watkins, Alfred J. *Red Ink II: A Guide to Understanding the Continuing Deficit Dilemma.* Lanham, Md.: University Press of America, 1988.

Wetterau, Bruce. *Congressional Quarterly's Desk Reference on American Government.* Washington, D.C.: Congressional Quarterly, 1995.

Wetterau, Bruce. *World History: A Dictionary of Important People, Places, and Events from Ancient Times to the Present.* New York: Henry Holt, 1994.

Wildavsky, Aaron B. *The New Politics of the Budgetary Process.* 2d ed. New York: Harper Collins, 1992.

INDEX

References in the index correspond to question numbers in the text.

Adams, Brock
  Budget Committee chair, 328
Administration for Children and Families, 255
AFDC. *See* Aid to Families with Dependent Children
Agencies
  agency debt, 137
  Book of Estimates, 283
  budget process, 272, 274
  budget writing, 276, 277
  budgeting and, 9
  chief financial officer, 315
  close of fiscal year, 277
  defending the budget, 366
  earmarking, 360
  iron triangles, 166
  legislative requests, 311
  management reforms, 314
  offsetting receipts, 291
  procedural reforms, 313
  reprogramming, 317
  spending, 3, 289, 290
  spending powers, 285
  supplemental appropriations, 353
Agency for International Development
  budget, 153
Agricultural Adjustment Act of 1933
  court test, 321
Agricultural extension service
  budget, 239
Agriculture, Department of
  agricultural extension service, 239
  budget share, 147
  Commodity Credit Corporation, 239, 240
  federal crop insurance program, 239
  Food and Consumer Service, 239
  food stamps, 239
  Forest Service, 239
  Rural Housing Service, 216, 218
  spending by category, 239
  Women, Infants, and Children (WIC), 239
Aid to Families with Dependent Children (AFDC). *See also* Welfare programs
  benefit distribution, 213
  spending (table), 215
  total recipients, 210
  welfare reform, 209
Aid to the Permanently and Totally Disabled
  merged with Social Security, 427
Air Force
  budget, 226
  F-22 fighter, 231
  size of, 228
Air National Guard, 224
Airports and airways trust, 95
Albert, Carl
  defends social spending, 449
Appropriations
  annual, 371
  backdoor spending, 165
  baseline projections, 280, 281
  biennial, 371
  committee reports, described, 357
  Constitution on, 78
  defined, 274
  general, 354
  largest bill, 323
  origins of, 349
  process, 2
  regular, 272, 273, 277, 350, 353, 369
  special, 354
  supplemental, 277, 353
  two-step, 285
  veto and, 304
Appropriations Committee (House), 366
  budget timetable, 277
  budget writing, 272
  established, 284, 338
  organization, 337
Appropriations Committee (Senate), 366
  budget timetable, 277
  budget writing, 272
  created, 284, 338
  organization, 337
Arab-Israeli War
  oil embargo, 454
Archer, Bill
  chair, Ways and Means, 335
Architect of the Capitol
  budget for, 154
Army
  size of, 228
  spending by category, 227
Army Corps of Engineers
  budget, 227
Army National Guard, 224
Audits
  General Accounting Office, 342, 343
  IRS, 106
Authorizations
  annual, 344
  bills, defined, 274
  bills, origins of, 349
  committee powers, 344
  two-step, 285

Automatic spending cuts. *See* PAYGO, Sequester
Automatic stabilizers, 20, 431
defined, 60
recessions and, 471

Baby boomers
economy and, 82
effect on work force, 459
Social Security and, 204
Backdoor spending
defined, 165
Bailouts
costs, 447
Baker, James A. III
disinvesting, 282
treasury secretary, 309
Balanced budget agreement (1997)
capital gains tax, 86
deficit and, 16
described, 397
Gingrich, 395
Medicaid reforms, 192
Medicare reforms, 191
set, 284
supplants amendment, 387
tax cut, 397, 488
Balanced budget amendment, 484
described, 387
Balanced Budget and Emergency Deficit Act of 1985
need for, 382
Balance of payments
annual total (table), 509
deficits, 509, 511
described, 508
devaluation and, 510
history, 440, 509
surpluses, 509
with Japan, annual (table), 512
Banks
Depository Institutions Deregulation and Monetary Control Act (1980), 500
Depository Institutions Act (1982), 500
deregulation, 500
discount rate, 494
discount rate (table), 494
federal funds rate, 494
federal funds rate (table), 494
Federal Reserve and, 490
money supply, 490
prime rate (table), 494, 496
reserves, 490, 494
reserves and inflation, 54
tight/easy money, 502
Treasury bills, 501
Base closings, 376
Baseline projections, 300
accuracy of, 281
defined, 280
Bentsen, Lloyd
Finance Committee chair, 331
treasury secretary, 309
Biennial appropriations, 371
Blue Dogs, 324
Book of Estimates, 283
Borrowing
agency debt, 137
authority, 2, 289
congressional powers, 78
constitutional authority, 124
credit crunch, 129
credit limit, 123, 126
debt and, 19
debt limit, 282, 377, 378, 379
default averted, 497
Federal Financing Bank, 451
foreign, 19
incremental budgeting and, 316
interest, 127
marketable securities, 138
need for, 125
non-marketable securities, 138
public debt, 137
securities, 451
sources of, 128
special issues, 139
Treasury bills and, 501
World War II financing, 420
Bottom-up budgeting, 316
Bracket creep. *See also* Taxes
Carter years, 409
eliminated, 468
Brady, Nicholas Frederick
treasury secretary, 309
Bretton Woods system
advantages, disadvantages, 504
described, 424
dismantled, 446
Bridges, Styles
chair, Senate Appropriations, 339
Budget
annual, 21, 305, 344
appropriations, 337, 347
approval, 2
balanced, 329, 330, 387, 488
balanced budget amendment, 484
balancing, 5, 14, 20, 71, 158, 162, 165, 284, 286, 293, 322, 324, 372, 388, 397, 399, 430, 460, 471, 483, 484
biennial, 313, 371
Contract with America, 484
controls, 288, 362, 372, 374
credit limit, 123, 126
current budget shares, 147
cuts, 286, 364, 386, 466, 467, 468, 472, 476, 477, 478, 482, 484, 485, 486
default averted, 497
defense spending, 376
deficit reduction, 122, 361, 372, 430, 457
deficits, 125, 126
deficits (string of), 16
described, 1, 271
economy and, 5, 44, 376
expected growth, 396
first formal, 9
fiscal policy and, 67
government-owned corporations, 294
government-sponsored enterprises, 294
growth of, 143
history, 303, 304, 311, 338, 348, 399, 403, 422, 430, 439, 441, 444, 450, 453, 457, 464, 467, 473, 476, 478, 482, 484, 486, 487, 497
inflated CPI and, 41
information sources, 21, 310
interest groups, 287
largest share, 144
limitations, 1
mandatory spending share, 162
National Performance Review, 313
net interest, 126, 127, 129, 146, 286

1995-1996 shutdowns, 485
obligations-based, 288
on- and off-budget, 279
origins of debt, 18
president's role, 272, 299, 430
printed version, 1
reconciliation, 284, 467
reform history, 9, 282, 283, 284, 312, 314, 322, 327, 355, 374, 380, 381, 382, 386, 387, 388, 390, 394, 397, 415, 455, 483
revenue growth (table), 83
spending control, 146, 176
spending growth, 83 (table), 439
spending patterns, 146
summits, 323, 476, 478
supply-side theory, 71
surplus, 15, 397, 423, 430, 432, 444
timetable, 276, 277, 345, 383, 487
types of funds, 94
Budget and Accounting Act
and budget process, 9
described, 283
Budget authority, 288
defined, 3, 289
Budget authority balances
defined, 289
Budget Committee (House)
budget timetable, 277
chairs, 328
described, 327
scorekeeping, 367
Budget Committee (Senate)
budget timetable, 277
chairs, 328
described, 327
scorekeeping, 367
Budget control
balanced budget agreement, 397
Budget and Accounting Act, 283
Budget Control and Impoundment Act, 382
Budget Enforcement Act, 284, 362, 390
Chief Financial Officers Act, 284
debt origins, 18
Executive Order 12857, 284, 394
Gramm-Rudman-Hollings Act, 388
history, 372, 374
president's influence, 375
Budget deal (1990), 327
Budget Enforcement Act of 1990, 390
enacted, 284
need for, 388
PAYGO, 362
Budget process
agencies, 285, 315
appropriations, 272, 274, 337, 344, 346, 350, 351, 353, 355, 357, 360, 363, 366, 370, 371, 382, 383, 388
authorizations, 274, 344, 360
balanced budget agreement (1997), 397
balanced budget amendment, 387
baseline projections, 280, 281
Book of Estimates, 283
borrowing authority, 289
bottom-up budgeting, 316
budget authority, 289
budget authority balances, 289
budget balancing, 401
Budget Committees, 327
Budget Enforcement Act (1990), 390
Budget and Impoundment Control Act, 382, 455
budget resolution, 272, 277, 365, 367, 368, 382, 383, 455, 457
budget summits, 284
budget writing, 272, 276
budgeting history, 484, 485
committee reports, 357
conference committee, 277, 350, 356, 363
Congressional Budget Office, 341
congressional committees, 352
continuing resolution, 354, 369, 370
contract authority, 289
debt ceilings, 377, 378, 379
debt limit, 282
deferrals, 382
described, 271
discretionary spending, 368
earmarking, 360
Executive Order 12857, 394
fiscal year, 277
functions, 292
General Accounting Office, 342
Gephardt rule, 463
Gramm-Rudman targets, 478
Gramm-Rudman-Hollings Act, 386, 388
history, 311, 323, 327, 338, 348, 369, 370, 372, 377, 379, 380, 381, 382, 386, 387, 388, 390, 394, 397, 401, 415, 441, 455, 457, 464, 467, 472, 473, 476, 478, 497
House, 349, 350
impoundment, 375, 382, 455
incremental budgeting, 299, 316
interest groups, 166, 271, 287, 322
Legislative Reorganization Act of 1946, 374
limitations, 357
logrolling, 358
mandatory spending, 368
National Performance Review, 313
Nixon, 455
obligated balance, 289
offsetting receipts, 291
OMB, 272
Omnibus Budget Reconciliation Act of 1990, 478, 482
outlays, 290
PAYGO, 327, 362
pork-barrel spending, 359
president's budget, 272, 283, 299, 300, 305, 366, 375, 382
President's Commission on Budget Concepts, 441
president's role, 375
reconciliation, 368, 464, 467
reform history, 284, 312, 314, 371, 374
Reorganization Plan Number 1, 415
rescission, 382
scheduled completion, 345
scorekeeping, 367
Senate, 350
Senate Finance Committee, 331
sequestering funds, 362, 389
shutdowns, 1995–1996, 485
Statement of Administration Policy, 303
summits, 323, 476, 478

Budget process *(continued)*
tax legislation, 365, 368
timetable, 277
"too big to butcher," 364
transfer payments, 293
two-step procedure, 347
undistributed offsetting receipts, 291
unified budget, 441
veto, 304
Budget resolution
adopted, 380
deadline for, 277
debt limit and, 378
described, 382, 383
first, 457
introduced, 455
scorekeeping, 367
Senate and, 365
Budget surplus. *See* Surpluses (budget)
Bureau of Alcohol, Tobacco and Firearms
budget, 232
Bureau of Indian Affairs
budget, 252, 253
Bureau of Labor Statistics
budget, 254
Bureau of Land Management
budget, 253
Bureau of Mines
budget, 253
Bureau of Reclamation
budget, 253
Bureau of the Budget
created, 9, 311
Reorganization Plan Number 1, 415
revamped, 305
Bureau of the Census
budget, 235
Bush, George
agrees to tax hike, 478
budget deal, 327
budget summit, 476, 478
budget woes, 388
budget writing, 301
capital spending grants, 163
defense budget, 223
deficits, 12, 18
economic record, 477
economy and elections, 43, 477, 480
income tax cut, 410
lowest economic growth, 405
NASA, 243
"Read my lips—no new taxes!", 480
rescission requests, 385
shutdowns, 479
tax hike, 411, 480
unemployment, 406
veto, 375
Business cycle
defined, 25
fiscal policy and, 298
indicators, 39
productivity, 27
stabilization, 64, 398, 431
Byrd, Harry Flood
chair, Senate Appropriations, 339
Finance Committee chair, 331
pork-barrel spending, 332

Cannon, Clarence
chair, House Appropriations, 339
Capital gains tax
Congress balks at cut, 476
cut, 488
defined, 86
Capital goods, 34
Carter, Jimmy
anti-inflation strategy, 460
bank deregulation, 500
budget writing, 301
Commerce budget, 235
deficits, 18, 461
economic policy, 457, 460
economy and elections, 43
full employment bill, 458
high tax rate, 71, 409
income tax hike, 410
inflation and, 50, 460
Misery Index, 59
recession, 1980, 465
reelection and economy, 460
rescission requests, 385
Social Security benefit cuts, 462
spending growth, 475
taxes, 411
Census Bureau
census cost, 236
Centers for Disease Control, 255
Chief Financial Officers Act (1990), 284, 315
Children
health care, 397
health insurance, 192
Medicaid, 189
nutrition benefits, 179
Chiles, Lawton
Budget Committee (Senate) chair, 328
Christmas treeing
defined, 356
Chrysler
bailout, 447
Civil service
OPM, 248
retirement fund, 497
Civil War
deficits, 145
and income tax, 7
mounting debt, 399
Clinton, William
balanced budget agreement (1997), 387, 397, 488
Blue Dogs and, 324
budget, 1997, 487
budget battle, 1995, 304
budget concessions, 484
budget stand, 1996, 486
capital spending grants, 163
Commerce budget, 235
corporate welfare, 164
deficits, 12, 16, 393, 481
downsizing government, 45, 393
economy and elections, 43
education, 219
Executive Order 12857, 284, 394
federal default averted, 497
health care spending rise, 184
increased EITC, 482
limits cuts, 375
line-item veto, 318
NASA, 243
opposition to spending cuts, 484
rescission requests, 385
shutdowns, 304
social spending benefits, 181
tax hike, 1993, 482
veto, 304, 375, 485
White House fund raisers, 151
wins shutdown standoff, 485

Coal miners
benefits paid, 179
Coast Guard
budget, 244
Cold War
Marshall Plan, 426
military size and, 228
College of Cardinals
defined, 337
Commerce Department
budget share, 147
spending by category, 235
Committee reports
earmarking, 360
Commodity Credit Corporation
239, 240
Community Action Program, 437
Conference committee
appropriations, 350
budget timetable, 277
money bills, 356, 363
Congress. *See also* Budget, Budget process, Spending, Taxes, Tax legislation
agencies and, 313
Appropriations Committee (House), 337, 338, 350, 352, 366
Appropriations Committee (Senate), 337, 338, 350, 352, 366
appropriations subcommittees, 337, 350
authorization committees, 352, 353
bailouts, 447
balanced budget agreement (1997), 397
bank deregulation, 500
baseline projections, 280, 281
Blue Dogs, 324
borrowing authority, 124
borrowing limit, 126
borrowing power, 126
budget, 1997, 487
Budget Committee (House), 327, 328, 352, 367, 382
Budget Committee (Senate), 327, 328, 352, 367
budget control, 165, 166, 288, 322, 372, 381
budget cuts, 286, 468
Budget Enforcement Act of 1990, 390
budget powers, 2
budget process, 154, 271, 272, 273, 299, 350, 351, 352, 354, 355, 356, 357, 359, 362, 369, 371, 380, 382, 383, 388
budget reform, 283, 327, 382, 455, 464, 483
budget resolution, 383
budget summits, 284
budget timetable, 277, 369
budgeting history, 283, 284, 286, 303, 304, 319, 322, 323, 345, 348, 369, 370, 377, 379, 382, 388, 390, 401, 455, 457, 472, 473, 476, 478, 480, 482, 483, 497
conference committee, 272, 350, 356, 363
continuing resolution, 369, 370
Contract with America, 484
debt and, 19
debt interest, 127
debt limit, 126, 282, 377, 378, 379
defense of social spending, 455
earmarking, 313
economic policy, 295, 434
entitlement programs, 172
Fed and, 491
Finance Committee, 325, 365
fiscal policy and, 65, 67, 68, 298
General Accounting Office, 342
Gramm-Rudman-Hollings Act, 388
Great Society program, 437
history, 381, 390
imposed income tax, 7
income tax and, 80
inflation, 444, 464
interest groups, 287
Joint Taxation Committee, 326
members salaries, 155
Omnibus Budget Reconciliation Act of 1990, 478, 482
104th Congress, 395
opposition to Bush 1990 budget package, 480
opposition to spending cuts, 444, 449, 455, 466, 468
overspending, 18, 20
power of the purse, 168, 320, 375
president's budget, 277, 300, 375
reconciliation, 368, 464
reform, 284
reprogramming, 317
Republican control, 483
rescission, 384, 385
revenue-sharing, 448
salaries and expenses, 154
scorekeeping, 367
Senate Finance Committee, 331, 356
shutdowns, 304, 485
spending cuts, 467, 468, 484
spending history, 3, 18, 285, 321, 322, 361, 373, 374, 380, 403, 422, 444, 448, 449, 450, 453, 456, 458, 461, 462, 464, 474, 475, 487
Statement of Administration Policy, 303
summits, 323, 476, 478
taxing and spending powers, 78
trust funds, 96
United States v. Butler, 321
UN payments, 234
Ways and Means, 325, 336, 356
Congressional Budget and Impoundment Control Act of 1974
adopted, 284, 381
budget committees, 382
budget resolution, 457
CBO, 341, 382
history, 374,455
reconciliation, 368
rescission, 384
scorekeeping, 367
Congressional Budget Office
baseline projections, 280, 281
budget for, 154
duties, 341
scorekeeping, 367
sequestration, 389
Conservatives. *See also* Liberals
balanced budget amendment, 387
Blue Dogs, 324
budget control, 455
Bush and, 480
capital gains tax, 86
dominate budget agenda, 484
downsizing government, 45
economic goals, 430, 433
entitlement cuts, 372

Conservatives *(continued)*
fiscal policy, 298
full employment opposed, 422
Gingrich, 395
opposition to 1990 budget deal, 478
pass Reagan cuts, 467
spending limits, 380
supply side theory, 71
tax reform, 117
Consolidated Omnibus Budget Reconciliation Act (1985), 122
Constant dollars, defined, 53
Constitution
balanced budget amendment, 387
borrowing authority, 78, 124
impoundment, 381
income tax and, 80
power of the purse, 320, 321
revenue bills, 349, 365
spending powers, 78, 168
spending procedure, 346
taxing powers, 78, 79
Consumer goods
defined, 34
Consumer Price Index (CPI)
annual change (table), 40
basis for indexing, 450
defined, 40
inflation and, 40
Consumer prices
inflation effects, 52
Consumer spending
expansion and, 46
Continuing resolution
budget process, 272
Bush veto, 473, 479
described, 369
history, 369
most passed, 370
1981 shutdown and, 473
Contract authority
defined, 289
Contract with America
described, 484
Gingrich, 395
Kasich, 329
line-item veto, 484
shutdowns and, 484, 485
welfare reform, 484
Cooper, Jere
chair, Ways and Means, 335
Corporate taxes
Clinton increase, 482
hiked, 1982, 470
history, 120, 81
inflation effects, 52
IRS audits, 106
minimum tax, 488
1964 tax cut, 436
payroll tax share, 120, 121
percent of revenue, 73
revenue drop, 115, 120
special, 100
Corporate welfare
defined, 164
Corporation for Public Broadcasting
federal funding, 258
Cost-of-living allowance
benefits of, 196
cost of, 196
delayed, 474
elections and, 61
inflation and, 52
Council of Economic Advisers, 297
budget, 152
created, 422
described, 307
Court system. *See* Judiciary
Credit crunch, 19, 126, 129
Currencies
control of, 505
exchange rate, 503
G-7 meetings, 507
U.S. devaluations, 509
Currency exchange
Bretton Woods System, 424
Nixon reforms, 446
Current account. *See* Balance of payments
Current services estimates, 300
Customs Service
budget, 232

Daycare assistance, 179
Debt
agency, 137
amount, 130
borrowing and, 125
ceiling, 126
Civil War and, 399
default averted, 497
defined, 11
effect on budget, 1
financing, 451
fiscal policy and, 66
foreign borrowing, 19
foreign investment, 136, 440
growth spurt, 131
history, 130, 131, 133, 134, 136, 145, 399, 497
increase, 373
increase, causes of, 399
inflated CPI and, 41
interest, 19, 126, 127, 129, 132, 133, 399, 429
limit, 282, 377, 378, 379, 463, 497
net interest (table), 133
origin, 18
paying down, 17
per capita cost, 132
percent of GDP, 133
political issue, 20, 123, 126
public, 137
rapid rise begins, 18
relative to annual revenue, 18
repaying, 123, 135
size, 17, 123, 130, 131, 133 (table), 135
spending limits, 380
stabilization crisis, 136
who holds, 128, 136
World War I, 399
Defense Department
Air Force, 226
armed forces size, 228
Army, 227
base closings, 229, 376
budget categories, 224
budget share, 144, 147, 222, 223
civilian employment, 159
current spending, 224
cuts, 453
debt contribution, 18
drug control, 269
Golden Fleece, 169
largest budget, 223
medical spending (table), 184
military size, 159
Navy, 225

nuclear missiles, 228
peace dividend, 230, 453
Reagan and, 475
spending, 146, 224, 439, 466, 475
spending history, 222, 444
weapons spending, 224, 231
World War II spending, 419
Deferral
described, 382
Deficit. *See also* Debt, Budget
amount (1996), 281
annual (table), 83
balanced budget agreement (1997), 397
borrowing and, 125
Budget Enforcement Act, 362, 390
budget estimates, 300
Carter, 460, 461
causes, 459, 475
Clinton, 481, 482
current size, 4
debt and, 135
defined, 11
Domenici, 330
economy and, 44
elections and, 61
end in sight, 16
entitlement growth, 475
first, 145
fiscal policy and, 66
Gramm-Rudman targets, 478
Gramm-Rudman-Hollings Act, 388
history, 134, 141, 143, 145, 167, 322, 381, 393, 399, 423, 430, 431, 453, 456, 459, 461, 464, 466, 470, 471, 472, 475, 477, 478
increase, 459, 461, 464, 471, 472, 475
Keynesian economics and, 63
largest, 12
longest string, 16
mandatory spending, 165
Monthly Statement of Receipts and Outlays, 499
net interest and, 132
Omnibus Budget Reconciliation Act, 482
overspending and, 13
passes World War II high, 456
percent of GDP (table), 167
political issue, 466
Reagan, 306, 475
Reagan era, 471
recent economic growth, 83
reduction, 133, 361, 362, 372, 388, 390, 393, 397, 457, 460, 476, 478, 480, 481, 482
and savings and loan crisis, 12
sequestration, 389
size, 481
supply-side theory, 71
tax indexing and, 114
taxes and, 14
unified budget and, 279
user fee increase, 122
wasteful spending, 13
Deficit spending
defined, 13, 20
economic effects, 20
employment and, 422
history, 431
legitimized, 401
New Deal, 413
new role, 400
Roosevelt, 418
Deflation
defined, 57
depression rate, 412
Demand. *See also* Supply and demand
Keynesian economics, 63
Democratic party
balanced budget amendment, 387
Blue Dogs, 324
Carter years, 464
Clinton budget package, 482
defending social programs, 475
fiscal goals, 1940s, 423
full employment, 458
Great Society programs, 437
guaranteed annual income, 449
impoundment, 381
income redistribution, 6
income tax hikes, 410
1997 budget, 487
Omnibus Budget Reconciliation Act of 1990, 478
O'Neill, 386
opposition to Reagan, 472
opposition to spending cuts, 444, 455, 466, 484
procedural reforms, 355
revenue-sharing, 448
social spending, 375
support for Reagan cuts, 467
tariffs, 513
taxes and, 14
Depository Institutions Act (1982), 500
Depository Institutions Deregulation and Monetary Control Act (1980), 500
Depression. *See also* Great Depression
defined, 55
Deregulation. *See also* Regulations
1980 bank deregulation, 500
1982 bank deregulation, 500
savings and loan crisis, 37, 500
savings from, 37
Devaluation
described, 510
of peso, 515
Discount rate
defined, 495
Fed control, 490
Discretionary spending. *See also* Spending, discretionary
budget share, 162
defined, 162
Disinflation
defined, 57
Disinvestment
averts federal default, 497
defined, 282
Disposable income
annual (table), 35
defined, 35
District of Columbia
funding reforms, 397
Dole, Robert
Finance Committee chair, 331
Dollar
devaluation, 510
floating exchange rates, 504
G-7 meetings, 507
Mexican financial crisis, 515
pegging currencies on, 504
strong, weak (defined), 506
Domenici, Pete
Budget Committee chair, 328
profiled, 330

Doughton, Robert L.
chair, Ways and Means, 335
Downsizing
Clinton, 45, 393
Contract with America, 484
defense, 228, 229
deficit and, 12
described, 392
Gingrich, 395
research grants, 247
Drug Enforcement Administration
spending, 241
Durable goods
defined, 34

Earmarking
academic earmarks, 360
committee reports, 357
described, 360
Earned Income Tax Credit (EITC)
benefits paid, 179
described, 182
increased, 482
refund amount, 109
total recipients, 161
Easy money
defined, 502
Economic and Statistics Administration
budget, 235
Economic Development Administration
budget, 235
Economic Opportunity Act
passed, 437
Economic policy
bailouts, 447
Bush, 477
Carter, 460
Council of Economic Advisers, 307
deficit and, 477
Democratic Congress and, 456
economic growth, 433
Economic Opportunity Act, 437
Eisenhower, 430, 431, 433
elections and, 445, 446
Employment Act of 1946, 422
failure of Keynesian economics, 459
Federal Reserve, 295, 491
fine-tuning, 436
Ford, 456
full employment, 433
GATT, 425
guaranteed employment, 458
history, 422, 423, 424, 425, 426, 428, 429, 430, 431, 432, 433, 434, 442, 445, 446, 447, 454, 460
Hoover, 412
inflation, 435
inflation-unemployment relation, 443
interest rates, 429
international, 424
Johnson, 435
Kennedy, 433, 434, 435
legislation, 422
limits of, 442, 477
Marshall Plan, 426
monetary, 490
New Economic Policy, 446
oil embargoes and shocks, 454
partisan goals, 423
post-depression, 398
postwar era, 422
presidential leadership, 295
Reagan, 306, 466, 468, 470, 475
recession, 1959, 431, 432
recession, 1981–1982, 471
Roosevelt, 401, 412, 418
setting priorities, 401
seventies, 459
sixties, 435, 442
stabilization, 431
stabilization crisis, 516
tax cut, 1964, 436
tax cut, 1975, 456
tax surcharge, 435, 442
Treasury, 308
Truman, 421, 426, 428
unified budget, 441
wage-price controls, 445
Economic Recovery Tax Act of 1981, 468
Economic Stabilization Act of 1970, 445
Economic theory
classical, 398
fine-tuning, 68
Keynesian, 63, 401, 422, 428, 430, 443, 459
laissez-faire, 62
policy options, 66
stabilization policy, 65
supply side, 71, 433, 436, 459
Economy
anti-inflation measures, 471
automatic stabilizers, 60
budget and, 281
Bush, 477
business cycles, 398
capital gains tax and, 86
Carter, 465
credit crunch, 129
debt effects on, 19
deficit and, 12, 481
devaluation of peso, 515
discount rate, 494
disposable income, 35
disposable income (table), 35
economic emergencies, 400
effect on budget, 281, 393
1800s, 62
elections and, 43, 445, 465, 61
employment, 23
expansion defined, 46
expansion, longest, 47
federal borrowing, 19
Federal Reserve, 489, 490
federal spending and, 142, 376
fine-tuning, 68, 436
fiscal policy and, 65, 67, 422, 442, 443, 456
forecasts, 341
full employment, 458
GDP and, 23, 29
GDP growth (table), 28
government effect on, 23
Great Depression, 412
growth, 28 (table), 82, 404, 405, 422, 425, 435, 436, 477
highest growth rate, 405
history, 404, 418, 421, 423, 442, 445, 446, 447, 454, 459, 460, 465, 466, 471
housing starts, 36
indicators, 37, 39, 40, 42, 68
individual and, 24
inflated CPI and, 41
inflation and, 48, 52, 54, 435, 442
influence of Fed chairman, 492
marginal taxes and, 87

monetary policy, 69
money supply (table, growth), 490, 493
1900s, 62
1990s growth, 83
oil shocks, 49, 454, 460
OMB, 297
productivity declines, 459
protectionism, 513
recession, 423, 432, 434, 456, 471
regulations and, 23
seventies, 459
spending cuts, 442
stabilization crisis, 516
stabilization policy, 64, 431
stagflation, 58
strong, weak dollar effects, 506
supply and demand, 26
supply shocks, 454, 459
tax cut, 1964, 436
tax cuts, 302
taxes and, 14, 442
tight/loose money, 502
Treasury Department, 296
unemployment, 406, 407, 435
unregulated, 62
U.S., size, 22
wage-price controls, 445
World War II demobilization, 421
Education, Department of
Clinton tax incentives, 488
elementary and secondary aid, 220, 437
spending, 147, 219
Eighteenth century
debt history, 145
Eighties
debt and, 18, 131
economic expansion, 25, 47
Medicaid spending, 189
monetary policy, 69
peak interest rate, 496
productivity, 27
taxes, 113
tight money policy, 502
Eisenhower, Dwight
budget surpluses, 15
economic growth, 404
economic policy, 430
inflation and, 51
1959 recession, 432
taxes, 411
unemployment, 406
Elderly
Administration on Aging, 255
Medicaid, 189
Medicare, 187
population, current and future, 199
rising population, 204
Social Security, 194
social spending and, 181
Election
economy and, 61, 446, 460, 465, 477
1960, 432
1995 shutdown and, 485
Nixon reelection, 445
Ellender, Allen J., 339
Employers
payroll tax payments, 438
Employment
annual growth (table), 32
demobilization and, 421
downsizing government, 392, 393
economic policy and, 433
Employment Act of 1946, 33, 422, 458
federal, 143, 159, 248
full employment, 33
growth, 435, 477
guaranteed employment, 458
inflation and, 49
lowest growth, 477
NAFTA and, 514
participation rate, 32
reducing government, 393
total civilian, 32
unemployment rate (table), 32
war years, 419
Employment Act of 1946, 33, 422, 458
Energy
effect on productivity, 27
inflation and, 459
low-income assistance, 179
Energy Department
atomic energy, 245
budget, 147, 245
defense work, 224
electric power, 245
history, 245
Strategic Petroleum Reserve, 246
Engraving and Printing, Bureau of
budget, 232
Entitlements. *See also* Social programs, Social Security, and other headings for specific programs
aging population and, 171
benefits of, 170, 179, 181
block grants, 180
budget share, 146, 286
caps, 390
changing programs, 160, 172
cost factors, 146
debt and, 18, 131
deficits and, 13
defined, 160
Executive Order 12857, 284
growth, 286, 396
indexing, 171, 450
mandatory spending, 162, 165
means-tested (definition), 181
PAYGO, 362
recessions and, 60
recipients (table), 161
and spending, 4
spending caps, 176
spending growth, 131, 146, 171, 453, 459, 460, 471
spending growth rate, 1970s, 461
transfer payment, 177, 178, 293
voters and, 173
Environment, 448
Environmental Protection Agency
budget by category, 242
budget share, 147
crude oil tax, 122
superfund, 242
Ervin, Sam J. Jr.
Budget and Impoundment Control Act, 455
Estate and gift taxes
defined, 98
percent of revenue, 73
Exchange rates
control of, 505
described, 503
falling peso, 515
Federal Reserve and, 505
floating, 504, 505

Exchange rates *(continued)*
G-7 meetings, 507
pegged on dollar, 504
Excise taxes
defined, 92
depression and, 75
percent of revenue, 73
revenue drop, 115
World War II and, 420
Executive branch. *See also* Office of Management and Budget, Presidents
annual appropriations, 273
budget powers, 2
budget process reform, 312
budget responsibility, 9
employment, 159
spending, 3
Executive Office of the President, 284
Budget Bureau, 311
budget share, 147
current budget, 152
Reorganization Plan Number 1, 415
staff size, 152
Expansions. *See also* Business cycle
budget and, 44
and business cycle, 25
defined, 46
history, 298
individual and, 24
longest postwar, 404
money supply, 493
Reagan era, 466
sixties, 435
stabilization policy, 64
Export Administration
budget, 235
Export-Import Bank
budget status, 441

Fannie Mae. *See* Federal National Mortgage Association
Farm credit banks, 294
Farm subsidies
created, 414
history, 240
reform, 240
spending, 240
Federal Aviation Administration
budget, 244
Federal Bureau of Investigation
budget, 241
Federal drug control programs, 153
Federal employee retirement trust, 95
Federal Financing Bank
described, 451
Federal funds rate
described, 494
Federal government
annual appropriations, 273
bankruptcy, 123
credit limit, 123, 126
cutting size of, 45
default, 497
divided government, 483
downsizing, 392, 393
economy and, 23
employment, 23, 159
expanded role of, 45, 62, 141, 168, 171, 320, 400
foreign indebtedness, 128
grants, 163
growth of, 143
insolvency, 282
limited role, 399
major spending growth, 419
power of the purse, 320
public confidence, 158
social spending, 170
spending, 141, 146, 376, 419
spending control issue, 372
spending per second, 140
trust fund borrowing, 207
Federal Highway Administration
budget, 244
Federal Home Loan Bank, 294
described, 218
Federal Home Loan Mortgage Corporation, 294
described, 218
Federal Housing Administration
described, 218
housing loans, 216
Federal Housing Authority, 256
Federal National Mortgage Association
described, 218
Federal prison system, 241
Federal Railroad Administration
budget, 244
Federal Reserve system
bank reserves, 494
Carter years, 460
currency control, 505
current deposits, 73
depression and, 412
described, 489
discount rate, 490, 494 (table)
economic policy, 295
economy, 490
exchange rates, 505
federal funds rate, 494
governors, 489
independence of, 70, 429, 491
inflation fight, 54, 64, 69, 70
influence of chairman, 492
monetary policy, 69, 456, 460, 466, 489, 502
money supply, 489, 493
policy meetings, 491
powers of, 429
recession, 1937, 418
recession, 1981–1982, 466, 471
tight money policy, 460, 502
Treasury bills, 501
Volcker chairman, 466
Federal Transit Administration
budget, 244
Fifties
debt and, 131
economic growth, 28
economic policies, 430, 433
inflation, 428
1959 recession, 432
surpluses, 15
taxes, 411
unemployment, 406
Finance Committee
tax bills, 325
Financial Management Service
budget, 232
checks written by, 3
described, 498
Fiscal policy. *See also* Economic policy
Congress and, 67
debt and, 19
deficits, 66
defined, 65
disadvantages of, 70
economy and, 23

fine-tuning, 68
full employment and, 33
history, 298
inflation and, 49
Keynesian economics, 63
limits of, 456
recessions and, 25
stabilization policy, 64
stagflation, 58
Fiscal year
closing out, 277
defined, 10
Fish and Wildlife Service
budget, 253
Flat tax, defined, 102
Food and Consumer Service
spending, 239
Food and Drug Administration
budget, 255
Food stamps
benefits paid, 179
cost, 239, 453
recipients total, 161
total recipients, 210, 214
welfare reform, 209
Ford, Gerald
budget writing, 301
deficits, 18
and Democratic Congress, 456
economic growth, 405
economic record, 456
opposition to full employment, 458
rescission requests, 385
spending limits, 380
taxes, 411
unemployment, 407
veto, 375
Foreign affairs
Bretton Woods System, 424
Marshall Plan, 426
State Department budget, 233
UN payments, 233, 234
U.S. loans to Mexico, 515
Foreign investors
balance of payments, 509
credit crunch, 129
debt and, 128
debt share, 136
stabilization crisis, 516
tax breaks, 440
Treasury bills, 501
Forest Service
budget, 239
Forties 404, 419
debt, 18, 130, 131
deficits, 16
demobilization, 421
depression ends, 63
federal spending, 376, 419
fiscal policy, 423
full employment, 422
inflation, 423
Marshall Plan, 426
taxes, 100, 409, 420
unemployment, 406
Freddie Mac. *See* Federal Home Loan Mortgage Corporation
Full employment
Employment Act of 1946, 422
Humphrey-Hawkins bill, 458
Functions
budget resolution and, 383
described, 292
Funds Appropriated to the President
budget, 147, 153
defined, 153

Gasoline tax. *See* Taxes, gasoline
GATT. *See* General Agreement on Tariffs and Trade
GDP. *See* Gross Domestic Product
General Accounting Office (GAO)
audits, 343
budget for, 154
created, 9
duties, 342
SSI investigation, 203
General Agreement on Tariffs and Trade
described, 425
General funds
defined, 94
General Services Administration
budget share, 147
George, Walter F.
Finance Committee chair, 331
Gephardt, Richard
debt limit rule, 463
GI bill
demobilization and, 421
Giaimo, Robert N.
Budget Committee chair, 328
Gibbons, Sam M.
chair, Ways and Means, 335
Gift tax. *See* Estate and gift taxes
Gingrich, Newt
balanced budget agreement, 397, 488
Contract with America, 484
Kasich, 329
named House Speaker, 483
profile, 395
scuttles 1990 budget deal, 478
shutdowns hurt popularity, 485
GNP. *See* Gross National Product
Gold reserves
current, 5
drain on, 446, 504
Golden Fleece awards, 169
Gore, Al
National Performance Review, 313
Government Accounting Office
established, 283
Government National Mortgage Association, 218, 256, 294
described, 218
Government-owned corporations
described, 294
Government Performance and Results Act
reforms, 314
Government Printing Office
budget for, 154
Government shutdowns
Bush, 473, 479
1981 budget battle, 473
1990, 479
1995–1996, 304, 485
Government spending. *See* Spending
Government-sponsored enterprises
budget status, 441
described, 294
Grace, J. Peter
government waste, 361
Grace Commission
wasteful spending, 361
Gramm-Rudman-Hollings Act
debt crisis, 282
described, 388

Gramm-Rudman-Hollings Act (*continued*)
  sequestration, 389
  superseded by BEA, 478
Grants
  block grants, 180
  budget share, 163
  history, 163
  line-item veto, 319
  revenue-sharing, 448
  welfare, 209
Gray, William H.
  Budget Committee (House) chair, 328
Great Depression
  causes, 412
  classical economics, 398
  debt origins, 18
  deficits and, 16
  deflation, 412
  economic policy and, 412
  economic theory and, 62
  expanded government, 400
  farm subsidies, 240
  Federal Reserve and, 412
  federal spending, 400
  government's new economic role, 295
  Keynesian economics, 63, 398
  need for spending, 141
  New Deal and, 413
  1937–1938 recession, 418
  spending and, 63
  unemployment rate, 62, 398, 400
  World War II spending, 413
Great Society
  cutbacks, 455
  debt and, 131
  deficits and, 374
  inflation and, 50
  Medicare, 186
  program described, 437
  rising costs, 171, 381, 439
  social programs, 402
  spending, 141, 146, 373
  stagflation, 58
Greenspan, Alan
  Fed chairman, 492
  influence of, 492
Gross Domestic Product (GDP)
  annual growth (table), 28
  constant dollar growth (table), 28
  defined, 29
  economic growth, 404
  inflated CPI and, 41
  revenue as percent of, 83
  spending and, 403
  spending as percent of, 83
  transfer payments, 177
Gross National Product
  defined, 30
  World War II growth, 419
Group of Seven (G-7)
  described, 507
  members, 507
GSE. *See* Government-sponsored enterprises
Guaranteed annual income
  McGovern campaign pledge, 449

Hamilton, Alexander, 309
Harding, Warren
  first formal budget, 9
Hatfield, Mark O.
  chair, Senate Appropriations, 339
Hayden, Carl
  chair, Senate Appropriations, 339
Hazardous waste superfund
  spending, 242
Health and Human Services, Department of (HHS)
  Administration for Children and Families, 255
  budget (table), 255
  budget share, 144, 147, 149
  Centers for Disease Control, 255
  Food and Drug Administration, 255
  Health Care Financing Administration, 255
  Health Resources and Services, 255
  Indian Health Services, 255
  Medicaid, 255
  Medicare, 255
  National Institutes of Health, 255
  projected cost, 149
  spending growth, 255
  Substance Abuse, 255
Health care
  Congress voted increases, 450
  history, 184
  HMOs, 193
  Medicaid reforms, 192
  Medicare, 186, 190
  revenue-sharing, 448
  Senate Finance Committee, 331
  spending rise, 184, 185, 188, 189, 190
  uninsured, 183
Health Care Financing Administration
  budget, 255
Health insurance
  balanced budget agreement, 192
  people not covered, 183
  Ways and Means, 334
Health Insurance trust fund, 95, 438
Health Maintenance Organizations
  described, 193
Health Resources and Services
  budget, 255
Highway trust fund
  revenues, 95
Hollings, Ernest
  Budget Committee chair, 328
"Hoover economics," 430
Hoover, Herbert
  depression causes, 412
  spending rise, 403
  tax hikes, 412
House of Representatives. *See also* Congress
  appropriations amendments, 351
  appropriations bills, 350
  appropriations committee, 272
  appropriations timetable, 277
  Budget Committee created, 382
  budget writing, 272
  conference committee, 363
  Contract with America, 395
  debt limit, 463
  Gephardt rule, 463
  members' salaries, 155
  originates appropriations bills, 274
  Republicans control, 483
  revenue bills, 349, 356
  salaries and expenses, 154
  Speaker Gingrich, 395
  spending limits, 380
  two-step procedure, 348
  two-step waiver, 347

Ways and Means Committee, 284, 325
Housing and Urban Development, Department of
budget share, 147
described, 256
homeless, 256
rent subsidies, 216
Housing assistance
benefit distribution, 213
benefits paid, 179
HUD, 256
mortgage loans, 218
programs, 216
programs created, 414
recipients total, 161
Rural Housing Service, 216, 218
Section 8, 217
spending, 216
total recipients, 210, 216
Housing starts, 36
Humphrey, Hubert H.
employment bill, 458
Humphrey-Hawkins full employment bill
described, 458

Impoundment
barred, 382
Nixon, 381, 444, 455
rescission, 384
sparks congressional action, 455
as spending control, 375
Income redistribution. *See* Income tax
Income tax. *See also* Corporate taxes, Payroll tax, Revenue, Taxes, and other specific taxes
amount collected, 105
compared with foreign, 112
filing cost, 118
first, 7, 8
foreign earnings, 91
highest revenues, 116
hike, 410, 420
history of, 7, 75, 80, 436
income redistribution, 6, 23, 413
indexation, 113, 468
inflation and, 52, 113
IRS audits, 106
lowest revenues, 116
McCulloch v. Maryland, 79
need for, 6
negative, defined, 101
per capita tax, 111
percent of revenue, 74, 115
presidents and, 410, 417
Reagan tax cut, 469, 470
reform, 117, 119
refunds paid, 105
revenue share, 6
Sixteenth Amendment, 79
tax cut, 1964, 436
tax cut, 1981, 468
Incremental budgeting
described, 316
Indexing
of entitlements, 171
inflation and, 52
Social Security, 450
taxes, 113, 468
Indian Health Services
budget, 255
Inflation
annual (table), 59
anti-inflation measures, 471
Carter, 50, 51, 460, 465
causes, 459
constant dollars, 53
defined, 49
demobilization and, 421
Economic Stabilization Act of 1970, 444
eighties, 50
Eisenhower, 51
end of high, 466
energy conservation and, 459
expansion and, 46
fifties, 50, 51, 432
fiscal policy and, 298
Ford, 456
full employment and, 33
Greenspan controls, 492
history, 50, 51, 58, 298, 428, 432, 435, 442, 443, 444, 445, 446, 454, 456, 457, 458, 459, 460, 464, 466
indexing, 113
interest rate policy, 429
Johnson, 435, 439, 442
Kennedy, 51
Keynesian economics and, 63
Korean War, 50, 428
Nixon, 50, 51, 443, 444, 445, 446, 449, 454
oil embargoes and shocks, 454
paychecks and, 48
periods of, 50
productivity and, 27, 459
recession and, 432
revenue and, 113
seventies, 50, 51, 58, 443, 444, 445, 446, 454, 456, 457, 458, 459, 460, 464
sinks Bretton Woods System, 504
sixties, 50, 51, 435
spending and, 142
stabilization crisis, 516
stabilization policy, 64
stagflation, 58
supply shocks, 454
tax cuts, 423
tax surcharge, 435, 442
Truman, 50, 421, 428
unemployment and, 443
Volcker "cures," 54
Insular Affairs
budget, 253
Inter-American Foundation
budget for, 153
Interest groups. *See* Special interests
Interest on the debt, 373
budget effects, 1, 286
Carter, 465
credit crunch, 129
discount rate (table), 494
economic effects, 19
Fed and, 429, 490
federal funds rate (table), 494
growth of, 132, 146
history, 429
individual and, 24
mandatory payment of, 127, 165, 399
per capita cost, 132
prime rate (table), 494
Interest rates
prime rate
S and L crisis cause, 500
stabilization crisis, 516
tight/easy money, 502
Treasury bills and bonds (table), 501

Interior, Department of
budget by category (table), 253
budget share, 147
Bureau of Indian Affairs, 253
Bureau of Land Management, 253
Fish and Wildlife Service, 253
National Park Service, 253
Internal Revenue Service
audits, 106
budget, 232
collection costs, 107
compliance rate, 108
current spending, 109
Earned Income Tax Credit, 109
employment, 110
filing costs, 118
forms processed, 104
funds collected, 105
refunds paid, 105, 109
tax cheats, 108
International development assistance
budget, 153
International finance
Bretton Woods system, 424
exchange rates, 446
Marshall Plan, 426
International Monetary Fund (IMF)
created, 424
corporate welfare, 164
Mexico loans, 515
International security
budget for, 153
International Trade Administration
budget, 235
Iron triangle
defined, 166

Japanese American WWII internees
payments, 179
Jefferson, Thomas
impoundment, 381
Johnson
deficits and, 16
economic growth, 404
economic policy, 435, 442
Great Society, 437
income tax hike, 410
inflation, 435, 439, 442
lowest average unemployment, 407
Medicare, 186, 336
payroll tax, 121
social programs, 402
spending decline, 373
spending increases, 141, 439
tax cut, 437
tax cut, 1964, 67, 436
tax revenues, 116
tax surcharge, 435, 442
taxes, 411
unemployment, 406
unified budget, 441
Joint Taxation Committee
described, 326
Jones, James R.
Budget Committee chair, 328
Judiciary
budget for, 147, 156
Court of International Trade, 156
district courts, 156
jurors, 156
legal defender, 156
U.S. Court of Appeals, 156
Justice Department
budget by category, 241
budget share, 147
drug control, 269
Drug Enforcement Administration, 241
FBI, 241
federal prison system, 241
Immigration and Naturalization Service, 241

Kasich, John R.
Budget Committee (House) chair, 328
profile, 329
Kennedy
assassination review, 270
deficits and, 16
economic growth, 404
economic policy, 434, 435
economy and elections, 43
highest economic growth, 405
income tax cut, 410
inflation and, 51
proposed tax cut, 67
spending tops $100 billion, 141
tax policy, 302
taxes, 411
unemployment, 406
Keynesian. *See* Economic theory
Knutson, Harold
chair, Ways and Means, 335
Korean War
and inflation, 50, 428

Labor. *See also* Employment, Leading indicator
budget share, 147
productivity, 27
Labor Department
budget by category, 254
Bureau of Labor Statistics, 254
Employment and Training Division, 254
OSHA, 254
unemployment compensation, 254
Laffer curve
defined, 103
Lagging indicators
defined, 37
Laissez-faire
defined, 62
Land and Water Conservation Fund, 97
Leading indicator
defined, 37
housing starts, 36
index of, 39
Legislative Branch. *See also* Congress, House of Representatives, Senate
budget share, 147
power of the purse, 320
Legislative Reform Act of 1970, 355
Legislative Reorganization Act of 1946, 374
Liberals. *See also* Conservatives
economic policy, 422, 433
fiscal policy, 298
full employment, 458
guaranteed annual income, 449
Medicare, 186
O'Neill, 386
opposition to 1990 budget deal, 478
opposition to spending cuts, 455
react to Reagan cuts, 468
social programs and, 45

Social Security benefits, 121
tax hikes, 372
tax reform, 117
Library of Congress
budget for, 154
Limitations
defined, 357
Line-item veto, 395
defined, 318
Liquor tax. *See* Excise taxes
Livingston, Bob
chair, House Appropriations, 339
Lockheed bailout, 447
Logrolling
defined, 358
Long, Russell B.
Finance Committee chair, 331
tax legislation, 333
Loopholes. *See* Tax exemptions

M-1, M-2, M-3. *See also* Money supply
annual growth (table), 493
defined, 493
Magnuson, Warren G.
chair, Senate Appropriations, 339
Mahon, George H.
chair, House Appropriations, 339
Mandatory spending. *See also* Spending, mandatory
budget share, 162
defined, 162
Marginal tax rate
defined, 87
Marine corps
budget, 225
size of, 228
Maritime Administration
budget, 244
Marshall Plan
described, 426
McClellan, John L.
chair, Senate Appropriations, 339
McCulloch v. Maryland
blocks income tax, 79
McGovern, George
guaranteed annual income, 449
McKellar, Kenneth
chair, Senate Appropriations, 339
Medicaid
benefits paid, 179
budget cuts and, 286
created, 437
described, 187
grant funds, 163
growth, expected, 396
Johnson created, 402
recipients total, 161
reforms, 192
rising costs, 453
sequestration, 389
spending growth, 184, 185, 189, 255
Medicare
bankruptcy, 190, 191
benefits paid, 179
budget cuts and, 286
budget share, 188
coverage expanded, 450
created, 437
described, 187
growth, expected, 396
Health Insurance tax created, 438
history, 186
Johnson created, 186, 402
Mills's opposition, 336
recipients total, 161
reforms, 191
reforms (1997), 397
spending, 184, 185, 190
spending growth, 185, 255
trust, 95
Mellon, Andrew William
treasury secretary, 309
Mexico
devaluation, 515
NAFTA and, 514
Milikin, Eugene D.
Finance Committee chair, 331
Mills, Wilbur D.
chair, Ways and Means, 334, 335
profile, 336
revenue-sharing, 448
Minerals Management Service
budget, 253
Minority Business Development Agency
budget, 235
Mint
budget, 232
Misery Index
annual (table), 59
Model Cities, 437
Monetarism
inflation and, 49
policy tool, 69
Monetary policy
advantages of, 70
anti-inflation measures, 471
Carter, 460
defined, 69
depression and, 412
discount rate, 494
Federal Reserve and, 429, 489, 490
Greenspan, 492
history, 429, 444, 456, 460
inflation fight, 70, 466
Nixon, 444
recession, 1981–1982, 466, 471
recessions and, 25
stabilization policy, 64
stagflation and, 58, 443
tight-loose money, 502
Treasury bills, 501
Volcker, 54
Money supply
annual growth (table), 493
described, 493
discount rate, 494
effect on economy, 69
Federal Reserve and, 490
government control, 23
inflation and, 49
inflation fight, 54
major expansion, 460
tight/easy money, 502
Morgenthau, Henry Jr.
treasury secretary, 309
Mortgage interest. *See* Tax exemptions
Most-favored-nation
defined, 425
Moynihan, Daniel Patrick
Finance Committee chair, 331
Muskie, Edmund
Budget Committee chair, 328

NAFTA. *See* North American Free Trade Agreement
Natcher, William H.
chair, House Appropriations, 339

National Aeronautics and Space Administration
budget history, 243
budget share, 147
spending cuts, 376
National Cemetery System, 250
National debt. *See* Debt
National Highway Traffic Safety Administration
budget, 244
National Indian Gaming Commission, 252
National Institute of Standards and Technology, 235
National Institutes of Health, 255
National Oceanic and Atmospheric Administration
budget, 235
National Park Service
budget, 251, 253
drug control, 269
entrance fees, 291
fee increases, 122
National Performance Review
biennial budget, 371
recommendations, 313
National sales tax
defined, 102
National Science Foundation
Golden Fleece, 169
National Security Council
budget, 152
National Telecommunications and Information Administration, 235
National Weather Service
budget, 238
National Wildlife Refuge Fund, 97
Native Americans
federal benefits, 252
Navy
largest share defense budget, 225
size of, 228
spending by category, 225
Negative income tax
defined, 101
New Deal
assessment of, 413
bigger government and, 62
effects of, 413
farm subsidies, 240
payroll tax introduced, 416
programs, 414
redistribution of wealth, 413
social programs, 402
spending, 141, 413, 419
United States v. Butler, 168
New Economic Policy
described, 446
New York City bailout, 447
Nineties
balanced budget agreement, 397, 488
Bush, 130, 477, 480
Clinton, 393, 397, 481, 482, 485, 488
Contract with America, 484
defense cutbacks, 228
deficit and, 12, 481
economy, 477
expansion, 25
line-item veto, 318
Republican party, 395, 397, 483
shutdowns, 479, 485
summit (budget), 478
taxes, 478, 482, 488
tight money policy, 502
Nixon, Richard M.
bank deregulation, 500
budget surplus, 15
budget writing, 301
created OMB, 305
currency devaluations, 509
economic policy, 444
economy and elections, 43, 432
ends Bretton Woods System, 504
impoundment, 374, 375, 381, 384, 455
inflation, 50, 51, 443, 444, 445, 446, 449, 454
New Economic Policy, 446
OMB, 311
revenue-sharing, 448
spending cuts, 449
spending limits, 380
tax refund review, 326
taxes, 411
veto, 375
wage-price controls, 445, 446
Nondurable goods
defined, 34
North American Free Trade Agreement
described, 514
devaluation of peso, 515
Nuclear Regulatory Commission
fee hikes, 122

OASDI. *See* Old Age, Survivors, and Disability Insurance
Obey, David R.
chair, House Appropriations, 339
Obligated balance, defined, 289
Obligations-based budget
described, 288
Occupational Safety and Health Administration, budget, 254
Office of Administration
current budget, 152
Office of Management and Budget
baseline projections, 280, 281
budget process, 366
budget timetable, 277
budget writing, 277
current budget, 152
described, 305
economic advice, 297
Office of Federal Financial Management, 315
sequestration, 389
Office of Mining Reclamation and Enforcement
budget, 253
Office of National Drug Control Policy
current budget, 152
spending, 269
Office of Personnel Management
budget, 147, 248
Office of Science and Technology Policy
budget, 152
Office of the U.S. Trade Representative
budget, 152
Offsetting receipts. *See also* Undistributed offsetting receipts
described, 291
housing, 256
Oil embargoes and supply shocks
balance of payments, 509
inflation and, 49, 454

price hikes, 460
recession, 1974, 456
Strategic Petroleum Reserve, 246
Oil spill cleanup spending, 242
Old age assistance. *See* Supplemental Security Income (SSI)
Old Age, Survivors, and Disability Insurance (OASDI)
bankruptcy, 204
described, 201
total recipients, 202
Omnibus Budget Reconciliation Act (1990), 482
deficit reduction package, 478
O'Neill, Tip
profiled, 386
Outlay
defined, 290
Overseas Private Investment Corporation, 294
corporate welfare, 164

Packwood, Bob
Finance Committee chair, 331
Panetta, Leon
Budget Committee chair, 328
Particle accelerator, 364
Patent and Trademark Office
budget, 235, 237
fees, 237
PAYGO. *See also* Budget Enforcement Act of 1990
defined, 362
established, 327
Payroll tax
Clinton increase, 482
current revenue, 93
defined, 93
described, 196
employer share, 121
Health Insurance tax created, 438
hikes, 427, 450, 474
history, 438
major hike, 462
Medicare funding, 186
originated, 416
percent of revenue, 73
rates, 121
regressive tax, 84
revenue rise, 115
revenue share, 416
Social Security benefits, 198
Social Security reforms, 208
Peace Corps budget, 153
Peace dividend, 230, 453
Pension Benefit Guaranty Corporation, 294
Perot, Ross
warning on NAFTA, 514
Persian Gulf War, 390
Strategic Petroleum Reserve, 246
Personal Responsibility and Work Opportunity Act of 1996, 209
Pollock v. Farmers' Loan and Trust Co.
and income tax, 7
Pork-barrel spending
deficit and, 13
described, 359
earmarking, 360
line-item veto and, 318
Sen. Byrd, 332
Postal Service
off-budget, 279
Poverty
persons below line, 211
race and, 212
regulations and, 62
social spending and, 181
Power Marketing Administration
described, 245
Power of the purse
congressional authority, 2
described, 320
Presidents. *See also* individual names
annual budget, 21, 272, 275, 299, 300, 366, 375
annual economic report, 465
balanced budget agreement (1997), 397
budget process, 2, 283, 299, 375, 455
budget reform, 312
budget writing, 272, 277
Council of Economic Advisers, 307
deficit spending, 401
economic advice, 296, 297, 307, 308
economic policy, 295
economy and, 62, 422
economy and election, 43, 432, 446, 460, 465, 477
Executive Order 12857, 394
Fed and, 491
first budget, 9
fiscal policy and, 65, 68
impoundment, 381, 382, 455
line-item veto, 318
OMB, 305
perks, 150
Presidential Election Campaign Fund, 257
procedural reforms, 313
rescission, 384
salary, 150
sequestration order, 389
stabilization policy, 64
Statement of Administration Policy, 303
veto, 318
Presidential Election Campaign Fund, 257
President's Commission on Budget Concepts, 284
described, 441
Prices
determined by, 26
expansion and, 46
productivity, 27
recession and, 432
Producer Price Index
defined, 42
Productivity
annual gains (table), 27
defined, 27
seventies decline, 27, 459
Progressive tax
defined, 84
Protectionism
described, 513
Proxmire, Sen. William, 169
Public Broadcasting Service (PBS)
funding cuts, 258
Public. *See* Voters
Public debt. *See* Debt
Public Debt, Bureau of
budget, 232
Public services
revenue-sharing, 448

Radiation exposure compensation program
budget, 241

Reagan, Ronald
average tax rate, 409
balanced budget amendment, 387
balanced budget promise, 466
bank deregulation, 500
budget cuts, 467
budget summits, 323
budget writing, 301
capital spending grants, 163
COLAs, 330
Commerce budget, 235
debt, 18
debt crisis, 282
defense spending, 146, 223
deficits, 12
economic policy, 306
economic record, 466
expansion, 404
government shutdown, 473
high deficits, 475
income tax cut, 410
income taxes, 116
Misery Index, 59
NASA, 243
opposition in Congress, 472
reconciliation bill, 464
rescission requests, 385
Social Security changes, 172, 197
spending, 403, 475
spending cuts, 386
spending tops $1 trillion, 141
Stockman, 306
summits, 388, 476
supply-side theory, 71
tax cut, 66, 302, 436, 468, 469
taxes, 103, 411
tax hike, 66, 470
tax indexing, 113
tax policy, 302
tax reform, 119
Tax Reform Act, 1986, 302
unemployment, 406, 407
veto, 375, 473
Reaganomics, 466, 475
Recession
automatic stabilizers, 60
Bush, 477
and business cycle, 25
deficit spending, 20
defined, 55
disinflation and, 57
durable goods and, 34
elections and, 43, 446
Federal Reserve, 412, 418, 466, 471
federal spending and, 142
fiscal policy options, 66
history, 298, 430, 431, 443
housing starts, 36
individual and, 24
inflation, 443
interest rate policy, 429
money supply, 493
1937–1938, 418
1948–1949, 421, 423
1959, 432
1969–1970, 443
1974, 456
1980, 460, 464, 465
1981, 466, 470
1990, 477
recent listed, 55
stabilization policy, 64
start of, 56
tax cuts and, 302
unemployment, 406, 443
Reconciliation
described, 368
Reagan cuts and, 467
Records, firsts, etc.
budget surplus (longest string), 15
Congress passes first revenue bill, 76
debt limit raised most times, 379
debt topped $1 trillion, 130
deficit, 145
deficit passes World War II high, 456
deficit tops $1 billion, 471
deficits, most consecutive, 16
first income tax, 7
first president to call for line-item veto, 319
first use of line-item veto, 318
inflation high, 50
inflation low, 50
largest appropriations bill, 323
largest budget share, 144
largest defense budget, 223
largest social program, 175
last budget surplus, 15
longest expansion, 47
lowest average unemployment, 407
lowest economic growth, 405
lowest postwar growth, 477
most continuing resolutions, 370
most rescission requests, 385
oldest extant price index, 42
Republicans regain House, 483
revenues top $1 trillion, 82
revenues top $100 billion, 82
top growth rate
Redistribution of income. *See* Income tax, income redistribution
Reed, Daniel A.
chair, Ways and Means, 335
Regan, Donald T.
treasury secretary, 309
Regressive tax, 102
defined, 84
excise tax, 92
Regulations. *See also* Deregulation
Democrats oppose rollbacks, 484
drag on productivity, 27, 459
in economic theory, 62
economy and, 23
grants, 180
inflation factor, 459
need for, 37
Reorganization Plan Number 1, 415
Republican party
balanced budget agreement, 284, 387, 488
balanced budget plan, 483
block grants, 180
Blue Dogs, 324
budget fight, 1995
budget, 1997, 487
capital gains tax, 86
Contract with America, 484
control of Congress, 483
deficit spending, 20
deregulation, 37
Domenici, 330
fiscal goals, 1940s, 423
Gingrich, 395
income taxes, 410
Kasich, 329
liberals and spending, 375
loses shutdown standoff, 485
1995 budget fight, 497

opposes tax hikes, 480
PBS and, 258
public opposes cuts, 483
shutdowns, 304
spending, 375
spending limits, 380
supply-side economics, 71, 103
tariffs, 513
tax cuts, 483
taxes and, 14
Repurchase agreements, 493
Rescission
described, 382, 384
most requests, 385
Retirement benefits. *See also* Social Security
civil service, 179
military, 179
Railroad retirement, 179
Revenue. *See also* Taxes
balanced budget agreement, 488
borrowing and, 123
budget and, 281
budget estimates, 300
budget resolution targets, 382, 383
capital gains tax and, 86
Congress powers, 78
current amounts, 99
declines, 471
defined, 72
disposable income, 35
economy and, 5, 44
estate and gift tax collections, 98
exemption losses (table), 89
GDP percent, 82, 408
general funds, 94
growth of, 82, 83 (table), 143
history of, 7, 75, 76, 77, 80, 81, 82
indexation, 114
inflation and, 113, 114
inflation swells, 460
leading source, 75
marginal taxes and, 87
mix of, 115
Monthly Statement of Receipts and Outlays, 499
special funds, 94
spending growth and, 475
tax cuts, 302, 436
taxes and, 14
tax increase yield, 1982, 470
Tax Reform Act, 1986, 119
trust funds, 94
types of funds, 94
user fees, 122
Revenue Act of 1913, 81
Revenue-sharing
described, 448
Roosevelt
activist government, 62
Budget Bureau, 311
budget process, 415
debt origins, 18
economic policy, 418
expands government, 143
free trade policy, 513
New Deal, 413
programs created, 414
Reorganization Plan No. 1, 284
social programs, 402
Social Security system, 194
spending cuts, 418
spending growth, 403
tax hikes, 412
taxes, 416, 417, 418
wealth tax, 417
Rostenkowski, Dan
chair, Ways and Means, 335
Roth, William V. Jr.
Finance Committee chair, 331
Rubin, Robert E.
avoids federal default, 497
treasury secretary, 309
Russell, Richard B.
chair, Senate Appropriations, 339

Sabo, Martin
Budget Committee chair, 328
Saint Lawrence Seaway Development Corporation, 244
Sallie Mae. *See* Student Loan Marketing Association
Sasser, Jim
Budget Committee chair, 328
Savings and investment
annual rates (table), 117
capital gains tax, 86
disposable income, 35
inflation and, 48
monetary policy and, 69
money supply, 490
prime rate (table), 496
supply-side theory, 71
taxes and, 117
Savings and loan crisis
budget and, 388
deregulation and, 37, 500
effect on budget, 478
interest rates and, 500
Savings bonds, 501
School lunch recipients, 161
Scorekeeping
described, 367
Secret Service
budget, 232
Senate. *See also* Congress
appropriations bills, 350
appropriations committee, 272
appropriations timetable, 277
balanced budget amendment, 387
Budget Committee created, 382
budget writing, 272
conference committee, 363
debt limit, 463
Finance Committee, 284, 325
originates tax bill, 365
revenue bills, 356
salaries and expenses, 154
senators salaries, 155
two-step procedure, 347, 348
Senate Finance Committee
budget resolution, 365
duties, 331
revenue bills, 356
tax bills, 365
Sequester
described, 362, 388, 389
Seventies
bailouts, 447
debt and, 18, 131
deficits, 167
economic growth, 28
economic woes, 459
enlarged social programs, 171
Ford administration, 456
inflation and, 50, 64, 443
monetary policy, 69
productivity, 27, 459
Social Security benefits, 121
spending history, 453
stagflation, 57, 58
supply-side theory, 71

Seventies *(continued)*
taxes, 113
unemployment, 406
Shutdowns. *See* Government shutdowns
Sixteenth Amendment, 79
income tax, 7
why passed, 80
Sixties
debt, 18
defense v. social spending, 439
economic expansion, 28, 47, 404, 405
economic policy, 434, 435, 442
economy, 404, 435
Great Society, 171, 186, 336, 437
inflation and, 50, 51, 435, 439, 442
monetary policy, 69
productivity, 27
spending, 141, 373, 439
taxes, 116, 121, 410, 411, 435, 437, 442
unemployment, 406, 407
Small Business Administration
budget share, 147
Social insurance taxes. *See* Payroll tax
Social programs. *See also* Entitlements, Welfare programs, specific programs
aging population, 171
automatic stabilizers, 60
benefits of, 170, 181
benefits paid, 179
block grants, 180
budget share, 174
Community Action, 437
Contract with America, 484
debt contribution, 18
Democrats defend, 449
direct payment programs, 178
education, 221, 437
entitlement growth, 396
Great Depression, 400
Great Society, 437
health spending, 255
history, 437
housing assistance, 216, 217, 256, 437
income security for disadvantaged, 450
inflated CPI and, 41
inflation and, 50
job training, 437
Medicaid, 437
Medicare, 437, 450
Model Cities, 437
Native Americans, 253, 255
number of recipients (table), 161
peace dividend, 453
poverty, 211, 212
ranked by spending, 175
revenue-sharing, 448
safety net spending, 402
Social Security, 200, 427, 474
social spending, 141, 146, 230, 293, 362, 386, 390, 397, 402, 437, 439, 459, 460, 461, 471, 474, 475, 485
spending cuts, 484
types, 174
War on Poverty, 437
welfare, 213, 216
welfare reform, 395
welfare spending (table), 215
Social Security. *See also* Medicare, Supplemental Security Income (SSI)
average benefits, 196
bankruptcy, 121, 196, 204, 462, 474
benefit cuts, 208, 462, 474
benefit increases, 121, 186, 427, 450, 461, 462, 474
benefit ratio, 198
benefits, 173, 186, 208
benefits paid, 179
budget cuts and, 286
budget share, 144, 149
cost-of-living adjustments, 208, 330
coverage, 427
created, 414
dependency ratio, 204, 205
described, 194
Disability Insurance created, 427
disinvesting, 282
diverting funds, 96
earmarked funds, 360
elections and, 61
eligibility, 196, 427, 474
financing, 121
growth, expected, 396
history, 194, 195, 200, 427, 437, 438, 450
impact of benefits, 199
indexing, 171, 450
inflated CPI and, 41
investment of funds, 207 (table), 208
major programs, 201
minimum benefit, 197
OASDI adopted as name, 427
payroll tax, 93, 121, 208, 468
projected cost, 149
recipients, 161, 202
reforms, 172, 208
rescue packages, 462, 474
rising costs, 453
Senate Finance Committee, 331
sensitive issue, 197
solvency, 450
spending rise, 200
SSI, 203, 215
support for, 287
system described, 196
tax breaks, 206
total recipients, 199
trusts, 95, 96, 196, 208, 279, 427, 438, 441
Ways and Means, 334
Social Security Administration
budget share, 144, 147, 200
Social Security Advisory Council
proposed reforms, 208
Space program. *See* National Aeronautics and Space Administration
Special funds
defined, 97
Special interests
budget and, 287
deficits and, 13
Senate Finance Committee, 331
Social Security, 197
spending and, 166
Spending. *See also* Spending limits
annual amount, 4
appropriations, 363
authority, 2
bailouts, 447
borrowing and, 123
budget and, 281

budget estimates, 300
budget resolution targets, 382, 383
caps, 176, 390
changing attitudes, 141
COLAs, 196
compared with foreign, 31
congressional powers, 78, 168
control, 165, 285, 372, 374
credit limit, 123
current amount, 4
cuts, 229, 230, 238, 247, 258, 302, 358, 376, 386, 389, 393, 396, 397, 421, 430, 431, 432, 444, 456, 464, 468, 476, 482, 486, 488
debt and, 126
deficit, 422
deficit spending, 13
direct payment programs, 178
discretionary, 162, 286, 390, 394, 396, 459, 482, 487
drug control, 269
economic effects, 5, 23, 44, 142
entitlements, 293, 368
expansion and, 46
fiscal policy and, 65, 66
foreign aid, 268
freeze, 482
GDP and, 31, 403
gold reserves and, 5
government checks, 3
Grace Commission, 361
Gramm-Rudman-Hollings Act, 389
growth, 83 (table), 143, 396, 403, 453, 475
health care cost rise, 184, 185
history, 140, 141, 146, 168, 171, 373, 400, 412, 419, 428, 430, 432, 434, 435, 439, 453
impact, 376
impoundment, 375, 381, 382, 444, 455
increase, 419, 428, 434, 439
inflation and, 50, 52
interest groups, 287
Keynesian economics, 63
Korean War, 428
limits, 380
line-item veto, 318
mandatory, 162, 165, 286, 293, 368, 394, 396, 453, 459
Medicaid, 189, 192
Medicare, 188, 191
Monthly Statement of Receipts and Outlays, 499
overspending, 13, 18, 20, 373, 374
patterns, 146
peace dividend, 230
per second, 140
philosophy on, 399
pork-barrel spending, 359
procedure, 346
reprogramming, 317
research, 247
revenue-sharing, 448
rewards of, 143
Social Security rise, 200
targets, 394
tax indexing and, 114
tops $1 billion, 141
tops $1 trillion, 141
Vietnam era, 435
wasteful, 158, 169, 361
who benefits, 142
who does the, 3
World War I, 399
Spending limits
caps, 390
Nixon and, 449
PAYGO, 390
Spotted owl program cost, 239
Stabilization crisis
debt and, 19
described, 516
foreign investors and, 136
Stabilization policy
Congress and, 67
defined, 64
Keynesian economics, 63
Stagflation, 443
defined, 57, 58
history, 432
State and local government
balanced budget amendment, 387
block grants, 180
federal tax exemption, 79
grants, 163
public confidence, 158
revenue-sharing, 448
State Department
budget by category, 233
budget share, 147
International Narcotics Control Program, 269
Statement of Administration Policy, 303
Stennis, John C.
chair, Senate Appropriations, 339
Stevens, Ted
chair, Senate Appropriations, 339
Stockman, David
OMB director, 306
spending cuts, 467
Stock market crash (1987), 388
effect on budget process, 476
Strategic Petroleum Reserve, 246
Student aid
loan recipients, 161, 221
loans, sequestration, 389
Pell grants, 397
Student Loan Marketing Association, 294
Subsidies
corporate welfare, 164
farm, 240
reform, 240
Summits (budget)
1987 budget summit, 284, 388, 476
1990, 478
Supplemental Security Income (SSI). *See also* Social programs, Social Security
abuse of, 203
benefits paid, 179
created, 450
described, 201
spending (table), 215
total recipients, 202
Supply and demand
classical theory, 398
defined, 26
seventies inflation cause, 459
supply side theory, 71
Supply-side economics. *See* Economic theory
Supreme Court
justice's salary, 157
McCulloch v. Maryland, 79
Pollock v. Farmers' Loan and Trust Co., 80
ruled against Gramm-Rudman, 388

Supreme Court *(continued)*
  salaries and expenses, 156
  United States v. Butler, 168, 321
Surpluses (budget)
  history, 134, 145
  listed (table), 83
  2002, expected, 397

Taber, John
  chair, House Appropriations, 339
Taft Commission on Economy and Efficiency, 284
Tariffs
  current revenues, 99
  defined, 99
  history, 76, 513
  main revenue source, 7
  NAFTA, 514
  percent of revenue, 73
  and revenue, 9
Tax Equity and Fiscal Responsibility Act (1982), 470
Taxes. *See also* Payroll tax, Revenue, Tax legislation, names of other specific taxes
  airline travel, 488
  balanced budget agreement, 488
  balancing the budget, 14
  bracket creep, 409, 460
  budget and, 281
  Bush reversal on, 480
  Bush tax hike, 478
  capital gains, 86, 488
  cheating, 108
  cigarette, 488
  collection costs, 107
  compared with foreign, 112
  congressional powers, 78, 79
  constitutional limits, 79
  corporate, 81, 115, 120, 121, 411, 436
  crude oil tax, 122
  cut, 1964, 67, 435, 436
  cut, 1975, 456
  cut, 1981, 66, 87, 113, 468, 469
  cut, 1997, 488
  cuts, 61, 66, 67, 71, 87, 103, 113, 114, 302, 397, 410, 423, 434, 435, 436, 456, 466, 468, 469, 484, 488
  direct, 79
  Economic Recovery Tax Act of 1981, 468
  effects, 142
  EITC, 109, 182
  estate, 488
  excise, 115
  exempt groups, 90
  exemption losses (table), 89
  fairness, 85, 417
  filing cost, 118
  first income tax rate, 8
  fiscal policy and, 23, 65
  fiscal policy options, 66
  gasoline, 482
  GDP percent, 408
  hidden tax hikes, 460
  highest GDP percent, 408
  highest, lowest, 409
  hike, 1977, 462
  hike, 1982, 468, 470
  hike, 1993, 482
  hikes, 114, 365, 393, 410, 412, 417, 420, 435, 442, 450, 462, 468, 470, 478, 480, 482, 488
  history, 80, 92, 98, 99, 101, 284, 411, 420, 468
  income taxes, 115, 116, 410
  indexation, 113, 114, 468
  inflated CPI and, 41
  inflation and, 52, 113, 114, 423, 460
  interest groups, 287
  Johnson surcharge, 435
  Laffer curve, 103
  liquor, 92
  marginal tax rate, 87
  mix of, 115
  necessity of, 6
  negative, defined, 101
  payroll tax, 416
  per capita tax, 111
  progressive, 84, 416, 417
  rates, 103, 112
  Reagan cuts, 466
  reform, 6, 102, 117, 119, 330
  refunds, 109
  regressive, 84
  revenue enhancers, 114
  revenue growth (table), 82, 83
  Senate Finance Committee, 331
  Social Security benefits, 482
  supply-side theory, 71
  Tax Equity and Fiscal Responsibility Act, 470
  tax policy, 114
  tax shelters, 119
  tax surcharge, 442
  tobacco, 92
  voters and, 14
  wealthy taxpayers, 87, 106, 117, 119, 417, 436, 469, 478, 482
  withholding tax created, 420
  World War II, 420
Tax exemptions
  capital gains tax cut, 86
  child tax credit, 488
  Clinton education incentives, 488
  corporate welfare, 164
  cut back, 119
  defined, 88
  effects, 142
  effects on poor, 181
  exemption losses (table), 89
  foreign earnings, 91
  foreign investors, 440
  groups exempted, 90
  Social Security benefits, 206
Tax expenditures. *See* Tax exemptions Tax fairness
  defined, 85
  progressive taxes, 84
  Reagan tax cut, 469
  Roosevelt and, 417
Tax legislation. *See also* Taxes
  amendments, 356
  baseline projections, 280, 281
  Christmas treeing, 356
  conference committee, 363
  House origins of, 349
  Mills, 334, 336
  1986 tax reform, 119
  procedures, 325, 326, 331, 356, 365
  reform, 102
  Senate, 365
  Sen. Long, 333
  tax reform, 6
  Ways and Means, 334
Tax Reform Act of 1986, 302
  changes detailed, 119
  fairness of, 85

Tax revenues. *See* Revenue, Taxes
Technology Administration budget, 235
Temporary Assistance for Needy Families (TANF)
program established, 210
Tennessee Valley Authority, 441
Thirties
economic policy, 398, 400, 402, 403, 412, 418
expansion of government, 62, 399
Federal Reserve, 412
free trade, 513
Great Depression, 398, 400, 412
New Deal, 402, 413, 414
Spending, 401, 403, 418
Social Security, 194, 196, 197
taxes, 412, 416, 417
Tight money defined, 502
Tobacco tax. *See* Excise taxes
"too big to butcher"
defined, 364
Trade
balance of payments, 508, 509 (table)
devaluation and, 510
exchange rate, 503
free trade, 513, 514
G-7 meetings, 507
GATT, 425
history of protectionism, 513
NAFTA, 514
strong, weak dollar, 506
tariffs, 99
trade deficit, 508, 511, 512
trade surplus, 508
Transfer payment
defined, 177
described, 293
GDP and, 29
Transportation Department
budget, 147, 244
demonstration projects, 164
drug control, 269
revenue-sharing, 448
Treasury, Department of the
borrowing, 377
Budget Bureau, 144, 415
budget share, 147, 148
close of fiscal year, 277
Daily Statement of the Treasury, 499
debt interest, 148
disinvested securities, 282, 497
drug control, 269
economic advice, 296
economic policy, 308
Fed and, 429
federal default, 497
Federal Financing Bank, 451
Financial Management Service, 498
financial responsibilities, 308
interest rates, 429
marketable securities, 138
Monthly Statement of Receipts and Outlays, 499
non-marketable securities, 138
profit on Mexico loan, 515
public debt, 137
secretaries (listed), 309
securities, 451
Social Security trust, 207
special issues, 139
spending by category, 232
Treasury bills and bonds (table), 501
Treasury bills
described, 501
interest rates, 501 (table)
Treasury bonds
described, 501
interest rates, 501 (table)
Truman, Harry
budget surplus, 15
demobilization, 421
full employment, 422
inflation, 423
lowest taxes, 409
unemployment, 406, 407
Trust funds. *See also* Special funds
airways trust, 96
annual receipts, 95
civil service retirement, 95
diverting funds, 96
federal borrowing from, 96, 128
Health Insurance trust, 95, 438
Highway trust, 96
interest earned, 96
major trusts listed, 95
off budget, 441
Social Security trusts, 96
special issues, 139
Ullman, Al
chair, Ways and Means, 335
Undistributed offsetting receipts. *See also* Offsetting receipts
in current budget, 147
described, 291
Unemployment
average rate, 406
Carter, 460
classical economics, 398
defined, 406
demobilization and, 421
1800s, 62
high, low, 407
history of, 406, 428, 446
Humphrey-Hawkins bill, 458
inflation and, 443
Keynesian economics, 63
1 percent rate, 422
rate (table), 32
recession, 1974, 456
spending cuts, 376
stagflation, 58
tax cut, 1964, 436
World War II drop, 419
Unemployment insurance
benefits paid, 179
created, 414
spending, 254
total recipients, 161
Unified budget, 441
adopted, 284
defined, 279
United Nations payments, 233, 234
United States Geological Survey budget, 253
United States Travel and Tourism Administration
budget, 235
United States v. Butler (1936), 168, 321
User fees
in budget, 291
energy, 245
increases, 122
National Indian Gaming Commission, 252
national parks, 251
patents, 237
revenue increase, 122

Value-added tax (VAT)
defined, 102
Veterans Affairs, Department of
benefits, 249
budget, 249
budget share, 147
drug control, 269
employment, 159, 249
National Cemetery System, 250
Veterans benefits
home loans, 216, 218
listed, 249
medical care, 179
medical spending, 184
pensions, 179
recipients, 161
Veto. *See also* Line-item veto
budget process and, 304
drafting, 415
shutdowns, 304, 473, 479, 485
spending control, 375
Statement of Administration Policy, 303
Vice presidents
perks, 150
salary, 150
Vietnam War
costs, 439, 452
debt and, 131
defense budget, 223
deficits, 374, 381
Great Society and, 437
inflation and, 50, 435
peace dividend, 453
size of military, 159
stagflation, 58
Views and estimates
in budget process, 277
Violent crime
reduction programs, 156
Volcker, Paul, 466
cures inflation, 54
Voters
budget and, 287
economy, 295, 432
entitlement support, 172, 173
fiscal policy, 65
monetary policy and, 70
shutdown reactions, 485
Social Security issue, 197
spending and, 166
supply-side theory, 71
tax policy and, 114
wasteful spending and, 158

Wage-price controls
Economic Stabilization Act, 445
failure of, 446
Truman, 428
Wages
annual gains, 27
inflation and, 48, 49
productivity and, 27
War on Drugs
spending, 269
War on Poverty
described, 437
Waste
Clinton cuts, 393
Grace Commission, 361
line-item veto and, 318
pork-barrel spending, 359
Reagan rescission requests, 385
Ways and Means Committee
established, 284
jurisdiction, 334
Mills, Wilbur, 336
revenue bills, 356
tax bills, 325
Welfare programs
Aid to Families with Dependent Children (AFDC), 210, 213
benefits paid, 179
block grants, 180
food stamps, 209, 210, 214
homeless aid, 216
housing assistance, 216
poverty, 211, 212
recipients, 161, 210, 213
reform, 209, 395
Senate Finance Committee, 331
spending (table), 215
Temporary Assistance for Needy Families (TANF), 210
welfare created, 414
welfare reform (1996), 209
White House
operating expenses, 151
Whitten, Jamie L.
chair, House Appropriations, 339
profile, 340
Windfall profits tax
defined, 100
Women, Infants, and Children (WIC)
spending, 239
World Bank
created, 424
World Trade Organization, 425
World War I
budget process and, 283
debt and, 399
federal spending, 141
and spending, 9
World War II
corporate taxes, 100
debt and, 18, 130, 131
defense budget, 223
deficits and, 16
demobilization, 421
economy, 376
ends depression, 63
federal spending, 419
how financed, 420
spending, 376, 412